The Biographical Dictionary of British Feminists
Volume One: 1800–1930

The Biographical Dictionary of British Feminists

Volume One: 1800–1930

Olive Banks
Professor of Sociology Emerita
University of Leicester

New York University Press
New York 1985

First published in the U.S.A. in 1985 by
NEW YORK UNIVERSITY PRESS
Washington Square, New York, N.Y. 10003

© Olive Banks, 1985

All rights reserved

Library of Congress Cataloging in Publication Data

Banks, Olive.
  The biographical dictionary of British feminists.

  Contents: v. 1. 1800–1930.
  Includes bibliographical references and index.
  1. Feminists——Great Britain——Biography——Dictionaries.
I. Title
HQ1123.B36   1985   305.4′2′0941   (B)   85–3110
ISBN   0–8147–1078–6   (v.1)

Printed in Great Britain

Contents

Introduction	vii
THE BIOGRAPHICAL DICTIONARY OF BRITISH FEMINISTS, 1800–1930	3
Index	233
Index of Topics	237

Introduction

This biographical dictionary was planned as a reference work for those interested in the British feminist movement. No other biographical dictionary provides this kind of emphasis, and existing dictionaries tend either to ignore feminists or, in some cases, seriously to misrepresent them. This is particularly true of the *Dictionary of National Biography (DNB)* which omits altogether all but the most eminent of the feminist leaders. Moreover, even an entry in the DNB does not guarantee that any particular attention, or even any attention at all will be paid to the subject's contribution to feminism. The *Dictionary of Labour Biography*[1] *(DLB)* is in some respects more useful since it provides important information on a number of hitherto unknown women and certainly does not neglect to discuss them as feminists, but, designed as it is to provide information on members of the Labour movement, the great majority of feminists find no place in it at all. The same kind of problem arises with the *Biographical Dictionary of British Radicals.*[2]

The attempt to compensate for the decidedly male bias of all these dictionaries by compiling a dictionary of notable women does not necessarily serve the purpose of a feminist dictionary either. *Women of the Day* by Frances Hays, published in 1885[3] devotes most of its pages to women who have succeeded as novelists, artists and actresses and contains very few feminists. The recently published *Women of Achievement*[4] has also been designed for quite a different purpose than the one attempted here, which is to provide biographical sketches of those women and, occasionally, men, who contributed their time, effort and money, and sometimes their health and happiness to forwarding the progress of the women's movement.

The meaning of the term feminism is of course controversial, and in any case changes over time. Modern feminism, in spite of many similarities, is by no means the same thing as the feminism which inspired women in the nineteenth century. In this volume we shall be concerned only with the feminist movement between 1800 and 1930 but in this very considerable span of time feminism changed in many different ways. Nor was the feminist movement ever a unity even at a single point in time. For this reason it is exceedingly difficult to provide a definition of feminism. At its simplest level it represents a criticism of the position of women in relationship to men and a desire to change that position, but it is much more difficult to find agreement on the precise nature and even direction of the changes required. While sometimes represented in terms of equal rights this does not by any means encompass the whole of even nineteenth-century feminism and is completely inadequate in understanding feminism today.

Feminists, it is true, have often seen the movement principally in terms of greater equality between the sexes, and have claimed for themselves the right to enjoy equal opportunities in education and employment, equal pay, equal guardianship rights over their children, equal citizenship rights and an end to the double standard of sexual morality. Indeed, these demands may be said to represent the very backbone of nineteenth- and early twentieth-century feminism. Behind and even partly concealed by these claims for equal rights have been other more fundamental needs and goals. Feminists have, for example, argued for a greater measure of economic and legal independence for themselves as women, and a greater recognition of their rights to individuality and self-expression. The demand of modern feminists for the right to choose was by no means absent from nineteenth-century feminism although it was usually applied to a completely different set of issues. Most important of all, perhaps, has been the desire for an end to women's subordination both in government and in the family. This is clearly evident in the demand for a single standard of sexual morality which, by imposing severe restrictions on male sexuality, would end the sexual exploitation of women by men, but it was also the motivation behind much of the support for women's suffrage. Even the demand for family allowances was inspired as much by the hope that they would increase the power of the mother in the family, as by the desire to mitigate poverty. In attempting to define feminism therefore, it is necessary to include in the definition concepts like subordination and exploitation as well as inequality.

If we look now at the history of the feminist movement in the light of this definition it is possible to discern three different intellectual traditions,[5] all of which deeply influenced its development but which tended to emphasise different goals as well as different conceptions of the nature and function of women. Of these traditions perhaps the most fundamental for understanding the origins of feminism is the equal-rights tradition, based essentially on the Enlightenment philosophy of human rights and expressed most clearly perhaps in the feminist writings of John Stuart Mill. Emphasising equality of opportunity this tradition tended to place most stress on the removal of restrictions on women's liberty of action to improve their circumstances, but also on the injustice of legal inequalities which denied women those rights that men enjoyed. It strenuously opposed, therefore, that doctrine of marriage which denied women their rights as persons, and the exclusion of women from higher education and the professions, which denied them the right to support themselves.

If equal-rights feminism can be seen as the backbone of nineteenth-century feminism it was strongly challenged as early as the 1830s by Owenite communitarian socialism which, when combined with feminism, was far more radical in its implications than the doctrine of equal rights. Without denying the need for equality between the sexes, the Owenite feminists[6] went on to advocate a system of communitarian socialism which would put an end to the economic dependence of a wife on her husband and, by the provision of community services, free her as well from the day-to-day routine of housework and child care.

The decline of Owenite socialism during the 1840s and 1850s virtually ended this co-operation between socialism and feminism, which were never again to be so closely aligned. Although socialism often continued to pay some attention to feminism in theory, in practice there were many areas which gave rise to opposition between the two movements. These emerged most dramatically in the struggle for women's suffrage, but were also very evident in the 1920s over the issue of birth control. The trade-union movement too was always decidedly ambivalent about the position of women workers. Women who were both feminists and socialists frequently found themselves in a situation where the issues of gender and class pulled in diametrically opposite directions and while some tried all their lives for a reconciliation between the two principles others, like Eleanor Marx for example, abandoned the issue of gender to work for socialism or, like Emmeline and Christabel Pankhurst abandoned socialism.

The third tradition within feminism is derived from the powerful evangelical element in nineteenth-century religious thinking, which, while often anti-feminist in ideology, nevertheless drew a number of women into the service of social reform through the exercise of philanthropy. Although initially often somewhat reluctant feminists, they were drawn into the women's movement by their recognition that women were needed in public service and ultimately in Parliament. The most vivid expression of this particular aspect of feminism is to be found in the career of Josephine Butler, who moved from the rescue of individual prostitutes to the leadership of the campaign against the Contagious Diseases Acts, a measure which by requiring the compulsory examination and if necessary treatment of women believed to be prostitutes was condoning the double standard of sexual morality by punishing the woman for what was essentially an abuse by men of their own sexuality and that of women.

Although evangelical feminists often worked for the same goals as the equal-rights feminists, there were many ways in which they differed. The equal-rights feminists, for example, tended to minimise the differences between men and women. Making use of what were essentially Enlightenment principles, they argued that such differences as occurred were the result of the limitations placed on women's experiences, and were caused especially by the frivolity of their education and upbringing; and John Stuart Mill, for example, was by no means alone in claiming that woman's true nature would not be revealed until all her disabilities were removed. The evangelical feminists, in contrast, accepted the fact that men and women differed in significant ways and emphasised in this connection the centrality to women's lives of their role as mothers.

Whereas the equal-rights feminists were concerned chiefly to enlarge women's opportunities for freedom and self-expression as individuals, evangelical feminists emphasised women's traditional virtue of service to others. Now, however, women no longer had the single duty to serve their own families; for many of the evangelical feminists women's new mission was to serve, if not indeed to save, the whole nation and even the whole world. Moreover where the equal-rights feminists emphasised women's need for autonomy, evangelical feminists were much more aware of the extent of women's exploitation. From the 1880s onwards, for example, campaigns were aimed at the protection of women in industry, some at least of which protected them from exploitation at the cost of their freedom of action. A particularly good example of this was the attempt to prevent women working as barmaids, which was designed to protect them chiefly from sexual exploitation, and which was opposed vehemently not only by the barmaids but by a number of equal-rights feminists.

There were, therefore, tendencies within evangelical feminism which led it into potential and sometimes actual conflict with feminism based upon the equal-rights tradition. At other times however, the two kinds of feminist formed alliances, as they did most effectively in the struggle for women's suffrage. The movement to improve the education of girls and women also gained from such an alliance, since both feminist traditions saw better education as necessary to women's intellectual and moral development. Evangelical feminism also came into conflict with Owenite feminism which was often strongly secularist in tone as well as very radical in its attitude towards the family. By the end of the century, however, the emerging Labour movement had lost its radical attitude to the family and there were times, as for example over the issue of protective legislation, when the Labour movement, especially on its non-Marxist side, had more in common with evangelical feminism than with the equal-rights movement.

Although individual feminists can be selected to represent different feminist traditions, it would be a mistake to conclude that all biographies in this volume can be categorised in any simple way as falling within one particular tradition rather than another. Individuals frequently changed their position over time, sometimes even moving out of feminism altogether. Emmeline Pankhurst, for example, began her career as a feminist under the influence of her husband, who was firmly within the equal-rights tradition, but later her views were much closer to evangelical feminism and, at the end of her life, she can scarcely be described as a feminist at all.

In choosing subjects for the *Dictionary*, therefore, an attempt has been made to convey both the variety and the complexity of feminism, and no attempt has been made to impose either my own version of feminism or one which would be acceptable to the modern movement. Indeed it would probably be as difficult to find a simple definition acceptable to all feminists today as it has been to find a way of characterising feminism in the nineteenth century. Most of the entries are for women, but a number of men have been included who were significant in the various feminist campaigns. At a time when women themselves had no voice in the centres of power, it was vitally necessary for them to secure male allies who would act on their behalf and a dictionary of feminists for this period would be incomplete without them. At the same time, for neither men nor women, has sympathy with the feminist cause been a sufficient reason for inclusion. Many people, both men and women, who have held feminist attitudes chose to spend their lives in support of other causes. Eleanor Marx is a good example of this kind of woman who, although she had strong feminist sympathies, chose to put socialism first.

The time-limit of the *Dictionary* also set some problems. The date 1930 does not represent the end of the feminist movement as such, but the final granting of complete suffrage in 1928 did indicate the close of an era during which suffrage had been the most important feminist goal, if only because it represented for women at the time, the means to achieve all the other goals they wanted. Those women whose careers as feminists began after 1930 therefore have necessarily been excluded. However, a small number of important feminists, including Dora Russell and Vera Brittain, were in fact already active as feminists while still very young women in the 1920s. But since they are in general part of a later generation of feminists facing different kinds of problems they have not been included.

Entries in the *Dictionary* have been made alphabetically under the name by which the individual concerned is most likely to be recognised. In most instances this has presented no problem but in the case of a number of married women there is the possibility of confusion since they are known under both their single and their married names at different periods of their lives. For example, Bessie Rayner Parkes later became Bessie Belloc, and Barbara Leigh-Smith later became Barbara Bodichon. In such cases the woman concerned is entered under her married name but indexed under both her married and single names. In a number of other cases women retained their single names after marriage or linked them with that of their husbands so that Teresa Billington became Teresa Billington-Greig. She will be found under Billington-Greig but is also indexed under Greig since she sometimes appears elsewhere under that name.

Finally, I would like to thank all those who have encouraged me in writing this *Dictionary* by making comments and suggestions. I would also like to pay particular tribute to those scholars who in various ways are pushing forward our knowledge of feminist history. Without their work this *Dictionary* would hardly have been possible and would certainly have been much less valuable.

Notes

1. *The Dictionary of Labour Biography*, ed. John Savill and Joyce Bellamy, Vols. I–VI, (London, Macmillan 1972–82).
2. *Biographical Dictionary of Modern British Radicals 1770–1830*, ed. Joseph O. Baylen and Norbert J. Gossman (Brighton, Harvester Press, 1979).
3. *Women of the Day: a biographical dictionary of notable contemporaries*, Frances Hays (London, Chatto and Windus, 1885).
4. *Women of Achievement*, Susan Raven and Alison Weir (New York, Harmony Books, 1981).
5. See *Faces of Feminism*, Olive Banks (Oxford, Martin Robertson, 1981).
6. For a recent account of Owenite feminism see *Eve and the New Jerusalem. Socialism and Feminism in the Nineteenth Century*, Barbara Taylor (London, Virago, 1983).

The Biographical Dictionary of British Feminists
Volume One: **1800–1930**

AMBERLEY Lady Katherine Louisa (Kate) 1842-1874

Kate Amberley, an early suffragist, was the fourth daughter of Lord Stanley of Alderley, a Liberal politician who had held minor office in several governments. Her mother, however, was more influential in forming her opinions. Brought up in Florence, Lady Stanley had a great contempt for all forms of feminine silliness and gave her daughters as well as her sons a good education, wanting them above all to be intelligent. She took a deep interest in the higher education of women and was, later in life, closely connected with Girton College.

As Kate Stanley grew up she began to take part in the social round of balls and parties typical of young women of her period and social class, but she had already started to take a keen interest in intellectual issues, partly under the influence of an older brother, and was soon an admirer of John Stuart Mill and familiar with his views, and those of his wife Harriet Taylor Mill, on the enfranchisement of women. Late in 1863, when she was twenty-one and he the same age, she met John Russell, Viscount Amberley, the eldest son of Earl Russell, and they were immediately attracted to each other, drawn as much by the similarities of their views, and their admiration for each other's intellect as by the charm which both seemed to have had in good measure. In spite of some opposition from his mother, they were married in 1864 and were to remain devoted to each other until the end of their short lives.

Earl Russell was a distinguished statesman, and more than once Prime Minister. He married three times, John's mother being his third wife, but John was his first son. A member of the Whig aristocracy, his views were not particularly Radical, but he never seems to have objected to those of his son, and letters between them show deep affection on either side. His mother however seems to have been more important in forming his character. A deeply puritanical woman who hated compromise and never doubted her own rightness, she may have been responsible for his remarkable intellectual honesty and his determination to act upon his beliefs.

Kate Amberley's admiration for Mill was shared by her husband and was deepened for both of them by a friendship with him which gradually developed in the early years of their marriage. She also became close friends with Helen Taylor, Harriet Taylor's daughter by her first marriage, and through Helen she was gradually drawn into the small circle of women then becoming increasingly active in the cause of women's rights. In 1866 there was an influential meeting with Elizabeth Garrett, later Garrett Anderson, the pioneer woman doctor who later became the family physician, and with Emily Davies, the principal pioneer in the field of higher education for women. To both of their causes Kate gave generously. In addition she became a member of a committee to support the Married Women's Property Bill.

In the meantime her husband was pursuing his own political career. He served for a short period in Parliament but in the 1868 general election was defeated in South Devon largely owing to an election campaign which grossly exaggerated some cautious remarks he had made at a private meeting in favour of birth control. The campaign also reflected back on Kate, since Emily Davies, while continuing to accept her donations, refused to place such a dangerous name on the Girton College committee.

From this time on, although now living in the country, Kate Amberley played an increasingly large part in the women's movement. She continued her work for the Married Women's Property Bill, and in 1870 gave her first lecture on suffrage, at Stroud.

This was published as 'The Claims of Women' in the *Fortnightly Review*, 1870. Throughout both 1870 and 1871 she worked hard organising a local committee on women's suffrage, and collecting signatures for a petition. Interestingly, however, neither she nor her husband supported the movement for the repeal of the Contagious Diseases Acts, in spite of the fact that almost all her co-workers were in sympathy with the campaign. The Acts were designed to protect the Armed Services against venereal disease by providing for the compulsory examination and if necessary treatment of women believed to be prostitutes and these Acts were seen by many feminists as condoning the double standard of sexual morality as well as making state provision for vice. In taking their stand both Kate and John Amberley were influenced by Elizabeth Garrett Anderson, who publicly supported the Acts on the grounds that they helped to protect innocent wives and children.

Unfortunately the public involvement of Kate Amberley in the women's movement was tragically brief. Her husband had always been troubled with poor health, and during 1872 this worsened, to be followed in 1873 by an epileptic seizure. The winter of 1873 was spent abroad for John's health and in the following spring both Kate and her only daughter Rachel died from diphtheria. Her husband, his health already poor, never recovered from the blow, and two years later he too was dead from bronchitis. They left two sons, John Francis born in 1865, and Bertrand born in 1872.

From the time of their marriage her husband seems to have supported Kate in her feminism and, indeed, to have shared in it himself, although it was Kate who took the more active part. Nevertheless, his support was important because she received a great deal of criticism for her views, both from her family and his, and from the public at large. Her willingness to overcome a natural diffidence and to speak in public was also helped by his encouragement.

Kate Amberley did not live long enough to make any great impact on the feminist movement. Nevertheless she was involved in three of the most significant campaigns of the time: married women's property, the higher education of women, and suffrage. Unlike some feminists she was not drawn to the cause by any dissatisfaction with her own position, but seems to have derived her ideas initially from John Stuart Mill and Harriet Taylor, and later to have had them strengthened by contact with activists within the women's rights movement. Like Mill she disliked the dependent status of women, and claimed, in a latter to a friend in 1869, that woman was 'a rational feeling, thinking animal, and not only a sensuous creature made for man' (*The Amberley Papers*, Vol. II, p. 299). In this respect her feminism, like that of Mill, derived ultimately from the Englightenment.

There is no full-length biography of either of the Amberleys but a brief sketch of their lives is given in *The Amberley Papers. The Letters and Diaries of Lord and Lady Amberley*, ed. Bertrand and Patricia Russell, Two Vols. (London, Hogarth Press, 1937). There is also a very short entry for Lord Amberley in *DNB* Vol. XLIX, p. 454.

See also ANDERSON Elizabeth Garrett, DAVIES Sarah Emily, MILL John Stuart.

ANDERSON Elizabeth Garrett 1836–1917

Elizabeth Garrett Anderson was the first British woman doctor. At the time that she was born her father, Newson Garrett, ran a pawnbroker's shop in London, but five years later he bought a corn and coal warehouse in Aldeburgh in Suffolk, and by 1850 he was a rich man. Of considerable ability, he was also an extreme individualist with a powerful will. Elizabeth's mother, Louise Dunnell, was a conventional and deeply religious woman, whose influence on Elizabeth was largely a negative one. Twelve children were born to the Garretts, but two died in infancy.

An intelligent and often rebellious child, Elizabeth Garrett was mainly educated at home by ill-equipped governesses although, with her elder sister Louisa, she spent two years at a school in London. From 1851 she spent nine years as the daughter at home. There was plenty to do, for her mother's final child was not born until 1853, but she was soon bored and discontented and desperately anxious to find something useful to do with her life. Her elder sister Louisa married in 1857 and moved to London, but Elizabeth found no attraction in the young men she met. She had been introduced to Emily Davies in 1854 while visiting some old school friends, and it was through her influence that, after several years of correspondence, Elizabeth was brought into contact with the group of young women centred around Barbara Leigh Smith, (later Barbara Bodichon) who were active in various feminist causes and particularly, at that time, in expanding employment opportunities for women. It was under their influence, and that of Elizabeth Blackwell, the first American woman doctor then on a visit to England, that Elizabeth Garrett after an initial period of doubt, resolved in 1859 to become a doctor herself.

The initial reaction of her parents to the idea was hostile and indeed her mother continued with tears and entreaties long after she was studying in London. But once her father's support was forthcoming, her mother's protests were ignored. From the first, too, there were individuals like Emily Davies' brother John, who were willing to encourage her, and others prepared to give her help with the tuition she required. Although she was never able to gain acceptance as a bona fide student either in London or Scotland she hoped through private study to gain a qualification by examination from the Society of Apothecaries.

During this long and disheartening period she received several proposals of marriage which were rejected without any apparent regret. Only her rejection in 1864 of Henry Fawcett, later to marry her young sister Millicent, seems to have caused her any distress. It is not altogether clear why she turned him down, but certainly marriage to him would have meant the abandonment of her studies and she may well not have cared for him sufficiently to do this.

In 1865 after some dispute she was allowed to sit the examinations of the Society of Apothecaries and so was able to practise as a doctor. Subsidised by her father, now one of her staunchest supporters, she set up in practice in London. At the same time she continued her interest in feminism and in 1866 was one of the committee to collect signatures for John Stuart Mill's suffrage petition. Yet she never allowed herself to become prominent in the suffrage campaign, believing it might interfere with her practice. She did, however, continue her active support of Emily Davies in her attempt to raise funds for what was to become Girton College.

In 1870, now well established in her medical practice, she was invited to serve as medical officer to a newly opened children's hospital and here she met James Skelton Anderson of the Orient Steamship Line and the financial advisor to the hospital. They became close friends, working together not only at the hospital but also in her successful campaign to be elected to the London School Board. Before the end of the year he had asked her to marry him and she had accepted. This time Elizabeth was deeply in love, but she had to face the problem of reconciling marriage with an independent career. Some of her friends, and also her father, were uneasy at the prospect, but Emily Davies gave her unqualified approval. Moreover, although James Anderson was a fairminded man and totally behind her in her professional career he was not happy with all her suggestions. He was hurt, for example, when she insisted that she take legal control of her earnings. These early difficulties were quickly overcome and there is no doubt that the marriage brought her a great deal of personal happiness.

The wedding took place in 1871, and there were three children, Louisa, Margaret who died of meningitis when only just over a year old, and Alan, born in 1877. Undoubtedly there was some curtailment of her activities during this time. For example, she decided not to continue on the school board. Nevertheless she remained very active. In 1872, with the assistance of a number of friends, she had opened a hospital for women, staffed entirely by women, and this continued to prosper. She was also involved in a dispute with Sophia Jex-Blake who wanted to open a medical school for women in London. Elizabeth believed this to be premature, and was in any case distrustful of Sophia Jex-Blake's rather tempestuous personality. However, Sophia persisted and Elizabeth agreed to join the council to prevent a split. She became a lecturer at the school in 1877 and in 1883, to the chagrin of Sophia, was made its dean.

In 1902 both she and her husband retired to Aldeburgh where in 1907 her husband died. A year later she joined the militant branch of the suffrage movement drawn in largely by her love for her daughter Louisa, now an active militant. In 1908 in spite of her age she joined in a raid on Parliament but owing to the intervention of her sister Millicent she was not arrested. By the end of 1911 she decided she could no longer go along with the militants, now growing increasingly violent, although Louisa persisted with her support and was sent to prison in 1912. By this time Elizabeth's health was breaking down and after several years as an invalid she died in 1917.

Although remembered chiefly as Britain's first woman doctor, it is clear that Elizabeth Garrett Anderson's desire to study medicine was deeply rooted in feminism. Originating in her own discontent with what she saw as a useless life, it was fanned by her association with Emily Davies and the small feminist circle active in London in the 1860s. When she fell in love, she feared marriage as a challenge to a woman's independence of mind and action. Nevertheless in some ways she was by no means a typical feminist. In 1870 she antagonised her feminist friends by her public support of the Contagious Diseases Acts which, in order to protect the Armed Forces against venereal disease, provided for the compulsory examination and, if necessary, treatment of women believed to be prostitutes. She recognised the strength of moral feeling against the Acts but believed them to be necessary for the protection of innocent wives and children.

Moreover, when in 1885 W.T. Stead exposed the traffic in young girls in a series of articles in the *Pall Mall Gazette*, she was one of the few feminists to disagree with his findings, writing to her sister Millicent, who was appalled by his disclosures, that his articles were both disgusting and untrue. She also, unlike the bulk of her feminist contemporaries, including Dr Elizabeth Blackwell, supported vaccination and vivisection. In this, as in other ways, she demonstrated the independence of mind which she shared with her father, and the determination to go her own way which accounted for her success in broaching the sternly defended citadel of medicine.

The biography by Jo Manton, *Elizabeth Garrett Anderson* (London, Methuen, 1965) is detailed and gives a full account of all her feminist involvement. There is also a detailed and thorough treatment of her relationship with Emily Davies in *Emily Davies and Girton College*, Barbara Stephen (London, Constable, 1927) and a memoir by her daughter Louisa Garrett Anderson, *Elizabeth Garrett Anderson 1836-1917* (London, Faber and Faber, 1939). See also the entry in *DNB* 1912-21, pp. 6-7.

See also DAVIES Sarah Emily, FAWCETT Millicent Garrett.

ASHURST William Henry 1792-1855

Nothing is known about William Ashurst's early life, or, indeed, his family background. He had little formal education, attending only a dame school, and later entered a solicitor's office where his industry led his employers to give him his articles. He soon developed a good practice as a solicitor, although an early marriage, at nineteen, led him to supplement his income by some copying, and by writing for the press. It is not known where or indeed how his feminism developed although he himself, when asked, would tell how he had seen a girl tried for child murder, who had been betrayed by a man, was convicted by men, sentenced by a man, and hanged by a man.

It is possible that William Ashurst was indeed deeply moved by such an incident, but it is also likely that his sympathies were already aroused by the radical milieu in which he lived, and in which feminism as a principle was a frequent subject of discussion. As a young man he had been influenced by Paine and he took an active part in supporting the Reform Bill of 1832. Even more significantly, he was a friend of Robert Owen and a warm supporter of Co-operation. For a time he carried on the 'Spirit of the Age' founded under Robert Owen's influence and as part of this circle he would certainly have been familiar with Owenite feminism and the Saint-Simonian doctrines on women and the family which were actively propagated in London in the 1830s. A friend of the American feminist and abolitionist Lucretia Mott as well as Lloyd Garrison, he would have been aware of the debate in British abolitionist circles when women delegates from the United States were refused admission to the World Anti-Slavery Convention in London in 1840.

Underlying his Radicalism was a deep concern for the underdog, and throughout his life he defended many men who had been oppressed for their views, but it is probably his championship of Mazzini which reveals most clearly this side of his character. They met for the first time in 1844 and for the rest of his life Mazzini was to remain deeply attached not simply to William Ashurst, but to his children, who continued to support the Italian cause after their father's death in 1855.

We know nothing of his wife and her views, although he seems to have been deeply attached to her, and his health broke down completely after her death. There were five children; a son William A. Ashurst, who became solicitor to the Post Office, and four daughters. These were brought up in habits of independence unusual for the time, and all in different degrees adopted the feminism taught them by their father. It is perhaps in this way that he gave the most practical effect to his own principles. Mathilda married a Joseph Biggs of Leicester and her feminism was handed on to her daughters, one of whom, Caroline Ashurst Biggs became an editor of the *Englishwoman's Review* from 1870 until her death in 1889. Both she and her sisters were active in the campaign for women's suffrage. Caroline Ashurst gave much of her enthusiasm to the cause of Mazzini but her husband James Stansfeld is chiefly remembered for his contribution to the campaign for the repeal of the Contagious Diseases Acts, and other feminist causes. Eliza, the most romantic of the sisters, ran away to Paris where she fell in love with a Frenchman and married him against the advice of her family only to die shortly after in childbirth. Emilie, the most unconventional, was for more than twenty years the ardent disciple and aide to Mazzini but later on, as Madame Venturi, was prominent in several feminist causes, particularly the campaign against the Contagious Diseases Acts.

William Ashurst belonged to a generation of feminists who lived in the decades immediately prior to the emergence of feminism as a political movement, at a time when it was still largely a set of principles advocated by a small number of Radical thinkers. His feminism was part of a more general concern for the oppressed which expressed itself in his interest in the anti-slavery movement, in the cause of Italian freedom, and in his work for individual victims of injustice.

There is an entry for William Ashurst in *DNB* Vol. II pp. 182-3. Material on the Ashurst family is also to be found in *Mazzini's Letters to an English Family*, ed. E.F. Richards, Three Vols. (London, John Lane, Bodley Head, 1920-2), and in *James Stansfeld. A Victorian Champion of Sex Equality*, J.L. and Barbara Hammond (London, Longmans, 1932). Some information on Caroline Ashurst Biggs can be found in *Women's Suffrage, a Record of the Women's Suffrage Movement in the British Isles*, Helen Blackburn, (London, Williams and Norgate, 1902).

See also STANSFELD James, VENTURI Emilie Ashurst.

AYRTON Phoebe Sarah (Hertha) 1854–1923

Hertha Ayrton achieved distinction as a scientist. Born Phoebe Sarah Marks, her father was a jeweller and clockmaker. He was the son of a Polish innkeeper who had fled to Britain to avoid persecution as a Jew. He married the daughter of a glass merchant, but appears to have been a somewhat inadequate provider, and his death in 1861 left the family in poverty. There were eight children in all, two girls and six boys. The youngest child Winnie was an invalid all her life, needing care as well as support. Hertha loved her dearly and later came to take full responsibility for her.

When Hertha was nine she was taken to live with her mother's sister who, with her husband, kept a school in London. It was a fortunate move, for not only was the school a good one, but the family into which she had moved was distinguished both intellectually and artistically. At sixteen she started work, first as a governess, then by taking private pupils. Through her cousin, Marcus Hartog, she met Otilie Blind and the two women became life-long friends. It was Otilie who gave her the name Hertha, encouraged her in her studies, and introduced her to feminism. Eventually Hertha applied for a scholarship to Girton and this led to a meeting with Emily Davies and Barbara Bodichon to whom she eventually became virtually an adopted daughter. There were still hurdles to overcome, as she was by now caring for her sister Winnie and there were also problems with her own health. In the end, although she failed to get a scholarship, money was forthcoming, largely from Barbara Bodichon, and she entered Girton in 1876.

For a short period after leaving Girton she maintained herself and Winnie by teaching private pupils but in 1884 she started serious studies in electricity, encouraged by Professor William Ayrton whom she married in 1885. Professor Ayrton was then thirty-eight years old and a recent widower with a young daughter Edith. In 1871 he had married his cousin Matilda Chaplin and shortly afterwards went with her to Japan on the offer of a position as professor of physics and telegraphy. In 1879 he returned to England and took up a professorship at the City and Guilds of London Institute for the Advancement of Technical Education, where he was working when he met Hertha. His first wife Edith, after an early training in art, had turned to medicine and after some initial attempts in England and Scotland had embarked on a course of study at the Sorbonne. This was interrupted by her marriage, but in Japan she opened a school for midwives and did some teaching herself. In 1877 she returned to Europe and obtained her MD in Paris in 1879. There were however already signs of consumption and although for a time she practised medicine in London, her health worsened rapidly and in 1883 she died.

William Ayrton had encouraged his first wife in her ambitions to be a doctor and he willingly agreed that Hertha too should go on with her studies. But in 1888, after the birth of a girl, a serious illness forced her to give up work. In 1891 Barbara Bodichon died, leaving Hertha a legacy which enabled her to engage a housekeeper. The death of her sister Winnie also relieved her of a burden of responsibility which had been an anxiety for many years. In 1893, her own health now fully restored, she began the work on electric arcs which was to make her reputation. In 1899 the Institute of Electrical Engineers opened their door to a woman for the first time when she was elected a member. In the same year she was also the first woman to give a paper at their meeting.

In 1901 her husband's health began to deteriorate and from then until his death in 1908 her scientific work was interrupted by his illness. A man of restless energy, he had had a distinguished career as a scientist, teacher and inventor, but was now feeling the effects of years of overwork. Nevertheless, she continued her investigations of the electric arc and also started her important studies into sand ripples which led eventually to the Ayrton fan, a device which could be used to clear the air of noxious gases. In 1904 she was the first woman to read a paper before the Royal Society, and in 1906 she received the Hughes Medal. This honour was a great joy to her husband. He had always been anxious that she should be recognised in her own right, and had avoided joint work with her for this reason.

Although Hertha Ayrton had been a supporter of women's suffrage since she had attended her first suffrage meeting when she was eighteen, she had always believed that her scientific work was the most important way in which she could serve women. In 1906 her daughter Barbara—named after Barbara Bodichon—joined Emmeline Pankhurst's militant organisation, the Women's Social and Political Union, and devoted herself to its work. Although previously a member of the constitutional suffrage society, the National Union of Women's Suffrage Socienties under the leadership of Millicent Fawcett, Hertha herself came increasingly to support the militant side of the movement. She gave money lavishly, and also hospitality, on many occasions sheltering Emmeline Pankhurst and other ex-prisoners when they were evading the police. She also walked in processions and occasionally made speeches. Israel Zangwill, who had married her step-daughter Edith in 1903, also became a speaker for the WSPU. In 1910 Barbara married Gerald Gould, himself involved in the suffrage movement as speaker and writer. Hertha, however, became increasingly disturbed at the escalating militancy. In 1914 both she and Barbara left the Pankhursts and joined the United Suffragists along with other previous supporters of the WSPU like the Pethick-Lawrences.

During the war her scientific work continued. She was now developing the Ayrton fan, which she hoped might be used to protect soldiers from gas. After the war she continued to study the industrial applications of the fan in spite of problems with her health, and with sponsorship. She died in 1923 from blood poisoning.

In her early days Hertha Ayrton had been deeply impressed by the ideas of Emily Davies and Barbara Bodichon, but her own feminism was expressed mainly in her scientific work. She saw herself not only as making a contribution to science, but as leading the way for the wider recognition of women scientists. In 1903, for example, she tried to dispel the rumour that Madame Curie's husband was the real discoverer of radium. She also took up cudgels on behalf of both herself and Madame Curie when, in 1912, Sir W. Ramsey alleged that eminent women scientists did their best work in collaboration with a male colleague. She must be seen therefore as an important pioneer in changing attitudes towards women.

There is a biography: *Hertha Ayrton 1854–1923. A Memoir*, Evelyn Sharp (London, Edward Arnold, 1926). The DNB contains no entry for her, but does have one for William Ayrton, *DNB* 1901–1911 pp. 72–5, and for Matilda Chaplin Ayrton *DNB* Vol. II, pp. 292–3.

See also BODICHON Barbara Leigh Smith.

B

BALFOUR Lady Frances 1858–1930

Frances Balfour, an eminent suffragist, was born Lady Frances Campbell, the daughter of the Duke and Duchess of Argyll. The tenth of twelve children, she had an exceptionally spartan childhood, in which there was not only a stoic disregard of comfort but an actual neglect of hygiene and health. As a result of a hip-joint disease which was probably mismanaged she limped from early childhood and suffered pain in the affected leg all her life. She was also severely short-sighted but it was not until 1871 that she was given her first pair of spectacles by her elder brother's bride, Princess Louise, the daughter of Queen Victoria.

Politically the family was intensely Whig, and her father, a somewhat eccentric man, was an active supporter of Gladstone until a difference of opinion on Gladstone's Irish Land Bill led to a breach between them. Both her grandmother, the Duchess of Sutherland, and her mother were active in the anti-slavery movement, and she grew up in this atmosphere, her own contribution the knitting of innumerable woolly garments for children freed from slavery. Later she was to apply the arguments about slaves to the cause of women. The Duchess of Sutherland, a noted Whig hostess, was a woman of independent mind, not at all afraid of courting unpopularity by her actions. A friend of Garibaldi and the campaign for Italian unity, she was his hostess on the occasion of his visit to England. She also befriended Caroline Norton at a time when she was shunned by many of her friends in society.

Because of her limp, Frances feared that she would not marry although she was anxious for the independence of a home of her own. During her first season, however, she attracted the attention of Eustace Balfour, and very soon after they met he asked her to marry him. There was some hesitation on the part of her parents, since he came from a Tory family and was a nephew of Lord Salisbury, but these objections were overcome and they married in 1879. Eustace Balfour came from an intellectual family, many of whom distinguished themselves in later life, and his elder brother Arthur Balfour became a Conservative politician and eventually Prime Minister. Eustace showed a talent for art and was trained as an architect, and in the early years of her marriage Frances Balfour mixed mainly with his artistic circle, falling, like her husband, completely under the spell of the pre-Raphaelites.

This period did not last long. Eustace does not seem to have been a great success as an architect and, perhaps for this reason, he began, in 1882, to take an interest in the idea of a Volunteer Army which eventually became his life-long passion. Frances found herself totally out of sympathy with the Army society in which he increasingly spent his time and eventually his holidays were spent away from his family. Five children were born, including Blanche in 1880 and the first son in 1884. In 1889 a second daughter was born, and in 1891 a third. Then in 1894 another son, Oswald, completed the family. Of these children only Oswald became really close to his father, and it is perhaps significant that, according to Frances Balfour, his interest was largely reserved for his sons.

Although she had married into a Tory family, Frances Balfour remained a Whig in most of her political attitudes, opposing any notion of a divinely appointed governing glass and approving Liberal Party policy on the extension of the franchise. Although she also believed passionately in women's rights, at first she found no one to take her seriously. Eventually, however, she was brought into contact with some of the leading suffragists through her work with the Women's Liberal Unionist Association. In 1887 she joined the women's suffrage movement, eventually serving on its central committee where she made a particular friend of Helen Blackburn.

For the next twenty-five years suffrage was one of the central issues in her life. No good at organisation, she was an able speaker and served the constitutional campaign well in this capacity. She was also well placed through her contacts to act as liaison between the suffrage movement and the Houses of Parliament, and this she did with zeal and efficiency. Her sister-in-law and friend Betty Balfour, who had married Gerald Balfour in 1887, was also a constitutional suffragist and the two frequently worked in harness. Later, Betty's sister Constance Lytton joined the militants, and her brother Lord Lytton himself became an energetic worker in the suffrage cause. Within the Balfour family itself, Eustace's sister Nora and her husband Henry Sidgwick were also sympathetic, although their main energies were given to women's education. Arthur Balfour, potentially the most influential, was prepared to accept the justice of the women's case, but his enthusiasm was never aroused and he held himself for most purposes aloof from the struggle in spite of the efforts of Frances and Betty Balfour to bring him into a closer involvement. This was in sharp contrast to Lord Lytton who gave himself whole-heartedly to the cause.

Both Frances and Betty Balfour remained constitutional suffragists throughout the whole of the campaign and neither followed the example of Constance Lytton who endured prison and forcible feeding before a breakdown in health ended her active involvement. Frances admired the Pankhursts, and believed that they brought necessary publicity to the cause but could not bring herself to accept their tactics. In no sense a socialist, she was at first alarmed when in 1912 the National Union of Women's Suffrage Societies adopted Millicent Fawcett's suggestion of giving support to Labour Party candidates. Later she accepted the policy, recognising the work that men like Philip Snowden had done for the campaign.

During these years Eustace Balfour became a hopeless alcoholic, and, his health impaired, died in 1911 at the age of fifty-seven. The Volunteer Army remained his chief interest, and his greatest disappointment was that failing health prevented him serving overseas in the Boer War. Frances Balfour was never anything but loyal to him, and the relationship between them remained, outwardly at least, an affectionate one to the end of his life. Nevertheless the marriage was clearly a disappointment to her, and she turned to Arthur Balfour for the intellectual companionship she could not get from her husband. Passionately interested in politics, she followed every stage of his career, not hesitating to criticise him when she thought he was wrong. Eustace appears to have been a tolerant husband who interfered very little with her activities, but he made no secret of the fact that he disagreed with her profoundly on a number of political issues, and particularly on women's suffrage, which he thought totally mistaken.

Although the suffrage issue was perhaps the most important, it was by no means the only one on which she took a determined and outspoken stand; others ranged from Irish home rule to protection and free trade. She was also deeply involved in promoting the interests of the Scottish Church. Moreover, although suffrage was her main preoccupation she was alive to other issues concerning women. For example, she was very concerned to defend the rights of barmaids when the temperance lobby tried to prevent women working in bars. In 1910 she was asked to serve on the Commission on Matrimonial and Divorce Laws. In later years she wrote widely for the periodical press and wrote several biographies and an autobiography.

Lively, intelligent and intensely loyal, Frances Balfour has also been criticised as quarrelsome and domineering. Certainly she was adept at the use of her sarcastic wit. Her chief passion was politics and it was indeed the tragedy of her life that because she was a woman she could take no part in the life of the House of Commons. She tried her best to work through others, but this was often intensely irritating to one of her forthright temperament. So it is not surprising that her feminism took the form of a plea for women to be granted equal rights as persons, and particularly as citizens. Her desire was to break into what had hitherto been a man's world and it is no contradiction that, as her daughter recalls, she did not in general enjoy women's company. She loved her children, but had little interest in the social and domestic world which imprisoned most women of her class. Nor did she share in the consciousness of a fellowship of women which was so characteristic a feature of the militant movement, and she was totally unsympathetic to any idea of a sex war. For her the vote was the key which would unlock the door to the equal citizenship she craved and she does not seem to have shared in the conception, prevalent especially amongst the militant suffragists, of the vote as a weapon to right the wrongs of women. Her conception of feminism was rooted in nineteenth-century concepts of freedom and democracy; the heritage of her Whig forebears and their stand on slavery which had influenced her childhood.

Frances Balfour has written her own memoirs, *Me Obliviscaris*, Lady Frances Balfour (London, Hodder and Stoughton, 1930). Her daughter Blanche gives some recollections of her mother in *Family Homespun*, Blanche Dugdale (London, John Murray, 1940). For her relationship with Arthur Balfour and also with her husband see *A Life of Arthur Balfour*, Max Egremont (London, Collins, 1980). See also *DNB* 1931–1940, pp. 34–5.

BARMBY Catherine Isabella ?1817–1853

Catherine Barmby, a communitarian socialist, was born Catherine Watkins. By the 1830s she was already a feminist, although not yet out of her teens, and it is tantalising that we know nothing of her background or the early circumstances of her life. The first we know of her, indeed, is as a contributor to Robert Owen's *New Moral World* under the pseudonym of 'Kate'. An early essay of hers, on 'Female Improvement', published in the *New Moral World* in 1835, argued for legal and educational equality between men and women, and a later essay in the same journal attacked the current laws for their injustice to women.

In 1840 she met Goodwyn Barmby, a young man only twenty years old but already deeply and passionately devoted to both Chartism and Owenism. He came of a well-to-do family and was intended for one of the professions but the early death of his father left him free to pursue his own interests. At first he was attracted by Chartism and his name appears among twelve signatories to the Manifesto issued after the Manchester Convention in 1840 which set up the National Charter Association, but already by 1840 his main interest was Owenite socialism.

Goodwyn and Catherine were married in 1841 and afterwards worked closely together in the communist church, a small communitarian sect which combined Owenite Socialism with a religious millenialism and owed something to both the Saint-Simonians and Joanna Southcott. Together he and Catherine toured the streets of London with a hooded cart, dispensing tracts demanding the re-instatement by the Church of England of the communist practices of the early church. In 1843 they opened the Moreville Communitorium but this failed to attract converts and lasted less than a year. The communist church however lasted until 1848 at which time Goodwyn became a Unitarian minster, and he and Catherine abandoned millenarian socialism for more orthodox belief. During the 1840s two children were born, a son Moreville in 1844 and a daughter Julie in 1846.

Goodwyn's feminism during the 1840s was founded very largely on his religious beliefs and looked forward to a transformation of society which would also transform the meaning of both womanhood and manhood, and the coming of a new type of androgynous personality. In this future, which was about to come into being, men would possess woman-power as well as man-power and women man-power as well as woman-power. Consequently he opposed all restrictions on women's social role.

During these years Catherine Barmby not only shared in her husband's work but developed her own ideas on women which were published in a number of progressive journals, as well as in millenarian literature. In a long essay, 'The Demand for the Emancipation of Woman, Politically and Socially', *New Tracts for the Times*, Vol III, (1843), she demanded women's emancipation under three headings: political, through universal suffrage, ecclesiastical, through their entry into the priesthood, and domestic, through economic independence which would free women from both domestic tyranny and the tyranny of the husband. She also wanted women's societies in which women could prepare themselves to use their influence as 'apostles' in society at large. The plea for economic independence was also made in 1848 when she published 'Women's Industrial Independence' in *Apostle and Chronicle of the Communist Church*, Vol. I, No. 1, 1848. She argued forcibly that only employment made women free, and complained that women had been turned out of their traditional occupations like midwifery. She also pointed out the isolation of domestic life and advocated common nurseries for children. Both she and her husband approved the principle of votes for women, and in 1841 in a Declaration of Electoral Reform they demanded that the People's Charter be amended to include women's suffrage, but Catherine always argued that the vote without socialism would not free women.

After 1848 Catherine Barmby's activities declined. She had tried unsuccessfully during the late 1840s to start a feminist journal, but after the birth of her second child in 1846 her health declined and she died in 1853. Goodwyn, in spite of his loss of faith in millenarianism, retained his interest in social reform supporting, for example, the campaign for Polish, Italian and Hungarian liberation. In 1861 he remarried, his second wife being Ada Marianne Shepherd, and another daughter was born in 1865. He had not lost his faith in feminism and in 1868 both he and his second wife supported the campaign for women's suffrage. He died in 1881.

Catherine Barmby is a very good example of the attempt to combine feminism and communitarian socialism and by doing so to transform not simply the legal and political status of women, but the very structure of the family itself. Views such as these disappeared with communitarian socialism and were not to reappear within feminism until the early twentieth century. Catherine Barmby herself is a rather elusive figure known to us chiefly through her writings and through the activities of her husband. Unlike some socialist feminists, she was not so far as we know introduced to feminism by some unhappy personal experience, and her conversion both to feminism and to socialism while she was still in her teens must remain a mystery, although it is possible that her family, of which we know nothing, had Owenite sympathies.

The best source of information on the Barmbys is *Eve and the New Jerusalem*, Barbara Taylor (London, Virago, 1983). This contains Catherine Barmby's *The Demand for the Emancipation of Women*. The other source is *DLB*, Vol. VI, pp. 10–18. Goodwyn Barmby is in the *DNB*, Vol. III, pp. 23–5, although this gives Catherine's maiden name incorrectly.

BARNES Annie 1887–?

Annie Barnes was a suffragette whose father ran a fruiterers' and confectioners' shop in Stepney. Her mother had an income of her own and this enabled her to have some help in the house, although with a total of twelve pregnancies it is unlikely that she had very much leisure. Nevertheless, Annie was spared any real poverty. She loved her mother but her father seems to have been a thoroughly hard and selfish man. Annie did well at school and was destined to be a teacher but in 1902, when she was fifteen, her mother became seriously ill and Annie, the eldest child, had to leave school and take her mother's place. When her mother died in 1910, at the age of forty-five, there were seven children for Annie to care for, four having died early. Moreover, several of them were still very young, including Rose aged five, Ernie aged three, and a baby only a year old. These children Annie cared for as if they were her own.

In the meantime she had become interested in the suffrage movement from hearing women speaking at open-air meetings. After her mother's death she joined the East London Federation of Suffragettes and got to know Sylvia Pankhurst who became a friend. She would slip out of the house without her father's knowledge, and although she limited her commitment because of the children, she joined in the work of distributing leaflets, and similar activities. In 1914, when Sylvia set up the *Workers' Dreadnought*, she would slip out to deliver copies.

For a long time Annie had determined that she would not marry. She felt strongly her responsibility to her young brothers and sisters, especially as her father cared little for them. Finally, however, Albert Barnes, a furniture maker, proved exceptionally persistent in his courtship and when he promised that he would help take care of the children she agreed to marry him. At first the children remained at home, but her fears that they would be neglected were soon realised and as soon as it could be managed the children were reunited with her. Perhaps because she felt her brothers and sisters were family enough, perhaps for other reasons, she had no children of her own, and as her brothers and sisters were now growing up, Annie soon had time to take an interest in politics.

Sylvia Pankhurst had persuaded her to join the Independent Labour Party and later she joined the Labour Party. When Sylvia joined the communists, Annie disapproved, although they still remained friends. In the 1920s she became a school manager, the secretary of the local women's section of the Labour Party, and in 1929 became involved in the Women's Co-operative Guild. In 1934 she became a Labour councillor for Stepney. Interested particularly in housing and public health, she was involved in the controversy over whether clinics for maternity and child welfare should give advice on birth control, and became embroiled with the Roman Catholics as a result of her support for birth control. During this period she was still friendly with Sylvia Pankhurst and through her was involved in the work of giving homes to illegal Italian refugees.

Her husband, a cheerful sociable person, was never really interested in politics. His hobby was gardening. He did not, however, raise any objections to her own absence at meetings. She recollected that the only time he ever stopped her doing anything was going on a plane trip to Switzerland with a group from Toynbee Hall. He could not bear the thought of her travelling on a plane. It was her practice during her years of involvement in local government to do all her housework from 6 to 9 am, leaving the day free. Food would be left in the house for her husband. In 1949 they moved to Pitsea and this ended her political work. Later they returned to East Ham but by then she had lost contact with her old friends. In 1980, when she was interviewed and tape-recorded, she was crippled with arthritis but still mentally alert and able to record her memories.

Annie Barnes is a good example of those East End women who were drawn into the suffrage movement by Sylvia Pankhurst. Her life clearly illustrates the problems faced by these women, especially when they had young children to care for. Annie Barnes is interesting because she continued her active involvement in politics after the war, although the issues she was involved in, with the exception of the birth-control controversy, were not necessarily concerned with women. Nevertheless, with others like her, she carried the voice of working-class women into local government.

Information on Annie Barnes is derived

from her own recollections in *Tough Annie. From Suffragette to Stepney Councillor*, Annie Barnes, in conversation with Kate Harding and Caroline Gibbs (London, Stepney Books Publications, 1980).

BEALE Dorothea 1831-1906

Dorothea Beale, a notable headmistress, was the daughter of Miles Beale, a London surgeon, and his wife Dorothea Margaret Complin. There were eleven children of the marriage, and Dorothea was the fourth child, and the third daughter. Her mother came from an intellectual family, and Dorothea's aunt Frances Cornwallis was the author of several devotional books. Her daughter, Dorothea's cousin, also enjoyed considerable literary success, writing books on philosophy and history, as well as journal articles. Something of a feminist herself, she was critical of the low estimation in which women's intellect was generally held. Although influenced mainly by her mother's family, Dorothea also had the sympathy and support of her father, who was always ready with encouragement and help.

Although her parents took care with her education, Dorothea Beale was critical both of her governesses and of the school to which she was sent. She left at the age of thirteen, because of ill-health, and afterwards, apart from a year at a school in Paris when she was sixteen, she was self-educated. A serious and studious girl, she had the advantage of several good libraries as well as the experience of teaching her younger brothers. Then, shortly after it opened in 1848, she enrolled at Queen's College for Women, in company with such other pioneers of women's education as Sophia Jex-Blake and Frances Buss. So well did she progress that in a very short time she became the first woman mathematics teacher.

At no time in her life, however, was Dorothea Beale able to work within an institution of which she disapproved, and she soon became dissatisfied with the college, and especially with the declining influence of the women visitors. Already she had become firmly convinced that women were the best teachers for girls, and in 1856, followed a dispute on the issue, she resigned and accepted the post of Head Teacher at Casterton School, the 'Lowood' of *Jane Eyre*. Again her disagreement with the way the school was run, and the failure of her efforts at reform, led to what was virtually a dismissal after only one year of service.

For a while, after the events at Casterton, Dorothea Beale seems to have lost her strong sense of vocation and considered other kinds of work. A broken engagement also contributed to her unhappiness although the background to this failed romance is unfortunately unknown to us. It is possible, however, that her high standards both for herself and others, may have been a contributory factor. Later in her life there were other proposals, the last when she was nearly fifty, but never again does she seem to have taken them seriously. She retained, throughout her life, a very high ideal of marriage, but came to believe that for women like herself the deepest satisfactions were to be obtained through work.

It is indicative of her character that even in this period of crisis she did not remain idle. She wrote a *Textbook of General History* for the use of teachers and a short account of the Deaconesses' Institution at Kaiserworth. During this same period she also wrote a devotional book for schools. Then in 1858, still only twenty-seven, she applied for the headship of Cheltenham Ladies' College, at that time a conventional and financially insecure school for girls. There were problems about her appointment, largely springing from her experiences at Casterton and concentrating mainly on doctrinal issues concerning baptism, but these were overcome and Dorothea Beale embarked on what was to be her life's work.

Her early years at Cheltenham were by no means without problems, since it was some time before the school was placed on a really secure financial base. It was difficult, also, to convince parents that the education of a daughter was something to be taken seriously. But by 1864 anxiety for the future of the school was at an end, and the rest of her years as principal were spent in consolidating and extending her success. For example, she was responsible for the opening of St Hilda's College at Oxford.

Although her life was chiefly bound up with her own school, her significance was much wider than this, since the school's success was a demonstration of what a good school could achieve. She also used her own experience effectively in the campaign for the improvement of the education of girls, and in 1865 was one of the small number of women who gave evidence to the Schools Inquiry Commission. In addition she played a part in a number of organisations for the improvement of education, taking an interest, for example, in the Head Mistresses' Association, The Teachers' Guild, the Froebel Society and the Child Study Association.

Nor were her activities confined to education. In the 1880s in particular she began to take a keen interest in rescue work, along with many other prominent women at that time, largely as a result of the disclosures of W.T. Stead. She was a supporter of the National Vigilance Association to which she left a legacy, and advocated women policemen as early as 1886. Moreover, she believed firmly in women's suffrage as the best way of getting the reform needed by women, and was a vice-president of the Central Society for Women's Suffrage.

In 1878 a long period of overwork resulted in a near breakdown and in 1882 an agonising period of religious doubt made her incapable of work and almost led to her resignation from the college. These were temporary difficulties, and the 1890s in particular were successful years during which her work for women's education was rewarded by a number of honours. Perhaps the most important was the granting of an honorary LLD by Edinburgh University in 1899. In 1898 she published *Work and Play in Girls' Schools* which was a distillation of her own ideas and experiences. Still principal of the college, she died in 1906 after an unsuccessful operation.

Although in some respects advanced in her views, in other ways Dorothea Beale was conservative in her thinking. Always profoundly religious, she saw the position of women principally in terms of duties rather than rights. Thus, she opposed the plan to open university local examination to girls since she feared it might foster a spirit of rivalry. High on her goals as an educationist was the need to encourage obedience to duty, and self-restraint. Later she was forced to accept public examinations for girls, but she delighted to be able to show that girls who did well in examinations could also excel in domestic duties. She stressed that women had a subordinate role to play in life, and were men's natural help-meets and companions, a belief oddly out of character with the way she had lived her own life. At the same time however she justified the need to educate women on the grounds that women as well as men must use the talents God had given them.

Dorothea Beale had an authoritarian personality and great energy and force of character. This was combined with a strong and religiously inspired sense of mission which gave her confidence in her destiny, and it is significant that when she was for a time assailed by religious doubt it almost destroyed her. The conflict between her sense of duty and her drive for independence was reconciled for her by her sense of a God-given mission and this produced a version of feminism which often stressed women's traditional qualities. Moreover, her strong absorption in the life of her own school kept her somewhat aloof from the rest of the women's movement in spite of her support for women's suffrage. Nevertheless she remains, like that other great Victorian headmistress Frances Buss, an important figure in nineteenth-century feminism.

The main biography of Dorothea Beale is *Dorothea Beale of Cheltenham*, Elizabeth Raikes (London, Constable, 1908). A somewhat shorter version is provided by Elizabeth Shillitoe in *Dorothea Beale. Principal of the Cheltenham Ladies' College 1858-1906* (London, Macmillan, 1920). See also *How Different from Us: a Biography of Miss Buss and Miss Beale*, Josephine Kamm (London,

Bodley Head, 1958). A recent more critical assessment can be found in 'Some Victorian Headmistresses: a conservative tradition of social reform', Joyce Senders Pedersen, *Victorian Studies*, Vol. XXIV (4), 1981. See also *DNB* 1901–1911, pp. 116–8.

See also BUSS Frances Mary.

BECKER Lydia Ernestine 1827–1890

Lydia Becker, a leading suffragist, was born in Manchester, the daughter of Hannibal Leigh Becker, of German descent, and Mary Duncuft. She was the eldest of fifteen children, and like the rest of her sisters was educated at home apart from a year in Germany in 1844–45. We know little about her childhood, or indeed her life with her family although, while still only a child, she had been involved in the activities of the Anti-Corn Law League from which she was to draw tactical lessons when she became involved in the suffrage movement. In 1855 her mother died followed two years later by her eldest brother, an event which caused her a great deal of sorrow. This was followed by a period of bitter trouble for the family although whether these troubles were financial, or whether there were more bereavements is not known. During all these years she lived quietly at home in the country where her father owned a chemical works. It is possible, although we do not know this for certain, that both before and after her mother's death she was involved in the care and education of her younger brothers and sisters. She read widely, her chief interest being botany, and in 1862 she won the gold medal for the best collection of dried plants made within a year. In 1864 she published *Botany for Novices* and some time during this period she wrote a treatise on elementary astronomy although this was never published.

In 1865 the family moved to Manchester and this move was to transform her life. Her first step was to devise a plan for a Ladies' Literary Society, of which she became president, but in 1866 she attended the Social Science Annual Meeting held that year in Manchester and heard Barbara Bodichon read a paper on women's suffrage. It is not clear how deeply she had thought about this issue previously, although there are signs that she was discontented with the lack of opportunity for women like her. What is certain is that she not only became a convert to the idea, but wrote a paper of her own which she sent to Emily Davies who was so impressed that she sent it on to Elizabeth Wolstenholme then living in Manchester. A year later, when the Manchester Women's Suffrage Committee was formed, Emily Davies put her in touch with it. She joined and was appointed its secretary.

This was the start of a close association with the suffrage group in Manchester which included Jacob Bright and Richard Pankhurst, whom for a time she deeply admired. In 1868 she was closely involved with him in an unsuccessful effort to include women householders on the electoral roll, and from this time she went to him frequently for his advice and opinion. There were indeed rumours that she had an unrequited passion for him but there is no real evidence that this was so.

Lydia Becker was not, however, destined to exert her influence only in Manchester. In 1867 an article 'Female Suffrage' in the *Contemporary Review* made her name known. In 1870 she became a national figure in the movement when she founded the *Women's Suffrage Journal* and became its editor. Soon she became the chief parliamentary agent for the suffrage movement, and was a familiar figure in lobbies, developing in time an unrivalled knowledge of parliamentary procedures. Nor, at this time, was suffrage her only interest, since she was active on the Married Women's Property Committee, founded in 1868, serving for a time as its treasurer. More surprisingly, since a number of women in the suffrage movement stood aloof, she was drawn into the campaign against the Contagious Diseases Acts which, in order to protect the Armed Services against venereal disease, provided for the compulsory examination and if necessary treatment of women believed to be prostitutes. Because of its nature this was a particularly difficult campaign for an unmarried woman to undertake but Lydia Becker does not seem to have hesitated at all. She strongly admired Josephine Butler and stood firmly behind her throughout the campaign which opposed the Acts as condoning the double standard of morality and making state provision for vice, and was one of those who signed the *Daily News* protest in 1870. In 1870, too, she was elected to the Manchester School Board, where she took a particular interest in the education of girls. During these years she published two important pamphlets, one in 1872 on *The Political Disabilities of Women* and one in 1873 on *Liberty, Equality and Fraternity: a Reply to Mr. Fitzjames Stephen's Strictures on the Subjection of women*.

But in 1874 a controversy within the suffrage movement parted Lydia Becker from many of her Manchester friends, and from this time on she appeared to grow more rigid in her views. In that year there was a move to exclude married women specifically from a proposed suffrage Bill. Lydia Becker at first rejected the proposal, but was later converted to the idea, on the grounds that such a limitation to single women might give the Bill more support. This antagonised some of her radical suffrage friends like the Brights and Richard Pankhurst. Indeed, the friendship with Richard Pankhurst seems never to have been resumed. In 1884, when he stood as an independent candidate in Manchester, she refused him the support of the Suffrage Society on the grounds that he was a firebrand. In 1874, perhaps because of her quarrel with Richard Pankhurst, she resigned as treasurer of the Married Women's Property Committee.

Increasingly during the late 1870s and 1880s Lydia Becker concentrated on the suffrage issue and remained an absolutely central figure in the suffrage movement through the *Women's Suffrage Journal* and her role in the parliamentary lobby. By the winter of 1889–90 however, illness confined her almost entirely at home. A course of baths at Aix-les-Bains in the following summer seemed to bring an improvement but on an excursion to the Alps she was taken ill with diphtheria, from which she never recovered.

In spite of her somewhat controversial position in the suffrage movement, Lydia Becker was of enormous importance in sustaining it through the parliamentary defeats of the 1870s and 1880s. Indeed, with her devoted editorship removed, the *Women's Suffrage Journal* ceased to appear. Her devotion to the cause of feminism was never in doubt, and her quarrel with the radicals was entirely a matter of tactics, not principles. Her feminism was perhaps of a more radical kind than many of her contemporaries. In 1877, for example, when laying the foundation stone for one of the Manchester School Board girls' schools, she criticised the narrowly domestic education of girls in such schools, and argued that boys should be taught to mend their own socks and cook their own meals. She also defended the pit-brow women, arguing that women had a right to work, and that Parliament had no right to take that away without compensation. On marriage she took up the position that the husband ought to have no headship or authority over his wife, and that such authority was indeed the root of all social evil.

A plain woman, she was often made the butt of gibes in the press but bore this with fortitude. She seems to have been an extremely reticent and even, to some extent, a lonely person. The suffrage movement which she served so devotedly gave her the opportunity to make use of her abilities on a scale which would otherwise have been denied to her, as well as an emotional satisfaction in working with other women in a cause in which she deeply believed.

There is no biography of Lydia Becker, and our knowledge of her life before 1867 is based on a very brief sketch by her friend Helen Blackburn in *Women's Suffrage. A Record of the Movement* (London, Williams and Norgate, 1902). There is a rather critical account of her contribution in *The Suffragette*

Movement, Sylvia Pankhurst (London, Longmans, 1931; Virago, 1977). For a more recent and more friendly assessment, see *One Hand Tied Behind Us. The Rise of the Women's Suffrage Movement*, Jill Liddington and Jill Norris (London, Virago, 1978) and *Women of Ideas and What Men Have Done to Them*, Dale Spender (London, Routledge and Kegan Paul, 1982). For her involvement in the Contagious Diseases Acts campaign see *Prostitution and Social Reform*, Paul McHugh (New York, St Martin's Press, 1980). There is an entry in *DNB Supplementary Vol. I*, pp. 159–60. For her work on the Married Women's Property Committee see *Wives and Property*, Lee Holcombe (Oxford, Martin Robertson, 1983).

See also PANKHURST Richard Marsden.

BELLOC Bessie Rayner 1829–1925

Bessie Rayner Parkes, a pioneer in opening wider opportunities to women, was the daughter of Joseph Parkes and the granddaughter, on her mother's side, of the famous Radical and Unitarian scientist Joseph Priestley. Her father, a solicitor, was also a Unitarian of Radical sympathies and a friend of Brougham, Grote, and John Stuart Mill. We know nothing of her childhood or her education, but in 1846 she began the close relationship with Barbara Leigh Smith, later Barbara Bodichon, which was to have a profound effect on her life. Barbara Leigh Smith also came from a Radical background so the two young girls had much in common, but Barbara's unconventional background and forceful personality must have made her the leader in all their enterprises. Nevertheless if Barbara Leigh Smith was the leader, Bessie Parkes was a highly able lieutenant and they worked together in harness for a number of years.

In 1854 Barbara had published 'A brief Summary in Plain Language of the Most Important Laws concerning Women'. The Law Amendment Society was interested and a ladies' committee was formed on which Barbara and Bessie both served. A petition was drawn up with the purpose of giving women the right to their own earnings. Although their bid to change the law was unsuccessful, Bessie and Barbara were led to consider other necessary changes in the position of women and turned both to the better education of girls and women and the opening up of new employment prospects. In 1856 Bessie Parkes published *Remarks on the Education of Girls* and in 1858 she joined with Barbara in establishing the *Englishwoman's Journal* in order to propagate their ideas. The money was provided by Barbara, but Bessie was made editor and became a frequent contributor to its pages. In 1857 Barbara had married Eugene Bodichon, and subsequently spent part of each year in Algeria, and this left Bessie Parkes very much in charge both of the journal and of the little group of women involved in its affairs.

The journal was the first of its kind, and was important in providing a vehicle of propaganda which awakened many women to feminist ideas. Its office also provided a meeting place and the Langham Place Ladies, as they came to be called, were an important nucleus from which other organisations soon sprang. Perhaps the most important of these was the Society for the Promotion of the Employment of Women, founded by Adelaide Proctor, who was one of Bessie's closest friends.

Bessie was closely associated with the work of the Langham Place circle from its inception until 1867. In 1866 she published *Essays on Women's Work* (London, Alexander Strachan) which demonstrates very clearly both the source and the nature of her feminism during these years. Central to her concern was the growing number of women forced by the circumstances of their lives to be their own breadwinners, and it was the needs of this class of women, or 'surplus' women as they were called in the jargon of the day, which she saw as the chief cause of the rise of the women's movement. The laws of the country, she argued, were framed on the assumption that women were supported by their husbands or fathers, but this was becoming less and less the case. She suggested an improvement in the education of girls, and the opening of a wider range of employment as the remedy, but beyond this she would not go. The great mass of women, she argued, would always remain homemakers since this was their best and proper sphere. She also rejected any notion of strict equality between the sexes since women, because of the delicate organisation of their brains and bodies, were not fitted for equal competition with men. She was therefore less of a feminist than a number of her contemporaries, including Barbara Bodichon and Emily Davies.

Although she was active throughout most of the 1860s, working as editor of the journal until 1867 and involving herself in the early stages of the suffrage campaign, beneath the surface she was becoming deeply uncertain of the direction her life should take in the future. This may have been the result of a profound change in her religious beliefs which occurred between 1861 and 1864 when a growing interest in the work of the Irish Sisters of Mercy and Sisters of Charity led to a conversion to Roman Catholicism. This was a big step for someone who had been brought up a Unitarian and who, in 1857, had shown considerable interest in Secularism. The death of her great friend Adelaide Proctor, herself a convert to Roman Catholicism, may have been another factor in her conversion. The death of Adelaide Proctor was a great personal loss, and was followed by a breakdown in her own health. The year 1866 also saw the end of a long relationship with a man who had loved her devotedly and had many times asked her to marry him. Although she did not return his love, she could not free herself from his need to love her and on several occasions had almost yielded to his entreaties. Perhaps indeed she would have done so, if she had not been sustained by Barbara's admonition not to marry a man she did not love.

In 1867 she went on holiday to France with Barbara, who had been ill. There she met and fell in love with Louis Belloc, the son of a French painter Hilaire Belloc, and his wife, Madame Belloc, herself a writer of some distinction. Louis, a year or two younger than Bessie, had been an invalid for thirteen years and their marriage was almost universally opposed by his family, and hers, but by no one more strenuously than Barbara Bodichon. Bessie however was not prepared to accept Barbara's advice and the marriage took place in September after a very short engagement. Undoubtedly this marriage made Bessie Belloc idyllically happy. Whereas the love of the earlier man in her life had distressed her, Louis Belloc, she found, was able to love her in the right way, so that she felt protected and cherished but never threatened. Her happiness was totally destroyed however when five years later Louis Belloc died suddenly from sunstroke. The grief that followed for Bessie Belloc shadowed not only the remainder of her own life but the childhood of her two children. Although the period of intense and paralysing grief eventually ended, she was never able to speak of him without tears.

After her husband's death Bessie Belloc returned with her two children to England. For a time she lived with her mother, but upon her mother's death moved to Sussex where she lived for the rest of her life. Nevertheless, in spite of her return, her ties with the women's movement, broken on her marriage, were never re-opened. Her friendship with Barbara Bodichon had survived the disagreement between them and, after Barbara's illness and paralysis in 1877, Bessie Belloc and her two children were frequent visitors until Barbara's death in 1891. She was however never more than a sympathetic bystander in the various campaigns which were actively pursued during the 1880s and 1890s. Nor did she take any part in the renewed suffrage campaign after 1900, which was of such interest and concern to her contemporaries Emily Davies and Elizabeth Garrett Anderson. Moreover, unlike Elizabeth Garrett Anderson, whose daughter became a militant suffragist, Bessie's daughter, a successful novelist, remained uninvolved and her son, Hilaire Belloc, became one of the leading anti-feminists, registering his disapproval not only of women's suffrage but of the higher education of women.

Apart from her feminist writing, Bessie Belloc published two volumes of poems and several collections of essays and recollections. It is perhaps significant that her reminiscences of Adelaide Proctor, published in 1895 in a collection of essays *In a Walled Garden* (London, Ward and Bowney), pay no attention to Adelaide's very significant services to the women's movement.

For almost ten years, between 1857 and 1867, Bessie Rayner Parkes was one of the most prominent of the little group of women who between them turned women's rights from an ideology into a social and political movement. Her own particular concern was the problem of women's employment but she also gave her support to many other issues, including education, the right of married women to their property and earnings, and the vote. But her period of active involvement was brief and ended completely with her marriage in 1867. To give her marriage as the sole reason for her abandonment of her work for women would however be an oversimplification. For several years previously there had been signs of weariness and disillusion, and the great happiness of her marriage may have come from the fact that she had found a haven from the doubts which were besetting her. Her feminism was a long way too from the passion for independence displayed by Barbara Bodichon, or the singlemindedness with which Emily Davies fought for equality in higher education, and derived perhaps more from her friendship with Barbara Bodichon than from any deep personal commitment. Nevertheless, we should not, on this account, forget her positive achievements.

There is no full biography of Bessie Belloc, but her daughter has written of her marriage to Louis Belloc in *I, too, have lived in Arcadia. A Record of Love and Childhood*, Mrs Belloc Lowndes (London, Macmillan, 1941). Her relationship with Barbara Bodichon is described by Hester Burton in *Barbara Bodichon 1827-1891* (London, John Murray, 1949). See also *The Life of Hilaire Belloc*, Robert Speaight (London, Hollis and Clarke, 1957).

See also BODICHON Barbara Leigh Smith, PROCTOR Adelaide Anne.

BESANT Annie 1847-1933

Annie Besant, a pioneer in the birth control movement, was the daughter of William Wood and Emily Roche Morris. Her father had lived his early life in Ireland where he took a medical degree, but came to London where he was offered a good opportunity in commerce by a relative. A versatile man and a good scholar, he was also an affectionate husband and father. In 1852 he died suddenly from an infection, leaving his wife and three young children almost destitute. Shortly afterwards the youngest child Alfred also died. Mrs Wood moved to Harrow where she supported herself by means of a boarding-house for Harrow pupils, and when Harry, the surviving son, later went to school as a day boy, Annie herself became the protégée of Ellen Marryat, sister of the novelist Frederick Marryat, with whom she lived until she was sixteen years old. She developed into a studious child, with a strong interest in religion which was to continue to fascinate her all her life, although her reading was to lead her at first into disbelief and finally into theosophy.

In 1866 she met Frank Besant, a young clergyman, and when, shortly after the meeting, he proposed she accepted him although not without misgivings and even one ineffectual attempt to get out of the engagement. From the start the marriage was a failure. Her first experience of sex, totally ignorant as she was, shocked and horrified her, and she never became reconciled to it. There were also incompatibilities of temperament since he expected submission and Annie was proud and independent. Moreover, he was a cold man without tenderness, who when roused to anger would sometimes strike her. In 1869 a son, Digby, was born, and eighteen months later, in 1870, a daughter Mabel, but they seem to have done nothing to reconcile her to the marriage. Deeply unhappy, she sought consolation in religion, only to find herself beset with doubt. Eventually she refused to attend communion and this was to prove the end of the marriage. Her furious husband demanded that she either obey him or leave him, and she chose to go. A separation was arranged, in which Digby stayed with his father, and in 1873 she went to London with Mabel.

In the final years of her marriage, in her search for a solution to her religious questions, she had come under the influence of Thomas Scott for whom she wrote a series of pamphlets. After the break-up of the marriage and, shortly afterwards, the death of her mother, she was befriended by Moncure D. Conway but her pilgrimage into doubt continued. In 1874 she joined the Secular Society, and began her long friendship with Charles Bradlaugh the secularist leader. At that time forty years old, Bradlaugh was a lonely man, his own marriage having broken down in 1870 as a result of the hopeless alcoholism of his wife. Immediately attracted by his new convert, he offered her a job on the *National Reformer*, and before long she was one of the society's most popular lecturers. Apart from the issue of secularism she also spoke and wrote on such issues as marriage and the political status of women.

Charles Bradlaugh was in love with Annie Besant, and in other circumstances would have made her his wife. Instead they remained friends, although never lovers. Bradlaugh's high moral standards prohibited any such alliance and it is likely that after her experiences with her husband, Annie was glad of a loving companionship which excluded sex.

In 1877 the decision was taken jointly to re-issue a pamphlet on birth control, *The Fruits of Philosophy*, which Henry Cook had been prosecuted for selling and Charles Watts for publishing during the previous winter. This action was intended as a stand on the issue of free speech, as well as a defence of the public discussion of birth control. Their eventual trial, which lasted four days, attracted enormous public interest and, although they were found guilty, no further proceedings were taken. It was an important milestone in the birth-control movement and led to considerable publicity for the birth-control cause. For Annie Besant herself, however, the result was the loss of her daughter Mabel. An unsuccessful attempt to gain custody had already been made by her husband in 1875 but this time, largely because of her conviction for publishing *Fruits of Philosophy*, her husband won his case. Later she was granted some access to both children but on such limited terms that for their own sakes she did not either write to them or see them, until they were old enough to come back to her of their own choice. The fact that they both did come back as soon as they could, suggests that Annie's account of her husband's character was probably very close to the truth.

The main result of the removal of Mabel was a hardening of Annie's feminism. In her writing and lectures she claimed legal equality in both marriage and divorce, and women's suffrage. She also, at this time, started to study for a science degree (later abandoned for lack of opportunities to study) which led to her meeting with Edward Aveling. By 1881 the two were inseparable as Aveling was drawn into the secular movement, and they may even, for a time, have been lovers for Aveling, a totally unscrupulous man, was a notorious seducer. Certainly when he abandoned her in 1884 to set up house with Eleanor Marx she was deeply hurt, and there is no doubt of the strength of her feeling for him. For a short while she found consolation in a close friendship with George Bernard Shaw but this did not last for very long. He deeply admired her but had no wish for any entanglement.

Although the break in her friendship with Shaw was hard for her, leading to a period of very considerable despondency, this mood did not last. Already moving away from secularism towards socialism, she had joined the Fabians. Soon, under the influence of a young socialist, Herbert Burrows, she joined the Social Democratic Federation and flung herself enthusiastically into the socialist struggle. In 1888 she organised the now famous 'match girl' strike, but the match girls were only one group who were helped in this way during 1888 and 1889. At this time she also campaigned successfully for a seat on the London School Board.

By 1889 her own brief involvement with socialism was almost over. During that year she was converted to Theosophy, and was to remain faithful to it for the rest of her life. It is not easy at first to see the appeal of Theosophy to someone like Annie Besant, and it can only be assumed that secularism had never been completely satisfying to her emotionally. There is some evidence, too, that what particularly attracted her to Theosophy was its element of the occult, and it was the hope of mystical experiences which bound her so closely to the homosexual Leadbetter. Once converted to Theosophy she spent much of her life in India, which she came to look on as her adopted country. During the first world war she became involved in the struggle for Indian Home Rule and was interned by the British. After the war however, Gandhi took over the leadership and, now an old woman, she retired from Indian politics. Yet she was a significant figure in Theosophy until her death in 1933.

After she embraced Theosophy, Annie Besant did not abandon her feminism. In India she worked to try and raise the position of women by the establishment of schools for girls. Moreover, during her visits to England she worked for the women's suffrage movement and in 1911 she was one of the speakers at a great rally in the Albert Hall. Nor had her ideas changed very much since the days of the match girls. In a letter to *The Times* in 1911 she argued that the vote was necessary to raise the economic status of working women.

Her own feminism sprang very directly from the circumstances of her marriage. She resented her husband's attempts at domination, not from any prior familiarity with feminist arguments, but from a sense of her own personal worth. An extraordinarily vivid and compelling personality, she seemed destined to take a leading role in whatever movement she was involved in. She was never, however, a feminist leader, and indeed was never more than marginally involved in the feminist movement itself, probably because both her secularism and her Malthusianism cut her off from the more conventional women in the movement. Nevertheless, it is probably as a pioneer in the advocacy of birth control that she is most important as a feminist.

There have been several biographies of Annie Besant, but these have been superseded by the comprehensive two-volume study by Arthur H. Nethercot, *The First Five Lives of Annie Besant* (London, Rupert Hart Davis, 1961) and *The Last Four Lives of Annie Besant* (London, Rupert Hart Davis, 1963). There is also her *Autobiography* (London, T. Fisher Unwin, 1893). See also 'The Bradlaugh Besant Trial and the English Newspapers', J.A. and Olive Banks, *Population Studies*, Vol. VIII (1), 1954, 22-34. There is an entry in both the *DNB* 1931-1940, pp. 72-4, and in the *DLB*, Vol. IV, pp. 21-31.

BILLINGTON-GREIG Teresa 1877-1964

Born in Blackburn in 1977, Teresa Billington, a suffragette, was the daughter of a shipping clerk. As a husband and father he seems to have inspired neither affection nor respect and she describes him as unfaithful, selfish and insensitive. She was closer to her mother, but even here the relationship was basically unsatisfactory as the mother would withdraw from her for long periods of praying and meditation. Since we have only Teresa Billington's memories, it is impossible to say to what extent her mother's withdrawal from her family contributed to her husband's own neglect, but Teresa's own sympathies were with her mother, a fact which certainly contributed to her own attitude to marriage. Eventually, however, she rejected both her parents, running away from home while in her teens. She also rejected the Roman Catholicism in which she had been raised, becoming, while still very young, a convinced and outspoken agnostic.

A pupil-teacher, and then a teacher, Teresa Billington, early in her career, came into dispute with Manchester Education

Committee over the issue of religious instruction, which she absolutely refused to teach. At this point, Emmeline Pankhurst, then a member of the education committee, intervened and Teresa was sent to a Jewish school where she would not be expected to teach religion. While still a young teacher she became honorary secretary of the Manchester Equal Pay Committee as well as being secretary of the Ancoats University Settlement.

In 1903, possibly at the instigation of Emmeline Pankhurst, she joined the Manchester Independent Labour Party, and a year later was appointed an ILP organiser. Soon, however, she was drawn into the Women's Social and Political Union, and in 1907 went to London as its second London organiser. At this stage she was a highly important figure on the London scene and was nicknamed 'Parnell in petticoats' long before the title was accorded to Christabel Pankhurst. She was one of the first of the Holloway prisoners although her stay was a brief one. Her friendship with the Pankhursts was not, however, to last very long. In that same year she revolted against the increasing despotism with which Emmeline and Christabel Pankhurst were running the WSPU, as well as their growing alienation from the ILP. There was a brief but sharp struggle and eventually she, along with Charlotte Despard and a number of other women, was virtually elbowed out to form their own organisation which they named the Women's Freedom League.

So far Teresa Billington had avoided marriage, and Sylvia Pankhurst tells how she rejected the doglike devotion of a young working-class man who served with her on the Ancoats University Settlement. In 1907, however, she met and married a Scotsman, Frederick Louis Greig. We know nothing of his background or character, but he must have had sympathy with her views, because he agreed to adopt Billington-Greig as their joint name.

At the end of this same year, in December, she joined with Margaret Bondfield in a debate on the resolution 'that the immediate granting of the Parliamentary Franchise to women on the same terms as men is the speediest and most practical way to real democracy'. In the debate Teresa Billington-Greig took the view that sex disqualification was a greater bar to democracy than disqualification on grounds of property, so that even a limited extension of the franchise to women was justified. To Margaret Bondfield's argument that such an extension would only increase the Conservative vote, she argued that many working-class women would also be enfranchised. In the voting that followed the debate, 171 voted for Teresa Billington-Greig and 139 for Margaret Bondfield, a clear victory for Teresa's arguments.

But this debate was to mark the end of Teresa Billington-Greig's prominence in the suffrage movement. She was frequently away in Scotland and the leadership of the Women's Freedom League was very much in the hands of Charlotte Despard. Moreover, Teresa quite quickly became disillusioned with the Women's Freedom League and what she viewed as its suicidal weaknesses. To some extent this was due to an inability to get on with the eccentric and wayward Charlotte Despard, but the League itself was in considerable difficulty particularly in its confrontation with the successful WSPU. There were disputes over tactics, since most but not all of the members of the league were against the militancy which was increasingly becoming the policy of the WSPU. Instead the league adopted policies of passive resistance, in particular refusing to pay taxes. Like the other suffrage groups they organised deputations and marches, usually on a fairly small scale, although frequently culminating in arrests and imprisonment, but there was not the overt violence associated with the WSPU. Its policy was also wider than suffrage, and it organised protests, for example, against the scandalously short sentences imposed by the courts for child molestation.

Immediately after leaving the league Teresa Billington-Greig published her most important book, *The Militant Suffrage Movement* (London, Frank Palmer, 1911). This was largely an attack on both the tactics of militancy itself and the style of leadership adopted by the Pankhursts, whom she accused of emotionalism, personal tyranny and fanaticism. She was made anxious, too, by the increasing number of wealthy women in the WSPU and feared that once they had achieved the vote for themselves their 'clamour for change' would cease. Nor did she agree with the Pankhursts' claim that women have a higher moral nature than men, and she disliked their attempts to turn the struggle for suffrage into a battle between the sexes. The Women's Freedom League also came under fire and she announced her intention to work for suffrage independently.

Having made this decision, she seems to have turned to writing as a way of influencing events, and in the following two years produced two more books, *Consumers in Revolt* (1912) and *Woman and the Machine* (1913), but neither enabled her to regain her short-lived prominence in the movement. She did not lose her feminism however even as an old woman, serving between 1946 and 1949 as chairman and honorary director of Women for Westminster, a group which campaigned for women to have improved access to the political process and desired that they should participate more fully in parliamentary politics and the professions. She was also one of a group of women who met at this time to emphasise the necessity for making what they called the feminine point of view more effective in national life. As one of the surviving suffragettes she also became of interest to historians in the last few years of her life. She died late in 1964.

Teresa Billington-Greig was one of the earliest recruits to the WSPU, influenced, most likely, by her friendship with Emmeline Pankhurst. Nevertheless, she was already strongly feminist in her attitudes. A natural rebel, she was not afraid either to hold unconventional views or to stand up to authority. Aggressive in manner, she was said to enjoy an argument, and this may have made it difficult to fit comfortably into any organisation, but more especially into the autocratic WSPU, and it is not surprising that she clashed with the Pankhursts. After this she does not seem to have found a suitable niche anywhere and her considerable talents were apparently dissipated. Although writing was not her real métier, her principal significance today seems to lie in her book *The Militant Suffrage Movement.* Although shrill and emotional in tone, it does expose many of the weaknesses in both the tactics and the ideology of militancy.

Teresa Billington-Greig has not proved attractive to biographers, and information on her life is hard to find. The fullest account is provided in *The Militant Campaign of the Women's Social and Political Union*, Andrew Rosen (London, Routledge and Kegan Paul, 1974). There is some additional information in *Votes for Women*, Roger Fulford (London, Faber and Faber, 1956). A brief pen-portrait is given in *The Suffragette Movement*, Sylvia Pankhurst (London, Longmans, 1931; Virago, 1977). A view of the debate with Margaret Bondfield is given in her *A Life's Work* (London, Hutchinson, 1949). The debate itself was published by the Women's Freedom League in 'Sex equality versus adult suffrage' (London, Women's Freedom League, 1908). Although it does not give much information on Theresa Billington-Greig, there is a good account of the Women's Freedom League in *An Unhusbanded Life. Charlotte Despard, Suffragette, Socialist, Sinn Feiner*, Andro Linklater (London, Hutchinson, 1980). See also the Billington-Greig Papers in the Fawcett Library.

See also BONDFIELD Margaret Grace, DESPARD Charlotte.

BLACKBURN Helen 1842–1903

Helen Blackburn, a suffragist, was born in County Kerry, the only surviving daughter of Bewicke Blackburn, a civil engineer and the manager of a slate quarry, and Isabella the youngest daughter of Humble Lamb of Ryton Hall, County Durham. On her mother's side she could trace her descent from a brother of John Knox.

Nothing is known of her childhood and

youth, or even the manner in which she was drawn into the suffrage movement, but in 1874 she became secretary to the Central Committee of the National Society for Women's Suffrage, a post which she held until 1895. She was also, between 1880 and 1895, secretary of the Bristol and West of England Suffrage Society. From 1881 until 1890 she was editor of the *Englishwoman's Review*. In 1881 she published *A Handbook for Women Engaged in Social and Political Work* (Bristol, 1881).

Throughout these years she seems to have remained a humble figure very much in the background while at the same time putting her knowledge and experience at the disposal of everyone who needed it. Frances Balfour, who knew and admired her, described her face marked by long illness, and her selfless and loving personality.

In 1895 she gave up much of her public work to look after her father, and when he died at the age of eighty-six, she spent the extra time at her disposal in writing. In 1902 she published her most important book, *Women's Suffrage. A Record of the Movement in the British Isles* (London, 1902; New York, 1971). This is a most scholarly history of the suffrage movement, and still an important source for historians. It also contains the only knowledge we have of the early life of Lydia Becker, a woman Helen Blackburn obviously very much admired. In these last few years of her life she also published *Supporters of the Women's Suffrage Movement* (1897), *The Condition of Working Women*, with J. Boucherett (1896) and *Women under the Factory Acts* with N. Vynne (1903). Like other feminists of her generation she was a strong opponent of protective legislation for women. After her death in 1903 a loan fund for training young women was established in her memory. She left her books to Girton.

There is an entry in *DNB* 1901–1911, pp. 168–9. She is also mentioned briefly by Frances Balfour in *Me Obliviscaris* (London, Hodder and Stoughton, 1930).

See also BALFOUR Lady Frances.

BLATHWAYT Mary 1879–1962

Mary Blathwayt, a suffragette, was the daughter of Colonel Linley Blathwayt, who retired from service in India in 1882 and bought Eagle House, Batheaston, three miles to the east of Bath. Colonel Blathwayt was a naturalist, who achieved some distinction in entomology, and also an accomplished photographer, while his wife Emily had an interest in music. There were two children, Mary and a son William.

Mary, a rather shy girl, seems to have lived the typical life of a girl of the period. She was educated at Bath High School, and then lived quietly at home, paying calls, helping in various charitable events, and gardening. In 1905 and again in 1906 she, more unusually, spent several weeks on a university extension course, firstly at Oxford and then at Cambridge.

It is possible that she was introduced to the suffrage movement by the Tollemache family, who had also come to Batheaston after service in India, so that it was natural for the two families to become friends. The Reverend Tollemache had died in 1896, leaving a widow and three daughters all of whom became militant suffragettes. Mary herself attended her first suffrage meeting in Bath during 1906 and soon afterwards joined the Women's Social and Political Union, supported sympathetically by both parents. Soon she was drawn in to become an active worker, at first putting leaflets through letterboxes, and later she helped to organise meetings, arranged collections, and eventually, in spite of her shyness, was persuaded to take the chair at a meeting. Before long she was spending more time at Bristol than at home. She also paid a visit to London to join in a march, but escaped arrest. During this period she met Annie Kenney, then acting as an organiser in the Bristol area. The two women, so very different in their backgrounds, became friends and Annie Kenney became a frequent weekend visitor to Eagle House where Mary Blathwayt, who adored her, would wash and mend her clothes. In the meantime Mary extended her own activities into Devonshire and South Wales, selling tickets, chalking pavements, and chairing open-air meetings.

In 1909 Colonel Blathwayt conceived the idea of a gallery of suffrage photographs, and this ideas was extended to include an arboretum known as Annie's Arboretum, in which eminent suffrage workers were invited to plant a tree. An area of ground was marked out for the purpose, four apple trees were felled, and during the next four or five years a large number of trees were planted, each with its commemorative plaque, while Colonel Blathwayt photographed the ceremony.

Although her parents were not prepared to let Mary go to prison, many hunger-strikers were invited to Eagle House to get well. Mary Blathwayt herself tried unsuccessfully to get Bath doctors to sign a petition against forcible feeding. As the violence of the militant protest increased, and especially after window-smashing became a major tactic, the Blathwayts began to be disturbed at the direction the movement was taking. Mary herself was forbidden to take militant action, although she still continued to organise meetings and take part in peaceful protests. Eagle House, too, continued to offer hospitality to suffrage women, and the arboretum continued to grow. Only in the last phases of militancy, when houses were burned down, did Mary Blathwayt and her parents finally withdraw their support, and Mary joined the constitutional society, the National Union of Women's Suffrage Societies under the leadership of Millicent Fawcett.

Colonel Blathwayt died in 1919, but Mary continued to live in Eagle House with her mother, who lived until 1940, and her brother William. During these years she seems to have reverted completely to the traditional role of daughter at home. Her brother William died in 1952 and Mary herself in 1962, by which time Annie's Arboretum was neglected and overgrown. Later, when the land was sold for building, it was totally destroyed, although a few of the plaques were saved and deposited in the museum of the Batheaston Society.

Mary Blathwayt is a typical example of the young women who, without any previous involvement in the suffrage movement, were drawn into the militant campaign, often by personal contact with the Pankhursts themselves, or by one of their lieutenants, like Annie Kenney. Clearly, for Mary, the episode—for it was clearly no more than that—represented excitement and adventure, as well as the challenge of new experiences. There was also, perhaps, a sense of being part of a historic mission which the Pankhurst family so successfully conveyed to their followers. Ultimately, like many more, the Blathwayts lost their faith in militancy, and Mary Blathwayt withdrew once more into the shelter of her home.

The source for Mary Blathwayt is *A Nest of Suffragettes in Somerset. Eagle House Batheaston*, B.M. Willmott Dobbie (Bath, Batheaston Society, 1979). This includes many of the photographs of the suffragettes taken by Colonel Blathwayt.

See also KENNEY Annie.

**BODICHON Barbara Leigh Smith
1827–1891**

Barbara Leigh Smith, an outstanding feminist pioneer, active in many causes, was the daughter of Benjamin Leigh Smith and Anne Longden. Her grandfather, William Smith, had been Wilberforce's lieutenant in the House of Commons during the campaign for the abolition of the slave trade, and his sympathy for the French revolution nearly cost him his life. Her great-grandfather, similarly, had shocked public opinion in the eighteenth century by sympathising with the American colonists. Her father was a Radical MP who, at the age of forty, had seduced a young milliner only seventeen years old. He never went through a form of marriage with her, for reasons that are not clear, but she remained his common-law wife until she died seven years later of tuberculosis, after bearing him five children of whom Barbara was the eldest. Whatever his shortcomings with respect to Anne Longden, Benjamin Leigh Smith was an enlightened and affectionate father. More unusually he treated his daughters and his sons equally, and when Barbara came of age she was given an independent income just as if she had been a boy. This unorthodox background was undoubtedly an important factor in Barbara's later feminism. So was the atmosphere of her father's house, which was a meeting place for Radical abolitionists and political refugees from Europe.

In 1849 Barbara studied for a time at the newly formed Ladies' College in Bedford Square. Shortly afterwards she founded and taught in an experimental school in which boys and girls from different classes and different religious backgrounds were mixed and which was a most daring innovation for its time. Meantime she began to take a more active interest in the position of women. In 1851 she had read John Stuart Mill's article on the 'Enfranchisement of Women' which appeared in the *Westminster Review* and perceived correctly that it had been written by Harriet Taylor. Although she believed firmly in women's suffrage she accepted that the time for such a campaign had not yet come and turned her attention to women's legal disabilities.

In 1854 she wrote 'A Brief Summary in Plain Language of the Most Important Laws concerning Women' in which she set out in full the disadvantages suffered by married women in consequence of their position in law which placed them totally in the power of their husbands. She went on to persuade the Society for the Amendment of the Law, to which her father belonged, to introduce a Married Women's Property Bill to safeguard the property and earnings of married women, and Barbara Leigh Smith herself formed a ladies' committee to collect signatures for a petition in support of the measure. In 1857 the Divorce Act protected the property rights of divorced women but opinion in the House of Commons was not yet ready to accept that married women living with their husbands needed protection and it was left to a later generation of feminists to secure this particular change in the law.

Undoubtedly however, Barbara Leigh Smith was deeply affected by her work for this measure. Not only did it strengthen her consciousness of the need for reform, but it aroused in her a deep distrust of marriage. During this period she came very close to accepting a 'free-love' association with John Chapman, the editor of the *Westminster Review*. A married man with children, his marriage had not been happy and he had amused himself with a series of mistresses, one of whom had been the young George Eliot and it is strange that Barbara Leigh Smith should have been attracted by such an obvious philanderer. The rejection of his proposal cost her considerable effort and she went through a period of intense unhappiness. Although she felt a great longing to love and be loved by a man, she had an equally strong need for independence and a great fear of marriage. Her ideas at this time were expressed in an essay, *Women and Work*, published in 1857, in which she insisted that dependence was degrading, and that paid work for women was both natural and desirable. She also argued that fathers should help their daughters just as they helped their sons, and that women could and should be anything they wanted. In this she was doing no more than describing her own situation, but she was well aware from her own researches into the legal situation how her independence could be totally destroyed by marriage.

In 1856, soon after her final rejection of John Chapman, Barbara Leigh Smith went with two of her sisters to Algeria and during the visit met Eugene Bodichon, a French colonial from an old Breton family and a man of radical and independent views who had worked for the abolition of slavery in Algeria. There was a strong intellectual sympathy between them but also considerable physical attraction, on her part at least, and she found him 'the handsomest man ever created'. In 1857 they were married, Barbara then being thirty years of age and her husband forty-six. It is clear that she trusted him to respect her independence and in this she was not disappointed. They both agreed to allow each other the freedom to follow their own interests and this agreement was honoured throughout the marriage. In order to continue her work part of the year was spent in England and part in Algeria although Eugene Bodichon was never particularly happy in England and did not get on well with her friends, and for her part Barbara Bodichon missed England, particularly her work for the women's movement. She was also deeply disappointed that the marriage did not produce a child. Nevertheless there is no evidence that she ever regretted her marriage. Her husband's minor eccentricities, which worried some of her friends, did not bother the more unorthodox Barbara and she was grateful for the willingness with which he accepted what was for its time an extremely unconventional marriage.

A few weeks after the wedding Barbara Bodichon and her husband went on an extended trip to America. During this tour, which was mainly concerned with the issue of slavery, she also met and talked with women prominent in the American Women's Rights Movement who were pleased to learn of recent developments in England. On her return she was plunged into the affairs of the *Englishwoman's Review* founded in 1858 with her own money, and with her closest friend, Bessie Rayner Parkes as editor. She also took an active part in the promotion of the idea of women doctors and, through her friendship with Emily Davies, became involved in the movement for the higher education of women. Then, in 1866, she was largely responsible for the foundation of the Women's Suffrage Committee from which may be dated the real start of an organised and sustained campaign for women's suffrage. This committee organised the women's suffrage petition which John Stuart Mill presented to the House of Commons on their behalf. Barbara Bodichon also read a paper to the Social Science Society meeting in Manchester of that year which brought many recruits to the idea of women's suffrage, including Lydia Becker, destined in time to become the movement's leader. Published as a pamphlet, the paper sold many thousands of copies.

Barbara Bodichon also became very closely involved at this time with the foundation and development of Hitchin, later Girton, College at Cambridge. She took an active part in raising money for the new venture, although her name was left off the committee because of her connection with the suffrage movement which, it was feared, might antagonise some potential supporters. When the college opened in 1873 she helped with the furnishings and continued to give advice and encouragement. On the actual administration of the college, however, she and Emily Davies by no means always agreed, since Barbara was much too unorthodox for the conventionally minded Emily and, in disputes with the students, Barbara was often to be found on the students' side.

By the 1870s Barbara Bodichon's keen energy was flagging and she turned more and more to her painting. A serious and successful artist, her career as a painter was a source of great significance to her in her quest for independence. In 1873 moreover she met the young Hertha Marks, a Girton student who became virtually a daughter to her. As Hertha Ayrton she later achieved fame as a scientist and was as devoted to Barbara as Barbara was to her. In 1877 Barbara Bodichon was taken suddenly and dangerously ill, and, although she recovered, she was partially paralysed for the rest of her life. Unable any longer to travel, this meant increasing separation from her husband who, ill himself, could not winter in England. By 1881 he was confined to Algeria where he died in 1885. Barbara Bodichon herself lived on as an invalid until 1891, still maintaining close contact with friends like Bessie Rayner Parkes, now Bessie Belloc, with Emily Davies and with Hertha Ayrton. She maintained her interest in the progress of the women's movement, signing her last suffrage petition in 1891, the year of her death. She also kept up her involvement in the affairs of Girton, and in her will she left a large sum of money to the college, mostly from the sale of her paintings.

Although clearly sexually attracted to men, Barbara had a special liking for and sympathy with women. Her friendship with Bessie Rayner Parkes dated from their teens and lasted the rest of their lives. She was also an intimate friend of George Eliot and the first person to whom George Eliot confessed her love for George Lewes. Indeed, Barbara's sympathy with and concern for women was a fundamental characteristic of her feminism. Perhaps because of her upbringing, she saw more clearly than most what needed to be done and her feminism was more far-reaching than that of many of her contemporaries. At the same time it was also very strongly rooted in the anti-slavery movement which had deeply influenced her in her childhood, and she constantly made the analogy between the position of women and the position of the slave. Both were rooted, she believed, in man's willingness to countenance injustice, and when justice at last prevailed both slaves and women would be set free. There were tensions in her life between her role as artist and her role as social reformer as well as between her desire for the love of a man and her desire for independence, and she did not give the women's movement the undivided dedication of an Emily Davies or a Lydia Becker. Nevertheless, she was an important source of drive and inspiration in the years which saw the establishment of a women's movement in nineteenth-century Britain.

There is a rather reticent biography, *Barbara Bodichon 1827–1891*, Hester Burton (London, John Murray, 1949). Her role in the establishment of Girton College is described in *Emily Davies and Girton College*, Barbara Stephen (London, Constable, 1927). Her relationship with John Chapman, and her American journey, are to be found in *An American Diary 1857-8*, (ed.) Joseph W. Reed (London, Routledge and Kegan Paul, 1972). There is a recent assessment of her feminism by Jacquie Matthews, 'Barbara Bodichon: Integrity in Diversity' in Dale Spender, *Feminist Theorists* (London, The Women's Press, 1983). See also *Wives and Property*, Lee Holcombe (Oxford, Martin Robertson, 1983) and *DNB* Supplementary Vol. I, p. 229. Her letters to Emily Davies held at Girton College, Cambridge, are also available on microfilm, published by Harvester Microform, (Brighton 1984).

See also BELLOC Bessie Rayner, DAVIES Sarah Emily.

BONDFIELD Margaret Grace 1873–1953

Margaret Bondfield, a trade union leader and politician, was the daughter of William Bondfield and Ann Taylor. Her father started work as a bobbin boy in a lace factory, but later, as a designer, invented many new patterns, although he himself never benefited personally from them. As a young man he was an enthusiastic Radical, active in the Chard Political Union, leading many protests and demonstrations for reform. He was, however, sixty-one years of age when Mary was born, an old and embittered man, and in her recollections her mother was the most important figure. The daughter of the Reverend George Taylor, a non-conformist preacher active in reform, she married William Bondfield when only nineteen years of age, and bore him seven sons and four daughters. By the time Margaret was born she was already in her forties but still a woman of boundless energy. In spite of the cares of a large household she had an interest in politics and was an enthusiastic chapel-goer.

At fourteen years of age Margaret Bondfield left home to serve an apprenticeship in a Brighton shop. There she was much encouraged by a Mrs Martindale, an advocate of women's rights. In 1894 she moved to London where her brother Frank was already an active trade unionist. There they both became involved with the Hicks family, and for a time lodged with Amelia Hicks' daughter. At Amelia Hicks' house she met and became friendly with Margaret Gladstone, soon to become the wife of Ramsay MacDonald, a friendship which was to continue until Margaret MacDonald's death in 1911.

On arrival in London, Margaret Bondfield

joined the Shop Assistants Union, and very soon was a member of the London District Council. In 1896 when the journal *Shop Assistant* was founded she contributed articles under the pseudonym Grace Dare. Perhaps under the influence of the Hicks family she joined the Social Democratic Federation, only later moving to the Independent Labour Party. In 1898 she raised a storm of protest by an article in the *Shop Assistant*, painting the ideal married couple as one in which both went out to work and shared the household tasks between them. It was essentially a plea for individual choice for women.

In 1896, possibly through her acquaintance with Margaret MacDonald, she joined a two-year investigation of shop workers conducted by the Women's Industrial Council. In 1898 she became assistant secretary of the Shop Assistants' Union, a post she held until 1908 when she resigned for health reasons. Soon she was something of an authority on shop workers, and gave evidence in 1902 to the Select Committee on Shops and in 1907 the Select Committee on Truck.

From 1908 she worked for a time at freelance lecturing, including propaganda for the ILP. She was for a time secretary of the Women's Labour League and also worked closely with Margaret Llewellyn Davies and the Women's Co-operative Guild on minimum-wage legislation and a campaign for the improvement of infant mortality and child welfare. She was instrumental as a member of the Advisory Committee on the Health Insurance Bill in securing the inclusion of maternity benefits in the Act of 1911 as well as the amendment which made them the property of the mother. During these years too she was closely associated with a small group of women in London including Margaret MacDonald, Mary MacArthur whom she had met in 1903 and who became one of her dearest friends, and Gertrude Tuckwell, all involved very closely in the issues of working women and focussed around the journal the *Woman Worker*.

Like some, but by no means all, socialist women she was a firm opponent of a limited franchise. Chairman of the Adult Suffrage Society, she believed that a limited franchise would tip the scales against the worker, and even operate as a barrier against the granting of adult suffrage. In 1907 there was a public debate on the issue with Teresa Billington-Greig who took the opposing view. Her outspokenness on this issue made Margaret Bondfield very unpopular with women suffrage workers, who saw limited suffrage as an important point of principle.

During the war she gave nearly all her time to the Federation of Women Workers. She also stood staunchly by Ramsay MacDonald in his stand against the war, supporting a negotiated peace and opposing conscription. After the war, without relinquishing her trade union involvement, she turned her attention to politics and in 1923 was elected to Parliament for Northampton, the same year in which she was chairman of the General Council of the TUC. In 1924 she was made parliamentary secretary to the Ministry of Labour but was soon to earn the enmity of the left wing of the Labour Party. In 1926 she was heavily criticised for signing the Blanesborough Committee report which advocated some lowering of benefits and contributions. She became still more unpopular in 1929 when as Minister of Labour in MacDonald's administration, the first woman to achieve such a position, she supported Philip Snowden's financial caution. In 1931 she accepted a Bill which deprived some married women of unemployment benefit. However, she stayed with the Labour Party when MacDonald formed his national government, losing her seat in the election of that year. This was the end of her career in Parliament, although she continued her trade union work until 1938. Her public work continued however, and from 1939 to 1945 she was chairman of the Women's Group on Public Welfare. She died in 1953.

Early in life she appears to have given up any idea of love-affairs, explaining, in her autobiography, that she had 'seen too much too soon'. Instead she lived for the trade-union movement. The greatest romance of her life, according to her biographer, was her friendship with Mary MacArthur which lasted from their first meeting in 1903 until Mary MacArthur's death in 1921, and which was based essentially on their joint work together for the trade union movement. With M.M.A. Wood, a lecturer in cookery who became chief woman inspector for the Health Insurance Service, she enjoyed a different kind of friendship. They shared holidays together, and lodgings, and later a house in Hampstead.

Over time Margaret Bondfield grew more conservative, moving from the SDF to the ILP and finally to the right wing of the Labour Party. Her feminism also changed until by the end of her life she was emphasising the importance for women of the nurture of children, a task which, she alleged, had been assigned to women by nature. The majority of women, she argued, would always be homemakers and the task of women in public life was to demand for them housing reforms and the development of social amenities. Her support for equal pay too was couched in essentially trade-union terms, as necessary to protect men from the unfair competition of women.

It is not easy therefore to evaluate Margaret Bondfield's contribution to feminism. She was one of those women who always put socialism first, but as a young woman had been an enthusiastic supporter of a woman's right to independence. In the years before the first world war she was active in the defence of working women and did much to improve welfare services for women and children. In spite of her attitude to the suffrage issue, she was by no means opposed to votes for women, and her rejection of the limited suffrage campaign was based essentially on loyalty to the women of her own class. After the war, however, her growing conservatism in politics also expressed itself in a conservative attitude towards the family which was outside feminism altogether.

There is a biography *Margaret Bondfield*, Mary Agnes Hamilton (London, Leonard Parsons, 1924) and her autobiography *A Life's Work* (London, Hutchinson, 1949). She has an entry in the *DNB* 1951-1960, pp. 122-3, and in the *DLB* Vol. II, pp. 39-45. For the debate with Billington-Greig see, 'Sex equality versus adult suffrage: a verbatim report of a debate held on 3 Dec 1907 with Teresa Billington-Greig', Margaret Bondfield (Women's Freedom League, 1908).

See also BILLINGTON-GREIG Teresa, HICKS, Amelia Jane, MACARTHUR Mary Reid.

BOUCHERETT Emilie (Jessie) 1825-1905

Jessie Boucherett, a pioneer in the widening of opportunities for women, was the youngest daughter of Ayscogne Boucherett and Louisa, daughter of Frederick John Pigou. Her father was a Lincolnshire country squire, lord of the manor of Willingham who, in 1820, became High Sheriff of Lincolnshire. In 1840 he published 'A few observations on corn, currency, etc., with a plan for promoting the interests of agriculture'. An elder sister Louisa was a pioneer in the movement for the boarding out of pauper children. Jessie Boucherett was educated at a school in Stratford on Avon and afterwards engaged in philanthropy, supporting a dispensary and cottage hospital in Market Rasen. She enjoyed country pursuits and rode to the hounds with great ardour.

In 1858, catching sight of a copy of the *Englishwoman's Journal* on a railway station bookstall, she was so enthusiastic about its contents that she travelled to London to the office of the journal in Langham Place. There she met Bessie Parkes and Barbara Leigh Smith along with other women connected with the journal, and very soon afterwards, in association with Adelaide Proctor, she started the Society for Promoting the Employment of Women. A member of the Kensington Society, a discussion group from which sprang the whole of the women's suffrage campaign, she, along with Barbara Leigh Smith, by now Barbara Bodichon, and Emily Davies, drafted the petition which John Stuart Mill took to Westminster in 1866. In 1865 she revived the *Englishwoman's Journal* , which had ceased publication, changing its name to the *Englishwoman's Review*, and was its editor until 1871. She was also, at this time, involved in the foundation of Girton and, as part of her interest in the employment of girls, she founded a school in London to train young women as book-keepers, clerks and cashiers.

From the time of her involvement in the women's movement until the end of the 1890s, by which time she was an old woman, she was a frequent writer, particularly on issues relating to women's employment. In 1863 she interpreted Samuel Smiles for women by publishing *Hints on Self Help. A Book for Young Women* (London, 1863). In it she urged them to develop reason, self-reliance, common sense and perseverance. Above all they needed independence. She suggested that they might try for employment in nursing, copying law papers, and working as clerks or shopkeepers. In 1869 she was one of the contributors to Josephine Butler's volume of essays, *Woman's Work and Woman's Culture* (London, 1869). Entitled 'Provisions for Superfluous Women', her essay was, like so much of her writing, a plea for suitable work for women. In 1884, still on the same theme, she contributed 'The Industrial Movement' to *The Woman Question in Europe* ed. Theodore Stanton (New York, 1884). Finally, in collaboration with Helen Blackburn, she wrote *The Condition of Working Women and the Factory Acts* (London, 1896). She died in 1905, the last survivor of the family.

Coming as she did from a long-established and Conservative Lincolnshire family, Jessie Boucherett was an unexpected recruit to feminism. Clearly her involvement was a development from her philanthropy, although, significantly, it was the *Englishwoman's Review* which drew her into the women's movement and drew her attention specifically to women's need for economic independence through work. Once converted she worked for the movement for the rest of her life. Very little is known about her and she remains one of the most elusive of the Langham Place circle.

There is an entry for Jessie Boucherett in *DNB* 1901–1911 pp. 196–7. Further information is given in *Women of the Day*, Frances Hays (London, Chatto and Windus, 1885) and in *Women's Suffrage. A Record of the Movement*, Helen Blackburn (London, Williams and Norgate, 1902).

See also BELLOC Bessie Rayner, BODICHON Barbara Leigh Smith, PROCTOR Adelaide Anne.

BRAILSFORD Henry Noel 1873–1958

Henry Noel Brailsford, a journalist, was the only son of the Reverend Edward John Brailsford and his wife Clare Pooley. He was educated at Dundee High School and Glasgow University, where he studied classics and philosophy under Gilbert Murray, Edward Caird and A.C. Bradley. After achieving his MA in 1894 he studied at Oxford and Berlin before returning for a short period as an assistant at Glasgow teaching women undergraduates at Queen Margaret College. After this he served briefly as a sub-editor for the *Scots Pictorial* before enlisting in the Philhellenic Legion, a volunteer army fighting alongside the Greeks against the Turks. In 1897 he was wounded and returned home, describing his experiences in his first book and only novel *The Broom of the War God*. In 1898 he married Jane Edson Malloch, who had been a fellow student with him at Glasgow.

From 1899 to 1909 he acted as leader-writer for a number of newspapers, including the *Daily News*, writing mainly on foreign and imperial affairs. He also went on a number of foreign assignments and became an authority on Russia, Egypt and the Balkans. In 1903 he led a relief mission to Macedonia, accompanied by his wife. His book *Macedonia*, published in 1906, became the standard work on the subject. At this time, too, he was active in giving aid to foreign exiles in London, and this led to his trial in 1905, at which he was convicted and fined £100 for helping terrorists. In 1907 he became a member of the Independent Labour Party, having become disillusioned with the Fabians over their attitude to the Boer War.

From 1908, however, he gave his time and effort increasingly to the cause of women's suffrage. Sparked off to some extent by his wife Jane's sympathies with the Pankhursts, his concern was deepened by the increasing brutality with which the protesting women were treated. In 1908, with his friend Henry Nevinson, he founded the Men's League for Women's Suffrage. When forcible feeding was introduced the following year, as a result of the policy of hunger-strikes, he and Henry Nevinson both resigned from the *Daily News* when the editor A.G. Gardiner refused to repudiate government policy. In 1910 he was adopted as a women's suffrage candidate for South Salford in opposition to Hilaire Belloc, but stood down when a pro-suffrage liberal was nominated.

Meanwhile, in 1909 his wife Jane, in company with Lady Constance Lytton, had travelled to Newcastle where Lloyd George was to speak. There she struck with an axe the barricade erected to prevent women entering the meeting. Although clearly only a symbolic gesture, she was sentenced to six weeks in prison but was quickly released on the grounds that she was medically unfit. Her husband, however, was growing disillusioned with the policy of militancy. Determined to find some way to reach a solution peacefully, he took the initiative, in 1910, in forming a Conciliation Committee as it came to be called, which attempted to sponsor legislation acceptable to all parties. As its secretary he was also responsible, with Dr Jessie Murray, for a report *The Treatment of the Women's Deputations by the Metropolitan Police* which took evidence from a large number of women and was able to provide many instances of police brutality. By 1912, however, it was obvious that this attempt to find a solution to the problem had been a failure, and this was an important factor in producing the final and most violent phase of militancy. Brailsford had himself, however, broken completely with the Pankhursts, and was, indeed, regarded by them as a traitor. Instead he turned to Millicent Fawcett and the National Union of Women's Suffrage Societies, and it was largely on his advice that this organisation abandoned its non-party policy and came out in support of the Labour Party as the only party to endorse women's suffrage.

This marked the end of his active period with the suffrage movement. He again turned to writing, and in 1913 published *Shelley, Godwin and their Circle*. In 1914 he published *The War of Steel and Gold* which became an important textbook for those on the left. He was a determined opponent of the war and afterwards was one of the foremost critics of the Versailles Treaty.

Brailsford's associations with the suffrage movement were not, however, altogether over. In 1917 he was included in a small committee called by Eleanor Rathbone which consisted mainly of women associated with her in NUWSS, to consider the case for family allowances as a means of securing to the mother a greater degree of economic independence and a higher status within the family, provided always, of course, that the allowances were paid to her. The allowances were also conceived at this time as a contribution to the equal-pay debate since, without some scheme of family endowment, it was argued that equal pay would be to the detriment of the man with a family. A Family Endowment Society was formed to act as a small pressure group and the NUWSS, renamed after the war the National Union of Societies for Equal Citizenship, was converted to its policy. Henry Brailsford became an active member, occupied chiefly in forging links with the ILP. In 1918 he published, with K.D. Courtney, herself a suffragist, *Equal Pay and the Family* and in 1926 *Families and Incomes. The Case for Children's Allowances*. Between 1922 and 1926 he edited the ILP journal the *New Leader*, and during that period it carried numerous articles warmly supporting family allowances, as did his book *Socialism for Today* (1925).

Henry Brailsford's support for the ILP ended when it split with the Labour Party. During the 1930s he remained to the left, a supporter of Stafford Cripps against MacDonald. His pacifism, however, was changed by the war in Spain and the need for military action against Hitler. He was also deeply interested and involved in the affairs of India before and after the second world war when, as a friend of Gandhi, Nehru and Pethick-Lawrence, he acted as an intermediary between them. His links with feminism also continued at least until the 1930s when he became a vice-president of the Abortion Law Reform Society. By this time his marriage with Jane Brailsford was over. They separated soon after the first world war, and later he formed a successful relationship with the artist Claire Leighton. In 1937 Jane Brailsford died, and in 1944 he married Eva Maria Perlman Jarvis. His final work was his book *The Levellers and the English Revolution* which, although incomplete, was published posthumously. After a period of failing health he died in 1958.

A reserved man, Henry Brailsford nevertheless had an enormous capacity for indignation. He was so moved by the Spanish civil war that, although in his mid-sixties, he was dissuaded with great difficulty from enlisting in the International Brigade, and this romantic chivalry is clearly seen in his attitude towards the struggle of the Greeks against the Turks. Nor was he unique in this respect since a number of men sympathetic to feminism have also allied themselves with the cause of subject nations. In the nineteenth century the most outstanding example was James Stansfeld who devoted his life almost equally to the campaign for the repeal of the Contagious Diseases Acts and the freedom of Italy. Feminism appealed to men like James Stansfeld and Henry Brailsford because it too presented itself to them as the oppression of the weak by the strong, and it was this hatred of oppression which drew them to the women's side.

Henry Brailsford's involvement in the suffrage campaign is described in most accounts of the suffrage movement. See, for example, *The Fighting Pankhursts. A Study in Tenacity*, David Mitchell (London, Jonathan Cape, 1967); *Rise Up Women! The Militant Campaign of the Women's Social and Political Union*, Andrew Rosen (London, Routledge and Kegan Paul, 1974) and *The Suffragette Movement*, Sylvia Pankhurst (London, Longmans, 1931; Virago, 1977). For his involvement in the family allowance campaign, see *The Movement for Family Allowances 1918-1945*, John Macnicol (London, Heinemann, 1980). There is no full length biography but an entry in the *DLB*, Vol. II, pp. 46-53, and the *DNB*, 1951-60, pp. 137-9.

See also NEVINSON Henry Woodd.

BRIGHT Jacob 1821-1899

Jacob Bright, a major spokesman for the women's movement in the House of Commons, was the son of Jacob Bright and Martha Wood, his father's second wife who bore him eleven children before she died in 1830, leaving Jacob only nine years old. Jacob Bright the elder, a strict Quaker and proud of his Quaker inheritance, was strongly patriarchal both at home and at the mill which he owned. Jacob, however, was of a critical turn of mind and unable to accept any definite faith, although his daughter describes him as longing to be certain of a future life. He also came to reject his father's patriarchal attitude.

Throughout his life Jacob was involved in the family firm, John Bright and Brothers, of Rochdale. In 1855 he married Ursula, daughter of Joseph Mellor, a Liverpool merchant, and in 1867 he entered Parliament for Manchester. Unfortunately we know nothing of him during these years, but already he and his wife were both convinced suffrage supporters, and in that same year he took the chair at a Manchester meeting which was the origin of the Manchester Society for Women's Suffrage.

After John Stuart Mill lost his seat in 1868, Jacob Bright became the leader of the suffragists in Parliament and he carried out his task energetically until he too lost his seat in 1874. In 1869 he won for unmarried women householders the right to the municipal franchise by moving an amendment to the Municipal Franchise Bill, and in 1870 he and Sir Charles Dilke introduced what was in fact the first women's suffrage Bill, since John Stuart Mill's attempt to bring about women's suffrage had been in the form of an amendment to a suffrage Bill already before Parliament. At its second reading this Bill was carried by 124 votes of 91, but its further progress was defeated by the determined opposition of Gladstone.

Apart from his work for suffrage, he was very actively engaged in the married women's property campaign, believing firmly that the passage of such a Bill would bring an increase in respect for women in all classes of society. He was a member of the Married Women's Property Committee from its foundation in 1868, and worked long and hard in Parliament, sponsoring Bills in both 1869, which led to a very limited Act in 1870, and in 1872. He was also active behind the scenes on behalf of the committee in the events which led up to the successful Acts of 1881, for Scotland, and in 1882 for England.

1870 also saw the involvement of Jacob and his wife Ursula in the campaign for the repeal of the Contagious Diseases Acts, designed to protect the Armed Forces from venereal disease by requiring the compulsory examination and, if necessary, treatment of women believed to be prostitutes. The nature of the campaign, which required the outspoken treatment of sexual matters, divided the suffrage movement into opposing camps. Those who saw the repeal campaign as a danger to the suffrage cause tried to remove Jacob Bright from his position as suffrage leader in the House of Commons, but the attempt was made unnecessary when he lost his seat in 1874, his place being taken by a suffrage supporter from the Conservative Party. By the time of his return to Parliament in 1877 most of the controversy over the repeal campaign had died down within the suffrage movement and he once again became the suffrage leader, introducing another Bill in 1878 which was talked out in disorder. Later in the year, however, because of illness, he handed over the leadership permanently to a younger man.

Jacob Bright was always one of the more radical of the suffragists, protesting when a suffrage Bill in 1875 specifically excluded married women. Moreover, although there is no record that he came out publicly in her support, his daughter has recorded that he liked Annie Besant, and admired her for her courage.

In 1889 the issue of married women was raised again, when a Bill was introduced which would have expressly excluded them, and a new organisation was formed, the Women's Franchise League, which included the Brights, the Elmys and the Pankhursts. Its foremost plank was the defence of the married woman and, apart from the suffrage issue, it included equality with respect to divorce, inheritance and the custody of children. This, however, was to be the end of Jacob Bright's work for women. In 1895 illness forced him to retire from Parliament and he died in 1899 without recovering his health.

Jacob's more famous brother, John Bright, although also a Radical in his politics, is remarkable in contrast for his determined opposition to women's rights. He admired John Stuart Mill, and had indeed voted for his Amendment, but he thought Mill's *Subjection of Women*, published in 1869, a most pernicious influence and voted repeatedly against all the women's suffrage Bills while he was in Parliament. He believed firmly that women's place was in the home, and to grant them the vote would lead to the neglect of their domestic responsibilities. He also feared that women's suffrage might increase the influence of priests and parsons.

It was a cause of great irritation to him that women's rights were taken up not only by his brother and sister-in-law but by his two surviving sisters, Priscilla, who married Duncan McLaren, MP for Edinburgh, and Margaret, the wife of Samuel Lucas, both of whom were enthusiastic workers for women's suffrage. They were also, like Jacob and Ursula Bright, deeply committed to the campaign for the repeal of the Contagious Diseases Acts, and Duncan McLaren, like Jacob Bright, was a repeal leader in the

House of Commons. John Bright, however, although voting for repeal, disliked the style of what he considered to be an offensive campaign. Clearly he was influenced in this, as in the case of women's suffrage, by a profoundly conservative view of women and an essentially patriarchal view of marriage. He even went so far as to discourage his wife from discussions on the subject of women's suffrage with his sisters and sister-in-law. This is in sharp contrast to Jacob, who championed all the moves during his period in Parliament to raise the status of the wife in marriage and contrasts too with what we know of his own marriage, which appears to have been an essentially equal partnership.

Not only is there no biography of Jacob Bright, but there is only an exceptionally brief and uninformative entry in the *DNB Supplementary Vol. I*, p. 291. His involvement in the suffrage movement is described briefly in *Votes for Women*, Roger Fulford (London, Faber and Faber, 1956) and *The Suffragette Movement*, Sylvia Pankhurst (London, Longmans, 1931: Virago, 1977). On his involvement in the campaign for married women's property see *Wives and Property*, Lee Holcombe (Oxford, Martin Robertson, 1983). On the involvement of the Bright family in the Contagious Diseases Acts repeal movement see *Prostitution and Victorian Social Reform*, Paul McHugh (New York, St Martin's Press, 1980). His daughter has some comments on her father in *Old Memories and Letters of Annie Besant*, Esther Bright (London, Theosophical Publishing House, 1936). On John Bright's attitude to women's rights see *John Bright. Victorian Reformer*, Herman Ausubel (London, John Wiley and Sons, 1966).

See also BRIGHT Ursula, PANKHURST Richard Marsden.

BRIGHT Ursula ?1830–1915

The daughter of William Mellor, a Liverpool merchant, Ursula Bright, a leading equal rights feminist, married Jacob Bright in 1855. Like Jacob Bright she came from a Quaker background and her father was a subscriber to the Married Women's Property Committee. Otherwise we know nothing of her life until the founding of the Manchester Society for Women's Suffrage in 1867, although some time during that period a daughter, Esther, was born. Ursula, with her husband, became a valuable support of the Manchester Society, where they met and made what was to be a life-long friendship with Richard Pankhurst. It was in the cause of married women's property, however, that Ursula Bright was to make her particular contribution.

In 1868 a Married Women's Property Committee had been founded which included men like Richard Pankhurst and Sir Charles Dilke, and women like Lady Kate Amberley, Elizabeth Wolstenholme, Lydia Becker and Emilie Venturi, the daughter of William Ashurst. In 1874 Lydia Becker, who was treasurer, resigned and Ursula Bright took her place. Under her management she considerably increased the number of subscribers and the amount of money subscribed. It was Ursula Bright's opinion that lobbying would be a more useful tactic than popular agitation and so eventually, through the conversion of influential friends, and a large number of unsuccessful tries, a Married Women's Property Bill was passed for Scotland in 1881 and extended to England, Ireland and Wales in 1882. So a fight which had been begun by Barbara Leigh Smith as a young girl in the 1850s was brought to a successful conclusion.

In 1870, along with her husband, she became involved in the movement for the repeal of the Contagious Diseases Acts, and was indeed a founder member of the Ladies' National Association executive. The Acts were designed to protect the Armed Forces from venereal disease by requiring the compulsory examination and treatment of women believed to be prostitutes, and were seen by their opponents as not only condoning vice but supporting the double standard of sexual morality. The nature of the campaign led to a division within the suffrage movement, the more cautious element fearing that any association in the public mind between the two would harm the suffrage cause.

In 1874 there was another breach when a suffrage Bill was proposed excluding married women. The Brights, along with Richard Pankhurst and others in the Manchester Society, came into opposition with Lydia Becker and other suffrage leaders on this issue. Later this proposal was dropped but in 1889, when it seemed—wrongly as it turned out—that a Bill enfranchising only spinsters and widows would become law, the Brights, the Pankhursts, and a number of others formed the Women's Franchise League. This body was committed not only to married women's suffrage but also to other measures affecting the married woman, including equality in divorce, inheritance, and the guardianship of children. Ursula Bright was its secretary during most of its existence, and it was as a result of her endless and deeply frustrating working behind the scenes that the Local Government Act of 1894 ensured the inclusion of married women in all local franchises.

By this time Ursula Bright had spent some twenty years in ceaseless lobbying and, although her efforts had finally been crowned with success, she now felt tired of the struggle. Moreover, at this time she was becoming interested in Theosophy. Like her husband, her previous position had been one of agnosticism, but in 1890 her daughter Esther went to hear Annie Besant lecture on Theosophy. Ursula Bright had known Annie Besant at the time of the Bradlaugh Besant Trial and had admired her stand on birth control. At first it was only Esther who found Theosophy appealing and, in spite of opposition from her father, she joined the Theosophical Society in 1891. It is not clear exactly when Ursula Bright became converted, but by 1898 she was fully committed to its support. After Jacob Bright died in 1899 Annie Besant lived with Ursula and Esther Bright on all her visits to England, and with Esther alone after her mother's death in 1915. By 1907, however, Ursula was seriously ill and helpless, and in pain most of the time so that it is hardly surprising that the suffrage cause no longer moved her. Sylvia Pankhurst describes her in these years as very gentle and remote.

On the whole Ursula Bright remains a very elusive figure. Yet it seems clear that her efforts behind the scenes were largely responsible both for the Married Women's Property Acts of 1881 and 1882, and the securing of the local franchise for married women in 1894. Perhaps the very nature of her activities has helped to ensure her obscurity since she worked very much in the background, although the neglect of Jacob Bright has also contributed. She represents, alongside her husband and some other suffrage workers, most notably the Pankhursts and the Elmys, a protest against the narrowing of women's rights to the parliamentary suffrage issue. In particular she wanted to abolish the legal disabilities surrounding the married woman which kept her in legal subjection to her husband.

It is a pity that we know so little of her married life, although the evidence of her daughter suggests that it was a happy one, and it seems clear that in all her work for women's rights she enjoyed the full support and co-operation of her husband. Her daughter was later to recall only one instance in which her mother and father had disagreed with each other, and that was over Parnell. Jacob Bright stood by Gladstone on the issue, whereas Ursula was deeply indignant with Gladstone for throwing over the Irish leader. Esther, who seems to have admired both her parents deeply, called her mother 'an independent warrior soul' and she may even have been the inspiration behind her husband's loyal support for women's rights.

The last years of Ursula Bright's life have been described by her daughter Esther Bright in *Old Memories and Letters of Annie Besant* (London, Theosophical Publishing House, 1936). The best source for her activities on behalf of the Women's Franchise League is *The Suffragette Movement*, Sylvia Pankhurst (London, Longmans, 1931; Virago 1977). On her involvement in the repeal of the Contagious Diseases Acts campaign see

Prostitution and Victorian Social Reform, Paul McHugh (New York, St Martin's Press, 1980) and *Prostitution and Victorian Society*, Judith R. Walkowitz (Cambridge, Cambridge University Press, 1980).

For her work on the Married Women's Property Committee see *Wives and Property*, Lee Holcombe (Oxford, Martin Robertson, 1983).

See also BRIGHT Jacob, WOLSTEN-HOLME-ELMY Elizabeth Clark.

BROWNE Stella 1882–1955

Stella Browne was a pioneer advocate of greater sexual freedom for women. Little is known about her family background or early life. She was born in Canada but was educated in Europe and later at Somerville College, Oxford. For a time she worked as a librarian at Morley College in South London. Fluent in German, she made a number of translations of German texts. She was also widely read in German socialist thought. As a young woman she became interested both in the birth-control movement and in Havelock Ellis's writing on female sexuality and was convinced of the need of sexual freedom for women. She was also a committed socialist. In 1912 she developed some of her views on women and sexuality in the feminist paper *The Freewoman* under the pseudonym 'New Subscriber' and this early assertion of the rights of women, married or unmarried, to sexual pleasure was to be the key-note of her feminism throughout her life.

By 1914 she was involved in a campaign organised by the Malthusian League in South London to inform working-class women of contraceptive measures, and her connection with the Malthusian League continued into the 1920s. At about this time she met the American birth controller Margaret Sanger. Other friends she made at this time included Rose Witcop, a young anarchist deeply committed to birth control, and Cedar and Eden Paul. Cedar Paul had been associated with Sylvia Pankhurst's Workers' Suffrage Federation and Eden Paul supported both birth control and eugenics. In 1917 Stella Browne contributed to a book, *Population and Birth Control* edited by Cedar and Eden Paul.

In the years immediately after the war, Stella Browne, along with the Pauls, tried to bring the issue of birth control into the Communist Party. She based her case both on the immediate needs of working-class women and on the communist commitment to equality. Her failure led her to leave the Communist Party in 1923 and to take her struggle for birth control into the Labour Party. In 1923 a campaign began, organised largely by Dora Russell, to allow the centres which had been set up under the 1918 Maternity and Child Welfare Acts to give advice about birth control. Stella Browne was deeply involved in the campaign from the start, and lectured widely in London and other parts of the country, both on the birth-control movement and on practical methods of birth control.

By the 1930s the battle for birth control was well on the way to being won, but abortion was still a highly controversial issue. Stella Browne was one of the first to come out publicly in its favour, not simply in extreme cases, such as rape, but simply and straightforwardly as a woman's right. She made this claim as early as 1915 in a paper 'The Sexual Variety and Variability among Women and their Bearing upon Social Reconstruction', and continued to raise the abortion issue wherever she could even in spite of protest from more cautious colleagues. Dora Russell, for example, believed that to do so might prejudice the fight for birth control, which she thought should come first, and described Stella Browne, half admiringly, as a holy terror. Indeed, in giving evidence to the Birkett Committee in the 1930s, Stella Browne was courageous enough to admit that she had had an abortion herself. In 1936, she was one of the founder members of the Abortion Law Reform Association, although in her insistence on abortion as a woman's right, she was considerably in advance even of the Association itself at that time. During the second world war she moved to Liverpool to care for her sister, and by the time of her death in 1955 she was largely forgotten.

Stella Browne tried hard to reconcile socialism and feminism, arguing that economic changes alone could not give equality or self-determination to women and, in this way, she clearly anticipated some of the concerns of modern feminism. Her claim that abortion, like contraception, was essential if women were to have control of their own bodies, was also to become a major plank of the modern movement. She disliked patriarchal marriage and wanted to free sexual relationships from legal and economic coercion, believing the sexual impulse to be infinitely variable and individual. On the other hand, her acceptance of some of Havelock Ellis's ideas on fixed feminine characteristics and her belief that children born in free love were eugenically superior reflect her particular intellectual background. Described by her biographer as a 'little, indomitable, unrespectable, fanatical foghorn of a feminist' she was a remarkable pioneer.

The main source is *A New World for Women: Stella Browne—Socialist Feminist*, Sheila Rowbotham (London, Pluto Press, 1977). See also *The Tamarisk Tree*, Dora Russell (London, Virago, 1975).

BUSS Frances Mary 1827–1894

Frances Buss, an eminent headmistress, was the daughter of Robert William Buss, an engraver, and his wife Frances Eastwood. Never a very successful artist, at least financially, the burden of the family finance rested on Robert's wife, and later on Frances Buss herself, who was the eldest child and the only surviving daughter. Nine more children were born after Frances, but only four of them, all boys, survived beyond childhood. Frances was a studious child who enjoyed her lessons, and at the age of fourteen began to teach in the school in which she had been a pupil. When she was eighteen her mother opened her own school, with Frances taking charge of the older children. A family enterprise designed to ease their financial difficulties, Robert Buss also joined in the teaching, as did two of the young sons.

From the first Frances had an intense desire to improve her teaching and in 1849, encouraged by a family friend, the Reverend David Laing, she became an evening pupil at the newly formed Queen's College. David Laing was keenly interested in the education of women, and an active member of the Governesses' Benevolent Institution, the organisation responsible for the founding of the college, and Frances was one of its first evening pupils. A year later, in 1850, not quite twenty-three, she gained the Queen's College diploma and founded a new school, the North London Collegiate School for girls which she was associated with for the rest of her life.

From its inception the school attempted to achieve high standards. Some of the staff at Queen's College attended as visiting lecturers and Frances Buss, as headmistress, insisted on qualified teachers. She also had the support of David Laing until his death in 1860. A year later her mother also died. These two bereavements so close together caused her deep grief. At some time during the 1850s moreover she had made the deliberate decision to put aside marriage for the sake of her family, a sacrifice which, in her own words, caused her 'real heart-ache'.

By the 1860s however, in spite of her personal grief, Frances Buss was not only the headmistress of a successful school for girls but a pioneer in the movement for women's higher education. A friend of Emily Davies, she worked with her in the campaign to open university local examinations to girls, and in 1865 was one of those who gave evidence to the Schools Inquiry Commission. An ardent supporter of university education for women, she pressed its claims on both her pupils and their parents. She agreed with Emily Davies that there must be no lowering of standards for girls and was enthusiastically behind the establishment, by Emily Davies, of Girton.

In 1871 she took the unusual step of

changing her North London Collegiate School from a private school to an endowed grammar school. This involved her not only in a financial loss, but also in a loss of authority as she now had to work under the control of a board of governors. She was motivated, however, by a strong desire to see the benefits of a good education made available to a class of pupils who could not afford the fees of a private school.

Although her school was the real centre of her life, she was also active in a number of educational associations, of which the most important was the Headmistresses' Association, of which she was president from its inception in 1873 until her death. She also took a keen interest in medical education and was one of the governors of the London School of Medicine for Women. Another of her enthusiasms was the placing of women on school boards and boards of guardians. Although she felt she could not actively support Josephine Butler's work, she agreed with her stand. Moreover, when Stead was sent to prison for his work, in association with Josephine Butler, in exposing the traffic in young girls, Frances Buss wrote to Millicent Fawcett appealing to her to take up his case. She also placed great importance on the suffrage campaign. Throughout her life she was always on the side of reform, supporting such issues as the anti-slavery movement, the campaign for Italian unity, and the temperance movement. By 1880 however she was suffering from a debilitating kidney disease, although she continued her headship until her death in 1894.

Although Frances Buss greatly loved her father, it was her mother she most resembled, especially in her practical efficiency and in her devotion to duty. She was an affectionate and indeed overtly demonstrative person, with a great love of children. Her concern for others was manifest not only in the sacrifice of her own hopes of marriage, but in the decision to give up her financial interest in her own school. Of a practical, rather than a theoretical or introspective turn of mind, she was nevertheless forthright in the defence of her principles. Perhaps the issue she cared most deeply about was the need for women to be self-supporting. She saw education not only as a means to this end, but as one of the most important sources of a professional career for women, believing that the status of a headmistress should be equal to that of a headmaster. A firm supporter of training for teachers, she was active in the founding of a training college for teachers at Cambridge. She played, therefore, an important role in the professionalisation of women teachers as well as in the improvement she helped to achieve in the education of girls.

There is a biography of Frances Buss *Frances Mary Buss and her work for education*, Annie E. Ridley (London, Longmans Green and Co. 1895). Her life is also the subject of *How Different From Us: A Biography of Miss Beale and Miss Buss*, Josephine Kamm (London, The Bodley Head, 1958).

See also DAVIES Sarah Emily.

BUTLER Josephine 1828–1906

Josephine Butler, leader of the campaign against the double standard of sexual morality was the seventh child of John Grey and his wife Hannah Annett. Her father belonged to a prosperous Northumberland family and was the cousin of Lord Grey, the Whig who was Prime Minister during the struggle over the Reform Act of 1832. A man of deep if simple religious principles and strong family affections, he was also keenly interested in social reform. From childhood he had a hatred of slavery and this stayed with him all his life. Perhaps his chief characteristic was his respect for the rights and liberties of the individual, and he took a leading part in the agitation for the Reform Bill and, later on, in the campaign for the repeal of the Corn Laws. His sister Margaretta Grey had strong feelings about the lack of opportunities open to women and, as a schoolgirl, had dressed up as a boy in order to visit Parliament.

Brought up in the country, Josephine was educated mainly by her parents, although frequent visitors from all over Europe and America ensured that the household was far from intellectually isolated. She grew up to share the religious faith and moral principles of her parents, and early on came to appreciate the inequalities, injustices and cruelties in the world. In 1850 she met George Butler, a son of the headmaster of Harrow. Nine years her senior, he was then working as a lecturer at Durham University. Shortly afterwards a post at Oxford as examiner of schools gave him the financial security to marry, and the wedding took place in 1852. Two years later he was ordained, although he continued to hold academic appointments until 1882. By 1857, three sons had been born but Josephine's health was causing anxiety and she was advised to leave the damp environment of Oxford. For a time the family was split up, but shortly afterwards George Butler was offered the post of vice-principal of Cheltenham College.

The five years at Oxford had not been altogether successful for Josephine Butler, in spite of her happy marriage. The academic circle in which they moved was dominated by men to such an extent that sometimes she was the only woman present. Moreover, it was a largely unenlightened male society and she was frequently horrified by their casual attitude to moral and religious issues and particularly by their unthinking and indeed callous acceptance of the double standard of morality. They treated her interventions with contempt. While George Butler was not argumentative by nature, his views were in accord with her own and it was at his suggestion that they took the practical step of receiving into their own home a young deserted mother who had been in prison for the murder of her child.

The move to Cheltenham was followed by the birth of Eva, their only daughter, and brought a period of greater happiness, but it was not long before Josephine Butler once again found herself swimming against the tide of public opinion when the civil war broke out in the United States. Cheltenham was a conservative town and favoured the South, and both Josephine and George Butler's anti-slavery principles brought them not only controversy but even a certain degree of ostracism. Then, in 1863, their little daughter Eva fell to her death in front of their eyes. The parents were utterly grief-stricken and neither ever recovered completely.

In 1866 there was a further move, this time to Liverpool where George Butler had been appointed principal of Liverpool College. To try to assuage her grief, Josephine turned to workhouse visiting, but this soon grew into rescue work with prostitutes. At first, with her husband's full encouragement, girls were taken into her own home, but later a house was taken and a refuge started.

In the meantime both Josephine and George Butler were drawn into the work of the North of England Council for the Higher Education of Women. In 1867 she became its president, and in 1868 she was chosen to take a petition to Cambridge asking the university to set examinations to test women's educational qualifications. The petition was granted and the scheme grew eventually first into lectures for women at Cambridge and finally into the establishment of Newnham College. By accepting special examinations for women Josephine Butler was aligning herself with Anne Jemima Clough and Henry Sidgwick and was in opposition to Emily Davies who wanted women to take the same examinations and acquire the same qualifications as men.

Also in 1868 she published a pamphlet *The Education and Employment of Women* which was essentially a plea for widening and improving the educational and employment opportunities open to women who needed to support themselves. Josephine was however never a straightforward equal-rights feminist, as her support for special examinations for women had shown, and she took pains in the pamphlet to repudiate the argument that men and women were essentially the same, claiming that they existed to complement each other. Women's special role, in her view, was to protect and care for the weak, but also, and significantly in the light of her later work, to check the immorality in society which men were too ready to excuse. In the following year she was the editor of

Woman's Work and Woman's Culture in which, in her introduction, she once again argued that women should not try to rival men since they had a different part to play in society. Centred largely on the home, they were by no means bounded by it since their moral influence was badly needed outside. She painted a romantic picture of what marriage should be, based not on the abject dependence of the wife but on a 'sweet interchange of services'.

By 1869 Josephine Butler's involvement in the wider feminist movement was over, as she was drawn almost in spite of herself into the work for which she is now chiefly remembered. The Contagious Diseases Acts had been introduced during the 1860s in an endeavour to reduce the incidence of venereal disease in the Armed Services. The Acts applied however only to women, and provided for the compulsory and regular medical examination of those believed to be prostitutes. Those women found to be diseased were to be detained for treatment in special hospitals. The Acts were already in operation in several garrison towns, and it was the attempt to extend their provisions which eventually aroused opposition and led to the formation of the National Association for the repeal of the Acts. It was at this stage that Josephine Butler was asked to take part in the campaign and at first there is no doubt that she shrank from the task. She was acutely conscious of the effect her involvement was likely to have on her husband, who as a headmaster was in a vulnerable position, as well as the notoriety for herself which would follow from a woman breaking the taboo of silence surrounding the subject. Nevertheless both she and her husband believed she had been specially called to do this work and for the next few years she gave herself totally to its demands.

A brilliant speaker, she was able to hold audiences spellbound and with her beauty and her charismatic appeal she soon became one of the most outstanding figures in the movement. Although she spoke particularly to women, her audiences were mixed, and one of her earliest lectures was to a large meeting of railwaymen at Crewe. Her task however was by no means an easy one. The campaign roused violent hostility in some quarters and she and her husband had to face, in addition, coldness and even ostracism on the part of friends. At times too she had to face serious physical danger. The work also took its psychological toll and in 1875 she had a prolonged and serious breakdown. Her fears for her husband also proved justified and his career suffered badly. The consequence however seems to have been a strengthening rather than a weakening of the marriage and she found him a constant source of help and encouragement. In later years her sons too gave her practical as well as emotional support.

Josephine Butler's chief contribution was to bring into the open the whole issue of the double standard of sexual morality and the way in which it condemned the woman but excused and even protected the man. While she fully accepted that sexual immorality was a sin which required repentance, it was a sin for both sexes alike, whereas the Acts singled out only the woman for punishment. Moreover, while condemning the immorality involved, she was well aware that many women were driven into prostitution by low earnings and unemployment, while others were led astray by men who seduced and then deserted them. The result of this thinking on her part was to place the emphasis on the prostitute as victim as much as sinner. Moreover, she was horrified at the brutal operation of the Acts, especially the compulsory medical examination which, to Josephine Butler, who hated male doctors, was a kind of rape. Brought up in the anti-slavery movement, the treatment meted out to women suspected of being prostitutes seemed to her to be the most flagrant denial of human rights.

In 1874 Josephine Butler turned her attention to Europe, and the leadership of the campaign passed into other hands. It was James Stansfeld who eventually brought it to a successful conclusion when the Acts were finally repealed in 1886. On the other hand, her reports of the brutality and corruption of legalised prostitution in Europe helped to maintain the morale of the British workers at a time when, with a Conservative government in power, parliamentary success was hopeless.

By 1882 George Butler's health was failing and, after a period of financial anxiety, Gladstone offered him a canonship at Winchester. Josephine Butler turned her attention to the scandal of child prostitution and was actively involved with W.T. Stead in the plot in 1885 to expose the ease with which a young girl could be bought for immoral purposes. As a result W.T. Stead served a term of imprisonment as did his accomplice Rebecca Jarrett, a reformed prostitute under Josephine Butler's protection. This consequence of their action was a hard blow to Josephine, who felt partly responsible, but the public outcry led to a change in the law, and the age of consent was raised to sixteen.

The death of George Butler in 1890 was a great sorrow to Josephine who had come to rely on his companionship and support. To help overcome her grief she wrote a memoir *Recollections of George Butler* published in 1892. She also wrote her own memoirs, *Personal Reminiscences of a Great Crusade* published in 1896. By 1900 she had virtually retired from public life, and she died in 1906, at the age of seventy-eight.

Although she never took a very active part in the suffrage campaign, Josephine Butler believed firmly in its significance for women and indeed one of her most fundamental beliefs was in the need for women to play a much greater role in public life. This was based not on any abstract concept of equal rights but on the complementary role played by men and women and especially on woman's moral superiority. Her belief in men's moral weaknesses, which led them more easily into immorality, did not however lead her to pose any essential and necessary opposition between men and women, and, in spite of her awareness of the prevalence of the sexual abuse of women by men, there is never any indication of sex antagonism in her writings. Undoubtedly this belief was an expression of her relationship not only with her husband, her father and her sons, but with a number of other men with whom she worked in the repeal movement. Indeed, although all of Josephine Butler's work was for women, her closest colleagues were men. In later life, in particular, young men seem to have delighted in serving her. Consequently, whether in marriage and the family, in philanthropy, or in social reform generally, she always conceived of men and women working together, and this distinguishes her clearly from many later feminists.

The qualities of spirituality, of personal courage, and of faith in what she saw as God's mission, drew many men and women to follow her, but these qualities also produced a refusal to compromise with her principles which to some even of her sympathisers verged on fanaticism. Thus she was totally devoid of the political skills which enabled James Stansfeld to steer a Reform Bill through Parliament. Her role was a different but no less important one. As a feminist she spoke out on behalf of the most rejected and outcast of her sex, claiming for them not only the right to personal dignity and respect but the sympathy and support of other women. Moreover, by her stand, she forced the women's movement to face up to the implications of the double standard of sexual morality.

Biographies include *Josephine Butler. Flame of Fire*, E. Moberly Bell (London, Constable, 1962); *Portrait of Josephine Butler* by her grandson A.S.G. Butler (London, Faber and Faber, 1954), and *Josephine Butler. Her work and principles and their meaning for the twentieth century*, Millicent G. Fawcett and E.M. Turner (London, Association for Moral and Social Hygiene, 1927). Of autobiographical interest are her own *Recollections of George Butler* (Bristol, J.W. Arrowsmith, 1892), *Memoirs of John Grey of Dillon* (Edinburgh, Edmonton and Douglas, 1869) and *Personal Reminiscences of a Great Crusade* (London, Horace Marshall, 1898). For two recent assessments of her role in the Contagious Diseases Acts campaign see *Prostitution and Victorian Society*, Judith R. Walkowitz (Cambridge, Cambridge University Press, 1980) and *Prostitution and Victorian Social Reform*, Paul McHugh (New

York, St Martin's Press, 1980). For her religious views and their influence on her feminism see *Josephine Butler, Octavia Hill, Florence Nightingale. Three Victorian Women who changed their World*, Nancy Boyd (London, Macmillan, 1982). See also *DNB* 1901–1911 pp. 282–3. For a modern feminist interpretation see 'Josephine Butler from Sympathy to Theory' by Jenny Uglow in *Feminist Theorists* ed. Dale Spender (London, The Women's Press, 1983). Also *Significant Sisters*, Margaret Forster (London, Secker and Warburg, 1984).

See also CLOUGH Anne Jemima, SHAEN William, STANSFELD James.

C

CARPENTER Mary 1807–1877

Mary Carpenter, a pioneer in prison reform, was the daughter of Dr Lant Carpenter, a Unitarian minister, and Anna Penn. Mary was the eldest of six children, three of them daughters. Both parents were not only deeply religious but also over-conscientious about themselves and others, so that she was brought up under a very strict regimen of religious and moral training which had a very profound effect on her personality. Even as a tiny child she had a strong sense of duty and a desire to be useful which was to become something of an obsession later in life. She was educated by her father, and her studies were carried considerably beyond those normally open to girls at that time. Closer to her father than to her mother, he was probably the most important influence on her life.

In 1829, ill health forced Lant Carpenter to give up the school that he ran. To help to educate her brothers, Mary and her sister Anna opened a school for girls under the superintendence of their mother, and this situation was to continue until 1848. These were unhappy years for Mary. She did not enjoy teaching girls, since the subjects that interested her were not then part of a girl's education. Consequently she was often bored and frustrated. At times a deep sense of sin led to intense depression and even physical weakness. She was intensely self-critical and envied her sister Anna her gentle disposition. Much later in life she was to confess that, as a young woman, she longed to be a wife and mother, and there is indeed a distinct possibility that she was in love with James Martineau, the brother of Harriet Martineau, who was for a time an assistant in her father's school.

In 1839 her father had another breakdown and his death shortly afterwards, a suspected suicide, was a terrible blow to her. Nevertheless, this was followed by a growing confidence in herself, as she gradually came to better terms with her character and needs. The preparation of a book of meditation and prayer, published in 1844 in memory of her father, helped her over the first period of loss and then, in 1846, she opened her first Ragged School and embarked on what was to be her life's work. She may also at this time have become reconciled to her spinsterhood. In a moving passage in her journal she describes her dreams of someone combining rare intellectual power with wonderful gentleness and benevolence, and her gradual realisation that since God had denied her such a companion there must be a reason. This reason, she came to believe, was in her work for deprived and delinquent children.

With the closing of the family school in 1848, her time was now her own. At first she seemed to be seeking mainly an emotional satisfaction in the affection of her scholars, but her intellectual needs were also to find an outlet in the books and papers which were to make her an expert in her field. In 1850 she published *Ragged Schools: their Principles and Modes of Operation*. This was an attempt to pass on to others the result of her experiences. It was followed in 1851 by *Reformatory Schools for the Children of the Perishing and Dangerous Classes and for Juvenile Offenders*. Inspired by her own experiences with boys from this kind of background, it was an attempt to argue that prison was not the right place for child offenders.

At this stage she took a step that was still unusual, at this period, for someone of her sex. She organised a conference for workers in the field and, although she was still fearful of notoriety, and took no active part in the proceedings, it led directly to a Parliamentary Enquiry at which she was summoned to give evidence. The Reformatory Schools Act which followed in 1854 was a tribute to her ideas. In her own way, therefore, she was, like Florence Nightingale, challenging the right of the male sex to the exclusive manipulation of political influence. Her ability to make impersonal relationships with men, aided her in her work, and may also have been a source of personal satisfaction.

Meanwhile, in Bristol, she opened a Reformatory School for boys in 1852, and a similar school for girls, Red Lodge, in 1854. She took considerable personal interest in both, but particularly in Red Lodge, although in fact she found adolescent girls, unlike boys, difficult to handle, and does not seem to have had a great deal of sympathy with their problems. In 1853 she published *Juvenile Delinquents: Conditions and Treatment*, and in 1855 *On Reformatory Schools*. A further book on juvenile delinquents followed in 1857. The death of her mother in 1856 increased her independence and, after a period sharing a house with her sister Anna, now married, she took a house of her own near Red Lodge. In 1858, apparently on impulse, she adopted a little girl of five, but this does not seem to have been satisfactory for very long. At seven the child was sent away to school, where she remained, partly abroad, until 1876, when she returned as housekeeper. It is possible that, at fifty-one Mary was too old to take on the care of a small child, especially as she was, at that time, very absorbed in Red Lodge. From 1866 onwards, moreover, she made several lengthy trips to India.

Another effort to dispel the loneliness she felt after her mother's death was her acceptance of Frances Power Cobbe to live with her as companion and helper. Greatly admiring Mary Carpenter's work, Frances tried valiantly to succeed in this role, but was appalled both by the children she had to teach, and by Mary's excessively stoical way of life. In personality, too, the women proved totally incompatible, Frances Power Cobbe's warm friendliness unable to come to terms with Mary's extreme reserve. The experiment ended in 1860 and Mary never again sought to find a woman companion, relying, until her death, on her sister Anna for the affection she needed.

In 1864 her attention was drawn by Indian friends to the problem of women in India, and in 1866 she made the first of several visits. Her chief concern was to improve the education of girls, and she attempted to set up training colleges for women teachers, although she was also involved in Indian prison reform. On the whole however, in spite of the time and effort she expended, she was unsuccessful. She was totally ignorant of India, and of the difficulties she would face in bringing about any improvement, and managed to antagonise both the Indian government and the missionaries. It does however show that she was becoming receptive to problems affecting women.

Until the end of the 1860s Mary Carpenter had stood aloof from the British movement for women's rights. When John Stuart Mill wrote to her in 1867 she was at first very lukewarm on the issue of women's suffrage, although she eventually did agree, as a result of his persuasion, to sign the petition. The agitation for the repeal of the Contagious Diseases Acts was, however, a matter which appealed to her immediately, and she became a member of the Bristol committee as well as vice-president of the National Association. The Acts, which provided for the compulsory examination of women believed to be prostitutes, and their treatment if found to be diseased, roused the opposition of those who saw this as legalising vice as well as condoning a double standard of morality. The nature of the campaign meant that an unmarried woman in particular needed courage to make a public stand against the Acts, and her involvement demonstrates the extent to which Mary Carpenter had moved in the course of her life-time. Moreover, during the 1870s her involvement in women's rights grew rapidly. In 1877, just before her death, she signed a Memorial to the Senate of the University of London in favour of the admission of women to medical degrees. In the same year, now fully converted to the need for the vote, she spoke at Clifton to a meeting of the Bristol and West of England Society for Women's Suffrage.

Nevertheless, Mary Carpenter was always

rather ambivalent about the position of women, and, as late as 1873, she refused to speak at a mixed meeting, arguing that she had always kept within her own 'womanly sphere'. This was partly a matter of personality, since she was almost morbidly self-conscious about any public performance, and partly an apparent lack of any personal feelings of disadvantage that she was a woman. She had passionately wanted a husband and family, and there is no doubt that she idealised the position of wife and mother, calling it a noble work given by God. Unmarried women, if denied the happiness of husband and children need not, she believed, be unfulfilled since they, as she had demonstrated, could find ample work to do for the good of others. If she was resentful at the sacrifices she had made for her brothers it seems not to have been at a conscious level, although it may have contributed to the irritability she was constantly reproaching herself with. In this she contrasted strongly with her contemporary and fellow Unitarian Harriet Martineau, whose feminism developed at a comparatively early age. What is perhaps most surprising about Mary Carpenter is that, after a life-time of rather conservative views about women, she became in the end an active supporter of women's rights in such different fields as suffrage and the double standard of sexual morality, as implied by the Contagious Diseases Act. She also supported the higher education of women and their entry into the professions. To some extent this radicalisation of her views is an indication of the growing influence of the women's movement and the spread of its ideas during the 1870s in particular.

A biography of Mary Carpenter was written by her nephew J. Estlin Carpenter, *The Life and Work of Mary Carpenter* (London, Macmillan, 1879). A more recent biography is *Mary Carpenter and the Children of the Streets*, J. Manton (London, Heinemann, 1976). Shorter accounts can be found in *Some Eminent Women of our Times*, Millicent Garrett Fawcett (London, Macmillan, 1859); 'Mary Carpenter', Harriet Warm Schupf, *Victorian Studies*, 1974, 17, 301–17; *Mary Carpenter of Bristol*, Ruby J. Saywers (Bristol, Bristol University, 1964); *DNB* Vol. IX, 159–61.

See also COBBE Frances Power.

CHAPPELLSMITH Margaret 1806–1883

Margaret Chappellsmith was a little known Owenite socialist. Her maiden name was Reynolds and she was born in Aldgate, probably to upper working-class parents. Nothing is known of her early life, except that she was brought up a Baptist, but she became interested in the Radical politics of her time by reading Cobbett and later Owen, whose views were being propagandised at this time in his journal *The New Moral World*. By 1836 Margaret Reynolds, as she was still, was writing articles for the Owenite press on such issues as currency reform, communitarianism, and the position of women. In 1839 she became a salaried Owenite lecturer, and in the same year she married another Owenite, John Chappellsmith. Nothing is known about him except that he was very supportive of her position. There were no children of the marriage. In 1842 she opened a bookshop in London and, some time around 1850–2, she emigrated with her husband to America. She died at New Harmony in 1883.

In her lectures she associated the oppression of women with priestly power, thus relating her feminism to her attacks on religion. She also spoke regularly on divorce, arguing that new rules of marriage would produce more lasting associations while ending promiscuous relationships. Like other women lecturers associated with the Owenite movement, she was attacked both in the anti-Owenite press, and sometimes by her audience itself. In Paisley, for example, it is reported that women threw stones at her. She was called a she-devil, a witch, and a whore, and one journal, the *Antidote, or Anti-Socialist Gazette*, accused her of deserting her husband for a string of lovers. Later however, the journal was forced to admit that this was not true. Fortunately too, audiences were not always hostile, and lectures were often interrupted by the cheers of her largely female audiences.

Margaret Chappellsmith was one of that small but significant band of working-class or lower middle-class women preaching feminism to largely working-class audiences as part of the then vigorous Owenite socialist movement. Although not neglecting the issue of equal rights, such women preached a wider conception of feminism which, because of its association with communitarianism, envisaged the need for considerable changes in marriage and the family. Unlike most equal-rights feminism, it was often specifically securalist in its orientation, and attacked in particular the subordination imposed on women by the Church. Vigorous, especially during the 1830s, it was in decline during the 1840s, to be succeeded in the 1850s by the organised equal-rights movement which abandoned both the secularism of Owenism and its implications for the family.

The source for the life of Margaret Chappellsmith and other Owenite feminists is *Eve and the New Jerusalem*, Barbara Taylor (London, Virago, 1983).

CHEW Ada Nield 1870–1945

Ada Nield, a suffragist and trade unionist, was the daughter of William Nield and Jane Hammond. She was one of thirteen children, four of whom died in infancy. She was the second child and the eldest daughter in the family, and since the only other girl was an epileptic the whole responsibility for a daughter's household duties fell on Ada, as the boys were not expected to help in the house. Indeed she was taken away from school at the age of eleven for this purpose. Her father was a farmer in North Staffordshire and then near Malvern, but later he moved to Crewe where he worked in a brickworks. Ada herself worked in a shop in Nantwich, and briefly in a church school. In 1894, by then working as a tailoress in a Crewe factory, Ada burst suddenly upon the local political scene with a series of letters to the *Crewe Chronicle* under the pseudonym 'A Crewe Factory Girl'. We have no knowledge of how Ada acquired the skills in expression which marked these letters. She had a passion for reading, but must have been largely self-taught.

At the time of the Crewe letters her ideas were still relatively undeveloped but she was already a feminist, pointing out that women did not yet have the vote, and deploring the attitude of male trade unionists to women workers. She was well aware of the low wages paid to women because they were women, and advocated trades unions as the remedy. On any criterion this series of letters was a remarkable achievement for someone of her background, and, as a result of the furore they caused, which lost her her job, she was drawn into active membership of the Independent Labour Party and was soon elected to the Nantwich Board of Guardians. Two years later she became a travelling organiser for the ILP where she rapidly achieved great success as a speaker.

It was at this time that she met and married another ILP organiser, George Chew. Like Ada, he was self-educated, having started work as a half-timer at the age of ten, and it was probably on a joint propaganda tour that they got to know each other and decided to marry. The wedding took place in 1897 but Ada continued her organising work until a girl, Doris, was born the following year. Ada, however, had no intention of tying herself down with a large family. She had wished for one—but only one—child, and was determined that there would be no more.

When Doris was two years old Ada started work again, this time as an organiser for the Women's Trade Union League, although she continued her connection with the ILP. Until Doris was seven, she took her with her on her organising trips, and later used her earnings to pay someone to look after her. From 1908 however, she worked only part-time. During her years with the Women's Trade Union League some of her most important work was in connection with the Potteries Fund Committee, set up to deal with hardship arising from lead poisoning. At this time she was strongly opposed to a limited suffrage campaign believing that only adult suffrage would benefit the working class. In 1912 however, when the National Union of Women's Suffrage Societies began its policy of support for the Labour Party and needed Labour sympathisers as suffrage speakers, Ada became a NUWSS organiser in the Rossendale valley where she spoke at meetings, organised propaganda and wrote for the local press. At this time, too, she began to produce lively sketches of working-class life which appeared in both the local press and in *Common Cause*.

The outbreak of war ended the suffrage campaign and Ada lost her job. She turned instead to business, determined to be economically independent, and eventually started a successful mail-order firm. Her husband, meanwhile, had given up his work as an ILP organiser at the time of their marriage, and, after a short period as a weaver, had set up as a market trader and later on owned a chain of shops in Rochdale mainly dealing in shoes and slippers. Ada Chew retired in 1930, but George Chew continued in business until his death in 1940. During the years between 1915 and her death in 1945, Ada seems to have lost most of her interest in both politics and writing, determined, her daughter has told us, to make enough money for her retirement. She still occasionally wrote letters to the *Women's Leader*, the organ of the National Union of Societies for Equal Citizenship, and these showed that her attitudes had not changed. With her daughter, too, now a school teacher, she shared an interest in the Manchester branch of the Women's International League for Peace and Freedom. After her retirement she developed a taste for foreign travel, mainly with her daughter, though occasionally with her husband or alone.

Although her political activities ended in 1915, Ada Chew had spent twenty years of her life working for both the women's trade union movement and women's suffrage. Her feminism, however, went far beyond these two issues and reveals that her main concern was for women's economic independence. These ideas developed gradually, and indeed, in 1894 in her letters to the *Crewe Chronicle*, she had criticised married women for taking work away from women who needed it for their livelihood. By 1912 she believed that it was essential for all women to have economic independence and not be dependent on either husband or state. In order to achieve this she advocated collective care for children and the improved organisation of domestic work. Nor did she believe that all women made good mothers, and opposed all policies which she believed forced women into motherhood. For example she was opposed to the emphasis on domestic teaching in schools for girls. After the war she objected to family endowments because they branded motherhood as a trade, and in 1926 was arguing in favour of separate tax assessment and allowances for married women.

In her own marriage she rejected the constant child-bearing typical of her mother's generation. She was also determined to be economically independent, earning enough throughout her married life to contribute to household expenses and provide for the domestic help which enabled her to take up paid work. Nevertheless she continued always to accept the traditional view that domestic tasks and child-care were a wife's responsibility and she never advocated, even in her writings, the greater involvement of the husband in housework or child-care. Her husband shared this view, and if he accepted the demands of her work, it seems to have been only so long as his own domestic arrangements were not inconvenienced. There are also indications that the marriage itself was a disappointment. George Chew is described by his daughter as a man of a somewhat sulky disposition who found it difficult to show his affection. He was inarticulate both in speaking and in writing, and may have been jealous of his wife's abilities. He was certainly jealous of the close tie between mother and daughter. Moreover, from as early as 1910 his political attitudes changed, and he became more Conservative.

There was never any open breach but the couple seem to have drifted further and further apart.

Her own marriage therefore may have contributed to the decidedly unromantic picture of married life presented in her sketches. So too did the years as a household drudge when she was little more than a child and which made her determined that her own life would be different. Her writings are devoid of any sentimentality about either marriage or motherhood and reveal her as a feminist of considerable originality whose ideas frequently ran counter to those of her time, but which, in a somewhat different form, were to be revived by the modern movement.

The main source of information on Ada Chew is her daughter's biography, *Ada Nield Chew, The Life and Writings of a Working Woman*, Doris Nield Chew (London, Virago, 1982). See also *One Hand Tied Behind Us. The Rise of the Women's Suffrage Movement*, Jill Liddington and Jill Norris (London, Virago, 1978) and *DLB* Vol. V, pp. 57–64.

CLOUGH Anne Jemima 1820–1892

Anne Jemima Clough, first principal of Newnham, was the daughter of James Butler Clough and his wife Anne Perfect who was the daughter of a Yorkshire banker. James Clough, the son of a Denbighshire clergyman, chose to go into business as a cotton merchant in Liverpool where Anne was born. There were four children of the marriage, and Anne, the third child, was the only daughter. Her father was an amiable and affectionate man fond of amusements and not really fitted for a business career in which he eventually failed. Her mother, in contrast, was shy and disliked society. She was an affectionate clinging woman, both to her husband and her children, with a fondness for reading, especially religious subjects and poetry.

In 1822 the family moved to Charleston, South Carolina, so that Anne spent her childhood in the United States, returning only occasionally for holidays with relations. The boys, however, were sent to school in England. In 1836 the family returned permanently to Liverpool. Her favourite brother, Arthur, was still at Rugby but a year later he went to Oxford as an undergraduate and soon became, as indeed he was always to remain, the most important influence on her life. He directed her studies and under his guidance she began to visit and teach the poor. During the next few years, however, she went through a period of inner doubt and deep insecurity, as she both longed for and feared marriage and daydreamed of doing something that would make her name live for ever. She had grown up shy, like her mother, and awkward in company, but strong-willed and while her introspective mood made her highly self-critical the assertive side of her nature longed for release.

In 1841 circumstances changed very drastically when her father's business failed. The family was forced to move into a smaller house, and Anne and her mother took on many of the household chores. Anne herself opened a small school to help pay off the family debts. The death of her young brother George in 1843, and her father in 1844 also added to her problems. Meanwhile, as the years went by, Anne herself was beginning to think less of marriage and more of the need of women like herself for satisfying work. A break came in 1848 when her brother Arthur resigned his Oxford fellowship as a consequence of religious doubts and spent a period at home. This enabled Anne, now twenty-eight, to spend a few months in London at a training school for teachers. Her ideas at this time reflect a strong desire for a wider sphere for women, but she also still dreamed of an ideal marriage of affectionate companionship in which her relationship with Arthur was the conscious model.

In 1852 her life changed again when she moved to Ambleside with her mother, now an invalid. A year later her brother Arthur married Blanche Smith, the niece of Florence

Nightingale, with whose work he was later to be closely associated. Meanwhile, at Ambleside, in spite of the claims of her mother, she found time to run a small but successful school for the children of tradespeople and farmers. Nevertheless, these were hard years for her. Feeling like a bird in a cage, as she later put it, she longed for a wider scope for her activities. In 1860 her mother died, leaving her at last free of family ties. A legacy on the death of a brother also gave her a measure of financial independence. But the death, in 1861, of her beloved Arthur was a blow from which she took several years to recover. She gave up both the Ambleside home and the school and lived for a time with Arthur's widow and young family but this break in her life was in fact to lead to her emancipation. Through Blanche she met educational pioneers like Emily Davies and Frances Buss and gradually became involved in their work, making use of her Ambleside experience to present evidence to the Schools Enquiry Commission and publishing a paper in *Macmillan's Magazine* under the title 'Hints on the Organization of Girls' Schools'.

By 1866 she had gained the confidence to initiate a scheme for lectures for women in Liverpool, which, although unsuccessful, led to the formation of the North of England Council for Promoting the Higher Education of Women. Meeting for the first time in Leeds in 1867, it involved, besides Anne Clough, such men and women as Josephine and George Butler, brought in by the persuasion of Anne herself, and Elizabeth Wolstenholme. From this council developed not only a scheme of lectures for women as originally envisaged by Anne Clough, but a special university-based examination for women which would provide teachers, especially, with a measure of their achievement. Even more important for Anne Clough's future was a proposal from Henry Sidgwick to organise a series of lectures for women at Cambridge to prepare them for this special examination. This immediately brought him into opposition with Emily Davies, to whom special examinations for women were anathema, and who was already trying to found her own college with the aim of opening university degree examinations to women. Henry Sidgwick, however, went ahead with his scheme, took a house in Cambridge to lodge the women students, and in 1871 invited Anne Clough to be in charge. At first Anne was doubtful since she had been invited to be headmistress of a new school, but when this fell through she accepted Henry Sidgwick's offer. By 1880 the initially modest venture had expanded to become Newnham College and Anne Clough was its first principal.

Unlike Emily Davies, Anne was quite happy with special examinations for women, which she saw not only as more acceptable to public opinion and therefore more likely to succeed, but also as better suited to the lack of preparation of many potential students. Consequently Newnham was more flexible than its rival Girton, although in time as the education of girls improved, and the university opened its examinations, although not its degrees, to women the differences eventually disappeared.

Apart from her work in Cambridge she maintained her interest in the teaching profession, helping, for example, in the formation of the Association of Assistant Mistresses. In 1882 she was one of those who set on foot the University Association of Women Teachers to serve as a registry for university-trained teachers. Nor was her feminism confined to education. She supported suffrage and believed firmly that a wife should have the right to her own property. Active until 1888, she died in 1892.

Anne Clough was much less inclined than Emily Davies to see the issue of women's education in terms of equality. A compromiser by nature, she simply worked to make things better. In many ways she was cautious, even timid, and on most issues, conventional. Nevertheless, beneath her ladylike manner and seeming diffidence, there was considerable persistence and determination. If in practice she counselled patience, she was by no means without visions for the future. She was deeply conscious not only of her own limitations but of the limitations forced on women by their narrow education and narrow lives, and it was this consciousness which drove her to try to secure for women a fuller and freer life in the future.

There is a comprehensive biography of Anne Jemima Clough by her niece Blanche Clough, the daughter of Arthur Clough, *Memoir of Anne Jemima Clough. First Principal of Newnham College* (London, Arnold, 1903). There is also an entry in *DNB*, Supplementary Vol. II, pp. 35–6. For the background to her life at Cambridge see *Women at Cambridge. A Men's University—though of a Mixed Type*, Rita McWilliams Tullborg (London, Gollancz, 1975). For a detailed account of the North of England Council see an unpublished M.Ed dissertation *The North of England Council for the Higher Education of Women*, Sheila Lemoine (Manchester, 1968).

See also DAVIES Sarah Emily, SIDGWICK Henry.

COBBE Frances Power 1822–1904

Frances Power Cobbe, journalist and anti-vivisectionist, was the daughter of Charles Cobbe, an Anglo-Irish landowner who had served in India as a young man and later married and settled down on the family estates in Ireland where Frances was born. There were five children of the marriage and Frances, the youngest, was the only girl. Her childhood was a happy one, and, although her father was always a remote figure, she was petted by her brothers and had a close and affectionate companionship with her mother. She was educated at home until she was fourteen, when she was sent away for two years to a fashionable and ineffective school for young ladies. On her return home Frances was introduced into the society of the neighbourhood, but disliked it from the first. Instead, she enjoyed running the house and had a real passion for study. Moreover, by the time she was twenty she was already preoccupied with the problem of religious doubt. Her gradual loss of faith was a source of anguish to her and was accentuated by the death in 1847 of her dearly loved mother. Unwisely she confessed some of her doubts to her father, only to be banished from the house to live with her brother. After a period of several months she was allowed home to act as housekeeper but in a sort of moral Coventry.

In the years that followed Frances continued to be preoccupied with religion and took no interest in the social and political concerns which were to fill her life later on. Some of her religious belief began to return to her, and she eventually set out her position on religion and morals in her *Essay on the Theory of Intuitive Morals*, which, much to her father's disapproval, was published in 1855. In 1857 her father died, and the family home passed into the hands of her eldest brother. Although she had only a small sum of money of her own, Frances refused to stay on as a dependant of her brother and sister-in-law, and determined to find some way of making a living on her own behalf.

Her first thought was some form of social work and she lived for a time with Mary Carpenter, who was looking for an assistant to help in her work with delinquent children. This was not, however, a success. The two women were quite incompatible in temperament, and Frances, who enjoyed comfort and good food, could not accept the extreme stoicism of Mary Carpenter's way of life. Nor was she happy as a teacher. For a time she tried workhouse visiting but eventually, after moving to London, she began to earn her living writing for the press. During the 1870s she was taken on to the staff of the newly founded *Echo* and later was on the staff of the *Standard.* She retained her interest in religion and continued to publish on the subject, but a great deal of her writing, during the 1860s especially, was on women.

She herself dated her interest in women's rights to her period with Mary Carpenter, when her attention was directed to the legal position of her sex, and from 1861 her many articles on the subject of women brought her into contact with leading feminists like Barbara Bodichon and Lydia Becker. She also met John Stuart Mill who encouraged her in her writing. Later, she joined the women's suffrage committee, and worked for a time on the Married Women's Property Committee. As early as 1862 she read a paper at the Social Science Congress on the proposed opening of university examinations to women. In it she argued for a free trade in knowledge to be established between the sexes. Her own particular contribution was, however, on violence to wives. In 1878 she published a pamphlet *Wife Torture* which proposed that wife assault should be made grounds for a legal separation, and her writing on the subject influenced the Matrimonial Causes Act of 1878 which gave a wife the right to a separation with maintenance, and with custody of any child under ten years of age.

Her feminism was in many respects aggressive in its attitude to men. In another of her pamphlets, *Criminals, Idiots, Women and Minors* published in 1868, she argued that men made women economically dependent so that their authority would go unchallenged. Moreover, it was women's economic dependence which made it possible for men to go on ill-treating their wives. The following year, in a paper 'The Final Cause of Women' contributed to Josephine Butler's *Woman's Work and Woman's Culture* (London, Macmillan, 1869) she argued strongly for the view that women existed for their own purposes and not simply for the services they could render to men. At the same time some of her views were decidedly conservative. In a later pamphlet, *The Duties of Women* (1881) she stressed that once a woman was a wife and mother these duties were of paramount importance and other interests must be subordinate. She was also firmly conventional in her attitude to sexual morality and, in the same pamphlet, condemned the loose living indulged in by 'advanced' women.

Her other main interest during these years was her campaign against vivisection. She was first aroused by accounts of cruelty to animals in veterinary schools in Paris and wrote an article in *Fraser's Magazine* on 'The Rights of Man and the Claims of Brutes'. In 1870 she became involved in work in England aimed at strengthening the law on experiments on animals, eventually becoming one of the leaders of the British anti-vivisection movement. Deeply devoted to a succession of dogs, Frances Power Cobbe's opposition to vivisection was based mainly on her concern for the suffering of animals but contained also a very strong hostility to the medical profession. There may also have been an identification on her part between man's brutality to animals and his brutality to women.

In 1884 a legacy enabled her to give up her journalism and retire to Wales, where she spent the remainder of her life, in the company of her friend Mary Lloyd. The two had met in 1860 and set up house together in London. This relationship, which seems to have been one of mutual devotion, replaced, for Frances, the love and companionship she had known with her mother. At no time in her life does she seem to have felt any attraction to a man and, according to her own account, no man was ever attracted by her.

A well-known figure in feminist circles, Frances Power Cobbe never became one of its leaders, possibly because from 1870 onwards her attention was taken up increasingly by the anti-vivisection movement. A formidable personality, especially in her later years, she was not always popular with her fellow-workers, and had a reputation for dogmatism and self-assertion. She could be a bad enemy, and her quarrel with Anna Kingsford, a fellow anti-vivisectionist, reveals in her nature an unexpected degree of malice. Indeed, although she gave her love to her gentle and affectionate mother, it was her moralistic and autocratic father whom she more closely resembled. Her chief contribution to feminism was as a journalist, and she became a well-known publicist for the women's movement on a wide variety of issues. Her thinking was probably most original on the issue of male violence against women and in this area her ideas had practical fruit.

Frances Power Cobbe wrote an autobiography, *The Life of Frances Power Cobbe by Herself* (London, Richard Bentley, 1894). There is also a brief entry in *Women of the Day*, F. Hays (London, Chatto and Windus, 1885). Her relationship with Mary Carpenter is described in *Mary Carpenter*, Jo Manton (London, Heinemann, 1976). For her role in the anti-vivisection movement see *Anti-vivisection and medical science in Victorian England*, Richard D. French (Princeton, Princeton University Press, 1975). For her part in the legislation against violent husbands see '"A husband is a beating animal"—Frances Power Cobbe confronts the wife-abuse problem in Victorian England', Carol Bauer and Lawrence Ritt, *International Journal of Women's Studies* Vol. VI (2), 1983, pp. 99–118.

See also CARPENTER Mary.

COOPER Selina 1864–1946

Selina Cooper, a suffragist, was born Selina Coombe, the daughter of Charles Coombe and his wife Jane Uren. Born in Cornwall she later moved to Nelson in north-east Lancashire where she lived the rest of her life. She went into the local mills at the age of twelve, and by the 1890s was closely involved in the growing trade-union and socialist movements. She became a member of her local trade-union committee and joined the Independent Labour Party. In 1897 she became a member of the Nelson Co-operative Women's Guild. Soon she came to realise that women workers, however well they organised into trade unions, lacked the power of the ballot box, and she became an ardent advocate of the suffrage cause. In 1901 she was one of the sixteen delegates who presented the cotton weavers' petition on suffrage to Parliament.

In 1896 she had married Robert Cooper, a post-office worker and later a weaver. A son was born shortly afterwards, to die when only a few months old, and in 1900 a daughter Mary was born. Her husband was sympathetic not only to her socialism but also to her belief in women's suffrage, which he actively supported, keeping the account books and helping to deal with correspondence.

Selina Cooper was firmly committed to the view that even a limited extension of suffrage to women was worth having and argued forcefully, if unsuccessfully, for this view within the Labour movement, refusing to accept the opinion of the majority that women's suffrage must wait until adult suffrage had been secured. On the other hand, she would not follow the Pankhursts in their rejection of the Labour movement on this issue. Nor does she ever appear to have been attracted by the tactics of militancy. In 1907 she was recruited by the constitutional National Union of Women's Suffrage Societies and was in great demand by them as a speaker. In 1910 she was one of a deputation to Asquith in which she was one of the four who made a speech. She remained with the NUWSS until the early 1920s.

While acting as an organiser for the NUWSS she had been brought into close contact with Eleanor Rathbone, and after the war she joined with her in the campaign for family allowances, speaking all over Lancashire and Yorkshire. Her record of public service was also impressive during these years. She served on a number of committees and in 1915 opened a Maternity Centre. In 1924 she became a magistrate with a special interest in battered wives. Other feminist issues which concerned her during these years included the dissemination of birth control knowledge, and opposition to the various attempts made at this time to bar married women from employment. Her husband died in 1934 after a long illness but she survived until 1946, cared for by her devoted daughter Mary.

Selina Cooper was one of the small but significant group of working-class feminists who tried to bring the suffrage issue to the attention of working women. Although her acceptance of the value of a limited suffrage Bill alienated her to some extent from the Labour movement at this time, she did not, like some women, reject socialism altogether. Her work for the largely middle-class

NUWSS from 1907 to 1914 served to heighten the tension between the claims of gender and class, and from time to time she was urged by her middle-class suffrage workers to drop her socialist beliefs. Her work for family allowances after the war also underlined the problems facing socialist feminists since the issue was a highly unpopular one within large sections of the Labour movement. Courageous, public-spirited and independent, Selina Cooper's life not only throws light on working-class feminism but on the complicated relationship between socialism and gender.

The source of our knowledge on Selina Cooper is *The Life and Times of a Respectable Rebel*, Jill Liddington (London, Virago, 1984). *One Hand Tied Behind Us. The Rise of the Women's Suffrage Movement*, Jill Liddington and Jill Morris (London, Virago, 1978). See also 'Women Cotton Workers and the Suffrage Campaign', Jill Liddington in *Fit Work for Women* ed. Sandra Burman (London, Croom Helm, 1979). For the Cooper Papers see Lancashire Record Office, Preston (DDX 1137) series of deposits 1977-83.

See also CHEW Ada Nield, DICKENSON Sarah, RATHBONE Eleanor, REDDISH Sarah.

D

DAVIES Margaret Llewelyn 1861–1944

Margaret Llewelyn Davies, for many years secretary of the Women's Co-operation Guild, was the daughter of the Reverend John Llewelyn Davies and Mary Crompton. Her father was the brother of Emily Davies and himself a good friend of the women's movement. After a distinguished career at Cambridge he spent four years at St Marks, Whitechapel, where he came under the influence of the Christian Socialists. In 1856 he obtained the living of Christ Church, Marylebone, which he held for thirty-three years. In 1859 he married into a well-known Unitarian family which itself had feminist links, since one of his wife's sisters married Professor George Croom Roberton, an active worker in the women's suffrage cause, and a close acquaintance of J.S. Mill.

John Llewelyn Davies was, through his sister Emily, a friend and advisor of Elizabeth Garrett from the very start of her attempt to study medicine. Once she was qualified he continued to support her in her undertakings, serving as a member of the managing committee of the New Hospital for Women and a member of the council of the London School of Medicine for Women. He was also closely associated with Queen's College for Women, and was its principal in 1873–4 and again between 1878 and 1886. Women's suffrage also commanded his support.

Margaret was one of seven children, the others all boys. Margaret was christened Margaret Caroline but subsequently adopted the family name of Llewelyn which had been given to each of her brothers. We know nothing of her childhood, but what knowledge we have of her father suggests that she was brought up in an atmosphere where high principles were combined with a tolerance for new ideas and an ever-present atmosphere of sympathy for others, qualities, indeed, which were later to characterise her own work. She was educated at Queen's College and then at Girton, subsequently acting as a voluntary social worker in Marylebone. Soon, however, she became involved in the Co-operative movement, probably under the influence of her father who was deeply interested in co-operation as well as in the trade-union movement. She joined the Marylebone Co-operative Society in 1886 and soon afterwards became secretary of the Marylebone branch of the Women's Co-operative Guild. A year later she was elected to the guild's national executive and in 1889 was appointed as its honorary general secretary.

In the same year the family moved to Kirkby Lonsdale where her father had been appointed to the living. Margaret set up her office in a room in the vicarage and was soon joined in her work by Lilian Harris, the daughter of a wealthy banker who had come to Kirkby Lonsdale about 1850. In 1893 Lilian Harris became cashier of the guild and in 1901 its assistant secretary. Thereafter the two women worked closely together until their joint retirement in 1922. Lilian Harris had practical and organising abilities, quite untapped as the unmarried daughter of a rich man, which were now brought to the service of the guild. It was soon obvious moreover that Margaret had found more than a co-worker, for Lilian was to be her life-long friend and companion.

From the start Margaret Llewelyn Davies showed herself to be a secretary of unusual drive and imagination. Clearly she had her own ideas about the guild and its future, and gently but firmly she pushed into the background such popular domestic occupations as sewing classes and steered the guild in the direction of practical social reforms. One of the earliest of these was women's suffrage. From 1893 there were branch discussions followed by the collection of signatures for suffrage petitions. In 1901 guild members took part in the Yorkshire and Cheshire female textile workers' petition in favour of suffrage and guild members took part in the deputation to the House of Commons. Margaret Llewelyn Davies favoured adult suffrage but she was sympathetic to provisional measures and did not take the view of, for example, Margaret Bondfield, that provisional measures were unacceptable.

Apart from the suffrage issue she also led the guild into closer collaboration with both the Women's Trade Union Association and the Women's Industrial Council. Under her influence the guild became involved in such issues as minimum wages and early closing in an attempt to raise the standard of work for women co-operative workers. After 1900 the guild was in the forefront of the struggle for better conditions for mothers and children. As part of their campaign for a better standard of maternal care, letters were collected from guild members and published as *Maternity. Letters from Working Women* (London, 1915). The guild also worked successfully not only for maternity benefits but that they should be paid to mothers as a step towards the economic independence of wives.

In 1910, Margaret Llewelyn Davies gave evidence on behalf of the guild to the Royal Commission on Divorce Law. A circular had been sent to all guild branches, who had returned their answers to a series of questions, and she had based her evidence on their replies. The branches had voted overwhelmingly for equal divorce laws, and an end to the double standard by which the adultery of a wife, but not a husband, was a ground for divorce. The guilds also wanted cheaper divorce, and divorce by mutual consent, as well as the right of women to sit on juries. This stand by the guild on divorce led to a bitter fight with the Co-operative Union whose Roman Catholic members objected and the quarrel was not indeed resolved, in the guild's favour, until the end of the first world war.

Margaret Llewelyn Davies had maintained the guild office at Kirkby Lonsdale until 1908 when the retirement if her father, now eighty-two, made possible a move to London. Henceforward she lived with Lilian Harris in Hampstead, making a home also for her father until his death in 1916. In 1922 she and Lilian ended their official connection with the guild although she continued to take a great deal of interest in its affairs. In 1922 also she was the first woman chairman of the Co-operative Congress. She had helped to found the International Women's Co-operative Guild in 1921 and, sympathetic to the Russian revolution, she was the first chairman of the Society for Cultural Relations with the USSR. During the 1920s her pro-Russian and pacifist activities occupied much of her time. In 1931 she edited *Life as We have Known It* (London, 1931), a collection of reminiscences on the part of women's guild members with an introduction by her friend Virginia Woolf. She died in 1944, Lilian Harris in 1950.

Like her aunt Emily Davies, Margaret Llewelyn Davies gave a life-time to the cause of women, but otherwise they did not have a greal deal in common. Both, it is true, remained unmarried, but whereas for Emily the needs of unmarried women for education and work were always paramount, Margaret worked almost exclusively for married women. Nor did Margaret Llewelyn Davies share any of the conservatism characteristic of Emily. Indeed, in spite of her Liberal background she was rather to the left of the Labour Party. Furthermore, whereas Emily Davies worked mainly for her own class, Margaret cared chiefly for women in the working classes. Perhaps the reason for the difference lies in their personal circumstances. Born into a family that regarded the education of a girl as important as that of a boy, Margaret, like her brothers, went to Cambridge, and there is no evidence that she ever felt the personal sense of lost opportunity that haunted Emily Davies for much if not all of her life.

What Margaret Llewelyn Davies cared about was the lot of working-class women. Moreover, she saw that their position derived not simply from inadequate wages, although this was part of the problem, nor from lack of knowledge of health care and birth control, although that too was important, but from a wife's lack of economic independence and the effect of this on the personal relations between a man and his wife. In the introduction to *Maternity* she writes of the 'strike against maternity' by which she means the desire for smaller families and which, she argues, arises from the excessive child-bearing forced on wives by men who can see no destiny for women beyond that of the care of the household and the satisfaction of a man's desires. The guild, she believed, broke down the isolation of women in married life and was an important way in which the voice of these women could be heard.

Although undoubtedly a profound influence on the guild, Margaret Llewelyn Davies was not an autocrat. Her particular talent was an ability to draw out working-class women to speak or write of their own experiences. She herself learned from them the realities of working-class married life, and this turned the feminism she had acquired from her family into new directions. Once she had left the guild her attention turned to a large extent in other directions, and more especially towards international affairs and peace, but for more than thirty years it was her guiding hand which made the Co-operative Women's Guild the most radical of all the organisations set up to serve the interests of working-class women.

Apart from the books already mentioned, she published a large number of pamphlets, articles, etc., mainly on the Co-operative movement. She also contributed 'The claims of mothers and children' in *Women and the Labour Party* ed. Marion Phillips (London, 1918). She was also the author of *The Women's Co-operative Guild 1883-1904* (Kirkby Lonsdale, 1904).

There is an entry in *DLB* Vol. I, pp. 96-9, contributed by two of her nieces, which is the only source of her life. For her contribution to the Co-operative Women's Guild see *The Woman with the Basket*, Catherine Webb (Manchester, CWS, 1927) and 'Women and co-operation', Jean Gaffin in *Women in the Labour Movement. The British Experience* ed. Lucy Middleton (London, Croom Helm, 1977) and *Caring and Sharing. The Centenary History of the Co-operative Women's Guild*, Jean Gaffin and David Thoms (Manchester Co-operative Union Ltd., 1983).

DAVIES Sarah Emily (Emily) 1830-1921

Emily Davies, pioneer in the higher education of women, was the daughter of the Reverend John Davies and Mary Hopkinson. The Reverend Davies was the son of a Welsh farmer who, after studying at Cambridge, was ordained and set up a boarding school for boys. Later, ill-health caused the school to be given up and in 1839 he accepted a living at Gateshead where the family lived for the next twenty-two years. There were five children, two girls and three boys, and Emily was the second daughter and the fourth child. Little is known of her early years, or indeed her relationship with her parents. She had, apparently, a rather staid and strictly evangelical upbringing but only a sketchy education. Nor later on, in spite of her life-long involvement in education, did she develop scholarly interests, her strength being in practical achievements.

Her brother, John Llewelyn, the eldest boy and four years older than Emily, seems to have been particularly close, and when he went on to a distinguished career at Cambridge, Emily felt strongly her disadvantages as a girl and it was this first sense of deprivation that started her thinking about the position of women. In 1854 she met Elizabeth Garrett when Elizabeth visited her old school friends, Jane and Emily Crow, who were also friends of Emily Davies. An even more significant meeting took place shortly afterwards in Algiers where Emily had taken her brother Henry for his health. There she met Annie, the sister of Barbara Leigh Smith, and this led to an acquaintance with Barbara herself and her friend Bessie Parkes.

In 1858 the deaths of two of her brothers and her only sister had left Emily and John the only two children, and in 1861, after her father died, her mother moved with Emily to London where John and his family now lived. This opened up a new life for Emily since she was not only able to spend more time with Barbara Leigh Smith (now Barbara Bodichon) and her friends, but to be at hand when Elizabeth Garrett, now embarked on her attempt to gain a medical qualification, might need her. At this time she even considered studying medicine herself, but her own sketchy educational background, and the needs of her mother, decided her against it. Instead, she started work on a campaign to induce London University to allow the admission of women, and when this failed turned her attack on to securing the admission of girls to the Oxford and Cambridge examinations, established as a test of efficiency for boys' schools. A committee was formed with Emily Davies as its secretary and its efforts were eventually crowned with success.

By this time Emily knew exactly what she wanted: the admission of women to higher education and the professions on equal terms with men. Even at this stage in her life she was not satisfied, as most other women working in education were, with simply improving the education of girls. Women, she believed, were entitled to the same education as men on the same terms. Otherwise their education would always be denigrated as second-rate and they would never be able to compete with men for a professional career. Consequently, Emily Davies firmly and indeed, as her critics pointed out, obstinately stood out against any proposals for special examinations for women.

The 1860s were active years for Emily in several different ways, and the move to London seems to have released energies in her, previously trapped by her confinement to Gateshead. She campaigned successfully in 1864 to get girls included in the Schools Enquiry Commission to which she herself gave evidence, and in 1866 she published her book *The Higher Education of Women*. She also gave frequent papers at the Social Science Association meetings.

For a time, too, she as active in the suffrage movement. Indeed she was a member of the original Kensington Society which gave birth to the suffrage petition of 1866. Later she played a central role in the first London Suffrage Committee, although her position became a difficult one when she clashed with Helen Taylor, John Stuart Mill's stepdaughter, and, by implication, with John Stuart Mill himself. The issue was one of tactics rather than principle, since Emily Davies wanted to ask for the vote for unmarried women only, whereas Helen Taylor, like John Stuart Mill, believed that, as a matter of principle, they should ask for the vote for women on the same terms as men. This issue was to continue to divide the suffrage movement for almost twenty years. Emily Davies was also afraid that if the suffrage movement was to be associated too closely with John Stuart Millit would become allied with the Radical wing of the Liberal Party. Nevertheless, even from the start she was anxious that the suffrage movement should not interfere with the movement for higher education to which she always gave priority, and by 1867 she had dropped out of any active involvement with women's suffrage. Instead her mind turned increasingly to the idea of founding a women's college.

In 1866 she had drafted a short leaflet on the idea which she showed to a number of friends. Later a small committee was set up, carefully excluding all those active in women's suffrage, and fund-raising started in earnest. Eventually a small beginning was made in 1869 at a house outside Cambridge at Hitchin, and Girton College was opened in 1873. In her work for Girton Emily showed a curious mixture of conservatism and radicalism which was indeed a permanent feature of her personality. The college was set up outside Cambridge, to avoid too much contact with the Cambridge environment and the girls themselves were disciplined on severely conventional lines. Her views on education were old-fashioned in their emphasis on classics and mathematics at a time when there was a strong move for curriculum reform. She also insisted that the new college must be Church of England in its affiliation.

At the same time, her insistence—as in the issue of the local examinations—that women should compete on equal terms with men was founded on an unswerving belief in equal rights, so that her own caution on such issues as suffrage was due to a difference in priorities rather than values.

Her uncompromising attitude led her into a number of controversies, and eventually to the founding of a second college, Newnham, based on more flexible principles. Henry Sidgwick, who was largely behind the new college, was a supporter of both higher education for women and women's suffrage, but believed that concessions must be made to women, at least temporarily, because of the state of girls' schooling. He was also a university reformer in a wider sense, which Emily Davies was not. He hoped to reform men's higher education and did not want to reproduce for women all the faults of men's education. This led to some rather bitter confrontations, especially on Emily's part, since this was an issue that passionately concerned her.

The affairs of Girton occupied Emily Davies throughout the 1870s and the 1880s, although her activities had to be somewhat curtailed after a severe illness in 1876. There was always a great deal to do in raising funds for the college, and in planning several extensions, and she was actively involved in these plans into the 1890s. There were also several controversies since she disapproved of expenditure on research, feeling the money would be better spent on more students. Later there was an even more serious disagreement, when she opposed the admission of resident staff to the governing body.

Meanwhile, for most of this time, she stayed aloof from the suffrage campaign, although in 1879 she gave her name to a list of eminent women approving of suffrage. Yet in 1889 she became a member of the general committee of the London National Society for Women's Suffrage and in 1891 joined the executive committee and became an active worker. She was never to approve of militant activity but she was part of a deputation to Campbell-Bannerman in 1906 and later to Asquith. She also, although nearly eighty years of age, took part in a demonstration in 1908. In 1910 she published *Thoughts on some questions relating to women*. Like some other suffrage workers, she did not approve of adult suffrage, and when, in 1912, the National Union of Women's Suffrage Societies offered its support to the Labour Party she joined the Conservative and Unionist Women's Franchise Committee. In 1919 she was one of the very few early suffrage workers alive to record her vote, dying in 1921 in her ninety-second year.

It is not easy in the case of Emily Davies to go beyond her public life to the person behind it. Indeed, to some extent her passionate concern for women's educational rights seems to have absorbed her so totally that there was little room for anything else. We know very little of her relationship with her family, although she cared very dutifully for her mother until her death in her eighties in 1886. She was, however, close to her brother John, who helped and supported her in her work throughout their lives.

She made a number of women friends, and for several years was the guide and inspiration of Elizabeth Garrett. She also maintained her friendship with Barbara Bodichon throughout Barbara's life. Perhaps her closest friend was Anna Richardson, whom she met in 1859 and with whom she shared a long correspondence until Anna's death in 1872.

But the mainspring of her life was her work and this had its source, plainly enough, in what she saw as the limitations placed on her own life. Once she asserted that she would die to give young women what she had never had, and from this aim she never swerved. With the exception of her limited commitment to suffrage, other causes taken up by the women's movement never seem to have aroused her interest. On most issues, too, her opinions were conservative, and even her desire to give women an equal education with men had its conservative side in so far as she refused to consider the extent to which men's education might need reform. Nevertheless, in her insistence that different can never be the same as equal, she was firmly within the tradition of equal-rights feminism and one of its most important pioneers.

The main source is *Emily Davies and Girton College*, Barbara Stephen (London, Constable, 1927), and most other accounts of her life are based on this. Her relationship with Elizabeth Garrett is described in *Elizabeth Garrett Anderson*, Jo Manton (London, Methuen, 1965). For her controversies with Sidgwick see *Women at Cambridge. A Men's University though of a Mixed Type*, Rita McWilliams Tullborg (London, Gollancz, 1975). There is an entry in the *DNB* 1912-1921 pp. 147-8. For a recent account of her brief involvement in the suffrage movement see 'Emily Davies and the Women's Movement 1862-67', Andrew Rosen (*Journal of British Studies* 19, 101-21, 1979). A new assessment of her life and work is in *Significant Sisters*, Margaret Forster (London, Secker and Warburg, 1984). There is also an unpublished autobiography in manuscript *Family Chronicle* in the possession of Girton College, Cambridge. See also The Papers of Emily Davies and Barbara Bodichon (Brighton, Harvester Microform, 1984).

See also ANDERSON Elizabeth Garrett, SIDGWICK Henry.

DAVISON Emily Wilding 1872-1913

Emily Davison, a suffragette, was born in London, into a fairly well-to-do family. She began her education with a governess, but later went to several schools, including one abroad, before at thirteen, she was sent to Kensington High School. As a child she was daring and mischievous, always the leader although she was the youngest but one of the family. At school, however, she was obedient and a good student, not brilliant but above average, with a special interest in literature and the theatre.

At nineteen she obtained a bursary at Holloway College where she studied literature. Then in 1893, her father, who was devoted to her, died leaving the family in poor circumstances. She was forced to leave college and take up a post as a resident governess. She continued to study in her spare time and eventually graduated from London University. For a time she tried work in schools, but eventually returned to a private post. Meanwhile her interest in the suffrage movement grew. She joined the Women's Social and Political Union in 1906, and in 1908 was a steward at the first of the great suffrage processions. In 1909 she gave up her teaching to give all her energy to the women's movement.

Her first imprisonment was in March 1909 and during that year she was in prison several times, and was involved both in hunger strikes and forcible feeding. Later in the year, while in Strangeways Gaol, she barricaded herself in her cell in an attempt to escape forcible feeding, and, by order of the visiting magistrate, a hose pipe was turned on her. Afterwards she was hastily taken to the prison hospital but there was considerable outcry and Herbert Gladstone, the Home Secretary, ordered her release. In January 1910 she brought a successful action against Strangeways Gaol but the episode seems to have strengthened her leanings towards militancy. A strongly religious woman, she began to believe that she had been called by God to serve the cause of suffrage.

Shortly after the hospital episode she attempted to penetrate the House of Commons to speak to Mr Asquith, hiding almost without food for more than twenty-four hours without being discovered. In June of that year she started window-breaking entirely on her own initiative and this was followed by further imprisonment. In December 1911 her militancy entered a new phase when she was arrested for setting fire to a pillar box. This was the occasion for a long prison sentence from February till June 1912, which seems to have been the signal for the desire for martyrdom which gradually grew stronger. In June she attempted to kill herself by jumping down an iron staircase but was saved by netting which broke her fall. Nevertheless, she was severely injured and it took her some time to recover. She began to express her belief that the vote would not be won without the deliberate sacrifice of a woman's life. Finally, in June 1913, at the Derby, she ran out on the course and flung herself at the King's horse. Her skull was fractured and she died without regaining consciousness.

Emily Davison is an example, if an extreme one, of the urge to martyrdom inspired in a number of women by the suffrage cause. She was the only one who deliberately risked death, but there was a similar heroic quality in the way in which very many women endured imprisonment, hunger-strikes and forcible feeding, and returned to them again and again for the sake of victory. The example of Emily Davison also illustrates the extent to which acts of militancy were spontaneous responses by individuals and not, at least in their initial stages, planned by the leadership. Indeed Sylvia Pankhurst has suggested that the WSPU leaders saw Emily Davison as a self-willed person who persisted in acting on her own initiative. Her own motivation is, however, clear. She believed in her own God-given mission to serve the cause of women's suffrage, and to this end she was prepared to sacrifice even her life. To understand her state of mind, however, it is necessary to consider her own experiences, and particularly the episode with the hose-pipe which initially at least seems to have been an act of defiance against the prison authorities. As a result she had suffered extremely, but out of the suffering had come a wave of public sympathy which helped to publicise the cause. This unsought martyrdom may well have turned her thoughts to the effect she might obtain from an act of self-sacrifice.

In the event her death was almost certainly in vain. The opponents of women's suffrage were both hard-headed and hard-hearted and unlikely to be stirred by such an act, especially when it could be blamed on her and not, as in the case of the hose-pipe incident, on the prison authorities. Asquith in particular hated passion and would have been totally unable to understand the meaning or purpose of her sacrifice. Even within the suffrage movement there were those who deplored her action even while they sympathised with her aims. Nevertheless, this does not take away the heroism of the deed, and Emily Davison, however misguided, remains one of the genuine martyrs of the suffrage movement.

There is a biography, *The Life of Emily Davison. An Outline*, G. Colmore (London, The Women's Press, 1913). Her exploits, and of course her death are described in all the standard histories. See for example, *The Suffragette Movement*, Sylvia Pankhurst (London, Longmans, 1931; Virago, 1977).

DESPARD Charlotte 1844–1939

Charlotte Despard, a suffragist, was the daughter of Captain William French of the Royal Navy and Margaret Eccles, an exceptionally wealthy heiress. William French was a hard man but a neglectful rather than a severe father. Her mother was burdened with frequent pregnancies and was of so withdrawn a nature that she was virtually a recluse. The children were left to run wild in the care of servants, and Charlotte was later to recall with pleasure these years of freedom. When she was ten years old her father died, and the development of insanity in her mother made it no longer possible to keep the children in her care. They were sent to relatives who imposed a severe Presbyterian regime on their previously undisciplined lives. The effect on Charlotte was to increase rather than reduce the rebellious streak in her nature.

As a young woman Charlotte, now a wealthy heiress, took part in the social life appropriate to her position, and she had a brief and unsuccessful love affair, but she seems never to have been altogether at home in London society. She felt strongly for the suffering of the poor, and conceived an admiration for Shelley, but her feelings at this stage in her life were literary and philosophical rather than practical and she made no attempt to ally herself with the emerging feminist movement. Instead, in 1866, she and two of her sisters went on an extended tour of Europe which was to last three years. Subsequently, on a visit to Paris, she met Maximilian Despard, a quiet young man who shared her Radical opinions, and in 1870 when she was twenty-six they were married.

Born in 1839, Maximilian Despard had made a fortune as a merchant in Hong Kong, and was an able businessman. As a child he had contracted chronic kidney disease, so that he was never in robust health and, as he grew older, the disease increased its hold until he became a complete invalid. Restrained, rational and sceptical, his Radicalism was of a very different kind from Charlotte's, and it is likely that she found herself constrained by him not because he was tyrannical, but because her genuine admiration for his qualities made her try, while he lived, to accept his ideas as her own. Her more ardent and romantic nature found expression in the writing of novels, in which she achieved a not inconsiderable amount of success. She wrote ten novels in all, but three remained unpublished. The first, *Chaste as Ice, Pure as Snow*, was published in 1874, not long after her marriage, and to a large extent this set the pattern for the rest. Wildly romantic, with improbably happy endings, they tried to show that suffering brought out the best in people. For the most part they bore no relationship to the causes which were later to interest her although the unpublished *A Voice from the Dim Millions*, which was the story of a factory girl, reflected her sympathy for the poor.

In 1890 her husband died, leaving her the prey of extreme and prostrating grief. For a time it seemed she might take the path to insanity followed by her mother, but she found solace in mission work in London, and before long this became an absorbing passion. She gave up the luxurious home in Esher she had shared with her husband and took a house in London, at first in Wandsworth, and later in Battersea, actually amongst the poor she sought to aid. Nor was this the only way in which she rejected her past life. She became a vegetarian, adopted a black lace mantilla instead of the fashionable hats of the period, and later on, sandals instead of shoes. She also abandoned the agnosticism she had learned from her husband and adopted her own brand of Roman Catholicism which in 1909, after her conversion by Annie Besant, she combined with Theosophy.

At first, when she settled in London, her action was motivated simply by philanthropy but fairly soon she became a convert to socialism, at first in the Social Democratic Federation and later in the Independent Labour Party. In 1894 she was elected as a Poor Law guardian in Lambeth, and for the next nine years she devoted herself to Poor Law reform. During these years she became a friend of George Lansbury and also met and admired Margaret Bondfield, who introduced her to the women's trade-union movement.

Like Margaret Bondfield, Charlotte Despard was a convinced supporter of adult suffrage and she stood aloof from the main suffrage movement with its claim for a partial franchise. She was convinced eventually by Keir Hardie that a limited suffrage would be of benefit not only to the propertied classes but to the working women who were her chief concern, and by the summer of 1906 she was ready to give all her energy to the Women's Social and Political Union. She was impressed particularly by the heroism of a prison sentence but her own efforts to achieve martyrdom in this way were at first frustrated by her own prominence and that of her brother Sir John French, a distinguished soldier. Later, disguised by a thick veil, she was arrested and imprisoned. But her career with the WSPU was short-lived as, unable to accept the move away from the Labour Party, she was one of those who in 1907 rejected the Pankhurst leadership and formed the Women's Freedom League. The league, of which she was president, endeavoured to avoid both the autocracy of the WSPU and the more violent forms of militancy into which the WSPU was gradually drawn. Its main tactic was the nonpayment of taxes, although it also conducted a campaign within the courts for heavier penalties for child molestation.

Although she had many weaknesses as a leader, Charlotte Despard commanded considerable respect and affection, partly because of her age and her commanding appearance, partly because of the reputation she had already built for herself in her work for and amongst the poor. Her honesty and integrity were beyond doubt and so was her generosity, and this made up for her impetuosity and her quite sublime determination to go her own way. The eccentricity of her dress, moreover, enhanced rather than detracted from her reputation, so that she appeared, as H.M. Swanwick later described her, as a 'fiery old prophetess'.

The outbreak of war turned her attention, as it did that of many others, away from women's suffrage, although she never dropped her membership of the league. An ardent pacifist, her main energies were now given to the Women's Peace Council. In 1918 she stood unsuccessfully for Parliament as a Labour candidate, but by 1921 her attention was completely captured by the Irish cause, to which she devoted herself for the rest of her life. Her father and her husband had both been of Irish descent, but she had never lived in Ireland. Now she left England and gave her time and money to the Sinn Fein cause. She also turned increasingly to communism, and her beliefs were confirmed by a visit to Russia in 1930. During the last years of her life she became increasingly frail but continued writing and speaking into her nineties. She died, in Ireland, in 1939.

For Charlotte Despard feminism was only one of many causes but, although without children herself, the problems of women and children were always of concern to her, and one of the reasons she supported suffrage was because she hoped the vote would be used to help mothers and children. In 1905 she adopted a child, but because of her public work was a guardian in name only. During her suffrage years she wrote four pamphlets, *Women's Franchise and Industry* (1908), *Women in the Nation* (1908), *Women in the New Era* (1909), and *Theosophy and the Woman's Movement* (1910). Her views on feminism were strikingly modern stressing, for example, the need for women not only to rely on themselves but in particular to see with their own eyes, and she came to believe that women could see more clearly than men. She was conscious, too, of the power that came from women working together. She was fundamentally a religious woman and her approach to feminism was spiritual rather than materialist; in one of her post-war speeches to the Women's Freedom League she argued that spiritual love was the women's movement, by which she seems to have meant that it was an expression of women's spiritual nature. What moved her most directly was an enormous capacity for indignation and this she brought to all the causes which she embraced during her long widowhood.

There is a recent biography, *An Unhusbanded Life. Charlotte Despard. Suffragette, Socialist, Sinn Feiner*, Andro Linklater (London, Hutchinson, 1980). This supersedes earlier biographical sketches, the best of which is *Votes for Women. The Story of a Struggle*, Roger Fulford (London, Faber and Faber, 1956).

DICKENSEN Sarah 1868-1954

Sarah Dickensen, a suffragist, was born Sarah Welsh, the second of five children, three boys and two girls, of John Welsh, originally from Scotland, and his wife Jane Ferguson. Her father was an enameller and coach painter, and she was born in Hulme. At eleven years old she started work in a cotton mill, and during the 1880s she became involved in the efforts of the Manchester and Salford Trades Council to organise women workers. In 1895 a Woman's Trade Union Council was formed in Manchester and she became one of its organising secretaries. In 1896 she married William Roger Dickensen, an iron enameller who had his own bicycle workshop. At this time she became a member of the North of England Society for

Women's Suffrage and took a leading part in its activities, believing in particular in the importance of convincing factory workers.

During 1900 and 1901 she was deeply involved in collecting signatures in support of women's suffrage from women textile workers, and was amongst the speakers when the petition was presented to the Lancashire MPs at the House of Commons in 1901. In the following year her commitment to suffrage increased. In 1904 she broke away from the Women's Trades Union Council which was divided on women's suffrage and joined a new organisation, the Manchester and Salford Women's Trades and Labour Council. In 1905, at a meeting at the Trade Hall to welcome Christabel Pankhurst and Annie Kenney after their imprisonment, she was one of the principal speakers and seconded a resolution calling for votes on the same terms as men. In the same year she joined the National Industrial and Professional Women's Suffrage Society, formed to organise support amongst women workers. In 1906 she took part in a large deputation to Campbell Bannerman, speaking on the rights of women wage workers to the vote. Between 1906 and 1910 she took part in a large number of demonstrations although she does not seem to have been involved in the later stages of militancy.

Her work for the promotion of trade unionism amongst women also continued during these years. It was her belief that separate branches for men and women were desirable until there was a general consciousness of the particular needs of women workers. During the first world war she worked on a number of issues touching on women's employment. She was also one of the delegates chosen to attend the Women's International Conference on Peace at the Hague in 1915, although government restrictions on travel prevented the party from sailing.

Nor did her activities lessen after the war. From 1920 to 1925 she was secretary of the Women's Group of the Manchester and Salford Trades Council. She was a JP between 1923 and 1939, in which year she was awarded an MBE for her services to Manchester. Her main interests during these years were war pensions, and deprived children. She died in 1954.

Nothing is known of her husband, not even the year of his death, although he seems to have been sympathetically disposed to her numerous activities which marriage hardly checked at all. The absence of children would also have made it easier to keep up her work. Her commitment to suffrage was obviously very strong and she was one of the working-class suffragists who were prepared to support even a limited extension of the suffrage to women despite the fact that many if not most working-class women would not qualify for a vote. Suffrage, indeed, was seen by her as a part of her life-long concern with the woman wage-earner, to whose problems she could bring her own experience as a textile worker. Unlike some other working-class women, however, she has not left us any record of her thoughts, and we can only infer the kind of experiences that led her into the trade-union and suffrage movements. Her abilities were clearly considerable and enabled her to play a prominent part locally, even if she did not achieve a national reputation. Moreover, she continued to serve Manchester as a JP until almost the end of her long life. She takes her place, therefore, as one of the small band of working-class suffragists who tried to demonstrate the significance of suffrage for the lives of working-class women.

There is a biography of Sarah Dickensen in *DLB*, Vol. VI, pp. 101–5. This includes information obtained from a niece and nephew. She is referred to in *One Hand Tied Behind Us. The Rise of the Women's Suffrage Movement*, Jill Liddington and Jill Norris (London, Virago, 1978).

DILKE Sir Charles Wentworth 1843–1911

Charles Dilke, a Liberal politician, was the elder of the two sons of Sir Charles Wentworth Dilke and his wife Mary Chatsworth. He was however educated largely by his grandfather, a scholar and a Radical in politics. As a brilliant student at Cambridge Charles Dilke came under the influence of Henry Fawcett and later became a great admirer of John Stuart Mill, both of whom must have encouraged his feminist leanings. He entered Parliament in 1868 when only twenty-five years of age, where he joined the Radical group surrounding Henry Fawcett. Almost at once he became involved in the struggle over women's rights, and in 1869 spoke at the first public meeting in support of women's suffrage. In that same year both he and Jacob Bright moved an amendment to the Municipal Franchise Bill to grant votes to women householders, but Jacob Bright's amendment, which was carried, was called first. The following year he carried an amendment to the Education Bill which allowed women both to vote for, and to serve on school boards.

In 1872 Charles Dilke married Katherine Sheil, a gifted amateur singer but only two years later she died two days after the birth of a son. For a time he grieved desperately but in 1875 he met Emilia Pattison, three years his senior, whom he had known when she was a young art student. In 1861 Emilia had married Mark Pattison, Rector of Lincoln College, Oxford but by 1875 they were already seriously estranged, and quite soon a close friendship sprang up between Charles Dilke and Emilia Pattison which turned in time to love. While Mark Pattison lived, however, discretion required that they never became lovers, but they corresponded frequently, sometimes writing once a day, and he asked her advice on every difficult decision he had to take. Emilia Pattison was herself a feminist and this must have reinforced his own support for women.

During the 1870s Charles Dilke became closely involved in the agitation for legislation on married women's property, and in 1878 was one of the sponsors of an unsuccessful Women's Property Bill. In 1880 he was made president of the Local Government Board and used his position to appoint several women members of the Metropolitan Asylum Board. He failed, however, to get cabinet support for a woman member on the committee on working-class housing in 1884. He also failed to achieve the appointment of women factory inspectors. In 1884 he almost lost his seat in the cabinet because he abstained from a Conservative amendment to the Reform Bill which would have given votes to women. Gladstone, however, thought him too valuable to lose.

In 1884 Mark Pattison died and Charles Dilke became engaged to Emilia Pattison. But in 1885 he was overwhelmed by a scandal which effectively ruined his parliamentary career and threatened his marriage. He was cited as co-respondent in a divorce case brought by his brother's wife's sister, and, although the case against him was never proved, many believed him guilty. The reasons for the allegations against him, if, as seems probable, they were false, have never been satisfactorily explained. It is possible that Mrs Crawford used his name to direct attention away from her real lover, a Captain Forster, but there may have been a conspiracy, either of a political kind or, more probably, the consequence of the jealousy of an ex-mistress. Certainly his past life had been by no means free from blame and his own realisation that he had much to hide may have contributed to the confusion surrounding his attempt to defend himself.

Feeling his life to be in ruins, he offered to release Emilia from the engagement but she refused, and, from India, where she was recuperating from typhoid fever, telegraphed the notice of the engagement to *The Times*. She always believed in his innocence of the charge against him, and struggled all through their very happy marriage to clear his name. He had resigned from Parliament but she was determined that he should resume his political career and in 1892 her efforts were rewarded when he was re-elected. He never again reached the cabinet but he worked hard as an effective backbencher and continued to be a good friend to the cause of women.

By this time Emilia Dilke was deeply involved in the work of the Women's Trade Union League, and Charles Dilke associated himself closely with her, correcting proofs, dissecting blue-books and suggesting new ideas for angles to be covered. Later he was active in the Anti-Sweating League and was a consistent and determined supporter of trade boards. His interest in the low-paid woman worker dated from the 1880s, perhaps influenced by Emilia, and in 1898 he introduced a Wages Board Bill although it was not until 1909 that, largely through his efforts, the first Wages Board legislation was achieved.

In 1904 Emilia Dilke died suddenly but his interest in Women's Trade Union League affairs ended only with his own death in 1911 and the last day of his life, indeed, was spent on business for the league. After his wife's death he was greatly helped and supported by his wife's niece Gertrude Tuckwell, who was also prominent in the affairs of the league. He continued to be actively involved in women's suffrage, but in later years strongly opposed any limited suffrage Bill, believing that it would be of benefit only to the Conservative party. He did however work for adult suffrage, and in 1906 introduced a bill which, if it had been passed, would not only have given adult suffrage but would have allowed women to be elected to Parliament. During the last years of his life he moved steadily towards the Labour party in his sympathies. By 1910 however his health was going, and he died suddenly from heart failure in 1911.

Charles Dilke's feminism was an aspect of his general Radicalism and owed a great deal to his admiration for John Stuart Mill, although it was strengthened later on by his relationship with his wife Emilia. After his marriage his concern shifted from issues like women's suffrage to the plight of the low-paid woman worker, and in time he came to see a limited suffrage Bill as harmful to the cause of working-class women. In one way or another however he served the women's movement both inside and outside Parliament for more than forty years and during all that time was one of its ablest and most sympathetic allies.

The official biography is *The Life of the Right Honourable Sir Charles W. Dilke*, Stephen Gwynn and Gertrude M. Tuckwell (London, John Murray, 1917). See also *Sir Charles Dilke. A Victorian Tragedy*, Roy Jenkins (London, Collins, 1958). For a life of Lady Dilke which discusses their relationship in detail see *Lady Dilke. A Biography*, Betty Askwith (London, Chatto and Windus, 1969). For his work for married women's property see *Wives and Property*, Lee Holcombe (Oxford, Martin Robertson, 1983). *DNB*, 1901–1911 pp. 506–8.

See also DILKE Lady Emilia Francis, TUCKWELL Gertrude Mary.

DILKE Lady Emilia Francis 1840–1904

Born Emily Francis Strong, she was the fourth child of Captain, later Major, Strong and his wife Emily Weedon. After a career in the East India Company her father retired early and settled in Oxfordshire as manager of an Oxford bank. Educated by governesses, she showed a considerable artistic talent and on the advice of John Ruskin was sent, in 1859, to classes at the South Kensington Art School. Brought up in a High Anglican tradition, she came at this time under the influence of the Tractarians. These beliefs were later modified but she always remained deeply spiritual in her religious attitudes.

In 1861 she ended her studies and returned to Oxford where she married Mark Pattison, Rector of Lincoln College Oxford and twenty-seven years her senior. She was undoubtedly influenced by his intellectual gifts, which were considerable, but he was an unattractive man and there was clearly never any physical attraction on her part, a fact which was in time to prove disastrous. For his part he no doubt thought a young wife could be moulded to suit his requirements but he soon discovered an unexpected resistance to his efforts. Nevertheless at first she learned a great deal from him and even tried to conceal the physical repugnance she found an increasing burden. Eventually however her health broke down and from 1867 she began to spend long periods abroad, ostensibly for her health, but undoubtedly also to escape her marriage.

In 1874 she had a serious attack of rheumatism and it was while she was convalescing in London in 1875 that she met Sir Charles Dilke, a handsome clever man three years her junior. They had known each other while she was an art student but had not met for many years. At this time he was a widower, his wife having died in childbirth in 1874. A friend of John Stuart Mill and a Radical member of Parliament, he had already emerged as a champion both of women's suffrage and married women's property rights. A close friendship developed between them which in time became love, although they were never lovers, and Emilia indeed was very conscious of the need for a woman to retain her reputation.

In 1876, perhaps because she was already in love with Sir Charles Dilke, Emilia Pattison refused any further sexual relationship with her husband, and revealed to him the extent of the physical aversion such a relationship caused her. Deeply hurt, Mark Pattison never forgave her and, although she returned to Oxford from time to time, the marriage was virtually over. Indeed by 1879 Mark Pattison was himself in love with Meta Bradley, a young girl forty years his junior who gave him the affectionate but subservient admiration his nature needed.

Mark Pattison's death in 1884 left Emilia Pattison free to marry, and she and Sir Charles Dilke became engaged. In 1885, however, while Emilia was visiting friends in India, he was overwhelmed by a scandal which threatened their marriage. He was cited as co-respondent in a divorce case, and, although his guilt was never proved, the doubt that remained in many people's minds, as well as revelations about his earlier sexual involvements, led him to offer to withdraw from the engagement. Emilia Pattison however refused to accept his offer. Writing from India where she was recovering from typhoid, she announced their engagement in *The Times*.

The marriage took place in 1885 and was exceptionally happy for both partners. She always believed in her husband's innocence of the charge against him and spent the rest of her life trying to restore his political prospects. He had lost his seat in Parliament in 1886, and was not in fact re-elected until 1892. Nor did he again achieve the cabinet rank he had once had but he remained an active back bencher, and continued the campaign on behalf of women until his death in 1911.

During the 1870s, in spite of frequent periods abroad, Emilia Pattison, as she then was, began to involve herself in the women's movement. She was active in the suffrage movement from 1872 but later, under the influence of Emma Paterson, whom she had met in the course of her suffrage work, she became involved in the Women's Trade Union League which Emma Paterson had founded in 1875. She made her first public speech in 1877 at the annual meeting of the Women's Trade Union League and continued to be very closely associated with its work, travelling extensively to give lectures and help to organise its branches. In 1886, on the death of Emma Paterson, she took over the affairs of the league, only giving them up in 1903 because of her failing health. Under her guidance the league changed its policy from an opposition to protective legislation for women to a belief in women's inherent need for protection. From 1889 to 1904 she represented the league at meetings of the Trades Union Congress and during these years her deep concern for the most exploited women workers led her in 1904 to leave the Women's Liberal Association and to announce her commitment to the Labour party.

Although her work for the league occupied a great deal of time she continued to add to her reputation as an art historian. She had begun work in this field in the early days of her marriage and in 1879 she published *The Renaissance of Art in France*, a major work which had occupied her throughout the 1870s. In 1888 she published *Art in the Modern State*, an analysis of the French Academy, and between 1899 and 1902 she produced no less than four volumes which between them covered almost every aspect of the visual arts in eighteenth-century France. The last years of her life were therefore intensely full, and led eventually to a warning that she must rest. The warning came too late, however, and she died suddenly in 1904.

Emilia Dilke is important as a feminist because of the leading role she played in the affairs of the Women's Trade Union League for a period of nearly twenty years. She believed firmly in the need for women to be free agents and for marriage to be a matter of free choice, and to this end argued for a system of technical education for girls, as well as a system of equal pay. Nevertheless she was romantic about marriage, believing that, given the right circumstances, it could be the 'greatest bliss that life can offer'. She also believed firmly that, although large numbers of women were forced into employment, a women's ideal place was in the home. Increasingly too, as she moved amongst women in the sweated trades, she began to see such women as helpless to protect themselves and she turned for a remedy to the help of Parliament through protective legislation. Her friendship and later marriage to Charles Dilke was also an influence on her thinking about women, since he himself was a passionate advocate of minimum-wage legislation. He also converted her original acceptance of a limited extension of the suffrage to women to his own belief in adult suffrage.

Her own life reflects some of these ambiguities, since she needed both independence and the companionship of a successful marriage. Her happiness was blighted, first by her disastrous relationship with Mark Pattison, and then by the scandal which overshadowed her life with Charles Dilke. She had the courage, however, not to allow either to destroy her, and her passion for work, learned in part from her first husband, enabled her not only to build up a considerable reputation in the world of art but also to give generously of her time and energy to the needs of the most exploited of women workers.

There is a biography of Emilia Dilke, *Lady Dilke. A Biography*, Betty Askwith (London, Chatto and Windus, 1969). Her husband also published a memoir after her death, *The Book of the Spiritual Life by the Late Lady Dilke, with a memoir of the author* by the Rt Hon. Sir Charles W. Dilke (London, John Murray, 1905), For a critique of her work as an art historian see 'Lady Dilke. 1840-1904. The Six Lives of an Art Historian', Colin Eisler in *Women as Interpreters of the Visual Arts 1829-1979* ed. Claire Richter Sherman and Adele M. Holcomb (London, Greenwood Press, 1981). For her life with Mark Pattison see *Oxford Common Room. A Study of Lincoln College and Mark Pattison*, V.H.H. Green (London, Edward Arnold, 1957). See also *DLB* Vol. III, pp. 63-7 and *DNB* 1901-1911 pp. 507-8.

See also DILKE Sir Charles Wentworth, PATERSON Emma Anne, TUCKWELL Gertrude Mary.

DRUMMOND Flora 1879(c.)–1949

Flora Drummond was one of the militant suffragettes. Almost nothing is known of her early life, not even her date of birth, although it was probably some time in the 1870s. She was born as Flora Gibson in Manchester but spent her childhood on Arran. The daughter of a widowed mother, she early on experienced injustice at first hand when, having trained for a career in the post office, a regulation was passed excluding anyone from postal employment who was under five feet two inches in height. An inch too short, Flora believed that women in particular were unjustly treated by this rule. Relatives stepped in at this stage and she was helped to train as a shorthand typist. Shortly after this she met Joseph Drummond, a journeyman upholsterer, who fell off the steamer when he was going to Arran on holiday. They were married and went to live in Manchester but he was frequently unemployed, and she returned to work, eventually becoming manager of a typing pool. Both she and her husband were early members of both the Independent Labour Party and the Fabian Society.

In 1905 Flora Drummond, after hearing

of the imprisonment of Christabel Pankhurst and Annie Kenney, joined the Women's Social and Political Union. In 1906 she enthusiastically followed Annie Kenney to London, borrowing a typewriter and joining in secretarial duties. Later she was active in most aspects of the movement, being a good organiser, a good speaker, and particularly adept at questioning Ministers since she had a loud voice which she could use to good effect. Soon she was nicknamed the General because of her pugnacity, and her habit of riding a horse at the head of the suffragette processions, in paramilitary dress. As a result of her activities she was imprisoned nine times, on one occasion, in 1908, being released when it was found that she was pregnant. The child, a boy, was named after Keir Hardie, then her idol. It is not known whether he was the only child or whether there were others before or after. Certainly the birth of this one did not put any brake on her activities, although she never seems to have been involved in the more violent activities of the later stages of militancy which involved the destruction of property. Sylvia Pankhurst described her as brimful of self-assurance and audacity. She was always able to make her audiences laugh at her jokes and stories. Annie Kenney became a particular friend and found her someone who always enjoyed a good meal and a good joke.

The General remained totally loyal to the Pankhursts all through the campaign and, during the war, joined in the anti-strike line advocated by Emmeline and Christabel in spite of her earlier attachment to socialism. After the war she founded the Women's Guild of Empire in association with Elsie Bowerman, herself a one-time suffragette. For a time it was highly successful and in 1925 had more than thirty branches and a membership of some forty thousand women, mostly wives of working men. It was financed by leading industrialists and its main message was that capital and labour must co-operate. It opposed strikes, believed that trade unions should keep out of politics, and was against all forms of state welfare, including family allowances. In London, in 1926, she led an enormous demonstration against strikes. In 1930 she presided when Baldwin unveiled a statue to Mrs Pankhurst. She died in 1949.

She married twice, the second time Alan Simpson, who was killed by a V1 in 1944. Little is known, however, about either of her marriages, and her first husband as well as her second, remains a shadowy figure in the background. Flora Drummond herself remains a colourful but somewhat enigmatic figure. Her liking for a fight is clearly evident in the reputation she earned but she was also a popular figure and capable of very considerable loyalty to her leaders. Intellectually she is more difficult to interpret, especially her move from her left-wing beginnings to an extreme right-wing point of view. To some extent this was a result of the influence of Emmeline and Christabel Pankhurst, but her post-war activities seem to have been carried out on her own initiative. She is a good illustration of the ability of the Pankhursts to command loyalty and enthusiasm from the most diverse sources.

There is very little information anywhere on Flora Drummond's life. Most of the personal details come from *The Suffragette Movement*, Sylvia Pankhurst (London, Longmans, 1931; Virago, 1977) but there is also some extra information in *Votes for Women*, Roger Fulford (London, Faber and Faber, 1956). For information on her later career see *The Fighting Pankhursts*, David Mitchell (London, Jonathan Cape, 1967).

See also PANKHURST Emmeline, PANKHURST Christabel.

DRYSDALE Charles Robert 1829–1907

Charles Drysdale, a physician, was born in Edinburgh, where his father, Sir William Drysdale, was at one time treasurer of the City. He was educated at Edinburgh schools, and later at Trinity College, Cambridge, Trinity College, Dublin and University

College, London. Trained in both engineering and medicine, he eventually made medicine his career, receiving his MD in 1859. Later he studied further in both London and Paris and became a Fellow of the Royal College of Surgeons and a Member of the Royal College of Physicians.

An early visit to Ireland during the famine awakened his interest in over-population, but his solution was not the moral restraint advocated by Malthus, but contraception. He may have been influenced in this belief by his elder brother George, also a doctor, who had published in 1854 *Elements of Social Science* in which he advocated contraception as a remedy for over-population, believing that abstinence was harmful for both men and women. George was of a retiring nature but Charles became an ardent propagandist for birth control, and was one of the witnesses for the defence in the Bradlaugh Besant trial of 1877. In the same year he founded the Malthusian League to propagate contraception as the solution to over-population and poverty. He was its president from its foundation until his death in 1907, and from its inception his life was devoted exclusively to this cause. Although his Malthusianism was always seen by him as of particular benefit to women, it is in other areas that his feminism chiefly manifested itself.

As a young man he served as physician to the Rescue Society which led him to take a special interest in both prostitution and venereal disease. In 1863 he published a pamphlet 'The Nature and Treatment of Syphilis' and this was followed in 1866 by 'Prostitution Medically Considered with some of its Social Aspects'. Although he recognised the complexity of the problem, he believed that the chief cause of prostitution was the low wage paid to women. As a recognised authority on venereal diseases and a member of the VD committee of the Harveian Medical Society of London, he was early drawn into the controversy over the Contagious Diseases Acts which required the compulsory examination and if necessary treatment of women living in certain garrison towns who were believed to be prostitutes. Initially he approved both of the original Acts, and later of the scheme for their extension but by 1879 he had been convinced by the arguments of the repealers that police regulation threatened the civil rights of working-class women. Consequently he not only withdrew his support but worked actively on the side of repeal, becoming secretary of the Metropolitan Anti-Contagious Acts Association. At a time when most doctors favoured the Acts he was one of their leading medical opponents.

He appears to have been strongly sympathetic to women's rights at least as early as the 1860s, perhaps because of his great admiration for John Stuart Mill. He supported all the attempts to extend the opportunities open to women but his own personal contribution was largely in the field of medical education since, as a doctor, he was in a position to give help of a very practical kind. For example, at a time when such experience was difficult to obtain, he allowed women students to attend his hospital sessions. In 1870 he published a paper 'Medicine as a Profession for Women'. It was while lecturing to women medical students in the early 1870s that he met his future wife Alice Vickery, subsequently Alice Drysdale Vickery. A son, Charles Vickery Drysdale was born in 1874. Charles Drysdale died in 1907, and his wife, who had fully shared in his enthusiasm for Malthusian principles, became president of the league in his stead.

Charles Drysdale was clearly a man of considerable compassion who gave freely of his time to a number of causes aimed at improving the lives of women. His devotion to the principles of Malthusianism cut him off from many feminists who feared the association between secularism, birth control and free love, but his own belief in the necessity for contraception was grounded in his conviction that it would be of particular service to women.

There is no biography of Charles Drysdale. The best source on his life and work is *A History of the Malthusian League 1877–1927*, Rosanna Ledbetter (Columbus, Ohio State

University Press, 1976). *The Birth Controllers*, Peter Flyer (London, Secker and Warburg, 1965) also describes his work for birth control. For his work in the campaign against the Contagious Diseases Acts see *Prostitution in Victorian Society*, Judith R. Walkowitz (Cambridge, Cambridge University Press, 1980) and *Prostitution and Victorian Social Reform*, Paul McHugh (New York, St Martin's Press, 1980). There is also some material in a memorial issue of 'The Malthusian', February 1908 Vol. XXXII (2).

See also, BESANT Annie, VICKERY Alice Drysdale.

FAITHFULL Emily 1835-1895

Emily Faithfull, founder of the Victoria Press, was the youngest daughter of a Surrey clergyman, Ferdinand Faithfull. After attending a Kensington boarding school Emily was presented at court and for a short while she lived the social life of a young woman of her class. While still in her early twenties however she became involved with Jessie Boucherett, Bessie Parker and Adelaide Proctor in the founding in 1859 of the Society for Promoting the Employment of Women. Although she had no experience of printing, Emily Faithful became convinced that as a trade it was eminently suitable for women and, as a first step, had herself taught typesetting. Confirmed in her opinion, in March 1860 she founded the Victoria Press, in which the compositors, although not all the employees, were women. It was her opinion that heavy manual work should not be done by girls or women, and it was the manual dexterity involved in typesetting which attracted her to it.

Under her guidance the Victoria Press was quickly successful, although not without attracting a greal deal of opposition from the printing trade unions. There was considerable hostility to the whole idea, and the women employees were subjected to a certain amount of actual intimidation. Nevertheless the work of the press gained the approval of Queen Victoria, and Emily Faithfull was appointed Printer and Publisher in Ordinary to her Majesty. In 1863 she founded the *Victoria Magazine*, which she edited and which consistently pressed the claims of women for remunerative employment.

In 1864, however, she was involved in a highly publicised divorce case which must have caused her personal distress and may for a time at least have harmed her reputation. Her involvement had its origin in a very close friendship with Helen Jane Codrington, wife of Admiral Henry Codrington, which had started when Emily Faithfull was only nineteen years old. At this time, in 1854, while Admiral Codrington was away in the Crimea, his wife and Emily Faithfull shared not only the house, but apparently a bed. On his return in 1856 this practice continued, and it was alleged that on one occasion he entered the bedroom and tried to rape Emily Faithfull. After this incident his wife refused any marital relationship with him, but in 1857 Emily Faithfull was forbidden the house by the admiral, and a mysterious sealed package, explaining her dismissal, was deposited with his brother.

In 1864 Admiral Codrington petitioned for divorce on the grounds of his wife's adultery and she countered with the story of the alleged attempted rape. Emily Faithfull was called in evidence but refused to confirm the attempted rape, although she had earlier signed an affidavit claiming that it had taken place. It is by no means clear whether her original story had been a lie, or whether she had been intimidated by the threat of the sealed package, but the incident and the publicity given to her part in the case must have been extremely painful.

In 1867 Emily Faithfull withdrew from the Victoria Press, and this may have been as a result of the divorce case and its hints of lesbianism. But her other activities continued and she was one of the first women to join the Women's Trade Union League, founded by Emma Paterson in 1875. She was also one of the leading spirits behind the Women's Printing Society. In 1877 she started the *West London Express,* which was so successful that it was necessary to introduce steam machinery and to increase her staff of women compositors. For some years, too, she was on the staff of the *Ladies Pictorial.* During these years she made three highly successful visits to the United States, which she later described in *Three Visits to America* (Edinburgh, 1884). On her return to England she found herself something of a celebrity and it appears that by this time the old scandal was forgotten.

During her career she published two novels. *Change upon Change. A Love Story* (London, 1868) and *A Reed Shaken with the Wind. A Love Story* (New York, 1873). She also published numerous articles and pamphlets, mainly on the issue of women's employment, which remained her chief preoccupation. Another venture, not specifically concerned with women, was the International Musical, Dramatic and Literary Association founded by her for the purpose of securing better protection in the matter of copyright. Her death occurred in 1895 at the age of sixty.

Although Emily Faithfull's major contribution was in the field of women's work, she was a supporter both of the suffrage movement and of the higher education of women. She was involved in the early attempts to set up a Women's Suffrage Society during the 1860s, and it is possible that one of the effects of the divorce case was to make her less acceptable as a colleague. Emily Davies, in particular, was very sensitive on the issue of respectability, but she was not the only one, and the fear was very widespread that any hint of notoriety on the part of its supporters would harm the suffrage cause. It is therefore mainly as a pioneer in promoting the employment of women that Emily Faithfull is remembered. An interesting and unusual woman, it is a pity that we know so little about so many aspects of her life.

The best source on Emily Faithfull to date is 'Emily Faithfull and the Victoria Press. An Experiment in Sociological Bibliography', William E. Fredeman. *The Library* Fifth Series, Vol. XXIX (2), pp. 143-5 1974. See also *Women of the Day*, Frances Hays (London, Chatto and Windus, 1885); 'Emily Davies and the Women's Movement 1862-67', Andrew Rosen, *Journal of British Studies*, Vol. XIX, pp. 101-21, 1979.

FAWCETT Henry 1833-1884

Henry Fawcett, a Radical politician, was the son of William Fawcett and his wife Mary Cooper. His father started life as a draper's assistant but rose to become mayor of Salisbury and his mother was the daughter of a solicitor who was agent for the Liberal Party in Salisbury. There were four children, a daughter and three sons of whom Henry was the second. Both parents were ardent reformers with a keen interest in politics and strong supporters of the Liberal Party and this urge for reform was passed on to their son. Henry was a scholarly boy, with a considerable ability in mathematics, and it was this which influenced his father to send him to Cambridge, although such a step was by no means usual for a man in his position. At Cambridge Henry became part of a group which was influenced by utilitarianism and looked to John Stuart Mill for inspiration.

In 1856 Henry Fawcett became a Fellow of Trinity Hall but his chief ambition was to enter politics. Without money, he decided to approach Parliament via a career at the bar, but his prospects appeared to be ruined when in 1857 he was accidentally blinded by a shot from his father's gun. Stunned at first, Henry later resolved that he would let it make no difference to his hopes for a parliamentary career. Perhaps he was influenced in this by consideration for his father, who was heartbroken at what he had done to his beloved son. To have let it ruin his own life would be to ruin the life of his father also.

Meanwhile Henry had to abandon his studies at the bar, and turned instead to his academic career, determined to make himself a master of political economy. In this decision he was inspired directly by Mill's own work in this field. In 1860 he met Mill and the two became friends. In 1861 he started to write a book on political economy which was published in 1863. It was an immediate success and led to his election as professor of Political Economy, an academic advancement which not only helped his confidence in himself but improved his financial position.

During these same years he was also

pursuing his political ambitions. In 1860 he unsuccessfully contested Southwark, and this was followed by an attempt at Cambridge, but finally he was accepted as a candidate at Brighton and entered Parliament in 1865, still only thirty-two years old. Once in the House of Commons he joined a group of Radicals of whom John Stuart Mill was the leader.

In 1864 Henry had met and proposed to Elizabeth Garrett, then in the middle of her struggle to enter the medical profession. Little is known about their relationship, but she hesitated, and then refused him. Shortly after this he met her young sister Millicent, then only eighteen, at a party. She herself recalled afterwards that he overheard a remark she made on the death of Lincoln, in which she described it as the 'greatest misfortune which could have befallen the world on the loss of one man'. He sought her acquaintance and eighteen months later they were engaged. There was some opposition to the marriage from her family, and especially from Elizabeth who cited his relative poverty and his blindness as reasons against the marriage. Elizabeth's own biographer hints at some resentment, possibly unconscious, that he could have turned so quickly to her sister, but these problems were quickly resolved and they were married in 1867. Their only child, a daughter, Philippa, was born a year later.

Throughout their marriage Henry continued to regard his wife with what can only be described as devotion, and she made a tremendous contribution to his happiness. Yet in spite of the demands made on her time and energy by his blindness he always treated her as an equal in the marriage, encouraging not only her work for suffrage but also her attempts to be a writer. Under his urging she wrote *Political Economy for Beginners* which was published in 1870, and following this they collaborated in *Essays and Lectures in Political Subjects* (London, 1872) in which four essays were written by him and eight by her. He also carefully acknowledged her suggestions in his own work. Moreover, apart from the support and encouragement he gave her, he also not only fully shared her views on the position of women but made his own contribution to changing that position.

As a member of Parliament, Henry Fawcett was in a position to give expression to his feminism in a number of ways. He supported Mill's attempt to give women the franchise in 1867, and continued to support further attempts at enfranchisement when these occurred. Moreover, he was part of the more radical wing of the movement, along with Richard Pankhurst and Jacob and Ursula Bright pressing that any Bill should include married women and not just widows and spinsters. In the 1883–4 session Gladstone strongly opposed the inclusion of women in the Bill to enfranchise further groups of men, and ordered his party to vote against the proposal. Henry Fawcett was at that time a member of the government and did not feel able to vote against the party whip. He did however abstain, earning himself a severe reprimand from Gladstone, although he was not, as he might have been, asked to resign his government post.

He also took a strongly feminist line on the Factory Acts, supporting them in principle, but objecting to the inclusion of special protection for women. He opposed the legislation of 1874 which restricted the labour of adult women in textiles, claiming that it would force women into a narrow range of employment and lower their wages. Indeed he argued that the Act was the work of male trade unionists anxious to restrict women's work. Instead of protective legislation he wished to see more women workers in trade unions. This view was widely held in the feminist movement at the time and was only later to be replaced by the belief that protective legislation, including minimum-wage legislation, was necessary if women's working conditions were to be improved.

In 1880, on the return of the Liberals to power, he became Postmaster General and this gave him the opportunity to further the interests of women in the Post Office. In 1872, for example, he appointed the first woman medical officer. After the passing of the Married Women's Property Acts in 1882 he gave women postmistresses on marriage the option of retaining the appointment in their own name, whereas previously this had automatically passed to the husband.

Tragically, however, Henry Fawcett's career was cut short by his early death. In the summer of 1882 he was taken seriously ill with diphtheria and although he recovered, his health was weakened. In 1884 he died from an attack of pleurisy.

Although undoubtedly influenced by her opinions, Henry Fawcett's attitude to women was not derived from his wife but from his own political convictions formed at Cambridge. His biographer, Leslie Stephen, claims that his feminism was based essentially upon his dislike of restrictions generally, but especially when they tied the hands of the weak against the strong. He wanted to give women every opportunity to develop whatever abilities they possessed and had from the first approved proposals for admitting women to Cambridge. His feminism, like that of his mentor John Stuart Mill, had a great deal to do with freeing women from artificial and harmful restraints, and this explains his determined opposition to protective legislation for women. It is no accident, indeed, that throughout his life he was not only a feminist but a passionate free trader. He also tried to express his feminism in his marriage, in which he encouraged his wife to develop her own talents and in which he was perhaps influenced by John Stuart Mill's ideal of marriage as an intellectual partnership. At a time when women were virtually excluded from all areas of public life they depended very much on male allies like Henry Fawcett who not only supported their claims in theory but were prepared to act on their behalf in practice.

The standard biography *The Life of Henry Fawcett*, Leslie Stephen (London, Smith, Elder and Co., 1886) gives a very full account of his work for feminism. There is also an entry in *DNB* Vol. XVIII, pp. 252-7 but this does not have much on his feminism. On his marriage see *What I Remember*, Millicent Garrett Fawcett (London, T. Fisher Unwin, 1924).

See also FAWCETT Millicent Garrett, MILL John Stuart.

FAWCETT Millicent Garrett 1847-1929

Millicent Garrett, the leader of the constitutional suffrage movement, was the daughter of Newson Garrett and his wife Louise Dunnell. Her father was a self-made man who at the time of her birth was a wealthy corn and coal merchant in Aldeburgh, Suffolk. Her mother was a conventional and deeply religious woman whose influence on Millicent was much less than that of her powerful and self-confident father. It was a large family, ten children surviving infancy, and the last child was not born until 1853. Millicent was eleven years younger than her famous sister Elizabeth, who was already starting her fight to become a doctor when Millicent was only twelve years old. Her adolescent years, therefore, were to some extent spent in the shadow of that struggle. Like Elizabeth and the eldest daughter Louise, Millicent was sent away to school, but was removed at the age of fifteen. Her outlook was however considerably broadened by her visits to Louise who had married in 1857 and lived in London, where she moved in Radical circles and was herself committed to women's rights.

In 1865, when she was nearly eighteen, Millicent was taken by Louise to one of John Stuart Mill's election addresses, and this made a deep impression on her, strengthening considerably her already aroused belief in women's suffrage. Shortly afterwards, at a party given by Mr and Mrs Peter Davies, she met for the first time her future husband Henry Fawcett. The assassination of Abraham Lincoln had just been announced and she, deeply moved by it, remarked that it was 'the greatest misfortune which could have befallen the world on the death of any one man'. Deeply impressed, Henry Fawcett sought her acquaintance and eighteen months later they became engaged to be married.

At first, there was opposition to the marriage from her family and especially from Elizabeth, who had in fact rejected a proposal from Henry Fawcett shortly before he met Millicent. She argued that Millicent was throwing herself away, citing his blindness and his poverty as reasons, although her biographer implies that some unconscious jealousy may also have been at work here. It is possible that Millicent never did know of the earlier proposal since it seems to have been kept a secret. Millicent was hurt by Elizabeth's attitude but, deeply in love, in no mood to listen to arguments based on his unworthiness and Elizabeth's opposition did not last very long. The marriage took place in 1867, and a year later Philippa, the only child of the marriage, was born.

Marriage, however, did nothing to alter Millicent's attitude to women's rights, and, indeed, increased her opportunities to play a part in the suffrage movement. Henry Fawcett was already an MP and much at home in Radical circles in both London and in Cambridge where he held the post of professor of Political Economy. For some years, too, Millicent acted as his secretary, and this did a great deal to improve her own political education. Moreover, her husband encouraged her both to take an active part in the suffrage movement and to try her hand as an author. Immediately after the marriage she joined the London Suffrage Committee and in 1868 made her first speech in Manchester. She was never to enjoy speaking in public but she was a good speaker, not eloquent but always lucid and well-prepared.

She also began to write for the Press and her first article, on lectures for women in Cambridge, appeared in *Macmillan's Magazine* in 1868. Urged by her husband, she also wrote *Political Economy for Beginners* (London, 1870) which went rapidly through ten editions. It was followed by *Essays and Lectures on Political Subjects* (London, 1872) to which she contributed eight essays and her husband four. In 1875 she published her first novel, *Janet Doncaster*. Mainly a tract against drunkenness, it was not a great success, and a second novel, published under a pseudonym, was a complete failure. This seems to have ended any attempt to become a novelist although she continued to write on a variety of subjects and was to do so for the rest of her life.

During the 1880s she slowly emerged as one of the leaders of the suffrage movement. The early death of her husband in 1884 left her a widow at the age of thirty-seven. She moved to live with a sister, and used the extra time at her disposal to increase her commitment to the suffrage cause. In 1890, on the sudden death of Lydia Becker, she took over the leadership of the National Union of Women's Suffrage Societies and maintained this position until 1919, by which time the principle of women's suffrage had been won.

Although she always regarded women's suffrage as, for her, the main issue, she cared deeply for the cause of women's education and shortly after her marriage was drawn closely into the scheme for women's lectures at Cambridge, which led, eventually, to the establishment of Newnham College. At the same time Emily Davies was working towards the foundation of Girton and it seems strange, in view of the close friendship between Elizabeth and Emily, that Millicent should have given her support to what Emily saw as a rival establishment. It is very likely, however, that Millicent was drawn into the support of Newnham because of Henry's membership of the reforming element at Cambridge and his friendship with Sidgwick who was the moving spirit behind Newnham. In consequence her daughter Philippa went to Newnham, not Girton, where she was placed first in the mathematical tripos, a triumph which meant a great deal to the whole women's rights movement.

In 1870 Millicent had stood aside from the Contagious Diseases Acts controversy, not on grounds of principle, since she never accepted her sister Elizabeth's view that the Acts were a necessary evil, but because she feared the effect of involvement on the suffrage cause. Indeed for several years the suffrage movement itself was split on the issue, with some, like Jacob Bright, becoming prominent campaigners for the repeal of the Acts. There were many others however who agreed with Millicent that the two campaigns should be kept distinct. The Acts themselves, designed to protect the Armed Forces from venereal disease by requiring the compulsory examination and if necessary treatment of women believed to be prostitutes, were seen by their opponents as condoning vice and supporting the double standard of sexual morality. By the 1880s however there were signs that Millicent's priorities were changing and she was beginning to appreciate, in a way that perhaps she was too young to understand in 1870, that Josephine Butler's campaign for equal moral standards was as central to the feminist cause as the fight for suffrage. In 1885 she was deeply moved by Stead's articles in the *Pall Mall Gazette* in which he exposed the traffic in young girls. She wrote several letters to the press in his support in which she argued the need for women to have a share in the control of the law. When Stead was prosecuted for his part in the exposure she wrote to him in prison in the warmest terms, and was one of those who took action to get him treatment as a first-class prisoner. For the first time she came to know Josephine Butler and was deeply impressed. Many years later she wrote her biography, in association with E.M. Turner, *Josephine Butler* (London, 1927) to celebrate her centenary in which she called her 'the most distinguished Englishwomen in the nineteenth century'.

Perhaps the most significant evidence of her growing appreciation of moral issues for feminism occurred in 1894 when she launched a campaign against Henry Cust, a Conservative MP who was currently standing for election in Manchester. Cust had seduced a girl of good family and then offered marriage to someone else. When the girl, who was pregnant, wrote him an imploring letter he showed it to men of his acquaintance with facetious remarks. Perhaps it was this last and particularly repellent aspect of his behaviour which so roused Millicent that she sent details to the honorary secretary of the Women's Liberal Unionist Association in Manchester. At first nothing was done but she continued to press her case and eventually the man involved gave up his candidature and married the girl he had seduced. Millicent however did not drop her campaign against him and her friends were finally forced to tell her that she was harming the suffrage movement by what was beginning to look like persecution. That the eminently reasonable Millicent could act so passionately is, however, a clear indication of the strength of her feelings on the issue. In the years that followed she argued strongly for equal grounds for divorce and in the guardianship of children. On the other hand, she believed firmly that moral standards should be raised, not lowered, in order to achieve equality, and was so horrified when she saw a copy of *The Freewoman*, which advocated more sexual freedom for women, that she tore it into small pieces.

Although, like her husband, a Liberal in politics, she never forgave Gladstone for his opposition to women's suffrage, and gradually became alienated from the party. In 1886 she joined with the Liberal Unionists on the issue of home rule, although she withdrew her support when they abandoned the principle of free trade in favour of protection. Finally, in 1912, she accepted the decision of the National Union of Women's Suffrage Societies to support Labour candidates once the party had committed itself to women's suffrage. At heart, however, she always remained a Liberal, believing firmly in free trade, self-help and individualism. In 1870 she opposed free education on the grounds that it diminished parental responsibility, and after the first world war she disagreed with family allowances which she believed would ruin family life. Indeed she felt so strongly on this issue that she renounced altogether her membership of the NUWSS, by this time the National Union of Societies for Equal Citizenship, when family allowances, under the urging of Eleanor Rathbone, became part of its policy. Her essential liberalism was also revealed in her persistent opposition to protective legislation for women workers, even after many feminists had become convinced that some protection was necessary. In 1898, for example, she protested at efforts which would have prohibited women working with phosphorus.

As the leader of the NUWSS. pledged to constitutional means, the foundation of the Women's Social and Political Union and its adoption of increasingly militant methods placed Millicent in something of a quandary. She believed firmly in persuasion, but she recognised the success of the new methods in awakening public interest in the suffrage issue. She was also deeply resentful of the way in which the militant protest was handled by the government, and even as late as 1913, when militancy was at its most extreme, she blamed the politicians, whose 'blind blundering' had caused it, rather than the militants themselves, whose courage she admired. Her position was made more difficult because her sister Elizabeth, and Elizabeth's daughter Louise were both active on the militant side of the movement. Moreover, under the influence of the WSPU, the NUWSS itself adopted more colourful, if always constitutional, methods, moving away from its preoccupation with political lobbying and embarking on a programme of processions, public lectures and other means of attracting mass support.

Where Millicent differed perhaps most significantly from the Pankhursts was in her identification of suffrage as something to be won slowly by reason and persuasion. She believed that women's suffrage would be of benefit for the whole society, men as well as women, and she never seems to have shown any antagonism towards men as a class, or interpreted the suffrage movement as a battle between the sexes. The Pankhursts, in contrast, constantly defined the struggle for the vote in military terms and justified their actions in this way. This is not to suggest however that Millicent was a pacifist. She had supported the Boer War, and at the outbreak of the first world war argued in favour of suspending the suffrage campaign in the interests of the nation as a whole. This was in sharp contrast to the attitude of many in her own organisation and in 1915 there was a battle for leadership between her and the pacifists, which she eventually won. Her non-violent stand on suffrage, therefore, was based on her belief that there was no *necessary* antagonism between men and women.

Millicent retired from active political work in 1919 but she continued to work for sex equality, and in particular helped to secure the opening of the legal profession to women. She travelled widely, and in 1929, her eighty-third year, and the last year of her life, she travelled with her sister Agnes to the Far East. She also continued to write. In 1912 she had published *Women's Suffrage. A Short History of a Great Movement* in association with E.C. Jack. After the war she published a sequel, *The Women's Victory—and After* (London, 1920). This was followed by *What I Remember* (London, 1924). Her final publication was *Josephine Butler* written in association with E.M. Turner (London, 1927).

Millicent lived long enough to see most of the goals she had worked for achieved, since the 1920s saw the success not only of women's suffrage but a wide range of other reforms which were part of the women's movement, and which included an end to the double standard in the grounds for divorce and improvement in women's rights of guardianship over their children, both issues which were particularly important to Millicent herself. Other developments within feminism were less congenial to her, particularly its association with family allowances. Nor was she likely to have approved of the growing recognition by feminists of women's own sexuality. Indeed Millicent Fawcett was essentially a nineteenth-century figure, representing all the major goals of nineteenth-century feminism in her emphasis on education, suffrage and moral reform.

As a person she was highly reticent and tried at all times to maintain a somewhat rigid self-control. Her deep grief at her husband's death was not shown publicly, and indeed she could hardly bear even others to refer to her own sorrow. Without any of the charismatic qualities of the Pankhursts, she based her appeal essentially on her reasonableness. An attractive, highly feminine person in appearance, she tended to disarm criticism at a time when women's suffrage was regarded as highly dangerous and decidedly unfeminine. Her happy marriage and early and tragic widowhood were also useful antidotes to the view that the vote was only sought after by unattractive spinsters. Her personal reticence and dislike of the dramatic has probably led to an undervaluation of her services to feminism, which covered in effect more than sixty years of her long life.

There is a somewhat reticent biography *Millicent Garrett Fawcett* by her friend Ray Strachey (London, John Murray, 1931). She herself wrote a memoir *What I remember* (London, T. Fisher Unwin, 1924). There is also an entry in the *DNB* 1922-1930 pp. 297-9. More recently Ann Oakley has written a brief reassessment from the standpoint of modern feminism 'Millicent Garrett Fawcett: Duty and Determination' in *Feminist Theorists* ed. Dale Spender (London, Routledge and Kegan Paul, 1983).

See also ANDERSON Elizabeth Garrett, FAWCETT Henry.

FITCH Sir Joshua Girling 1824-1903

Joshua Fitch, an educationalist, was the second son of Thomas Fitch, a clerk in Somerset House, and his wife Sarah Tucker Hodges. There were six sons and two daughters, and although the family was poor, his parents sent the boys to a good private day school near their home. In 1838 he became a pupil-teacher and later an assistant master at Borough Road, a model school attached to the Borough Road Training College. At this stage in his life he already showed the love of work and intense energy that was to mark his career, as well as the desire for usefulness derived from the evangelical piety in his home which expressed itself in a life-long involvement in voluntary social work. In 1844 he became a headmaster but in spite of his various commitments continued his part-time studies at London University and in 1850 he obtained a BA degree followed two years later by an MA.

In 1852 he was appointed as a tutor at Borough Road Training College, shortly afterwards becoming vice-principal and in 1856 its principal. In that same year he married Emma Wilks, the daughter of an official of the East India Company. There were no children of the marriage but in 1863 they adopted a niece, the daughter of Emma's sister. In that same year they moved out of London, on Joshua Fitch's appointment as inspector of schools based in York. In 1870 he was released from his duties to act as one of the assistant commissioners who had the task of giving effect to the Endowed Schools Act, returning to the inspectorate in 1877, this time in East Lambeth. In 1885 he was made inspector of training colleges for women in England and Wales, a duty which he filled until his retirement in 1894, five years later than the normal retiring age. He was knighted in 1896 and died in 1903.

The interest in the education of women and girls which was to become so significant a feature in his life seems to date from the early 1860s and may have been the result of his friendship with John Llewelyn Davies, the brother of Emily Davies. At the Social Science Congress in 1862 he read a paper on behalf of Emily Davies in which she outlined her ideas on the education of girls, and this seems to have been the start of his active involvement in the issue. In 1864 he contributed his own views on the education of women in a paper published by the *Victoria Magazine* and his attitude was strengthened by his researches on behalf of the Schools Inquiry Commission in 1865, which convinced him of the weaknesses of middle-class education for girls. In his own report to the commission he complained that the claims of girls had been ignored, and his appointment, in 1870, as an assistant commissioner under the Endowed Schools Act enabled him to secure for girls a larger share of available endowments.

At the same time he was gradually drawn more closely into the movement for the higher education of women, although it is clear from his letters to Emily Davies at the time that at first he had some misgivings about her policy of opening university degrees to women on the same terms as men. Believing that men and women had different intellectual needs he tended to favour a different curriculum for men and women. Later however he became an enthusiastic supporter of Emily Davies in her attempt to found what was later to be Girton College based firmly on the principle of equal treatment and equal standards for men and women. Moreover, as a member of the senate of London University he was in the forefront of the battle to secure the new charter which, in 1878, opened the university to women on the same terms as men. He was also in full support, from the beginning, of the entry of women into the medical profession. Welcoming any extension of women's influence in public life, he was also anxious to see it extended to a wider range of public bodies, and was in addition a consistent and firm advocate of women's suffrage.

It was in the field of women's education, however, that he was most active and throughout the latter part of his life he was associated with a very wide range of bodies to improve the education of girls and women. These included, amongst many others, the Girls' Public Day School Trust in which he took a very considerable and personal interest and the Cambridge Training College for Women. In 1890 his portrait by Ethel King was presented to him in recognition of his services to the cause of the higher education of women. Apart from his work for women he also gained a considerable reputation as an expert on school organisation and on teaching methods, largely as a consequence of his book *Lectures on Teaching* (1881). He was also well known for his advocacy of teacher training for secondary as well as elementary schools, and this, like his advocacy of higher education for women, illustrates his willingness to accept innovation.

In championing the cause of women Joshua Fitch was concerned above all to remove disabilities and impediments which discriminated against women and anxious that women should be allowed to make their own choice of career. In this he was reflecting liberal values on the importance of individual freedom and personal choice which to a large extent, particularly through the writings of John Stuart Mill, underpinned the nineteenth-century women's rights movement. Yet he remained convinced that woman's special nature, and her unique role as mother, would remain of paramount importance in most women's lives. Indeed he went further since he saw the influence of women in the public sphere as essentially complementary to that of men, bringing in particular the ideals of service out of the home and into public life. His feminism therefore rested on a belief in the moral superiority of women so that women's emancipation was seen by him as a way to lift society to a higher moral plane. In this way he was able to reconcile his view of the essential difference between men and women with a strong commitment to feminist goals.

It is unfortunate that we know so little of Emma Fitch, either in her influence on her husband or as a person in her own right. According to his biographer, their marriage was an exceptionally close one and she worked with him in his efforts for women's education, acting, in this as in other things, as his inspiration. She may therefore have been particularly important in providing him with his ideal of womanhood. His other inspiration was Emily Davies, who helped to form his ideas on women's education during the crucial 1860s. He was also a close associate of Frances Buss, sharing her interest in the training of teachers, and it is clear that he was able to make and keep the friendship of women. By no means the only man who made a contribution to the educational side of the nineteenth-century women's movement, he stands out by virtue of the enthusiasm and indeed dedication he gave to the cause.

The biography *Sir Joshua Fitch*, A.L. Lilley (London, Edward Arnold, 1906) gives a good account of his work for women. See also *Emily Davies and Girton College*, Barbara Stephen (London, Constable, 1927) and DNB 1901–1911 pp. 27–8.

See also BUSS Frances Mary, DAVIES Sarah Emily.

FORD Isabella Ormston c. 1850–1924

Isabella Ford, a suffragist, and her sister Bessie came from a well-known and well-to-do Radical Quaker family who lived at Adel

Grange near Leeds. Their father was a friend of John Bright; and Mazzini and other political refugees found hospitality in their home. Nothing is known of their childhood and early life but during the 1870s the Ford sisters came to know Edward Carpenter and formed a lasting friendship with him. Probably through Edward Carpenter they became admirers of Walt Whitman and when his complete works were published in one large volume he sent two copies to Britain, one for Edward Carpenter and one for Isabella and her sister. At about this time, too, they began to interest themselves in women employed in the tailoring trade in Leeds, following the example of their parents who had started one of the first evening schools for working-class girls. Gradually Adel Grange became a kind of informal centre where socialists, trade unionists and Radicals could meet.

During the 1890s Isabella's political activities increased. To some extent the impetus for this seems to have come from a long strike at Manningham Mills in Bradford. Isabella supported the girls, defending them on public platforms and demonstrating with them in the streets. Although at first she found speaking in public difficult, she was soon a frequent speaker on socialist platforms. Both she and Bessie joined the Independent Labour Party and in 1903 Isabella became a member of its executive committee. It is not known when, exactly, she became involved in the campaign for women's suffrage, but certainly by the early 1900s she was making determined efforts to convert the ILP and later the Labour Party to the suffrage cause. In 1905, for example, she supported women's suffrage at the Labour Party Conference. A close friend of Philip Snowden and his wife Ethel, she and her sister were two of the very small number of guests at their wedding, and it has been suggested that it was Isabella who converted them to women's suffrage.

During the 1890s Isabella had also emerged as a writer. In 1890 she published a novel *Miss Blake of Monkshalton* (London, 1890) and this was followed by *On the Threshold* (London, 1895) and *Mr Elliott* (London, 1901). Several other publications reflected her experience with working women, the first being *Women's Wages and the conditions under which they are earned*, published by the Humanitarian League (London, 1893). This was followed by another pamphlet for the Humanitarian League *Industrial Women and how to help them* (London, 1900?). During this same period she also wrote *Women as Factory Inspectors and Certifying Surgeons* for the Co-operative Women's Guild (London, 1898). The most important of her publications however was *Women and Socialism* published by the ILP (London, 1904) and re-issued in 1907. In it she argued that the emancipation of women and the emancipation of labour were different aspects of the same great force and that socialists should support the struggle of women, just as women should support socialism. She also tried to deny the charge that the women's suffrage movement was middle-class, arguing that it was well aware of the needs of working-class women.

Although Annie Kenney was a protégée of hers, she never followed her, or the Pankhursts, out of the Labour movement. She did however continue to work in her own way for suffrage and was involved in one of the deputations to Asquith at which she pleaded the cause of the working-class woman. Less is heard of her however in the later stages of the campaign and it is possible that increasing age or even infirmity limited her activities as she neared her sixties. Moreover, *Women and Socialism* was her last publication and this also suggests a decline in either energy or involvement. Nevertheless she still retained a lot of respect as a Labour veteran, and although she refused the offer, was invited to stand as a Labour candidate in the election of 1918. She died in 1924.

It is tantalising to know so little of Isabella Ford, since she represents an unusual kind of feminist for her time, in her strong commitment to both socialism and feminism. She refused either to place socialism first, as many socialists did, or to abandon her socialism as did Christabel and Emmeline Pankhurst and many of their followers. Her pamphlet *Women and Socialism* is instead an attempt to see them both as different sides of the same coin. In the years after the vote has won many socialist women drifted away from feminism and it has taken the modern re-emergence of feminism to raise the issues that Isabella Ford tried to solve.

There has been no biography of Isabella Ford and she does not appear in either the *DNB* or, more surprisingly, the *DLB*. There are a number of references to her but all are disappointingly brief. The best sources are *Hidden from History*, Sheila Rowbotham (London, Pluto Press, 1972); *The Suffragette Movement*, Sylvia Pankhurst (London, Longmans, 1931; Virago, 1977); and Philip Snowden's *Autobiography* (London, Nicholson and Watson, 1934). See also *Women in the Labour Movement. The British Experience* ed. Lucy Middleton (London, Croom Helm, 1977) and *Socialism and the New Life*, Sheila Rowbotham and Jeffrey Weeks (London, Pluto Press, 1977).

FOX William Johnson 1786–1864

Born in a Suffolk village, William Fox, a Unitarian minister, was the son of a peasant farmer who, early in life, was in trouble with the local gentry for poaching. His mother, a sensitive, delicate woman, was the daughter of the local barber who also served as a clerk in the Dissenting meeting house. Their family grew rapidly and William's schooling was irregular as he was forced to work from an early age. For some time he was a clerk in a bank, and during these years he continued to study. In 1806 he entered Homerton, a theological college for the training of Dissenting ministers, but soon became obsessed by religious doubts. By 1812 he was an avowed Unitarian and settled down as the minster of a small Unitarian congregation at Chichester. Here he fell in love with Eliza Florance, whose father was a barrister in his congregation. The love affair was, however, far from smooth and a semi-engagement was undertaken and then broken. In 1817, with a reputation enhanced by the publication of three sermons, he moved to London, but Eliza followed him and, possibly as a result of pressure from her family, they were married in 1820.

The marriage, however, proved a fatal mistake for them both. Incompatible in temperament, she was also a poor household manager and they were unhappy from the start. Nor did the birth of a deaf and dumb son a year later help to bring them together. In 1822 William Fox had a mental illness of a severe enough character to prevent him working for a year and which was believed by his biographer to have been caused by his unhappy marriage. The following year he began his association with Eliza Flower, then twenty years old, which was to result in the breakdown of his marriage.

Eliza and her sister Sara had lost their mother as children and had been brought up unconventionally by their father, the veteran reformer Benjamin Flower. Both sisters were unusually talented and Eliza was later to achieve distinction as a composer. William Fox, who had an affectionate nature that craved sympathy and was unsatisfied by his marriage, quickly responded to her ardent, unworldly, impulsive nature. She soon began to assist in his work, copying articles and speeches and hunting up materials, but their friendship was, not unnaturally, resented by his wife and in 1832 a crisis in their relationship led to a separation although they continued to live in the same house. His wife now carried her complaints to the congregation and matters were further complicated by protests at his public advocacy of a liberalisation of the divorce laws. In the dispute that followed he retained the majority of his congregation and continued to act as their preacher but he was disowned by the Association of Unitarian Ministers of London. At this stage he left his wife and set up house with Eliza and the two eldest of his children, although it is generally accepted that their relationship remained platonic.

During the 1820s and 1830s William Fox gained a considerable following as both a preacher and a writer. He contributed both to the *Westminster Review* and especially to the Unitarian journal the *Monthly Repository*, becoming its editor in 1827 and its owner in 1831. After 1834 he turned increasingly to journalism, and after 1840, to politics. Between 1840 and 1850 he was one of the most prominent orators of the Anti-Corn Law League. He was not a socialist and believed that, apart from the repeal of the Corn Laws, the way forward for the working classes was in the improvement of their education. Between 1844 and 1846 he delivered a series of Sunday Evening Popular Lectures to the Working Classes, and these were later published as *Lectures to the Working Classes*. Elected to Parliament in 1847 as Radical MP for Oldham, he introduced, unsuccessfully, a Bill for establishing compulsory secular education. His life with Eliza Flower ended in 1846 with her early death, and some years later he was reconciled with his wife. By 1860 his health was failing and he resigned from the House of Commons in 1863, dying the following year.

William Fox's public involvement in feminism dates back to 1832 when he published an outspoken article in the *Monthly Repository* advocating female suffrage as well as reform in the divorce laws. He continued to hold these beliefs all his life and in the House of Commons he deplored the want of any real respect for women and argued for women's suffrage on the grounds that the interests of men and women are not necessarily the same. He criticised the People's Charter for its avoidance of this issue. His feminism was based partly on general humanitarian grounds, partly on a belief, not shared by many men at this time, in women's capacity for intellectual achievement. His view of women was essentially both romantic and idealistic, and he saw their real task in the world as purifying and reforming it. By denying women education he believed men had crippled not only women's lives but also their own. Marriage, he argued, should be based on mutual affection, not economic or legal dependency, and indeed a sexual relationship not based on such affection was immoral. Consequently marriage should be a civil contract which could be dissolved.

It is likely that William Fox's feminism was influenced by his own relationships with women. His unhappy marriage was certainly a factor in his attitude to divorce, but even more important were four women he deeply admired. Eliza Flower and her sister Sara were both women of unusual accomplishment, and Eliza in particular clearly formed for him his ideal of womanhood. Sara was married to William Bridges Adams who himself wrote strongly feminist articles in the *Monthly Repository* under the pen-name 'Junius Redivivus'. Harriet Martineau had published her article 'On Female Education' in the *Monthly Repository* as early as 1823 and, although she disapproved of his relationship with Eliza Flower, they remained friends. Finally, he was a close friend of both Harriet Taylor and John Stuart Mill, having indeed brought the two together, and undoubtedly the exchange of ideas between them could only have served to reinforce his own attitudes.

Certainly there is something of the nineteenth-century notion of woman as 'help-meet' in William Fox's emphasis that education would make women better companions to men, but the companionship he sought was in a free and loving relationship and he strongly deplored the economic and legal dependency which made of women domestic slaves. Moreover, he was a feminist at a time when it was still an unconventional doctrine even in the Radical circles in which he moved. Although widely discussed within Owenite and socialist circles in the 1830s, his contribution was to bring the issue before a rather different and a wider public.

See William Fox's biography *The Life of W.J. Fox. Public Teacher and Social Reformer 1786-1864*, Richard Garnett (London, Bodley Head, 1910); *The Dissidence of Dissent. The Monthly Repository 1806-1838*, Francis E. Mineka (New York, Octagon Books, 1972); *DNB* Vol. XX, pp. 137-9.

See also MARTINEAU Harriet, TAYLOR Harriet, MILL John Stuart.

G

GAWTHORPE Mary 1881–c.1960

Mary Gawthorpe, a suffragette, was born in Yorkshire, one of a family of five children, four girls and one boy. Her mother had been forced, through poverty, to work in the mill from the age of ten. Later she helped an elder sister in dressmaking and as a result of their efforts a younger sister became a college-trained teacher. Her father, John Gawthorpe, had followed his own father into leather work, although his schoolmaster had wanted him to become a teacher. Both parents therefore saw themselves to some extent as the victims of educational deprivation.

As a young child, Mary had loved and admired her father but later what she herself described as a 'black cloud' descended on the family in the shape of some rather vaguely pictured sexual indiscretion on his part which caused her mother deep distress. Perhaps as a result of local disapproval her father, formerly active in the church choir, left the church, and began to drink. He never, it seems, was really a drunkard, although he did get drunk from time to time, but her mother, from a teetotal family, found any drinking distasteful. Moreover, the money he spent on drink could not easily be spared.

Nevertheless, in spite of his shortcomings as a financial provider, there was enough money for Mary to stay on at school to train as a pupil teacher, although at nineteen she refused the offer to go to college so that she could earn money as an assistant teacher to help at home. Meanwhile the relationship between her parents steadily deteriorated. At one point her mother tried to evade any sexual relationship with her husband by sleeping with Mary, but did not persist in the face of his disapproval. Finally, in 1901, Mary persuaded her mother to leave him. Together with her younger brother the three of them moved out, leaving him just a note to say that they had gone.

At this time Mary became friendly with a young man, known to us only by his initials F.L., who was a compositor on *The Yorkshire Post*. Before very long they were engaged although, for financial reasons, they envisaged a long engagement. Through his influence, Mary, who had previously taken no interest in politics, became interested in the Labour church and later the Leeds branch of the Independent Labour Party. Her liveliness and ability led quite soon to her appointment as vice-president of the branch, and she also contributed a woman's page to their local journal as well as acting as a local speaker. In 1905, through her ILP activities, she was appointed a member of the Lord Mayor's Central Committee of the Leeds Children's Relief Committee.

Up to this time, although converted to socialism, Mary seems to have played little or no part in the suffrage campaign, although she had met Christabel Pankhurst briefly at an ILP meeting. But in 1905 she read of the arrest of Annie Kenney and Christabel Pankhurst and their subsequent imprisonment, and was sufficiently moved to write to offer to go to prison herself. At first, however, she joined not the Women's Social and Political Union but the Leeds branch of the National Union of Women's Suffrage Societies where she worked closely with Isabella Ford. For a short time, too, she was involved with the Women's Labour League, working for Labour on their behalf at the Cockermouth election. In 1906, however, she was made an organiser for the WSPU and for the next few years was heavily engaged in their campaign.

She was described as one of the most popular speakers in the WSPU, although in the end her voice was ruined by overstrain. She was imprisoned in 1906, and attended the banquet given by Millicent Fawcett to honour the first batch of women who went to Holloway, and this was the first of several imprisonments. When the split came with Teresa Billington-Greig and Charlotte Despard she stayed loyal to the Pankhurst family. But in 1910 she fell seriously ill and afterwards was an invalid for several years. For a time in 1911 she served as editor of the feminist journal *The Freewoman* but her health forced her to give up. In that year she was also forced to give up her place on the WSPU ruling committee. Nevertheless her commitment to the cause did not weaken and as late as 1912 she broke a window at the Home Office as a protest against forcible feeding. She was arrested but because of her health released after a week on remand.

She did not marry F.L. although it is not known at what stage the engagement was broken. He did not at first oppose her commitment to the WSPU but may in time have wished to end an engagement which had lost its meaning. Alternatively, her serious illness may have led to her withdrawal. Years later she refers to the apprehension she felt at the idea of marriage as a result of her mother's experiences. Later, although it is not known when, she emigrated to Canada, took up journalism and eventually married.

Mary Gawthorpe was one of those women who entered the suffrage campaign from the ILP. She was inspired directly by the example of the Pankhursts whom she seems to have served loyally, although her move to *The Freewoman* in 1911 may be an indication of a change of mood. Her relationship with her parents may also be seen as predisposing her towards feminism, especially her disillusionment with her father, whose actions may well have seemed a betrayal of the whole family. Moreover, a life-time of reflection does not seem to have softened her view of him. Under these circumstances her commitment to the militant campaign may well have seemed a desirable alternative to marriage and a family, offering her not only adventure but the chance of service to a cause.

Mary Gawthorpe's memoirs *Uphill to Holloway* (Traversity Press, Penobscot Maine, 1962) do not take the form of a biography and dwell mostly on her childhood and youth. There is also a brief reference to her in *The Suffragette Movement*, Sylvia Pankhurst (London, Longmans, 1931; Virago, 1977).

GORE-BOOTH Eva Selina 1870-1926

Eva Gore-Booth, poet and mystic, was the third child of Sir Henry Gore-Booth, and was born at Lissadell, Co. Sligo in Ireland. Her father took pride in his reputation as a good landlord, and kept a store of food at Lissadell during the 1879-80 famine, giving it free to the hungry. This experience may have contributed to Eva's deep concern all her life for the poor and the suffering. A beautiful but fragile child, she also showed from an early age an interest in the mystical which was to permeate her life. Although, as a young woman, she was presented at court, she showed no liking for fashionable society. In 1895 a serious illness during which indeed her life was despaired of, was followed by a convalescence in Italy where, in 1896, she met Esther Roper, a university graduate who for two years had been working in Manchester for the political and economic emancipation of women. Eva Gore-Booth was already interested in women's suffrage and, in spite of the great difference in their background, the two women began a friendship which was to last for life.

In 1897 Eva joined Esther Roper in Manchester, and the two women became joint secretaries of the Women's Textile and Other Workers' Representation Committee. That same year, too, saw the publication of her first book of poems which earned her the praise of Yeats. The next ten years were filled with organising, speaking and writing, and she soon became a practised speaker. In 1900 she became co-secretary with Sarah Dickensen to the Manchester and Salford Women's Trade Union Committee and the two women, one working-class, the other from the Irish aristocracy, became close friends. She was also an active member at this time of the North of England Society for Women's Suffrage. Perhaps the most characteristic feature of her work was the attempt to bring women's suffrage to working women and to combine the issue of women's trade unionism and women's suffrage. She argued that to try to improve the conditions of work for women and children without the vote was 'like fighting without bayonets'. During these highly active years she served on the Manchester Education Committee where she protested against the exclusion of girls from scholarships at the Municipal College of Technology. For a time, with Esther Roper, she ran a paper, the *Women's Labour News*. She was also involved in the work of the Manchester University settlement where she ran a dramatic society for working women.

In 1901 she and Esther met and befriended the young Christabel Pankhurst and it was with them that she served her political apprenticeship. It was through their influence also that in 1903 she started her study of law. For a time Christabel adored Eva, and Sylvia Pankhurst has described how when Eva suffered from neuralgia, as often happened, Christabel would sit with her for hours, massaging her head. By 1905 Christabel was ready for more independent action but neither Eva Gore-Booth nor Esther Roper was prepared to accept her militant tactics and the friendship came to an end. Later the breach between them widened when the Women's Social and Political Union abandoned its ties with the Independent Labour Party and the Labour movement.

During these years Eva published a pamphlet *Women's Right to Work* in which she violently attacked the suggestion that married women should not be allowed to work. She also opposed all attempts to restrict women's labour and supported such varied groups ar barmaids, pit-brow workers, women acrobats and gymnasts and women florists. In 1908 she and Esther Roper founded the Manchester Bar Maids' Association to protest at aspects of the Liberals' Licensing Act believed to be unfair to barmaids. Another publication at this time was *Women Workers and Parliamentary Representation* and she was a frequent contributor to the NUWSS journal *The Common Cause*. Nor was her poetry neglected. In 1904 she published *The One and the Many* which included the well-known poem 'The Little Waves of Breffny', Further volumes of poetry followed in 1905 and 1912.

In 1913 there was a recurrence of her illness and, when she was forced to leave Manchester, she and Esther Roper moved to London. During the war she worked unceasingly for the Women's Peace Crusade and the No-conscription Fellowship and, in spite of her health, attended court-martials and tribunals up and down the country in support of conscientious objectors. Her sister Constance, the Countess of Markievicz, shared her concern for the poor, and had been working in the slums of Dublin for a number of years. Deeply committed to the cause of Ireland, Constance was arrested at the time of the 1916 rebellion and condemned to death. Later she was reprieved and served a period in prison. In 1918 she was the first woman elected to the House of Commons but did not take up her seat, and the honour later passed to Nancy Astor.

After the war Eva Gore-Booth worked mainly for prison reform and was an active member of the Committee for the Abolition of Capital Punishment, although worsening health greatly interfered with any active work. She continued to write however, and published a number of long mystical poems, including *The Shepherd of Eternity* (1925) and *The World's Pilgrim* (1927) which revealed her belief in the unifying force of love. Cared for by Esther during her long illness, she died in 1926.

Eva Gore-Booth was a woman of great charm, able to secure the friendship and affection of women of all classes. Passionate and romantic, she also had the ability to inspire enthusiasm and commitment in others. Her poetic gifts were by no means inconsiderable but her mysticism was combined with a very decided practical ability and a deep and even painful commitment to the victims of injustice. Her most important years as a feminist were those between 1897 when she arrived in Manchester, and 190. when the initiative began to pass to the WSPU. During these years however she and

Esther Roper together did more than anyone else to rouse the working-class women in the Manchester area to a concern for women's suffrage.

The main source of information is Esther Roper's *Biographical Introduction to the Poems of Eva Gore-Booth* (London, Longmans Green and Co., 1929) There is also information in *One Hand Tied Behind Us. The Rise of the Women's Suffrage Movement*, Jill Liddington and Jill Norris (London, Virago, 1978); in *Votes for Women*, Roger Fulford (London, Faber and Faber, 1956) and *The Suffragette Movement* Sylvia Pankhurst (London, Longmans, 1931; Virago, 1977).

See also ROPER Esther.

GREY Maria Georgina 1816–1906

Maria Grey, a pioneer in the reform of women's education, was born Maria Shirreff, the daughter of William Henry Shirreff, a career naval officer who eventually reached the rank of rear admiral, and Elizabeth Murray, daughter of the Hon David Murray. The family were resident in France between 1826 and 1829, and in Gibraltar between 1830 and 1834, after which they lived in England. Six children were born, two of them sons, but both the boys died young. Their mother was conventional in her attitude to the education of girls and they were left largely in the hands of governesses, but later their father guided their studies and in England they mixed with a number of intellectual families.

Maria's first literary work was written jointly with her elder sister Emily. Entitled *Letters from Spain and Barbary*, it was published in 1835 when Maria was only nineteen. In 1841, at the age of twenty-five, she married Thomas William Grey, the nephew of the second Earl Grey, Prime Minister between 1830–34. The marriage was a blow to Emily, but did not put an end to the close relationship between the two sisters. In 1850 they published their first feminist writing *Thoughts on Self-Culture addressed to Women* which was essentially a plea for women's education. In 1853 they published a joint novel, *Passion and Principle*. In 1859 Maria's husband fell ill, and she nursed him until his death in 1864. This marked the end of the first phase of Maria's life, in which a wholly domestic role out of the public eye was enlivened only by an occasional literary excursion. Within a few years however she was to enter a life of public enterprise and even, to a small extent, public controversy.

A few years after her husband's death, in 1868, Maria published another novel *Love's Sacrifice* but this was to be the last of her purely literary endeavours. She became active in the Charity Organization Society and in 1870 sought, although unsuccessfully, election to the London School Board. She also became involved in the women's suffrage movement and wrote a pamphlet 'Is the Exercise of the Suffrage Unfeminine?' in which she attacked arguments against the role of women in public life.

It was in the world of education, however, that both she and Emily were to be most deeply involved. In 1871 the two sisters launched the National Union for the Improvement of the Education of Women of all Classes, better known as the Women's Education Union. This in turn launched, in 1873, the Girls' Public Day School Company and in 1876 the Teachers' Training and Registration Society. The aim of the Women's Education Union was not only to provide a low-cost but efficient education for girls, but also to improve the social conditions of teachers. Later, a model teacher-training college was founded, the Maria Grey Training College, named in honour of her contribution.

Her involvement in the education movement led to friendships with women like Emily Davies, Dorothea Beale and Josephine Butler, whose work was deeply admired by Maria although she herself did not take part in it. She also continued to take considerable interest in the suffrage campaign although it was always peripheral to her main work for education. In 1877 she wrote another pamphlet, 'The Physical Force Objection to Women's Suffrage', and in 1879, when the National Society for Women's Suffrage issued *Opinions on Women's Suffrage* she was one of the contributors. In 1889 she wrote 'Last Words to Girls on Life in School and After' in which she called on women to become involved in politics.

During the 1880s Maria began to link women's suffrage to social justice. She attacked discrepancies in wealth and began to move in the direction of socialism, a move which caused something of a rift between the two sisters. By 1888 however she was a total invalid and, although she lived on until 1906, her public life was at an end.

Maria Grey's entry into feminism was primarily through an Enlightenment concern for women's right to knowledge. This continued to be central to her feminism and it was in this area that almost all her practical activities were concentrated. Nevertheless her feminism was by no means confined to educational issues and she strongly approved of women's suffrage and of women's entry into both professional employment and public life. Nevertheless this concern for women's rights was combined, somewhat uneasily, with a strong belief in women's moral duties and the central role of motherhood. In her novel *Love's Sacrifice* the heroine spends years in devoted care of her husband, and there is a strong affirmation of the value of a life devoted to the care of others. Similarly, in an article in the *Fortnightly Review* in 1879 she denied that men and women were endowed with completely different qualities but asserted nevertheless that women had prior responsibility for the care of children.

Like quite a number of her contemporaries, therefore, Maria Grey combined a somewhat conservative view of women's mission with a view of women's right to a life of their own that by implication transformed women's position in society. Her own life, too, showed a similar pull between women's duties and women's rights since she spent all her youth and early middle age fulfilling the role first of daughter and then of wife. Only in widowhood, at the age of forty-eight, did she move not only out into the world but into a view of women which emphasised their public rather than their private duties. Maria Grey is chiefly remembered for her contribution to the creation of an efficient system of secondary education for girls, but is equally important for the light she throws on the ambiguities and even the contradictions at the heart of nineteenth-century feminism.

There is a biography of Maria Grey and her sister Emily Shirreff, *Liberators of the Female Mind. The Shirreff Sisters. Educational Reform and the Women's Movement*, Edward W. Ellsworth (London, Greenwood Press, 1979). See also *DNB* 1901–1911, pp. 166–7.

See also SHIRREFF Emily Anne Elizabeth.

GRIMSTONE Mary Lemon c. 1790–?

Mary Grimstone was a poet and novelist who, during the 1830s, became a frequent contributor both to Robert Owen's paper *The New Moral World* and to the Unitarian *Monthly Repository* edited by W. J. Fox. The inadequacy of female education was perhaps her most persistent theme and she also urged both better employment opportunities for women and the adoption of a single moral standard. In an article in *The New Moral World* (21 February 1835) she argued that an improvement in women's education would help to protect them from the seducer's wiles. During 1835 and 1836 she contributed a series of nine 'Sketches of Domestic Life' to the *Monthly Repository* which were designed to illustrate the consequences of the inadequate education available to women. She also contributed an article 'Men and Women' to the *Edinburgh Review* (March 1834) which was reprinted in Robert Owen's *Crisis* (Vol. III, p. 236).

Her earliest publication, a volume of poems entitled *Zayda, A Spanish Tale*, appeared under the pseudonym 'Oscar' in 1820 and was followed by a second volume of verse, *Cleone*, in 1821. In 1830 she published a novel, *Louisa Egerton*, now using the name Mrs Mary Lemon Grimstone. Four more novels followed, the last *The Beauty of the British Alps* in 1840. William Fox much admired her novels, which were reviewed in the *Monthly Repository*, and compared her to Jane Austen. There are no publications after 1840 but she was active during the 1850s and 1860s in the emerging women's rights movement.

Mary Grimstone is known to us only through her writing and we have no details of her personal life. A plea in one of her articles for employment for women condemned to early widowhood suggests the possibility that she may have been such a widow herself, forced to earn her own living by her pen. later she became Mrs Gillies and this may have been why her publications ceased to appear after 1840.

The source of her feminism is unclear although it must have owed a great deal to the lively debate on women during the 1830s both in the Owenite press and in the *Monthly Repository*. Her own circumstances may also have played a part. Although she wrote for Owenite journals she does not appear to have had socialist connections and her ideas seem closer to those of William Fox and to other Unitarian feminists like Harriet Martineau.

The main sources of information on Mary Grimstone are *Tennyson and the Princess. Reflections on an Age*, John Killham (London, University of London Press, 1958) and *The Dissidence of Dissent. The Monthly Repository 1806–1838*, Francis E. Mineka (New York, Octagon Books, 1972). There is also a brief reference in *Eve and the New Jerusalem. Socialism and Feminism in the Nineteenth Century*, Barbara Taylor (London, Virago, 1983).

See also FOX William Johnson, and MARTINEAU Harriet.

H

HAMILTON Cicely 1872–1952

Cicely Hamilton, an actress and playwright, was born Cicely Mary Hammill, and later adopted the name Hamilton. Her father commanded a Highland regiment and the four children, two girls and two boys, spent much of their childhood 'farmed-out' while their parents were abroad. Her unhappy experiences contributed in later life to a distrust of marriage and motherhood, especially since her happiest times were with two spinster aunts. For a while she was at a boarding school in Malvern, where she learned to love acting, and later spent some time at a school in Germany. When she was eighteen her father died suddenly of malaria and the family, never very well-to-do, found themselves in poverty. The youngest child, a boy, was kept at school for a few years with the help of relatives, and the rest of the children had to start to earn their own living. Cicely became a pupil-teacher which she hated, and soon abandoned it to try to realise her dream of going on the stage. After a period of struggle, during which she supported herself by translating, she found work with a series of touring companies. This enabled her to experience at first hand the struggle a single woman had to make to secure economic independence. The pay of an actress was lower than that of an actor, and twice during the course of her life on tour she was thrown out of work to make room for a manager's mistress.

Eventually, realising she would never achieve her ambition as an actress, she turned to writing, attempting both short stories and plays. When one short play was performed however she was advised to conceal her sex since as a woman she was bound to get a bad press. Finally her play *Diana of Dobson's* brought her recognition as a playwright. It was at this time that she began to be drawn actively into the suffrage movement. For a short while she was a member of the Women's Social and Political Union but disliked its autocratic atmosphere and its emotionalism, and left it for the more democratic Women's Freedom League. She also, with some misgivings, joined the Women's Tax Resistance League. She was happiest however in the Women Writers' Suffrage League which she helped to found. She wrote two propaganda plays: a *Pageant of Great Women* for the suffrage exhibition of 1910 and *How the Vote was Won*, a comedy about a general strike of women, which had its debut in 1909. She also wrote the words for Ethel Smythe's *March of the Women*.

Perhaps her most important and long-lasting contribution was her influential *Marriage as a Trade*, published in 1909. This was a powerful defence of women's need for independence and a refutation of the view that a woman only exists in her relationship to a man, as wife, mother or mistress. She argued that women were brought up to look for success only in the marriage market and this expectation governed every single aspect of their lives, hindering both their intellectual and their moral development. By making marriage a choice for women and not an economic necessity, all women would be set free. She herself had grown up expecting to be married, but even as a child had resented the limitations marriage and motherhood would place on her ambitions, and when marriage failed to materialise she clearly had no regrets, rejoicing rather that her happiness did not depend on the good nature of another person.

After the war Cicely Hamilton settled down to a career of freelance journalism, although she also continued to write a succession of books and plays, including several novels and a series of travel books based on journeys through Europe. She continued her interest in feminist issues, writing for *Time and Tide*, then an important feminist journal, and becoming a member of the Open Door Council, an organisation formed for the purpose of opposing protective legislation for women. She also became a vigorous champion of voluntary motherhood, emphasising the need for improved facilities not only for birth control but also for abortion. Her memoirs, published in 1935, show that her feminism had by no means abated over the years.

Cicely Hamilton's feminism was at bottom an argument against women's dependency on men and was much more therefore than a straightforward demand for greater opportunities for women. Even the vote she regarded as in itself of no very great importance. She saw that women's dependence had crippled their lives, and she wanted above all to free them from that burden. Moreover, in her unsentimental and indeed cynical view of love and marriage she looks forward in many respects to the critique of romantic love put forward by many modern feminists. Standing aloof from the emotional involvement of the militant suffragettes, she made use instead of the literary weapons of wit and ridicule to present her case for voluntary marriage and against what she called the secondary existence of women.

The main source on Cicely Hamilton's life is her own book *Life Errant* (London, J.M. Dent, 1935). See also *Women of Ideas*, Dale Spender (London, Routledge and Kegan Paul, 1982) and *A Literature of their Own*, Elaine Showalter (London, Virago, 1978). There is a full list of her publications in *Who Was Who 1952*. Her book *Marriage as a Trade* originally published in 1909 (London, Chapman and Hall) has been reprinted (London, The Woman's Press, 1981).

HARDIE Keir 1856–1915

Keir Hardie, one of the founders of the Labour Party, was born in Lanarkshire, his mother a farm servant, his father unknown. Later his mother married David Hardie, a ship's carpenter who became a miner. A heavy drinker, David Hardie did not prove a satisfactory husband, and Keir Hardie and his six stepbrothers and two stepsisters grew up in poverty. Forced to start work at only eight years of age, he was often the breadwinner when his stepfather was unemployed. He retained, however, a deep admiration for his mother.

Keir Hardie grew up with a powerful urge for self-improvement. He attended night school and acquired a passion for reading, especially on literary and historical themes. His first cause was temperance, and in 1877 he joined the Evangelical Union, becoming a leading lecturer and organiser for the temperance movement. Drink, at this time, was seen by him as the root cause of human weakness. At the same time he was increasingly attracted by the trade union movement. In 1879 he married Lillie Watson, a Lancashire girl. Patient and hard-working, she was nevertheless not a suitable wife for the man Keir Hardie was to become, lacking understanding both of his political ambitions and his intellectual and emotional needs. There were three children, two sons, James and Duncan, and a daughter Agnes.

By this time Keir Hardie was no longer a working collier. For a time he kept a small shop, while spending most of his time trying to establish himself as a journalist. His political views were still deeply influenced by his temperance and he was a Liberal rather than a socialist. In 1886 he accepted the secretaryship of the Ayrshire Miners' Union, and from this time his opinions took a more radical and militant direction. He began to turn against the Liberal Party as the best way for working-class representatives to enter Parliament, and advocated instead working-class independence through a new Labour Party. His view of socialism however remained largely romantic and utopian, driven by a vision of a new and more moral society.

In 1892 his political ambitions, which had been slowly developing, came to fruition when he was elected to Parliament on a Lib-Lab vote. He lost his seat in 1895 but was returned for Merthyr in 1900. He was influential in the founding of the Independent Labour Party in 1893 and remained a dominant figure in its leadership, although his relationships with other ILP leaders like Philip Snowden and Ramsay Macdonald were often strained. A stubborn, proud isolated man, he remained to a large extent a political outsider.

Meanwhile his marriage was increasingly unsatisfactory to him. His work as a trade-union organiser had involved him in frequent absences from home, and these were intensified by his entry into Parliament. In 1893 he had an intense but probably innocent relationship with Annie Hines, the daughter of an Oxford Fabian, in which he poured out to her his personal unhappiness and his disillusionment with his marriage. This, though short-lived, was the first of several such relationships, of which his love for Sylvia Pankhurst was the most important.

Keir Hardie had been a close friend and political associate of Emmeline and Richard Pankhurst during the 1890s and his friendship with Emmeline and her children continued after her husband's death, although it is highly unlikely that he ever felt more for her, or she for him, than admiration. Through this friendship he was drawn into active involvement with the Women's Social and Political Union from its earliest days, since, unlike some members of the ILP, he was already sympathetic to the suffrage cause. In 1903 he helped to publish Christabel's *The Citizenship of Women: a plea for Women's Suffrage* and in the following year came out at the party conference as a committed supporter of the WSPU policy of a limited suffrage. From this time on his support did not waver, and he was one of the militant movement's most sympathetic allies in Parliament, pleading their cause to the House, protesting at their treatment in prison, and the cruelties of forcible feeding and the Cat and Mouse Act.

His most important battle however was inside the party, where no one fought harder than he did to get women's suffrage accepted as party policy. Most of his colleagues were either indifferent or found it acceptable only as an aspect of adult suffrage, and were opposed to a limited franchise for women (which Keir Hardie supported) as a threat to the Labour vote. Consequently he found little sympathy within the party, especially after the WSPU adopted the policy of opposition to Liberal and Labour candidates in protest at the refusal of the government to support their cause. This breach between the Labour Party and the WSPU was a great disappointment to Keir Hardie, but he did not abandon his efforts and in 1907 even threatened to leave the party in his distress at their lack of sympathy for the women's case. Later, in 1910, he supported the Conciliation Bill which attempted unsuccessfully to find a formula acceptable to all the parties, and later, when adult suffrage seemed a political possibility, he tried to persuade the Labour Party to vote against any extension of the franchise that did not include women.

The breach between the Labour Party and the WSPU also caused a rift in the friendship between Keir Hardie and Emmeline and Christabel Pankhurst, since they blamed him for his failure to convince his colleagues. Only Sylvia remained close to him and, indeed, their affection for one another deepened considerably during these years, and by 1911 they had a passionate relationship which, as their letters reveal, clearly had a sexual as well as an emotional side. Sylvia's involvement in militancy and her sufferings in her periods of imprisonment caused him deep distress and gave an added poignancy to his accusations against government policy.

By this time, however, he was failing in both health and spirits. In 1903 an attack of appendicitis had weakened him, and in 1907 a complete breakdown in health had necessitated a world tour. The growing militarism saddened him, and the actual outbreak of war in 1914 may have contributed to the stroke which left him a permanently sick man. Now totally alienated from Emmeline and Christabel Pankhurst, he was still close to Sylvia, and she was one of the last visitors he received before his death in September 1915.

Keir Hardie's Labour colleagues tended to attribute his commitment to women's suffrage to his friendship with the Pankhurst family, and this influence on his attitude cannot be discounted. It does not explain away his feminism, however, which was part of a more general attitude to both women and socialism. His search for a relationship with a woman which combined intellectual, emotional and sexual aspects reveals a romantic attitude to marriage common amongst male feminists which looked to a companionship based on equality between the sexes as the ideal. He also saw women's suffrage as part of a more general movement towards moral reform and a new and purified society. Consequently he looked forward to women's greater participation in social and political life. As a socialist too, he was essentially reformist so that he perceived a limited suffrage for women as a step towards a widening of the franchise for both sexes. In this respect his socialism still retained much of nineteenth-century Radicalism just as it still retained something of nineteenth-century evangelicalism. For this reason he was able to see a harmony between socialism and feminism not shared by some of his colleagues, which goes a long way to explain his total commitment to the suffrage cause.

The biography *Keir Hardie. Radical and Socialist*, Kenneth O. Morgan (London, Weidenfeld and Nicholson, 1975) deals fully and sympathetically with his feminism, which is often ignored, as for example, in the *DNB* entry Vol. 1912-21 pp. 239-40. For a subjective account of their relationship see *The Suffragette Movement*, Sylvia Pankhurst (London, Longmans, 1931; Virago, 1977). For Keir Hardie's own views see *The Citizenship of Women: A Plea for Women's Suffrage*, Parliamentary Debates, Fourth Series Vol. CLXIV, pp. 511-12 (1905).

See also PANKHURST Sylvia.

HICKS Amelia (Amie) Jane 1839/40-1917

Amie Hicks was the daughter of a Chartist and as a child came under the influence of her father's mother. Nothing is known of her early life, but in 1865, by this time married to William James Hicks, she emigrated with him to New Zealand, where she worked as a rope-maker. Her husband's occupation at that time is not known, although later he worked as a pianoforte maker. In the early 1880s the family, now with six children, returned to England where they settled in London. Soon Amie, her husband and the three eldest children were active in the Social Democrat Federation where they remained even after the breakaway of the Socialist League. Amie was elected to its executive committee and became very active as an open-air speaker. In both 1885 and 1888 she contested the London School Board elections as an SDF candidate but both times was unsuccessful.

Although the SDF was not noted for its feminism, Amie Hicks seems to have interested herself closely in issues concerning women. At that time a midwife, she was also a member of the Ladies Medical College. In 1885 she took an active part in the campaign which preceded the repeal, in 1886, of the Contagious Diseases Acts which, in order to protect the Armed Forces against venereal disease, required the compulsory examination and treatment of women believed to be prostitutes. She wrote two letters to the journal *Justice* on the issue. The first, published on the 1 August 1855, was called 'Lust and Legislation'. The second, published on 29 August, was a defence of prostitutes. Earlier in the same year she had written on the theme 'Women and Socialism' and this letter was published in the journal on the 25 April.

Interested particularly in working women, she helped in 1889 to form the Women's Trade Union Association, an organisation to help women and girls form trade unions. This was something of a rival to the older Women's Trade Union League, whose members were in fact forbidden to join the association. In 1889, too, she was elected secretary of the East London Rope-makers Union, on the strength of her experience in New Zealand. As secretary she gave evidence to the Royal Commission on Labour in 1891, testifying to the unhealthy and immoral conditions of the trades. She pleaded for women factory inspectors, medical inspection of women at work, and the government regulation of profits and wages. For a few months she represented the rope-makers on the London Trades Council, but was asked to leave because she had had no experience in the trade in England.

In 1884 the Women's Trade Union Association was broadened to become the Women's Industrial Council. Its intention was to set up specialised committees and to conduct enquiries. Amie Hicks served on its executive committee until 1908, her special interest being working girls' clubs, which aimed at the industrial education of the girls, and especially their knowledge of industrial law. She continued her association with the Women's Industrial Council until 1910, and in her last years was vice-president of the National Organisation of Girls' Clubs.

A firm supporter of the need for forms of protective legislation for women, she pressed for a prohibition on factory work for women for six weeks before and after confinement. The injurious effect on women's earnings was to be counteracted by a grant of maintenance from a state maintenance department. In 1896, as a result of her pressure a resolution to this effect was carried unanimously by the Socialist and Trades Union International Congress.

Her enthusiasm for socialism was shared by her family, which seems to have been an exceptionally close one, and both husband and children involved themselves in political work. Her daughter Frances was associated closely with her, acting as secretary to the London Tailoresses' Union. She was also elected to the London Trades Council in 1893 and the Technical Education Board of the LCC in 1894. In 1895 she became the first secretary of the Women's Industrial Council but left after a few months to marry. She continued, however, to serve the council in various ways.

During the 1890s Margaret Bondfield and her brother Frank came to know the Hicks family very well, lodging for a time with Frances Hicks, by then Mrs James. Margaret Gladstone, later to be the wife of Ramsay Macdonald, was also a friend of the family. Herself of middle-class origin, Margaret Gladstone was deeply inspired by Amie Hicks who represented for her all that was best in working-class women and the working-class family. Margaret Bondfield tells in her memoirs that it was in the Hicks' garden that Margaret Gladstone informed her of her forthcoming marriage.

Amie Hicks was most active in the 1880s and 1890s when she played a leading part in the movement to improve the working conditions of women and girls in industry. A working-class woman whose roots went back to Chartism, she introduced a genuinely working-class element into the largely middle-class world of the Women's Industrial Council, and her espousal of protective legislation was designed to protect and not to limit the opportunities of women. She died in 1917 after a long illness.

The main source of information on Amie Hicks is the entry in the *DLB* Vol. IV. pp. 89–92. There is a brief mention of her in *A Life's Work*, Margaret Bondfield (London, Hutchinson, 1949) and also in *Margaret Ethel MacDonald. A Memoir*, J. Ramsay MacDonald (London, Allen and Unwin, 1912).

See also BONDFIELD Margaret Grace, MACDONALD Margaret Ethel.

HUBBACK Eva Marian 1886–1949

Eva Hubback, Parliamentary Secretary to the National Union of Societies for Equal Citizenship, was born Eva Spielman, the eldest daughter of a Jewish family living in London. Her mother, Gertrude, was the daughter of George Raphael, a millionaire banker. She was brought up largely in the nursery where her nurse's preference for her brothers may have contributed to her later feminism. A solemn, rather lonely child, she showed from an early age considerable determination to succeed. She was conventionally educated at private schools and at a finishing school in Paris, followed by the social life appropriate to her background, but she had conceived the ambition to go to Cambridge. At first this idea was opposed by her parents, but later they consented and in 1905 she entered Newnham College, enrolling for the economics tripos.

Cambridge life was a tremendous change for her, since for the first time she moved out of the Jewish circle in which she had been born. She had a great capacity for making friends and this was now given full scope. Amongst her wide circle of friends, of both sexes, was Bill Hubback who later became her husband, although her emotional involvement at this time was with another man. She joined the Fabian Society, at this time strongly feminist, and became both a feminist and a socialist, although she was never to be very deeply involved in party politics. She was, however, elected to the LCC as a Labour candidate in 1945.

She left Cambridge with a first-class degree and, back at home, was drawn into social work. Her parents were themselves deeply involved in public service, her father having a very strong interest in the care of homeless and delinquent boys so that unlike her attendance at Cambridge her social work did not mean any break with tradition. She worked as an organiser of Care Committee work for the LCC and in 1910 was elected a Poor Law guardian for Paddington. Meanwhile her friendship with Bill Hubback deepened. Two years older, Bill Hubback was the son of a Liverpool corn merchant. More of an intellectual and less of a social reformer than Eva, his approach to life was less moralistic and more casual. In 1910 they became engaged, although there was some family opposition to the idea of a 'mixed' marriage. In 1911 they married, and their first child Diana was born in 1912. A second daughter Rachel followed in 1914 and a son David in 1916. A year later Bill, who had joined the Army in 1915, was killed in action and Eva's brief marriage was over. As a result of this tragedy of war, Eva Hubback was to spend the next ten years in the service of the women's movement.

Although she had joined the Women's Social and Political Union, Eva had strong doubts about militancy and soon withdrew her active support. She still attended suffrage meetings but her main concern at this time was with social work, and especially social reform. After her husband's death, faced with the need to earn her living, she obtained employment with the National Union of Societies for Equal Citizenship, working at first as its information bureau. In 1920 she became parliamentary secretary, a post of vital importance since it was her task to press for legislation to implement NUSEC policy. The aims at this time, immediately after the war, were equal pay and opportunities; an equal moral standard in both divorce and prostitution; pensions for widows; an equal franchise, which was then limited to women over thirty; the opening of the legal profession to women; and equal guardianship of children. Her main assistants in this work were Eleanor Rathbone, Elizabeth Macadam, NUSEC's honorary secretary, and Mary Stocks.

By no means all of these aims were of course realised by NUSEC, or indeed have been achieved to this day, but a surprising number did, in Eva Hubback's capable hands, pass into law. Most of her work was in and around Parliament and, apart from lobbying, she had to find parliamentary sponsors for the Bills NUSEC wished to promote. As well as parliamentary secretary, she was also general secretary, supervising the office, helping to edit the weekly paper *The Woman's Leader*, and organising summer schools and conferences.

The Bill for which she bore the greatest personal responsibility was the Matrimonial Causes Act of 1923 which provided equal grounds for divorce. She was also deeply concerned in the long campaign which ended with the Guardianship of Infants Act of 1925 which gave equal rights to the mother. Other legislation which she worked on included the Widows, Orphans and Old Age Contribution Act of 1925 and the Summary Jurisdiction (Separation and Maintenance) Act, also of 1925, which improved the position of the wife with regard to separation.

In 1927, feeling the need for a change, she applied for and obtained the post of principal of Morley College and, although she retained her membership of NUSEC, her interests from this time on turned to issues which had little to do with feminism. Indeed, convinced by this time that most of the legal changes had been achieved, she believed that the way forward for NUSEC was through a purely educational programme. Taking the Women's Institutes as her model she proposed, and NUSEC eventually accepted, a nation-wide system of women's clubs, to be known as Townswomen's Guilds which would aim at teaching ordinary women comradeship, arts and crafts, and citizenship.

Eva Hubback had always supported Eleanor Rathbone's scheme for family endowment, which had also become NUSEC policy. Intended by Eleanor Rathbone as essentially feminist in its implications, she saw it not only as a way of increasing the financial independence of the wife but also as giving her greater power in the family. By the end of the 1930s however Eva Hubback was beginning to see it as primarily an aspect of population policy which was itself coming to seem more and more important to her. In 1938 she argued that peace was the first objective of the women's movement, followed by the preservation and welfare of the racial stock, leaving the removal of economic inequality between men and women in only the third place. Other issues which concerned her during the 1930s were also removed from the feminism which had occupied her during the 1920s. Foremost amongst these issues was the Association for Education in Citizenship, and she was closely associated with its first publication *Education for Citizenship in Secondary Schools*. She was also one of the founders of the Children's Minimum Council whose intention was to improve the social services affecting children.

During the 1940s she continued to be preoccupied with the issue of population. Her influential book *The Population of Britain* (1947) betrays an uneasy relationship between her feminism and her anxiety at the fact of population decline. Although she wished to maintain freedom of choice for women, and condemned marriage bars, she wanted at the same time to strengthen all those forces which imposed on women the belief that the bearing and raising of children was their principal and most rewarding function. Schools, for example, should impress on girls in particular the importance of family life, and the teaching of child care should be compulsory. She emphasised the need to improve the facilities for mothers, and advocated family allowances and day nurseries. She also believed that husbands should be encouraged to play a larger part in the care of their children. Nevertheless she made it quite clear that economic independence for women should come about not by greater job opportunities but by adequate family allowances. A professional career, indeed, might be dangerous if it tempted a woman to limit the size of her family. Throughout the book there is an emphasis not only on the significance of motherhood, but on the happiness to be obtained from a large rather than a small family.

Although grounded in her anxiety about population trends, and also in her acceptance of eugenic principles, this idealisation of family life seems also to have been a consequence of her own personal experience of loss. She loved children and had hoped for a family of six. Although she never seems to have considered another marriage, she did, during her fifties, enjoy a brief but deeply satisfying friendship with Charles Grave, a *Punch* artist. This ended with his death in 1941, which Eva Hubback's daughter described as the greatest personal sorrow of her mother's life. Afterwards she was often depressed and came to feel that her widowhood had robbed her of the most important things in a woman's life, a mood accentuated by her sorrow at the death of her mother not long before her own death in 1949. Just before she died she embarked on a study of housewives, and far from chronicling their discontent as a modern generation of feminists have done, was delighted to discover the extent of their satisfaction.

By the end of her life, therefore, Eva Hubback had moved a long way from feminism and there are, indeed, in many of her ideas, the seeds of that 'feminine mystique' which, in the 1950s, was to penetrate most thinking about women in both Britain and the United States and which was essentially anti-feminist in its implications. The problems faced by Eva Hubback arose partly from her own situation, which led to an over-sentimentalised picture of the family, and partly from weaknesses within feminism itself. The nineteenth-century movement had looked mainly to legislation for the solution to its problems and, as Eva Hubback correctly realised, most of the issues that remained could not be resolved by a simple change in the law. What she, and the rest of her generation, failed to realise was the extent to which further change depended on a radical reappraisal of the family itself.

The main source for Eva Hubback's life is the biography by her daughter Diana Hopkinson, *Family Inheritance. A life of Eva Hubback* (London, Staples Press, 1954). For her part in the foundation of the Townswomen's Guild see *Organization Woman*, Mary Stott (London, Heinemann, 1978).

See also RATHBONE Eleanor, STOCKS Mary Danvers.

J

JAMESON Anna Brownell 1794-1860

Anna Jameson, a writer, was the first child of Dennis Murphy, an Irish artist, and his English wife. Her father, a witty and convivial man and a good talker, was never in a position to provide adequately for his family of five daughters. Indeed Anna became a governess at the age of sixteen and continued in this work for fifteen years. In the winter of 1820-1 she met Robert Jameson, a young man four years her junior and an engagement quickly followed, but was broken off by Anna shortly afterwards. Eventually, and in spite of her misgivings, the engagement was resumed and they were married in 1825. At first sight the marriage seemed a highly suitable one, since they had many artistic and literary interests in common and he was, besides, sincerely interested in her writing and did all he could to encourage her. Nevertheless the marriage proved a failure from the start. There is some evidence that it was never consummated and certainly there was an incompatibility of temperament which made it impossible for them to be happy together. There were also financial problems and in 1829 Robert Jameson took up an appointment on the Island of Dominica which began a separation between them which was eventually to prove permanent.

Meanwhile Anna was gradually making a name for herself as a writer. Her first book, *The Diary of an Ennuyée*, published shortly after her marriage, was a fictionalised travel-biography based on a tour of Europe she had undertaken as a governess. She followed this with *Loves of the Poets* in 1829 and *Celebrated Female Sovereigns* in 1831. A study of Shakespeare's heroines, published in 1832, for the first time showed clear indications of a fairly discreet feminist propaganda in her judgements on Shakespeare's female characters.

In 1832 Robert Jameson returned to England and he and Anna lived together for several months before he left again to take up an appointment as attorney general in Upper Canada. Anna however remained behind, where she was becoming something of a celebrity both in England and in Germany where she made a number of friends, including Ottilie von Goethe, Goethe's daughter-in-law. Another close friend at this time was Robert Noel, a cousin of Lady Byron, which led to a friendship between the two women and the involvement of Anna Jameson in some of Lady Byron's philanthropic interests. Meanwhile her husband was urging her to join him, and in 1836 she made the decision to go to Canada, but any possibility of a reconciliation was quickly dispelled. She could not bear the social isolation of a frontier society in which there was no appreciation of literature or art, and, although her husband had begged her to come, he seemed unable to show her the tenderness and consideration which her affectionate nature needed and which might have made her stay tolerable. A separation was mutually agreed and Robert Jameson made her an allowance of £300 a year. They parted in 1837, never to see each other again.

In 1838 Anna Jameson published a record of her American travels. Entitled *Winter Studies and Summer Rambles in Canada*, this was her first work to deal quite explicitly with the position of women, and was, indeed, condemned by a number of reviewers for its feminist stance. Although ostensibly dealing with the American Indians, she made it plain that they sometimes occupied a more honest and honourable position than their more civilised sisters. In particular she condemned an ideal of woman as existing solely as a happy wife and mother when thousands of women could be neither, and she demanded an improvement in women's education to fit them for useful employment.

Although the book was on the whole well received, it was followed by a period of severe financial difficulty, caused mainly by the illness and later the death of her father in 1842, and her need to be a support to the rest of the family. Often unhappy, her active feminism increased considerably, and during the 1840s she began to publish articles dealing explicitly with feminist issues. In 1843 she contributed an article to the *Athenaeum* under a man's name which reviewed the recent Royal Commission's report on the Employment of Women and Young People, in which she demanded increased educational facilities for women. Her move towards a genuinely feminist point of view is well illustrated by her argument that attempts at reforming the position of women always foundered because they were thought to interfere with the privileges of husband and father. In 1846 a pamphlet on the *Relative Position of Mothers and Governesses* also made the feminist point that the position of the governess was devalued by the inferior status and also the inferior education of women generally. Meanwhile she was rapidly making a name for herself as a writer on art. Her many books on the subject not only ensured her a reputation but were an important source of income.

It was during the 1850s that her feminism entered its most active phase. In 1851 her husband, who had become an alcoholic, was retired from his position as vice-chancellor of Upper Canada and ceased to pay his wife her allowance. In 1854 he died, and in his will excluded her from any share in his estate. Anna was bitter at this turn of events and this may have increased her sense of the injustice suffered by women generally. She became the virtual sponsor and patroness of a group of women which included Adelaide Proctor and Bessie Rayner Parkes, and provided support and encouragement in their work to improve the employment prospects of women. She also backed Barbara Leigh Smith's attempt to change the law with respect to the property and earnings of married women. Moreover, two public lectures, *Sisters of Charity* in 1855 and *The Communion of Labour* in 1856, which were later published, were to be a source of inspiration to many other women.

In these two lectures Anna Jackson set out very clearly the nature and limits of her feminism. She did not believe in, or press for, strict equality between the sexes and indeed believed that their function was different, with the ordering of domestic life and maternity the province of women and political life the domain of men. Nevertheless she made a powerful plea for more opportunities for women to be useful in the world, both in order to support themselves when it was necessary and to bring their civilising influence into play in fighting the evils prevailing in society. The lectures were also a powerful condemnation of the double standard of morality, since she argued that what is morally wrong for one sex is morally wrong for the other.

Anna Jameson was, therefore, a significant part of the feminist movement of the 1850s, although her own activity was gradually curtailed by a breakdown in her health. Undoubtedly her particular brand of feminism was a reflection of her own personal experience, and she was well aware of the limitations in her education and the difficulties faced by a woman who needed to earn her own living. On the whole she was a conventional person who took pains to maintain her reputation intact, aware of the dangers facing a married woman living apart from her husband. Her feminism too was conventional in character and, unlike the Owenite feminists of the same period, she made no claims for any revolutionary change in society, speaking chiefly for those women who were forced by circumstances to live an independent life. Nevertheless her own independence was to some extent a matter of choice and there is no doubt that she also represented that aspect of nineteenth-century feminism which sought self-expression rather than dependence.

The main biography of Anna Jameson is *Love and Work Enough. The Life of Anna Jameson*, Clara Thomas (London, Macdonald, 1967). There is also an earlier biography, *Memoirs of the Life of Anna Jameson*, Geraldine Macpherson (London, 1878). See also *Anna Jameson. Letters and Friendships* ed. Mrs Steuart Erskine (London, T. Fisher Unwin, 1915). For a recent account of her as an art writer see 'Anna Jameson 1794–1860). Sacred Art and Social Vision' by Adela M. Holcomb in *Women as Interpreters of the Visual Arts 1820–1979*, Claire Richtal Sherman and Adela M. Holcomb (London, Greenwood Press, 1981). There is an entry in *DNB* Vol. XXIX, pp. 230–2.

See also BELLOC Bessie Rayner and PROCTOR Adelaide Anne.

JEWSON Dorothea (Dorothy) 1884–1964

Dorothy Jewson was the daughter of Alderman George Jewson, JP, a wealthy coal and timber merchant, and Mary Jane Jarrold. Born in Norwich, where the family were well-known Liberals, she was educated at Norwich High School and later at Cheltenham College and Girton College, Cambridge, where she took the classical tripos in 1907. She went on to Cambridge Training College for Teachers and was an assistant mistress at a Richmond school from 1908–11. In 1911 she returned to Norwich where she became an assistant at a local school, and also joined with her brother in a large-scale enquiry into poverty in Norwich. She had become interested in Fabian socialism at Girton but later joined the Independent Labour Party. At some time during these years she also became a militant suffragette, although we do not know how she was led into this, or the actual extent of her involvement.

In 1916, at the invitation of Mary Macarthur, she left her teaching career to become an organiser for the National Federation of Women Workers, where she was associated closely with Margaret Bondfield. In 1921, when the NFWW amalgamated with the National Union of General and Municipal Workers she worked for its newly formed women's section. In 1923 she was elected as a Labour MP for Norwich, and, although defeated in 1924, contested the seat unsuccessfully in 1929 and 1931. Although her ambitions to serve in Parliament were therefore frustrated, she continued to be active in local politics and served on the City Council from 1929 to 1936.

Unlike some Labour women who entered Parliament, Dorothy Jewson never allowed her feminism to be submerged in her socialism. In her maiden speech she seconded a resolution to bring down the voting age for women to twenty-one. She also spoke in the debate in 1924 on the guardianship of infants, making it clear that this was for her a further step in the achievement of equal citizenship rights between men and women. She was an early supporter of family allowances at a time when there was considerable hostility to the idea from many in the trade-union movement. She raised the issue at both the 1928 and 1929 ILP conferences, arguing that it would not only alleviate poverty but raise purchasing power, and so help to relieve the depression.

It was the issue of birth control, however, which demonstrated most clearly the extent to which feminism directed her socialism. She was converted to the idea by Stella Browne in 1923, and became president of the Workers' Birth Control Group which was formed in 1924 with Dora Russell as secretary. At this time welfare centres were forbidden to give birth-control advice, and one of the main objects of the group was to change the government ruling in order to make such advice available to those working-class women who needed it. Apart from her activities for the group, Dorothy Jewson also took a leading part in the campaign to convert the Labour Party. At the Labour Party Conference in 1926 she seconded a resolution moved by Dora Russell asking for a commitment to the right of welfare centres to give birth-control advice. The executive committee produced no less a person than Ramsay MacDonald to oppose them, and his argument that it was not a political decision was used to prevent birth control being made an issue of party policy in spite of the very strong feelings expressed by women's groups in both the Labour and the Co-operative movement. As in the case of abortion later, the Labour leaders were frightened to antagonise the powerful Roman Catholic vote, but there were also many socialists, especially those influenced by Marxism, who saw the issue of birth control as an unnecessary irrelevance in the fight for socialism.

In 1936 Dorothy Jewson married R. Tanner Smith, but he died shortly afterwards in 1939. In 1945 she married again, this time Campbell Stephen, MP for Camlachie, but his death in 1947 ended her second marriage. She herself lived on until the age of eighty in 1964. Her own involvement in politics seems to have ended in the late 1930s, although it is recorded of her that she never lost her youthful enthusiasm. An ardent and life-long pacifist, she was in opposition to both world wars, and her pacifism led her into the Society of Friends.

Never a leading figure in either the feminist or Labour movements, Dorothy Jewson is interesting because she attempted to combine both feminism and socialism. Although a militant suffragette she did not, as many did, abandon the Labour Party. Moreover, in the 1920s she tried to carry feminist politics into the Labour movement even though that meant standing out against the Labour Party leadership. In her advocacy of birth control, in particular, she showed both courage and independence and it is a pity that so much of her life is unknown to us.

There is an entry for Dorothy Jewson in the *DLB* Vol. V, pp. 119–21. Her activities in the birth-control movement are described briefly in *A New World for Women*, Sheila Rowbotham (London, Pluto Press, 1977). There is also a brief mention in *The Movement for Family Allowances 1918–45*, John Macnicol (London, Heinemann, 1980).

JEX-BLAKE Sophia 1840–1912

Sophia Jex-Blake, a physician, was the daughter of Thomas Jex-Blake and Maria Emily Cubitt. Her father had been proctor of Doctors' Commons but, by then fifty years of age, was retired at the time of her birth. There were two other surviving children, Thomas William eight years, and Caroline six years her senior. Both her parents came from the landed gentry and were products of evangelical Anglicanism. She was therefore brought up very strictly, even repressively. An active and self-willed child, she was seen by her parents and herself as disobedient, especially in contrast to the much more docile Caroline. Persistent ill-health also gave her mother much less patience with her lively little daughter than she might otherwise have had. Sophia also suffered during the long periods she spent away at school where discipline was often harsh, and she was frequently unhappy. Only later on in her life did her relationship with her mother improve, although, in spite of considerable affection between them, they were in fact happier apart.

In 1858, after hearing about Queen's College from a friend. Sophia resolved to attend its classes herself. At first there was a struggle with her father, but he eventually gave his permission and Sophia found that she enjoyed not only the work itself but the feeling of independence it gave her. For the first time in her life her spirited nature was freed from the repressive discipline which had restrained it. Soon, so fast was her progress that she was offered a tutorship in mathematics. Her parents approved so long as she was not paid and it is entirely characteristic that she challenged her parents on this issue on strictly feminist lines, arguing that they would not have minded if she had been a man.

For the time being, however, her parents' views on pay prevailed and she gave up her salary. Sophia resisted her mother's more general anxiety about the unconventionality of her life as well as any idea of marriage. Indeed, neither at this time nor later was she attracted towards a man, recognising herself that she was drawn towards women. This was demonstrated very clearly in 1860 when she met Octavia Hill. The friendship which developed was at first mutual and plans were made for sharing a house with the Hill family, but Octavia Hill could not for long cope with Sophia's tempestuous nature. There were also problems with Mrs Hill and before the plan could be put fully into operation there was a complete and lasting breach in the relationship.

Deeply hurt, Sophia gave up her lecturing and returned to the comfort of her mother at home, but found no lasting remedy there. Yearning for Octavia, she found consolation eventually in her deepening consciousness of some great work for her to do. She had no interest, as yet, in medicine, and her great desire was to found a college, with perhaps herself as its head, and her various moves at this time were made from a desire to prepare herself for this task. She spent a period of time teaching in Germany, explored the idea of founding a girls' college in Manchester, and eventually, in 1865, after overcoming the opposition of her father, went to the United States. There she studied schools and colleges, including Oberlin, and was impressed by what she saw of co-education. Her experiences were later described in *A Visit to Some American Schools and Colleges*.

The most important consequence of her American visit was her friendship with Dr Lucy Sewell, the resident physician at the New England Hospital for Women and Children. This not only filled, to some extent at least, the gap in her life left by the loss of Octavia Hill, but turned her attention towards the idea of medicine as a career. At first her idea was to train in the United States but the death of her father in 1868 necessitated a return to England. At first she made up her mind that her duty was to stay with her mother, but later, in spite of some anxiety about leaving her mother alone, decided to try to secure a medical education in Britain. She made several approaches to sympathetic men, including one to Henry Sidgwick who advised her against Cambridge, and she finally settled on Edinburgh. Meanwhile she expressed her ideas on medicine as a profession for women in a chapter in Josephine Butler's *Woman's Work and Woman's Culture* (London, 1869).

Sophia Jex-Blake's attempt to storm the citadel of medical education at Edinburgh has often been described. Although she and a few other women started their training quite successfully, opposition mounted. The students, incited by some teachers, expressed their feelings in objectionable behaviour and eventually in a riot which both attracted sympathy for the women's cause and in other quarters hardened opinion against them. Sophia believed that she recognised one of the ring-leaders and in her fury was led into the indiscretion both of naming him and of alleging that he was drunk at the time. He denied his presence and, since she had no proof, he was able to win a libel case against her. Although sympathisers paid her costs, it was widely believed at the time that her action had harmed her cause. Meanwhile the universities were trying to use the law to get rid of what they saw as troublesome and unwelcome students. In 1872 the women appeared to have won their case, but the university appealed, and the final decision went against them, on the grounds that it had not been legal to admit them in the first place. There was no other course open but to admit defeat at Edinburgh and try elsewhere.

Sophia Jex-Blake's next move was to take the battle into Parliament. She secured a number of allies, including Russell Gurney, but she was the moving spirit behind the scenes, supplying facts and arguments and even a draft Bill. Meanwhile she made yet another attempt to qualify, this time through the licence in midwifery of the College of Surgeons, but this was foiled by the examiners who resigned en masse. In August of that year, however, the Russell Gurney Enabling Act empowered all medical examining bodies to examine women. The first to use this was the Irish College of Physicians, and in 1877 Sophia Jex-Blake qualified at Dublin.

While the parliamentary battle was in progress she turned her attention to the idea of a London Medical School for women. Elizabeth Garrett Anderson felt this to be premature, but plans went ahead, with Elizabeth on the council, and, later, as one of its lecturers. Not medically qualified, Sophia had to stay in the background. By 1877 the school was established, and Sophia, newly qualified, hoped that she would be put in charge. Unfortunately her fiery and headstrong nature had made her enemies, including Elizabeth Garrett Anderson herself. The two women had first met in 1862 when Sophia had hoped that they could be friends, but Elizabeth Garrett Anderson's cautious and controlled nature found Sophia too emotional and too outspoken. Sophia's later indiscretions at Edinburgh confirmed this view, and Elizabeth let it be known that she thought Sophia had contributed to the failure to win over the university at Edinburgh. Believing Sophia to be an unsuitable candidate, she let herself be proposed to take charge of the new medical school. Finally, a compromise candidate, Isabel Thorpe, was appointed.

The result was a bitter disappointment to Sophia Jex-Blake who ended all her connections with the London Medical School and retreated to Edinburgh where she established herself in a successful practice. She also founded her own medical school for women which ran for ten years before various difficulties caused it to close. The wider issues of feminism were not forgotten either, and she took an active part in the Edinburgh suffrage campaign as well as encouraging women to be Poor Law Guardians. In 1899 she retired and spent the rest of her life in Tunbridge Wells. Happiness in her private life continued to elude her however, and she was never able to achieve her hope of finding a friend who would share her home. Nor was she ever able to effect a reconciliation with Octavia Hill. Her last attempt was in 1910, only two years before her death, but nevertheless she left Octavia Hill all her property in her will.

Recognised as one of the pioneers in the medical education of women, her life is of interest as much for its failures as its successes. Her early years were a struggle to escape her parents' conventional attitudes to women, and her father's death almost trapped her into abandoning her own life to serve the needs of her mother. She was driven partly by a desire for the independence and self-expression which had been stifled in her by her family and school, partly by her strong religious beliefs which gave her for a long time a sense of personal destiny, although late in life she became virtually an agnostic. She never learned to subdue her impetuous and fiery temper and this caused her great suffering. In particular, it made her something of a loner, standing outside much of mainstream feminist activity and depriving her of the support and encouragement she needed. It is likely, however, that her indiscretions were of less importance than they appeared at the time. It is by no means certain that a more cautious approach would have succeeded where she failed and the controversies she provoked probably did as much to draw sympathisers to her cause as they did to harden her opponents against her. In retrospect, therefore, she stands out as one of the most important pioneers in the field of medical education for women.

The main source is *The Life of Sophia Jex-Blake*, Margaret Todd (London, Macmillan, 1918). For her relationship with Elizabeth Garrett Anderson see *Elizabeth Garrett Anderson*, Jo Manton (London, Methuen, 1965). There is an entry in *DNB* 1912–1921 pp. 297–8.

See also ANDERSON Elizabeth Garrett.

K

KENNEY Annie 1879–1953

Annie Kenney, a leading suffragette, was born near Oldham, the daughter of working-class parents. Her mother, Ann Wood, worked in a cotton mill throughout her married life, in spite of bearing eleven children, and Annie herself, the fifth child, became a half-timer at the age of ten and a full-timer at the age of thirteen. During her years in the mill she lost a finger, torn off by a whirling bobbin. Her father, Nelson Horatio Kenney, was a gentle affectionate man, and her mother, whom Annie greatly admired, was clearly the head of the family.

Annie was glad to leave school, and in her youth was something of a tomboy, but later she turned to serious reading and, by the time she was twenty, had started to read such authors as Walt Whitman and Edward Carpenter. Inspired by Robert Blatchford's writings in *The Clarion*, she joined the Oldham Clarion Vocal Group and it was through this activity that, in 1905, she first became acquainted with Christabel Pankhurst, who was speaking on women's suffrage to the local branch of the Independent Labour Party. This was the first time Annie had heard the case for women's suffrage and she was deeply impressed, not only by the arguments but even more by Christabel herself. A friendship quickly developed between the two, and soon Annie Kenney was a frequent visitor to the Pankhurst home in Manchester. She also, inspired by Christabel, began to take an interest in her trade union, serving on its local committee, and starting a correspondence course at Ruskin College.

Quite soon however she was drawn full-time into the affairs of the Women's Social and Political Union. When Christabel decided to challenge Edward Grey and Winston Churchill on government policy towards women's suffrage Annie Kenney was her chosen companion. Protesting when their question went unanswered, they were hustled out by the stewards, arrested by the police on a charge of assault, and together served the first imprisonment for the suffrage cause. After this Annie Kenney was virtually adopted into the Pankhurst family. She left her work in the mill for good, and was sent to London where she joined several other women already at work, including Christabel's sister Sylvia.

During the next few years there is no doubt of Annie Kenney's happiness. Her trust in the Pankhursts was complete, and she served them with utter devotion. She revelled in the excitement, the comradeship of her fellow organisers, and the friendship of men and women like Keir Hardie, W.T. Stead and above all Frederick and Emmeline Pethick-Lawrence who treated her as if she had been a daughter. Tremendously courageous, living from day to day, even prison held no terrors for her. In 1907 she was sent to Bristol as organiser for the west of England, and there she gained a devoted disciple in Mary Blathwayt of Eagle House. Mary Blathwayt was herself a dedicated suffrage worker, and Eagle House was always open to Annie for rest and recuperation.

The optimism and even lightheartedness of these years was not, however, to last. In 1912, when Christabel Pankhurst fled to Paris to avoid arrest, Annie Kenney was left in charge of the organisation in London. She also became Christabel's go-between, travelling weekly between Paris and London with Christabel's orders. The split between the Pankhursts and the Pethick-Lawrences in that year, over the issue of an extension of militancy, also tried Annie's loyalty almost to breaking point. Not only did she love the Pethick-Lawrences deeply, but she herself had some doubts about the wisdom of Christabel's policy. In the end however she stayed loyal to Christabel, although it clearly hurt her deeply to cut herself off from two of her dearest friends.

In the two years that remained to the militant movement Annie Kenney was the Pankhursts' loyal lieutenant, not only faithfully transmitting orders but taking an active part in the militant action. In 1913 she was sentenced to eighteen months in prison where she went on hunger and thirst strike. Released under the provisions of the Cat and Mouse Act, she adopted several disguises to escape arrest before she was caught, until she eventually became seriously ill from the effects of her imprisonment.

The outbreak of war ended both the militant campaign and the involvement of Christabel and Emmeline Pankhurst in the issue of suffrage. They turned their attention to the war effort and started an anti-Bolshevist campaign against strikes. Annie Kenney continued as their loyal lieutenant all through the war, and only when it was over did she finally break her ties with them. In 1920, now forty-one years of age, she married James Taylor, a civil servant, and they had one child, a son. From this time forward Annie devoted herself to Theosophy which had attracted her for a number of years, and eventually became an official of the Rosicrucian Order. She was joined in this by her sister Jessie who had earlier followed her into the suffrage movement. Although the date of her husband's death is not known, Annie Kenney herself died in 1953.

The tie that bound Annie Kenney to Christabel Pankhurst and thus to the suffrage movement was ultimately a tie of love. She adored Christabel to the end and gave her total loyalty even after she had begun to have doubts about the wisdom of some of the militant tactics. Until Christabel recruited her to the WSPU she was not a political activist in spite of a rather vague attraction to socialist ideas, and it was the magical effect of Christabel's personality which led her into a total commitment to the militant cause. Indeed she herself was aware of the extent to which her approach to feminism was closer to a religious conversion than to a political commitment. Both she and Christabel lost their faith in feminism once the vote was won, and spent the rest of their lives in the search for a religious experience.

Annie Kenney's value to the militant movement lay to a considerable extent in her unquestioning obedience to her leaders, although she also had undeniable talents as a speaker and organiser. She was also important because she was one of the very few WSPU leaders with a genuinely working-class background and this did something to counter the argument that the organisation existed to serve the middle and upper classes. She always retained an unsophisticated charm which appealed greatly to many men and women whose own background was very different. Nevertheless, in spite of her working-class origin, she was never a committed socialist and this enabled her to follow Emmeline and Christabel Pankhurst in their own move away from the Labour Party and towards their anti-strike stand during the war. It is not without significance that her own loyalties to the Pankhursts were strained, although not broken, by her personal allegiance to the Pethick-Lawrences. She was, however, completely unself-seeking and it was perhaps this quality more than any other which made her the perfect lieutenant to Christabel's autocratic but dynamic leadership.

There is no biography of Annie Kenney, but she published her own recollections in *Memories of a Militant* (London, Arnold, 1924). For her relationship with Mary Blathwayt see *A Nest of Suffragettes in Somerset*, B.M. Willmott (Bath, The Batheaston Society, 1979). For the recollections of Emmeline Pethick-Lawrence see her *My Part in a Changing World* (London, Gollancz, 1938). There is an entry in *DNB* 1951–60 pp. 572–3.

See also BLATHWAYT Mary, PANKHURST, Christabel, PETHICK-LAWRENCE Emmeline.

KNIGHT Anne 1792-1862

Anne Knight, an early suffragist, came from a Quaker family and had worked hard in the anti-slavery cause in its earliest years, together with her sister Maria, and her brother-in-law John Cander. It is not clear when she first began to be interested in women's rights, but by 1840 she was in correspondence with the American feminists Angelina and Sarah Grimké and they may have converted her to their views. Her own feminism was, however, deeply affronted by the refusal in June of that year of the World's Anti-Slavery Conference in London to accept the credentials of a small group of American delegates because they were women, and who, in consequence, were banished to the gallery. From this time forward, certainly, Anne Knight became a persistent advocate of women's rights, bombarding her friends and acquaintances with letters and leaflets on women's suffrage.

Nor did she confine herself to the anti-slavery movement. She also lectured on women's rights at both peace and temperance gatherings, and tried, though unsuccessfully, to attend the 1851 peace conference as a delegate. She corresponded with Owenite socialists like John and Catherine Barmby, and with Isaac Ironside, a leading Sheffield socialist who, in 1851, gave her the names of seven Chartist women eager to take action on the suffrage issue. She wrote to them and a month later the Sheffield Female Political Association was formed to work for women's suffrage. It did not survive for long, but it demonstrates the extent of her activity and involvement. One of the pioneers of the women's suffrage movement, her efforts met with little tangible success in her life-time but she deserves to be remembered.

There is a brief biographical reference to Anne Knight in *British and American Abolitionists. An Episode in transatlantic Understanding*, Clare Taylor (Edinburgh, Edinburgh University Press, 1974). See also *'Women's Mission' and Pressure Group Politics in Britain (1825-1860)*, Alex Tyrrell (Manchester, Manchester University Press, 1980); *Eve and the New Jerusalem*, Barbara Taylor (London, Virago, 1983); *Women's Suffrage. A Record of the Movement*, Helen Blackburn (London, Williams and Norgate, 1902); *The Petticoat Rebellion: a Century of Struggle for Women's Rights*, Marion Ramelson (London, Lawrence and Wishart, 1967).

L

LANSBURY George 1859-1940

The son of George Lansbury, a time-keeper working on railway construction, George's early childhood was spent in the nomadic existence of a migrant worker's family. His mother, Mary Ann Ferris, was of Welsh origin and had run away to marry when she was only sixteen. George was the second son of the nine children born before his father's early death in 1875. In 1868, however, the family settled in Whitechapel where his father started a small business unloading trucks, mainly of coal, and when he died George and his brother Jim took over the running of the business. In the same year he met fourteen-year-old Elizabeth or Bessie Jane Brine, and, in spite of opposition from her family who did not think he was good enough for Bessie, they married in 1880.

Politics had always interested George, even as a child, perhaps because of the influence of his Welsh grandmother who was a staunch Radical and non-conformist. As a young boy, he formed the habit of attending open-air political meetings which contributed considerably to his political education. He also came under the influence of the vicar of Whitechapel, the Reverend J. Fenwick Kitto, and joined the Whitechapel Church Young Men's Association. At this time too he was converted to teetotalism, perhaps because both his parents drank heavily, and this remained a life-long practice.

In 1884 he was tempted by the idea of emigrating to Australia and he and Bessie made the journey with their three babies and his young brother whom they had cared for since his mother's death in 1881. His stay was, however, only brief and he returned in 1885, horrified at the high level of unemployment in Australia and the appalling housing and working conditions. It was, however, an important step in his political career, since the campaign he proceeded to wage against the misleading information given to potential immigrants to Australia led directly to his involvement in the work of the local Liberal Association. Soon, however, he began to be attracted by the Social Democratic Federation, and by 1892 had finally broken with the Liberals, although his attempts to stand for Parliament as an SDF candidate in 1894 and 1900 were unsuccessful. He had become a Poor Law Guardian in 1892, and this was the start of an energetic and largely successful campaign to improve the workhouses in his charge, which uncovered not only weaknesses in the law, but many abuses in workhouse administration. In 1905, in recognition of the name he had made for himself, he was appointed as the only working-class member of the Royal Commission on the Poor Law.

In 1910, by now a member of the Independent Labour Party, he was elected to Parliament and at this stage in his career he began his active involvement in the militant suffrage movement. He had first met Emmeline and Richard Pankhurst in 1893 and seems from the first to have been sympathetic to the case for women's rights as part of his general belief in equality. Once in Parliament he entered vigorously into the political battle that the militants were waging against the government. Moreover, he took the woman's side with a fervour unmatched by any other member of Parliament. To his initial intellectual belief in the suffrage cause was now added the emotional impact of the suffering the militants endured. In 1912 there was an open row with Asquith over forcible feeding in which he shook his fist in Asquith's face. Forced to leave the chamber, the incident brought him the delighted approbation of the militants, whose hatred of Asquith was at its peak.

George Lansbury's next step, however, in which he asked the Labour Party to vote against every government measure till the introduction of an official measure for women's suffrage, took him further than the rest of the party in the House were prepared to go. Ordered to toe the party line on the issue, which was committed to oppose the government only if women's suffrage was omitted from a suffrage bill, George Lansbury resigned his seat and fought the resultant election as a woman's suffrage candidate. In the event he was heavily defeated and was not to regain a seat in Parliament till 1922. He himself later recognised that he had acted precipitously and unwisely.

The defeat did not, however, cool his enthusiasm for the suffrage cause. His home became a centre for organising illegal meetings, and his daughter Daisy once disguised herself as Sylvia Pankhurst to allow Sylvia to evade arrest under the Cat and Mouse Act. Moreover, several of his children joined in the window-breaking campaign. Finally, in 1913, after a speech in which he condoned violence against property, he was sent to prison only to be released after a few days. He also tried to advance the suffrage cause in more constitutional ways, arguing the case continuously in the *Daily Herald* of which he was now editor. At the same time he tried to make a private deal with Lloyd George but this was frustrated by the refusal of the Pankhursts to call a truce.

In 1914 the outbreak of war ended the militant movement and also George Lansbury's own crusade for women's suffrage. He turned his attention to other issues, taking a strong anti-war line, and after the war was over waged a successful campaign to prevent war against Russia. It was, however, his part in the battle between Poplar Borough Council and the government over the equalisation of the rates burden which brought him again into public prominence. With his fellow councillors he spent another period in prison in defence of his principles, and, as a result of the popularity his stand had brought him, was returned to Parliament in 1922.

Shortly after his re-election he became converted to the birth-control movement, convinced by the feminist argument that women should be allowed to control what happened to their own bodies. It is likely that the chief influence here was his daughter Dorothy Thurtle, a leading activist in the Workers' Birth Control Group. Her husband Ernest, a Labour MP, was a vice-president of the group, and on its behalf attempted to introduce a Bill on birth control into Parliament. George himself, in spite of a personal feeling that reticence should be observed on matters of sex, took an active part in the campaign, taking up the issue in his paper *Lansbury's Labour Weekly*.

Meanwhile his political career was going forward. In 1928 he was elected chairman of the Labour Party and in 1929 was made First Commissioner of Works with Cabinet rank. One of the few Labour leaders re-elected in 1931, he became leader of the party in the House, but eventually his position was threatened by his pacifism and he resigned his leadership in 1935. The rest of his life was spent in furthering the pacifist cause and in an unavailing attempt to halt the outbreak of the second world war. He died of cancer in 1940, seven years after the death of Bessie.

George Lansbury was one of the very few Labour men in the House of Commons who gave their wholehearted support to the women's suffrage movement. His involvement in the birth-control campaign also came at a time when the Labour Party as a whole was unwilling to come out publicly in its favour. His willingness to put issues of gender before issues of party was a consequence of his hatred of cruelty and oppression rather than a fully worked out adherence to feminist ideology. He was a man of great compassion, as his work as a Poor Law Guardian had already revealed, and it was his indignation at women's wrongs which drove him to embrace the militant cause with such total commitment. In addition he had a remarkable independence of mind, and was totally incapable of going against his principles for the sake of expediency. Once he had made up his mind that a course of action was the right one nothing could move him, and this quality was evident throughout his life until the very end.

Nevertheless, George Lansbury was on

the whole conventional in his attitude to women, and in his long and happy marriage there was a clearly marked division of roles which reflected Victorian rather than feminist values. His wife Bessie bore him twelve children, two of whom died young, and spent her life quietly behind the scenes as a devoted wife and mother. George was a loving husband but his passion for politics condemned her to a life of loneliness which he himself recognised and regretted. According to his son Edgar, he was a home-loving man who did his share of walking the floor at night with troublesome babies but, inevitably, his increasing involvement with politics kept him apart from his wife and family. But Bessie shared his socialist principles and this may have made her sacrifice easier. On women's suffrage there was less accord, and Bessie, who put socialism first, was inclined to resent the presence of the suffragettes in Bow. He was clearly the dominant partner, however, and when he made the decision to resign she came loyally to his support. Indeed it would seem that Bessie herself held traditional views of woman's place.

As a young husband in the 1880s, George Lansbury was strongly opposed to birth control and this attitude is reflected in his own large family. Indeed, there is every indication that, in spite of his general acceptance of the principle of sex equality, in practice George Lansbury gave little attention to feminist issues until he was awakened to the militant campaign in 1912. Even afterwards, with the single exception of birth control, issues like socialism and pacifism tended to hold all his attention. The extent, therefore, to which George Lansbury can truly be called a feminist is open to question. Nevertheless, at a time when most men in the Labour movement were indifferent to women's rights, it would be churlish not to recognise the generosity with which he made the woman's cause his own.

There is a biography, *The Life of George Lansbury* by Raymond Postgate who married his daughter Daisy (London, Longmans, 1951). George Lansbury himself wrote two memoirs, *Looking Backwards and Forwards* (London, Glasgow, Blacker, 1953) and *My Life* (London, Constable, 1928). There is also a memoir by his son Edgar Lansbury, *George Lansbury. My father* (London, Sampson and Low, 1934). For an account of his suffrage involvement see *The Suffragette Movement*, Sylvia Pankhurst (London, Longmans, 1931; London, Virago, 1977). See also *DLB* Vol. II, pp. 214-27 and *DNB* 1931-1940 pp. 524-6.

See also PANKHURST Sylvia.

LAW Harriet Teresa 1831-1897

Harriet Law, a secularist and feminist, was born Harriet Frost, the daughter of a farmer at Ongar, who later fell on hard times and brought his large family to London, where Harriet ran a school to help the family finances. Originally a strict Baptist, she came into contact with Radical free thought when she heard a number of Owenite lecturers in the East End of London. She challenged them to debate but soon her own views began to change. Significantly, in the light of her later career, her first doubts arose from St Paul's injunction to women to be silent in church. In 1855 she married Edward Law, the son of William Law of Newton Abbot, and shortly afterwards they both became secularists. In 1859 or 1860 she began her public career as a lecturer with a regular tour outside London, while her husband and a nurse cared for the children.

During the 1860s she appeared on Reform League, secularist and republican platforms, advocating universal suffrage, women's rights and the destruction of all religious influence. A bluff, stout woman with a loud voice and a good-natured humour, she was a popular lecturer. At one time she was the chief female advocate of secularism but she was later replaced by Annie Besant.

Apart from her work as lecturer, she also ventured into publishing, taking over George Reddall's *Secular Chronicle* in 1876. A penny weekly, its policy under her guidance included liberty, equality, fraternity, atheism, women's rights, and Owenite Co-operation. Its most unusual feature was a Ladies' Page which devoted itself to political, social and domestic matters especially affecting women. *The Secular Chronicle* ran for three years and she lost £1000 on it, financed by her husband, who made his living out of property dealing. In 1879 she retired from public life and died in 1897, survived by her husband, a son, and three daughters.

Harriet Law was primarily a secularist, and her feminism was an aspect of her revolt against religion. She was also one of the last of the line of feminists who drew their inspiration from Owenite socialism and which included Anna Wheeler, Catherine Barmby, Emma Martin, and Margaret Chapellsmith. Indeed Emma Martin, once of the most prominent of the Owenite lecturers, who had died in 1851, was Harriet Law's heroine, and was undoubtedly the inspiration of her own work.

There is an entry for Harriet Law in *DLB* Vol. V, pp. 134–6. See also *Eve and the New Jerusalem*, Barbara Taylor (London, Virago, 1983).

LYTTON Lady Constance Georgina 1869–1923

Constance Lytton, a suffragette, was the second daughter and third child of Robert, afterwards the first Earl of Lytton, and Edith Villiers. The granddaughter of Bulwer Lytton, the novelist, Constance was the great-granddaughter of the pioneer feminist Anne Wheeler, the mother of Bulwer Lytton's wife Rosina, and it is tempting to imagine the connection between them as an influence on Constance. In fact, however, she seems to have known little about the ideas of her great-grandmother and it is, indeed, unlikely that she would have had much sympathy with them, since her own brand of feminism was rooted very much in her own time.

Lord Lytton, her father, was a successful diplomat and much of her early childhood was spent in India, where he was Viceroy of India. Returning to England in 1880, the family lived several years in Hertfordshire before moving to Paris in 1887 on Lord Lytton's appointment as ambassador. Constance was a shy and submissive child with a love of neatness and order. Educated by a series of governesses, she had no liking for lessons, although at the age of thirteen she revealed an unexpected but considerable talent for music. Yet she remained shy and found the social life necessary in Paris a strain. The sudden death of her father in 1891 meant, however, not only a return to England but a considerable fall in income, and henceforward the family lived quietly in the country, where Constance performed the domestic duties of an unmarried daughter living at home.

Outwardly content, Constance did have a sorrow which she seems to have kept secret even from her mother, confiding only in her closest friend Adela Villiers. In 1892 she had fallen deeply in love, but owing to various obstacles, some of which may have been financial, no engagement was possible. For several years she hoped that the obstacles might be removed but this hope was never realised and, as the years went by, meetings with the man she loved grew fewer and more restricted. Unable to reconcile herself to her loss, she suffered deeply for many years.

Although living quietly at home, Constance was by no means unaware of the existence of the women's suffrage movement. Her sister Betty, who had married Gerald Balfour, brother of Arthur Balfour, was a keen supporter of the constitutional suffrage movement, as was Betty's sister-in-law, Frances Balfour. So was her sister Emily, wife of the architect Edwin Lutyens and indeed Emily later claimed that it was she who first interested Constance in the subject. For a long time, however, Constance held herself aloof from any active involvement in the movement. This was partly a lack of conviction, since she was unconvinced by some of the more advanced views, partly her natural shyness, and partly no doubt her own preoccupation with her unhappy love affair. Moreover, in 1902 she suffered an acute rheumatic attack which caused her much pain and left her heart permanently affected.

In 1908 she became involved in the Esperance Club which had the aim of reviving folk dancing and singing. Interested on behalf of the women in her village, she attended the holiday home of the club, and met Emmeline Pethick-Lawrence and Annie Kenney, and it was the force of their enthusiasm which led her to take an interest in the Women's Social and Political Union, already embarked on the early stages of its militant campaign. At first Constance, although intellectually convinced of the case for women's suffrage, was uneasy about the tactics of militancy, but she soon developed a deep admiration for the leaders, especially Emmeline Pankhurst, and a strong sympathy for those women suffering imprisonment for their ideals. At first she simply tried to enlist the help of leading politicians to grant the women prisoners political status, but the more she became personally involved the more certain she became that only militancy would win the vote for women.

In 1909 she joined the WSPU and took part in a deputation to the House of Commons. She was arrested in the struggle that followed and imprisoned, but, because of her heart condition and, even more significantly, in deference to her social position, she was given special treatment. Furious at being given privileges denied to her fellow prisoners she resolved to seek imprisonment again, this time in disguise. As Jane Wharton, a poor seamstress, she was again arrested and sent to prison for fourteen days. On this occasion there was no medical examination and she was forcibly fed eight times with great brutality before, her identity revealed, she was released. From this time on, in spite of frequent periods of illness, she gave herself devotedly to the cause. She was made a paid organiser, which allowed her to live in London, and she forced herself, in spite of her shyness, to speak in public. She also produced a short pamphlet *No Votes for Women*. In 1911 she was again arrested for window-breaking but was quickly released from prison because of her health. Then, in 1912, she suffered a stroke which left her partly paralysed and dependent for the rest of her life on her mother's care.

Even this, however, did not end Constance Lytton's participation in the struggle to change the position of women. Painfully and slowly she wrote a record of her experiences, which was published under the title *Prisons and Prisoners* in 1914. It was a powerful indictment of prison conditions and a plea for prison reform. She continued to give help to individual women when this was possible and to give support to causes she believed in. After the war, for example, she was one of the original sponsors of Marie Stopes' first birth-control clinic, believing that this knowledge was already available to the rich and should be made known to the poor, and on the occasion of Marie Stopes' trial sent her a letter of sympathy and support.

Constance Lytton was the only member of her family to take part in the militant suffrage movement. Although her sisters encouraged her to take an interest in the suffrage issue, they never followed her into militancy. Emily, indeed, admired her sister's courage, but feared imprisonment too much to become a militant herself. Moreover, in 1909 she was converted to Theosophy and the suffrage movement lost its interest for her. Perhaps the greatest encouragement to Constance came from her elder brother, Lord Lytton, who not only defended her at home but supported her cause in the House of Lords, where he became its chief protagonist. He was also, in 1910, one of the main initiators of the unsuccessful attempt to promote a woman's suffrage Bill which would meet with the approval of all the political parties. Her mother, however, was horrified at the danger to her daughter's health as well as her participation in acts which were a disgrace to the family. Nevertheless, the affection between the two women survived and she nursed Constance devotedly between 1912 and the death of Constance in 1923.

The life of Constance Lytton illustrates above all the power of the militant movement to take hold of the imagination of women whose capacity for service had previously been called upon by their immediate family and who had never been interested in politics. To some extent this was achieved through the personalities of leaders like Emmeline Pankhurst and Annie Kenney, but Constance Lytton shows us the significance of the experience of militancy itself. The tactics of the government, designed to halt militancy, turned many women into militants in what they saw as self-defence against a cruel and oppressive authority. The brutality of forcible feeding not only seemed to justify this belief but made those women who endured it into martyrs, and inspired other women to desire the same martyrdom for themselves. It also increased their consciousness of themselves as women. In the case of Constance Lytton her own experience in prison served to increase her commitment to the cause both of suffrage and militancy, partly through her own sufferings, but also because of what she saw of the sufferings of others. She serves to remind us, therefore, that the militant suffrage movement cannot be understood solely in terms of its leaders, and that the motivation of its followers is equally important.

There is no biography of Lady Constance Lytton but the collection of her letters edited by her sister gives a brief account of her life. See *Selected Letters of Constance Lytton*. Selected and arranged by Betty Balfour (London, Heinemann, 1925). See also the recollections of her sister Emily, *Candles in the Sun*, Lady Emily Lutyens (London, Rupert Hart-Davis, 1957). For an account of her involvement in the suffrage movement see *The Suffragette Movement*, Sylvia Pankhurst (London, Longmans, 1931; Virago, 1977). For Constance Lytton's own account see *Prisons and Prisoners*, Lady Constance Lytton (London, Heinemann, 1914).

See also BALFOUR Lady Frances.

MACARTHUR Mary Reid 1880-1921

Mary Macarthur, a trade union organiser, was the daughter of John Duncan Macarthur and Anne Elizabeth Martin. Her father, originally from the Highlands, had built up a big Glasgow drapery business and was a prominent and respected citizen. Her mother was quiet and home-loving, and it seems that Mary was more influenced by her successful and politically active father. Although six children were born, only three survived, all of them girls, of whom Mary was the eldest.

From early on Mary showed both the ability and the rebelliousness which was to characterise her life, and her schooldays at the local high school were somewhat stormy ones. She also displayed her initiative and determination, launching a school magazine with herself as editor. At this time her ambition was to be a famous writer. In 1895 the family left Glasgow for Ayr, and, after a period in Germany, she absorbed herself for a time in the Primrose League, of which her father was a prominent supporter. Soon bored with this, she persuaded her father to take her into the business as a book-keeper, and it was this that led her into the trade-union movement. She attended a Shop Assistants' Union meeting to scoff and was instead converted. Soon she was chairman of the Ayr branch and became involved in various socialist societies, where she met Will Anderson, a young man of her own age whose father had been a blacksmith. Self-educated, and a member of the Independent Labour Party, he led her deep into Labour politics.

In the meantime she progressed within the trade-union movement. In 1902 she met Margaret Bondfield at her union's annual conference and this was the start of what was to be a life-long friendship between them. In 1903 she was elected to the union's national executive, a place filled for the first time by a woman. At home, however, her relationship with her father had become strained. A Conservative in politics, he had nevertheless been able to swallow her trade-union activities, but socialism was hard for him to accept. In 1903 she left home for London, where she obtained a post as secretary to the Women's Trade Union League. From this time on, until her death, her life was given to the cause of women's trade unionism. Indeed, when, later in the same year, Will Anderson asked to marry her she refused, placing her work first. This meant a parting but later, as an organiser for the Shop Assistants' Union, he came to London and from that time they were in constant contact and he became increasingly important to her.

Her abilities, unable to find scope in Ayr, were now able to develop to the full. She had considerable talent both as a speaker and as an organiser, and these were important assets in her work. During these years she maintained her friendship with Margaret Bondfield and also with Gertrude Tuckwell, both active in the women's trade-union movement. She also moved closely in ILP circles and was a friend of Keir Hardie, and also of Ramsay Macdonald and his wife Margaret. Charles Dilke was another important influence, and she came to accept completely his views on the need for the legal regulation of women's wages. She was closely associated with the *Daily News* Exhibition of Sweated Industries in 1905 and the Anti-Sweating League in 1906. In that same year she founded the National Federation of Women Workers which operated on the model of a general labour union. In 1907 she launched the *Woman Worker*, a monthly, later a weekly newspaper, which focussed its energies mainly on the need for a minimum wage. Later she became involved in trying to improve the position of women under the Health Insurance Act, and this absorbed a great deal of her time between 1911 and 1914.

Meanwhile, in 1911 she had married Will Anderson and in 1913 to her great grief, a baby boy was born dead. Then in 1915 a daughter, Nancy, was born. She continued her work however, striving continuously for improved wages and conditions of work for women war workers, and arguing that equal pay for women was the only way to secure justice for men as well as women. At the end of the war she stood unsuccessfully as a Labour candidate, and her husband, who had been elected to Parliament for the first time in 1914, was also defeated. Then in 1919 Will Anderson died suddenly in the influenza epidemic of that year. Her marriage had brought her great, perhaps even unexpected, happiness and her friends believed that she never recovered from his death. Nevertheless she continued her work, making two visits to the USA and beginning the task of transforming the Women's Trade Union League into the Women's Section of the New General Council of the TUC. Shortly, however, cancer was diagnosed, and in spite of two operations she died on New Year's Day 1921.

It is not easy to place Mary Macarthur as a feminist. In her own life she rejected the traditional place allotted to women, choosing deliberately the active sphere of work rather than domesticity. Yet in some respects she was suspicious of the feminism of her day, distrusting especially any attempt to idealise women. She worked well with both men and women, and this may have influenced her in her belief in sex co-operation rather than sex antagonism. She was also at odds with some feminists at that time in her strong support for protective legislation for women, which she saw as complementary to her desire to involve women actively in the trade-union movement.

Although she believed that, as a result of their enfranchisement, politicians would take more interest in the questions that specially interest women, she did not expect that this would transform society. 'Women,' she argued in a contribution to *Women and the Labour Party*, Marion Phillips (London, 1918), 'in the main will vote pretty much as men have voted' (p. 28). Moreover, like her great friend Margaret Bondfield, she had consistently opposed all attempts to obtain a limited suffrage for women, on the grounds that this would deny the vote to working-class women, who most needed it. Indeed, although herself middle-class in origin, she was deeply committed to the women of the working classes, whose hardships appealed to her deeply emotional nature. She represents, nevertheless, an important aspect of socialist feminism which refused to place gender before class, but which tried to bring the needs of women to the attention of the Labour and trade-union movement.

The main source for Mary Macarthur's life is *Mary Macarthur. A Biographical Sketch*, Mary Agnes Hamilton (London, Leonard Parsons, 1925). There is an entry in the *DLB* Vol. II, pp. 255–60 and also in the *DNB* 1912–21 pp. 7–8 under her husband's name.

See also BONDFIELD Margaret Grace.

MACDONALD Margaret Ethel 1870–1911

Margaret MacDonald was the only child by his second wife Margaret King, of John Hall Gladstone, a professor of chemistry at the Royal Institution. His first wife, together with two of his children, had died from scarlet fever, leaving him with four young daughters, and five years later he remarried only to lose his second wife a year later soon after Margaret was born. As a child, therefore, she was brought up largely by servants and later by her elder sisters. Her father was a distinguished scientist who published a number of scientific papers of importance but whose greatest enthusiasm was for public service. He was a member of the London School Board for twenty years and a founder of the Young Men's Christian Association, and Margaret grew up in an atmosphere in which such service was taken for granted.

Educated at home by governesses, Margaret

Gladstone later went to Doreck College, a school for young ladies, but did not, at this stage in her life, show any aptitude as a scholar. Later, for a while, she studied political economy under Millicent Fawcett. She also became involved, like her elder sisters, in various branches of voluntary social work, including classes for servant girls. In 1893 she became secretary of the Hoxton and Hagerton Nursing Association and a visitor for the Charity Organization Society in Hoxton. Intensely religious as a young woman, by 1890 she had begun to move towards socialism, influenced at first by the Christian Socialists and later the Fabians.

In 1894 she joined the Women's Industrial Council and soon became involved in its work. She served on several of its committees and organised on its behalf an enquiry into home work in London which was published in 1897. The people she met, as well as her experiences, inclined her still further towards socialism, and it was through her growing political involvement that she became acquainted with Ramsay MacDonald. In 1895 she had sent him a contribution towards his election expenses and later she wrote to him while he was ill in hospital. Soon afterwards they met, and in 1896 were married.

He was far from being her first suitor, but she was searching for someone she described romantically in 1893 as 'her knight', and turned down four proposals before she found in the young working-class socialist the fulfilment of her dream. Indeed their shared principles and intellectual sympathy made for an exceptionally close and happy marriage. The difference in their backgrounds was never a barrier between them, and Ramsay MacDonald's lowly birth and early hardships may indeed have been part of his charm for her, as well as satisfying a strong need in her to practise austerity. She refused to dress up for her wedding and after the marriage set up house with no resident servants. She disliked fashionable dress and, although they entertained a constant stream of visitors, many from overseas, the setting was always informal.

Although marriage brought her domestic responsibilities, she was determined that it should not end her work for others. Her activities in subsequent years were wide, and included such varied issues as housing, sanitation, the management of hospitals, and the amendment of factory laws. She pressed in particular for more skilled work for women and especially for an extension of their technical education which was neglected in favour of men. As a result of her efforts, trade schools for girls were established, the first in 1904. She also pressed for more women on public bodies and in administration. Other interests were women in the sweated trades, and home workers, both of which occupied her attention for a number of years. Women's unemployment was also of great concern to her, and in 1905 for example she was involved in the organisation of a march of unemployed women in Whitehall.

Apart from her work for the Women's Industrial Council, which only came to an end in 1910, she was also an active member of the National Union of Women Workers, serving on both its industrial and its legislative committees. Between 1899 and 1909 she wrote most of the industrial section of the *Englishwoman's Year Book*. A good many of her articles, often anonymous, appeared in the *Women's Industrial News*, the organ of the Women's Industrial Council. She also read several papers before the British Association, including 'The Industrial Effect of Legislation for Women' (1900) and 'Day Trade Schools for Girls' (1907).

A suffrage supporter, she was a member of the constitutional National Union of Women's Suffrage Societies and for a time served on its executive. From the start, however, she was, like her husband, utterly opposed to militancy. Nor did she accept some of the more extravagant claims of the suffrage movement with respect to the effect of the vote on women's earnings or on issues like prostitution. Although she was unconvinced by Wages Boards as a solution to low wages, she differed from many in the suffrage movement in accepting the idea of protective legislation. Believing that men and women were different, she was opposed to the idea that equality meant sameness and argued that the natural differences that existed must be reflected in both legal and industrial provision. Her attitude to protective legislation brought her into considerable controversy with other feminists, particularly with respect to her attitude to barmaids. She had raised the issue of women in bars as early as 1902 and in *Women as Barmaids* published in 1905 she argued that such women were sexual decoys inciting men to drink and that the work itself involved a grave risk of degradation for the women themselves. She opposed the view that women had a right to work for any wage and under any conditions, and although she was prepared to safeguard existing jobs she wanted to prohibit women working in bars.

In 1906 she was one of those involved in the formation of the women's Labour League, an organisation through which women could work for the Labour Party. It was not, however, merely intended as an adjunct to the party, but as a means to educate women, to draw them out of their homes and to give them confidence in themselves. She maintained a strong interest in the league until her death.

In 1909 both Margaret and her husband went on a long visit to India, their last such visit abroad together. On their return she contributed two chapters to her husband's published account of his impressions, one on purdah and one on the cruelty of child marriage. In December 1910 Sheila, the last of their six children, was born. The following February their son David died from diphtheria and this was a shattering blow from which she never recovered. She continued to work hard, serving on a committee to safeguard women's interests under the new National Insurance Bill, but she was very tired. In April a close friend, Mary Middleton, died and shortly afterwards her own health broke down. After six weeks of illness she died from blood poisoning following an internal ulcer.

Although Margaret MacDonald believed in women taking a greater share in public and political life, and fought strongly against injustice and exploitation in their working lives, she was conscious of the differences between men and women, differences which made necessary a degree of protection which ran counter to the opinions of many of her contemporaries. Her temperament, too, was suspicious of too much enthusiasm and this cut her off not only from what she saw as the emotional excesses of the militant movement but also from their optimism with respect to what the vote would bring. Loving her husband deeply, she was also alienated by the elements of sex warfare which characterised some aspects of the suffrage movement and she was unsympathetic too to any tendencies towards a more bohemian style of life favoured by those who advocated 'free love'.

Her place was with the group of socialist women who held themselves aloof from many aspects of the suffrage struggle and devoted themselves to what might be called the industrial wing of the women's movement. These women often sought protection rather than equal rights, believing that women had special needs as actual or potential mothers. Often traditional in its views on the family, this version of feminism did not challenge existing views on the division of labour between the sexes. Nor did it concern itself with the problems of middle-class women who were often regarded as selfish in their attitudes.

Margaret MacDonald's own contribution was chiefly as researcher, and her carefully prepared reports were an important source of information on a wide variety of topics. Her work was not confined to research reports however, and she did valuable service as an organiser, committee member, journalist and lecturer. Her unassuming manner and deep sincerity won her many friends and her husband never fully recovered from her loss. Many of her ideas were controversial then, as they are now, but she represents an important strand within feminism which has been deeply influential within the Labour Party.

There is a biography *Mrs Ramsay MacDonald*, Lucy Herbert (London, Women Publishers Ltd., 1924). See also the memoir by her husband, *Margaret Ethel MacDonald*, J. Ramsay MacDonald (London, Hodder and Stoughton, 1912); *The Girlhood of Mrs Ramsay MacDonald* by her sister, Isabella Holmes (Ealing, Middlesex, County Times Printing and Publishing Co., 1938); *DLB* Vol. VI, pp. 181–5.

See also BONDFIELD Margaret Grace, HICKS Amelia Jane.

MALLESON Elizabeth 1828–1916

Elizabeth Malleson is best known for her work for the repeal of the Contagious Diseases Act. She was born Elizabeth Whitehead, the daughter of Henry Whitehead and Frances Maguire and the eldest of their eleven children. On her father's side her grandfather had been a rich and successful contractor, builder and architect who left his children well provided for, but Henry, who became a solicitor, was without business ability and gradually lost his property. His marriage to Frances Maguire was a successful one, but their children grew up in a casual and disorganised environment.

Both Elizabeth's parents held progressive views, her father throwing himself into the movement for the repeal of the Corn Laws with great conviction. He also became a Unitarian, to the further detriment of his business interests. Her mother was a keen Liberal and a follower of Gladstone. The family were on terms of close friendship with William Fox, and through Fox with Jacob Bright.

In 1853 Elizabeth learned from William Fox that Barbara Leigh Smith was seeking a teacher for an experimental elementary school she was about to establish. Elizabeth was accepted for the job but a serious breakdown in health shortly afterwards forced her to give up the idea of teaching. It did however bring her into contact with Barbara Leigh Smith and the two young women became friends.

In 1857 Elizabeth married Frank Malleson with whom she had been friends for some time, drawn to him by his sympathy, which she shared, for the 'Friends of Italy' movement. By mutual consent, the word 'obey' was omitted from the marriage ceremony, which suggests that Elizabeth's feminism was already well developed. Frank proved to be a loving and supportive husband who allowed her complete individual freedom. Indeed they were very much in accord in their ideas and worked side by side in most of the issues that she involved herself in. The marriage also drew her into a new circle of like-minded friends which included the Stansfelds and Emilie Ashurst, later Emilie Venturi. There were four children of the marriage, three daughters, two of whom went to Cambridge, and a son.

Soon after the marriage both the Mallesons became involved in F.D. Maurice's Working Men's College and gradually Elizabeth came to perceive the need for a similar education for working women. With gifts from sympathisers like Barbara Leigh Smith (now Bodichon), John Stuart Mill, George Eliot and Harriet Martineau, a College for Working Women was established in 1864. In time Elizabeth became convinced of the need for mixed classes, and in 1874 a College for Men and Women was founded.

Her interest in women's suffrage dated from the early 1850s when she and Barbara Leigh Smith discussed the subject and both she and her husband canvassed strenuously for John Stuart Mill in his 1865 election campaign. She joined the London National Society for Women's Suffrage, although she did not take an active part. By 1870 she and her husband were deeply engaged in the campaign for the repeal of the Contagious Diseases Acts, in which they both took a prominent part, and Elizabeth had been one of the signatories of the original 'Protest' to the *Daily News*. The Acts were designed for the protection of the Armed Forces against veneral disease, by requiring the compulsory examination and if necessary treatment of women believed to be prostitutes, but they were seen by their opponents as condoning vice and, by focussing only on the women, as contributing to the double standard of sexual morality. Both she and her husband were active on committees, Frank Malleson serving as vice-chairman of the National Association for Repeal, and Elizabeth as secretary of the London Ladies' Committee. She organised meetings, speaking when necessary, and attended deputations. One of her addresses at Portsmouth was later published as a pamphlet.

In 1877 Elizabeth had a serious breakdown of health and in 1882 she and her husband moved from London to Gloucestershire. This was the end of her active involvement in national causes although she still continued to work in local affairs. In particular she pressed for the provision of village nurses and midwives and this led to the formation in 1889 of the Rural Nursing Association with Elizabeth Malleson as its honorary secretary.

Frank Malleson died in 1903 but Elizabeth, in spite of her age, continued to maintain an interest in the suffrage cause. She disapproved however of the militant methods of the Pankhursts, although she admired their courage. In 1913, at the age of eighty-five, she was so outraged at the revelations in that year of the traffic in women for immoral purposes that she initiated a Gloucestershire branch of the National Vigilance Association.

Elizabeth Malleson was not a religious woman, and indeed owed allegiance to no particular religious body. Nevertheless she had a deep and idealistic commitment to reform which shaped her whole life. It was, however, rooted essentially in nineteenth-century Radicalism and she had no sympathy, in later life, with either socialism or the trade-union movement. Her feminism sprang from the same roots and was indeed a feature of the circles in which she moved, both before and after her marriage. Although a prominent worker in the campaign for the repeal of the Contagious Diseases Acts, her most distinctive contribution, for which she deserves to be better known, is her contribution to the education of working-class women.

The main source on Elizabeth Malleson's life is *Elizabeth Malleson 1828-1916. Autobiographical Notes and Letters with a Memoir*, Hope Malleson (printed for private circulation, 1926). Both the Mallesons are mentioned in histories of the campaign for the repeal of the Contagious Diseases Acts. See especially *Prostitution and Victorian Social Reform*, Paul McHugh (New York, St Martin's, 1980).

MARSDEN Dora 1882-1960

Nothing is known of Dora Marsden's parental background or early life. She appears, however, to have come from a relatively poor family and to have won a scholarship to Manchester University where she obtained an arts degree. For a few years she worked as a schoolteacher until she gave this up to join the Women's Social and Political Union where she was one of Mary Gawthorpe's aides in Manchester. Later, as district organiser for Southport, she came into conflict with Emmeline Pankhurst and Emmeline Pethick-Lawrence. For a time she was a member of the Women's Freedom League but in 1911, with Mary Gawthorpe, founded *The Freewoman*, a feminist weekly. Shortly afterwards Mary Gawthorpe was forced to resign because of illness. The paper took an anti-militant line and criticised the personal dominance of the Pankhursts. It was its outspoken discussion of female sexuality which was, however, its most distinguishing feature, especially the stand it took on greater sexual freedom for women.

In 1912 the original backer withdrew after the paper was banned by W.H. Smith for immorality, and Harriet Weaver, later the friend and financial support of James Joyce, offered her financial backing. The paper was renamed the *New Freewoman* with Dora Marsden as its editor and continued its policy of providing a forum for the discussion of controversial issues of sex and morality. In 1913 Christabel Pankhurst's articles on venereal disease in *The Suffragette*, later published as *The Great Scourge and how to End It*, were severely criticised by the *New*

Freewoman. Christabel Pankhurst had recommended that women avoid sexual relationships with men, but the *New Freewoman* preached a doctrine of sexual freedom which emphasised the dangers of abstinence.

By 1913 however Dora had lost interest in the journal and she became increasingly involved in the study of philosophy. The *New Freewoman* became *The Egoist* and took on a mainly literary character. It featured writers like Ezra Pound and James Joyce, whose book *A Portrait of the Artist as a Young Man* was serialised in its pages. In 1914 she resigned her editorship to write a book, based on an unorthodox form of Christianity, involving a female deity. Frequent episodes of poor health delayed her progress and the book *The Definition of the Godhead* (London, Egoist Press) was not published until 1928. It was not a success, nor was a second book also on religion *The Mysteries of Christianity* (London, Egoist Press, 1930). Her final publication was a pamphlet *The Philosophy of Time* (Oxford, Holywell Press, 1955) and she died in 1960 from a heart attack.

In her early days she was a compelling speaker and a successful organiser. Later, as editor of the *Freewoman* she revealed a willing acceptance of new ideas, even when they were of unorthodox and unpopular kind, and she provided a forum for the views on female sexuality developed by men like Havelock Ellis, and publicised by women like Stella Browne. This phase of her life was brief however, and she soon retreated into mysticism, living the life of a rather eccentric isolate and never succeeding in bringing her unorthodox ideas to the attention of more than a small number of readers. Her concept of a female deity suggests that she had not abandoned her feminism, but it became submerged in her attempt to express and propagate her own version of Christianity. It is as editor of the *Freewoman* therefore that she made her chief contribution as a feminist.

There is no biography of Dora Marsden and the main source of information on her life is *Dear Miss Weaver. Harriet Shaw Weaver 1876-1961*, Jane Lidderdale and Mary Nicholson (London, Faber and Faber, 1970).

See also BROWNE Stella, GAWTHORPE Mary.

MARTIN Emma 1812-1851

Emma Martin, an Owenite socialist, was the fourth child of William Bullock, a Bristol cooper, and his wife Hannah Jones. Her father died shortly after her birth and her mother married John Gwyn. Nothing is known of her childhood, but at the age of seventeen she joined the Particular Baptists and for the next four years was attached to the Bible Society as a collector and tract distributor. From the beginning, therefore, she took her beliefs seriously and tried to act on them. Not long after her conversion she married another Baptist, Isaac Luther Martin, the son of a brick and tile manufacturer, but this marriage was destined to be an unhappy one. The first child, a daughter, was born in 1832 or 33, a second in 1834, and a third in 1836 or 37, but by 1839 she had left her husband, taking her young daughters with her. The exact reasons for the break-up of the marriage are not known, but she later claimed that he had dissipated her inheritance. There may also have been an intellectual incompatibility exacerbated by her gradual conversion to free thought.

During the early years of her marriage Emma was the proprietor of a ladies' boarding school, in spite of the fact that her own education had been an indifferent one. In 1835 she also became the editor of a short-lived periodical entitled the *Bristol Literary Magazine*. In 1838 she delivered her first recorded public lecture which was on the subject of education. In the following year an Owenite missionary, Alexander Campbell, came to lecture in Bristol. Emma, still a Baptist, challenged his views in public debate, but in the process she was herself converted, both to free thought and, later, to Owenite socialism.

Later that year her marriage finally came

to an end. She settled in London with her daughters, her husband, so far as we know, making no attempt to claim them, and became one of the most prominent of the Owenite lecturers. These were difficult years financially, as she was supporting herself and her daughters on a very tiny salary. Moreover, she often had to leave them with friends while she travelled about the country. Apart from lectures, she was also an enthusiastic tractarian, distributing tens of thousands of pamphlets.

Her propaganda embraced not only free thought and socialism but also feminism, as indeed did many other Owenite lectures. Her own feminism, however, was not inspired by Owenism, although it may well have been strengthened by it. She herself maintained at the Owenite Congress of 1841 that she had been dissatisfied with the position of women even while she was still a member of the Baptist church. It is possible, therefore, that the origins of her feminism must be sought in her own experience. She was keenly aware, for example, of the limitations on women's education and claimed that this excluded women from all remunerative employment.

Such an argument, however, was to become fairly commonplace in the 1840s and 1850s. Emma Martin's conversion to free thought and socialism provided her with a much more far-reaching critique of women's place in society. She developed, for example, a feminist attack on the scriptures, in which she tried to free women from the rule of a patriarchal god and the shackling image of Eve. She also roundly condemned the marriage system linking it, in Owenite fashion, to the system of private property which condemned all relationships to the market place.

She was a good lecturer, mixing witty repartee with tub-thumping polemics. Nevertheless, like other socialist women lecturers, she was sometimes fiercely attacked by the crowds, and in Edinburgh in 1845 she and her little daughter narrowly escaped injury by stoning. In that same year, too, she spent two nights in gaol. In spite of the fact that her lectures were full of injunctions against loose living, she was called a witch and the devil's whore.

By 1845 Emma Martin was both physically and financially exhausted. She settled in London, where she lived with Joshua Hopkins, an engineer ten years older than her, who was deeply sympathetic to her views and took her surname. In 1847 a child, another daughter, was born. This was not, however, to be the end of Emma's work for women. She started a new career as a midwife, training at the Royal Adelaide Hospital in 1847, and almost immediately began a propaganda campaign against the growing male dominance of female health. She strongly supported the right of women to practise as obstetricians and gynaecologists, at a time when the efforts of women to train as doctors were still a long way in the future. In this area in particular, therefore, she was very much a pioneer.

For a few years Emma practised privately as a midwife. She also lectured on the physiology of women, believing that girls ought to be given factual knowledge unmixed with romantic stories. It is also possible that she gave advice on birth control. In 1848 she published *A Miniature Treatise on some of the Most Common Female Complaints.* Also, during these years, she ran an agency for the supply of nurses, and a surgical garments business. But her health was already breaking down and in 1851 she died from tuberculosis, Joshua dying only a year later.

Her esteem in Owenite circles was considerable, and her funeral oration was delivered by the leading Co-operator, George Holyoake, himself a strong sympathiser with the feminist cause. Her reputation, however, extended outside Owenite circles and Harriet Martineau was one of those who subscribed to a headstone for her grave. Regarded as second only to Frances Wright as a propagandiser for women, she was later to be almost forgotten within the feminist movement.

There is no biography of Emma Martin, although George Jacob Holyoake produced an appreciation *The Last Days of Mrs Emma*

Martin. Advocate of Free Thought (London, J. Watson, 1851). There is an entry in the *DLB* Vol. VI, pp. 188-91. She is also one of the socialist feminists featured in Barbara Taylor's *Eve and the New Jerusalem* (London, Virago, 1983).

MARTINEAU Harriet 1802-1876

Harriet Martineau, writer and journalist, was the third daughter and sixth child of the eight children born to Thomas Martineau, a Unitarian textile manufacturer from Norwich, and his wife Elizabeth Rankin, the daughter of a wholesale grocer and sugar refiner. The household was dominated by the mother, who ruled her children with sternness, demanding instant obedience and showing little tenderness or understanding. Harriet sought her mother's love desperately, yet found submission hard to bear so that her childhood, by her own account, was extremely unhappy. Teased by her older siblings and, as it appeared to her, rejected by her mother, she developed strong feelings of inadequacy which were increased during adolescence by her deafness, which first appeared at this time.

Nevertheless the Martineaus were not neglectful parents and she and her sisters were given an education which, if inferior to that of their brothers, was much better than that generally available to girls at this period. She was taught mainly by her older siblings, with two short periods away at school, and she soon grew to love learning which became her chief solace. Her most rewarding relationship was with her younger brother James. As children they were devoted companions and, as he grew older, they studied together so that when, in 1821, he went away to college, Harriet was desolated. Indeed this was a landmark in her life, because it seems to have brought home to her the educational discrimination suffered by girls, which was at the heart of her feminism. It was James who first suggested that she should take up writing to comfort her during his absence, and she was soon rewarded by success. Only a year after his departure her article 'Female Writers on Practical Divinity' was published by the Unitarian *Monthly Repository*, followed, in 1823, by 'On Female Education'. Very much in advance of its time, this second article attributed the differences between men and women entirely to educational discrimination, and sought for women the right to develop and use their potentialities.

In 1823 her brother James brought home a college friend, John Hugh Worthington. A number of other visits followed, and in 1826 he asked Harriet to marry him. After some hesitation she accepted although her motives are by no means clear. Undoubtedly she liked him and, believing herself to be unattractive as a woman, may also have been flattered by his attentions. She was also very conscious of how much he loved her. His health, however, was already causing grave concern and, probably for this reason, James was not happy about the match. Shortly after the engagement he fell ill with brain fever without hope of recovery. Harriet withdrew her consent to the marriage, returned his letters and refused to visit him. Her behaviour has been interpreted as hardhearted and was certainly not the action of a woman deeply in love. Its most likely explanation is that she felt a desperate need to escape a situation which had become more than she could face. Later she was to look back on his death without regret, convinced that she could never have made a success of marriage.

In 1826 Harriet Martineau's father died, leaving the family business in financial difficulties, and the final collapse came in 1829. She was now left with the knowledge that she must support herself. Her contributions to the *Monthly Repository* had continued and, in her altered circumstances, the editor, William Fox, offered her a small payment but it was by no means enough to keep her. She moved to London, living with an aunt and uncle, and maintained herself as best she could with needlework while still striving to make a living by her pen. Her life in London was rewarding however since through William Fox she became acquainted with the leading figures in London Unitarianism. She was therefore deeply resentful when she was ordered back home by her mother. Although she obeyed, the incident deepened her ambition, and quite soon her faith in herself was amply restored when she won a prize in a Unitarian essay competition. Her mother now permitted her to spend three months a year in London, and before long she was deeply immersed in a scheme to illustrate political economy for the ordinary reader by making use of fictional illustrations. The difficulties she faced were very great, she showed enormous persistence, and the nine volumes, published between 1832 and 1834, were an instant success not only bringing her financial independence but making her famous.

In 1834 Harriet Martineau decided on a visit to America. She travelled extensively during the two years of her trip, forging lasting bonds with the abolitionists, and, on her return, added to her reputation by the publication, in 1837, of *Society in America*. Mainly a critique of America's failure to live up to its democratic principles, it included a chapter entitled 'The Political Non-existence of Women' which was received somewhat uncomprehendingly by many of her readers, even those who were in general sympathy with her. Moreover, perhaps because it predated by some twenty years the rise of the women's movement in Britain, its arguments have been unjustly neglected. By arguing that it was wrong for men to represent women's interests, she was making a quite unambiguous claim for women's suffrage and, in a comparison between the positions of women and of slaves, she suggested that women were given indulgence rather than justice. She also entered a strong plea for better education for girls so that marriage need not be their only object in life.

On her return to England she set up house with her mother, an old aunt, and her brother Henry, but her mother still maintained her dominating ways and the years between 1836 and 1839 were anxious and even unhappy for Harriet. Nevertheless, she continued to work hard, writing numerous articles and also a novel, *Deerbrook*. In 1839, too, she was invited to edit a proposed new journal. The prospect tempted her, although it also aroused fears of failure. James however advised against it and she rejected the invitation. Later that same year she was taken seriously ill on a European holiday and placed herself under the medical care of Thomas Greenlow, her sister Elizabeth's husband. It has sometimes been suggested that this illness was psychological and was an unconscious attempt on her part to evade family responsibilities, particularly for her mother. In fact, however, the main source of the trouble was a cyst and for five years, suffering considerable pain, she was forced to live as a complete invalid. By 1844 there were distinct signs of improvement in her condition, due to a change in the position of the tumour, and by the end of that year she was able to go outside for the first time since the illness began. She herself however attributed her improvement to mesmerism, which she had recently turned to for help, and she became an enthusiastic convert, publicly proclaiming her new faith in the pages of the *Athenaeum*. Thomas Greenlow was antagonised and in the ensuing quarrel she found herself isolated from most of the rest of the family, including James.

This break with her brother was, however, far less harmful to her happiness than it would have been earlier. They now occupied very different intellectual positions and had also grown apart emotionally. Indeed there are a number of indications that James had become jealous of his more famous sister. Although hurt, she seems to have outgrown her former dependency. Moreover, her health now seemed completely recovered and she moved to the Lake District where she built herself a house near Ambleside. For ten years she was free from symptoms and lived a cheerfully active life, receiving her many visitors, going on long walks, and maintaining an astonishing output of writing. Indeed, while her health lasted, she was probably happier than she had ever been. Her first major publication from Ambleside was *The History of the Peace*, a history of England between 1816 and 1846, which was published in 1849–50. During 1846 and 1847 she travelled in the Middle East, and on her return published *Eastern Life Past and Present*. This was followed, in 1851, by *Letters on the Laws of Man's Nature and Development*, a record of her complete rejection of religion. It caused something of a sensation amongst her friends, and was the occasion of the final breach with James, who had written a fiercely hostile review. Her next work was a translation of Comte's *Positive Philosophy*, which she admired, although she rejected Comte's views on women.

By 1855, however, the cyst had moved again and was now pressing on her lungs and heart. Expecting her death at any time, she worked on her autobiography, and, when it was finished, devoted herself to journalism. Still needing to earn a living, in 1852 she had become a leader writer on the London *Daily News* and she contributed more than sixteen hundred leaders, letters, and obituaries in the sixteen years before she became too ill to continue. It was largely as a journalist, moreover, that she played her part in the growing women's movement during the 1850s and 1860s.

It was, for example, one of her articles, 'Female Industry', published in the *Edinburgh Review* in 1859, which inspired Adelaide Proctor's establishment of the Society for the Promotion of the Employment of Women. In an article in the *Cornhill Magazine* at the time of the Schools Inquiry Commission in 1864 she complained at the state of middle-class education for girls, and supported the new ventures in higher education for women. Other issues raised by her included the needs of seamstresses and domestic servants, and the injustices involved in the legal position of married women. As early as 1853 she had deplored the double standard of sexual morality which assumed that the conjugal infidelity of a wife was a greater sin than that of a husband. During the 1860s she supported the newly formed women's suffrage movement and in 1870 personally petitioned Parliament to admit women into the medical profession.

Perhaps her most important contribution to feminism at this time, however, was her involvement in the Contagious Diseases Acts controversy. In order to protect the Armed Forces, the Acts provided that, in certain garrison towns, women believed to be prostitutes were to be compulsorily examined and if necessary treated for venereal disease. She took her first action in 1864, when the first Act was introduced, warning, in the pages of the *Daily News*, of the dangers to women's liberty, but her words were little heeded. In 1869 it was proposed that the Acts should be extended to other areas, and once more she raised the issue in the *Daily News*, writing three letters, signed 'An Englishwoman'. She admitted to a friend the dreadful effort it cost her to write on such a subject, but was sustained by thoughts of the ordeal of Godiva, an illustration which illuminates for us the courage that was required of her. Her letters were followed by a memorial from the newly formed Ladies National Association for the Repeal of the Contagious Diseases Act, and it was signed by 128 women, with Harriet Martineau's name at the head of the list. Later Josephine Butler was to admit that Harriet Martineau had fired the first round.

To Harriet Martineau the most outrageous aspects of the Acts were the threat to women's liberties, and the personal violation involved, but she also protested bitterly with Josephine Butler that the Acts were designed to protect the sex which was the actual cause of the sin. Prostitution, in her view, was an aspect of women's lack of power in society, which allowed their exploitation. In spite of the increasing weakness caused by her illness she maintained her support into the 1870s, writing addresses for pamphlets and posters and contributing fancy work to be sold in aid of the funds. In 1876 she died from bronchitis.

Harriet Martineau, in spite of her feminism, was never one of the leaders of the women's movement and her contribution for this reason has often been overlooked. There are many reasons for this, including her particular personality which was too fiercely independent to be at home in any kind of organisation. It is also significant that during the 1830s feminist thinking was associated mainly with the Owenite socialists with whom Harriet Martineau had little sympathy and whose feminism would have been quite uncongenial to her. Not until the 1850s was there a woman's movement in which she could feel intellectually at home, and by this time she was confined to her house at Ambleside. Nevertheless, she gave the movement her active support as a journalist, and added her name to Barbara Leigh Smith's petition on married women's property in 1856. Most striking of all was the initiative she displayed with respect to the Contagious Diseases Acts when she was already an old and very sick woman who might have been forgiven for turning her back on such a topic.

Harriet Martineau believed firmly in the power of reason, and had a deep distrust of those women, like Caroline Norton, who based their case on their own personal unhappiness. Indeed it was her firm opinion that the best advocates were those who demonstrated not women's weakness, but women's strength. Conventional in her attitudes, she disapproved of the liaisons between William Fox and Eliza Flower, and John Stuart Mill and Harriet Taylor, believing them to be not only immoral, but detrimental to the causes they advocated. It was her belief that passion should always be subordinated to duty and she was probably incapable of understanding the kind of love which overcame reason. She had learned in early childhood the need for self-reliance and almost certainly it was a fear of commitment to others which made her decide that she was happiest alone. Even her brother James, perhaps the person she loved most, proved a traitor in the end. Her drive for achievement also had its origin in the consciousness of rejection which dominated her early years, and probably explains why self-determination for women played such a central role in her feminism. A fascinating and still enigmatic woman, her ideas deserve a more sympathetic appreciation than they have been given in the past.

There are a number of biographies of Harriet Martineau. The most recent, which pays considerable attention to her feminism, is *Harriet Martineau. The Woman and her Work 1802-76*, Valerie Kossew Pichanick (Ann Arbor, University of Michigan Press, 1980). The most scholarly of the earlier biographies is *Harriet Martineau. A Radical Victorian*, R.K. Webb (New York, Columbia University Press; London, Heinemann, 1960). For two papers which deal specifically with her as a feminist see 'The Rights and Wrongs of Women' by Margaret Walters in *The Rights and Wrongs of Women* ed. Juliet Mitchell and Ann Oakley (Harmondsworth, Penguin, 1976) and 'Harriet Martineau: a Reassessment' in *Feminist Theorists* ed. Dale Spender (London, The Women's Press, 1983). See also *Harriet Martineau's Autobiography with Memorials by Maria Weston Chapman* (London, Smith Elder and Co., 1877). *DNB* Vol. XXXVI, pp. 309-14.

MILL John Stuart 1806-1873

John Stuart Mill, political economist and philosopher, was the eldest of the nine children of James Mill and his wife Harriet Burrow. Intended for the Scottish church, James Mill instead came to London where he earned a precarious living as a writer and journalist before securing an appointment in 1819 at the India Office. His marriage in 1805 proved to be an unfortunate one since his disappointment in his wife's intellect led him to treat her with coldness and arrogance. The early years of their marriage were also years of financial stringency, and she was forced by these circumstances and by her frequent pregnancies into the role of household drudge. Amiable by disposition, she was no match for her clever but domineering husband, and submission must have seemed the only way out.

Neglectful of his wife's happiness, James Mill devoted his attention to the intellectual development of his children, and especially his eldest son, who received almost all his education at his father's hands. He started Greek at the age of three, and this was only the beginning of an arduous and intensive system made harder in some respects because in his turn John was expected to take charge of the lessons of his younger brothers and sisters. In 1820 he had learned all he could from his father and spent a year in France, followed by a period at home studying Roman law. It must have been during this period that, at the age of seventeen, John was involved with some young friends in helping Francis Place distribute birth-control pamphlets. Arrested by the police, he was released after a few days and the matter was successfully hushed up until the affair was revived after his death. This incident did not change his attitude towards birth control but it taught him discretion, and thereafter he was always cautious in the public presentation of his views, believing firmly that it was necessary to wait until it was politically expedient before challenging accepted views.

In 1823 he obtained an appointment with the East India Company and also commenced to write for a number of newspapers, especially for the Radical *Westminster Review*. For a time he became interested in Owenite socialism, but was never completely won over to its views, although he may have been influenced by the feminism of William Thompson who became his friend. In 1826, however, still only twenty years old, he fell into a deep depression which led him into new ways of thinking and a distrust of some of his father's ideas. In particular he became aware of poetry and the significance of feeling as opposed to reason. It was in this condition of mind that he met and fell in love with Harriet Taylor.

When John Stuart Mill met Harriet Taylor in 1830 she had been married four years and had two young sons. Her last child, a daughter, was born in 1831. She was already unsettled in her marriage and bored with her kind but dull husband, and was attracted by the intellectual abilities of Mill as he was by her beauty and charm. They found, too, a common dissatisfaction with the position of women. Convinced that men and women had an equal right to happiness, Mill had disagreed with his father's view that the interests of women could be represented by their fathers or husbands, and accepted that they should have equal legal and political rights with men.

By 1832 the couple could no longer hide the fact that they were in love. For a time indeed, Harriet Taylor, aware of her husband's distress, tried to break off the relationship altogether but eventually, torn between her feelings of affection for her husband and her passion for Mill, a compromise was reached. Harriet Taylor continued to maintain the external appearance of married life with her husband, while maintaining her right to the continued friendship with John Stuart Mill. It is certain that this arrangement was hard on Mill. He was required to accept a platonic friendship with occasional meetings in place of the passionate and intimate relationship he wanted, and it is possible that the resultant strain contributed to a serious physical breakdown in health in 1836. Moreover, the arrangement designed to protect the reputation of all three of the parties did not really work. Gossip and innuendo were rife, and even John Stuart Mill's friends frequently failed to believe that his relationship with Harriet Taylor was a platonic one. In time, however, the arrangement, with the consent of John Taylor, was relaxed somewhat to the advantage of Mill. Harriet, with her daughter, moved out of her husband's house, although she still paid him visits from time to time, and Mill regularly visited her at weekends. She and Mill, although discreetly, also found the opportunity to spend holidays together.

Meanwhile, in 1834 Mill had become editor of the *London Review* which later became the *London and Westminster Review*. Between 1834 and 1840 when he gave up the editorship this task took up most of his spare time. He had also started work on his *System of Logic* in 1830 and this was published in 1843, becoming at once an instant success. This was followed in 1848 by his *Principles of Political Economy*, the first of his books in which Harriet's hand is clearly discernible, chiefly in her greater practical sympathy with the working classes and in her socialist leanings. Both he and Harriet had earlier been interested in Owenite socialism, but it seems to have had a more permanent effect on Harriet and was probably the major source of her feminism. In 1849, however, the death of John Taylor from cancer opened up the possibility of a life together.

Both John Stuart Mill and Harriet Taylor had been hurt by the refusal of so many of their friends to believe in the innocence of their relationship, and the response of John Stuart Mill, in many ways a sociable person as a young man, was to retire from the world. The prospect of marriage, longed for as it was, roused in him fears of re-awakening the old scandal, and the wedding which occurred in 1851 was almost a secret ceremony. Afterwards the couple lived quietly, seeing only a few close friends. The next seven years were the most deeply fulfilled of his life, marred only by his own poor health, and the tuberculosis which eventually killed Harriet in 1859. They were, however, happy and fruitful years, filled with intellectual collaboration. Mill's biographer, indeed, goes so far as to argue that everything that Mill wrote afterwards was a product of their joint discussions during this period. They were also years during which Mill's feminism under Harriet's influence, became a more dominant theme in his writing.

During the first years of their acquaintanceship they had written down and exchanged their views on marriage. These written drafts, unpublished in their life-time, were made public by F.A. Hayeck in 1951. They reveal that already there was considerable common ground in their views on equal rights for men and women, although Harriet was the more radical of the two, since she believed that even married women needed a paid occupation in order to retain their independence. John Stuart Mill, in contrast, did not believe it necessary that a woman should actually support herself, only that she should be capable of doing so. Indeed, at this time, he held a very romantic view of women, believing that their occupation in life 'is to adorn and beautify', and that their function was fulfilled 'by being rather than doing'.

In 1851, not long after the marriage, an essay, 'The Enfranchisement of Women', was published in the *Westminster Review*. Ostensibly written by Mill, it was in fact a joint production. Certainly Mill had a hand in it, but it was based on a draft by Harriet Taylor and much of it may have been written by her. Essentially a plea for civil and political equality, it developed at greater length some of the arguments she had briefly sketched in 1832. 'The Enfranchisement of Women' was followed a year later by an article in the *Morning Chronicle* (28 August 1851) on the need for the protection of wives and children from brutal husbands and fathers. Under Mill's name, it was almost certainly inspired by Harriet, and a small pamphlet on the same theme in 1853 was under their joint names. Another important preoccupation was his *Autobiography* in which they hoped to give a true account of their life together.

In 1858 John Stuart Mill was finally in a position to retire from his job, but their hopes for a retirement together in a warmer climate were dashed by Harriet's death in the same year in Avignon. Mill, heartbroken, never recovered from her loss, although the continued presence of her daughter Helen compensated him in some degree. He made himself a home in Avignon near Harriet's tomb, and worked on the completion of those books, including his essay *On Liberty*, which they had started together. *The Subjection of Women*, which they had worked on together, was published in 1869, and, although it aroused more antagonism than anything else he wrote, it proved to be of enormous significance for the growing women's movement throughout the world. Dispassionate in tone and cautious in argument, it is essentially a plea for an end to the legal and political restrictions on women which result in their legal, political and domestic subordination. Appealing in particular to the ideals of reason and progress, he called the subordination of women 'a single relic of an old world of thought' and went on to attack all the arguments based on the nature of women, by arguing that in the present state of society we have no real knowledge of what the differences between the sexes really are. The important thing was to give women the chance to show what they could do.

Mill had always believed it necessary for women to take the lead in their own emancipation, and the women's suffrage movement in particular gained from his advice and encouragement. In 1866, when he was elected to Parliament, he was in a position to give more practical support, and in 1867 he rose to move that the word 'man' in the Reform Bill then before Parliament should be replaced by the word 'person'. Although success was hardly to be expected, he got a good hearing and John Bright, a determined opponent of women's rights, was moved for the first and only time to vote in their favour.

John Stuart Mill's last stand for women took place not long before his death in 1873. Like many others he had been deeply angered by the Contagious Diseases Acts which, in order to protect the Armed Forces against venereal disease, provided for the compulsory medical examination and, if necessary, treatment of women suspected of being prostitutes. Appalled at the threat to liberty that the Acts implied, Mill volunteered to give evidence to the Royal Commission appointed to consider the future of the Acts. Questioned by the commissioners, he did not hesitate to take a profoundly feminist stand, arguing that if action needed to be taken it must be against the man, since he, and not the woman, was the one to blame.

Mill's feminism was in essence part of his moral and political philosophy. It was based on a fervent belief in equal rights between men and women, and on the rights of women as well as men to achieve their maximum potential. For this reason he was concerned chiefly with the removal of legal and political restrictions on women's freedom of action. His relationship with Harriet Taylor, therefore, did not make him a feminist, although it provided him with a greater appreciation of the practical disabilities under which women laboured. Moreover, after her death the advance of women became a sacred duty to her memory.

His ideal of marriage was certainly drawn from the kind of relationship he had with Harriet, and its equality stands in sharp contrast to the life of dominance and submission shared by his parents. Unfortunately Mill's relationship with his mother is unclear, for he mentions her very rarely, and in later life they were estranged. He certainly draws no direct lesson from her submission to his father, and if anything blames his mother rather than his father for the situation between them. Nevertheless, it would be strange if he drew no conclusions from their relationship, and his willingness to sublimate his own sexual desires is in stark contrast to what he, with his views on the sexual relationship, must have seen as his father's cold lust.

Nevertheless, his own views on marriage and the family did nothing to challenge the accepted position on the division of labour between the sexes. Although he certainly wanted to end women's subordination in marriage, he did not, like Harriet, aspire to economic independence for married as well as single women. Indeed, in *The Subjection of Women* he argues that the best arrangement normally was where 'men earn and wives undertake the careful and economical application of their husband's earnings'. His ideas, therefore, embody both the strengths and weaknesses of equal-rights feminism, and *The Subjection of Women* in particular remains even today one of its most perfect representations.

The best discussion of John Stuart Mill as a feminist is in *Essays on Sex Equality: John Stuart Mill and Harriet Taylor* ed. Alice S. Rossi (Chicago and London, The University of Chicago Press, 1970). See also *The Life of John Stuart Mill*, Michael St John Packe (London, Secker and Warburg, 1954); *John Stuart Mill and Harriet Taylor. Their Correspondence and Subsequent Marriage*, F.A. Hayeck (London, Routledge and Kegan Paul, 1951); 'The Writing of John Stuart Mill's Autobiography' by A.W. Levi, *Ethics* Vol. LXI, 1951, pp. 284–96; *The Early Draft of John Stuart Mill's Autobiography*, Jack Stillinger (Urbana, University of Illinois, 1961); *Autobiography of John Stuart Mill* ed. John Jacob Coss (New York, Columbia

University Press, 1924); 'Marital slavery and Friendship. John Stuart Mill's "The Subjection of Women"', M.L. Shanley *Political Theory*, Vol. IX, 1981, 229–47.

See also FOX William Johnson, TAYLOR Harriet, THOMPSON William.

MILLER Florence Fenwick 1854–1935

Florence Fenwick Miller, a journalist, was born in London, the only daughter and second child of Captain John Miller and his wife Eleanor Fenwick. Her father was a sea captain who was abroad for long periods, and her mother seems to have been an important influence on her life, passing on to her, for example, her firm belief in temperance. Whether or not her mother had leanings towards feminism can only be conjectured but the very early emergence of such views in Florence suggests that this may have been so. Privately educated, Florence—named after Florence Nightingale—decided to become a doctor and in 1871, at the age of only seventeen, followed Sophia Jex-Blake to Edinburgh University, where she passed a portion of the preliminary examination. The collapse of the attempt to persuade Edinburgh to give medical degrees to women forced Florence back to London where she completed her studies with considerable academic distinction at the newly created Medical College for women. She soon decided however, that medicine was not the most effective way for her to work for women and after she qualified she was in practice for only a short while. In 1876 she was elected to the London School Board, where she served until 1885, giving so much care and attention to the interests of women teachers that in 1882 the Association of Board School Mistresses asked permission to bear her election expenses, a request which was refused. While on the board she was successful in reducing the amount of time spent by girls on fine needlework. She was also able to block a move to exclude mothers from teaching jobs.

In 1877 she married Frederick A. Ford, a stockbroker's clerk of twenty-nine who seems to have shared her views. By mutual consent she retained her own name, adding, however, the prefix Mrs as recognition of her married status. An attempt was made to upset her election to the school board on the grounds of the illegality of her name but, on taking the issue to law, her action was found to be perfectly legal. There were two children of the marriage, both girls, who took the name of Fenwick-Ford.

She gave her first lecture on suffrage while still a young medical student and in 1875, still only twenty-one, her reply to a hostile lecture from Admiral Maxse was printed by the Women's Suffrage Society. Her interest in suffrage continued, and in 1902 she became the first treasurer of the International Women's Suffrage Committee. She was also active in the English Women Writers' Suffrage League and in 1915 was its president.

It is probably as a writer and popular educator that Florence Fenwick Miller was best known in her own life-time. Her earliest publications derive from her medical training and include *Simple Lessons of Health* (1877) and *Physiology in Schools* (1881). She also wrote a school text-book, *Readings in Social Economy and Natural History* (1883). In a somewhat different vein she was responsible for a popular biography of Harriet Martineau (1884) whom she seems to have particularly admired.

She also built up a considerable reputation as a journalist, contributing weekly columns to a number of provincial newspapers under the pseudonym 'Filomena', and from 1886 she wrote the Ladies Notes for the *Illustrated London News.* Then, in 1895, she became the editor and sole proprietor of the *Woman's Signal*, a journal previously devoted mainly to temperance and to which she was already a contributor. Under her guidance the journal became an important feminist vehicle, intermingling book reviews and articles on current affairs with discussions on matters of interest to the women's movement. In order to maintain the circulation there were also lighter topics of interest to women. She also maintained a system of free subscriptions to other journals and to highly-placed and influential people, and in 1897 started a free circulation fund with contributions from readers to spread its influence even wider. Copies were placed in free libraries and other reading rooms, and members of Parliament and their wives were sent free copies.

The feminist issues dealt with by the *Woman's Signal* were varied, depending mainly on their topicality. Thus, for example, a bad case of wife-beating led to a discussion of violence against women. Three issues were, however, given especial prominence; women's suffrage, which was the subject of parliamentary debate in 1897; the unsuccessful attempt in that year to obtain degrees for women at Cambridge, and the attempt by the government to impose a Contagious Diseases Act in India. The opposition to the Acts in Britain had succeeded in obtaining their repeal in 1884, but in 1897 legislation on the same lines was proposed to solve the problem of venereal disease amongst British troops in India. As in the British case, women believed to be prostitutes were to be compulsorily examined and if necessary treated, and this was seen by Florence Fenwick Miller as condoning immorality.

By 1899 a combination of poor health and the drain of the journal on her own financial resources proved too much, and the *Woman's Signal* ceased publication. This did not, however, mean the end of her career as a journalist. She was on the staff of the *London Daily News* between 1902 and 1904, and continued to write the Ladies Notes for the *Illustrated London News* until 1918. She was never again, however, so prolific as a writer or so influential as a feminist as she had been between 1875 and 1899.

Less well known than her career as a writer and journalist is her strong commitment to neo-Malthusianism. This had its source in her friendship with Charles Drysdale, who had been her teacher while she was a medical student in London. Later she came to know him well and was converted to his views on birth control, which they saw as having particular importance for women. She became a member of the Malthusian League and in 1908 she was one of those who contributed to Charles Drysdale's commemoration service. Her views on religion were also unorthodox, and as early as 1877 in a lecture on Harriet Martineau she repudiated superstition and declared herself an agnostic.

It is clear that Florence Fenwick Miller was an enterprising and courageous woman, not afraid to take up unpopular causes. She once defined the new woman as one who wanted to earn her own living, to study for a degree, to vote, and to serve her generation by work in public affairs. Her name is now largely forgotten, but she was a fighter of no small significance on the side of women's independence and autonomy.

There is a brief biography of Florence Fenwick Miller and an account of her work for the *Woman's Signal* in *Florence Fenwick Miller, Feminism and the Woman's Signal 1895-1899*, Rosemary T. Van Arsdel (Washington, University of Puget Sound, 1979). There is an entry in *Women of the Day*, Frances Hays (London, Chatto and Windus, 1885) and also in *A Biographical Dictionary of Rationalism*, Joseph McCabe (London, Watts, 1920). For her contribution to neo-Malthusianism see *The Malthusian* Vol. XXXII (2), February 1908. See also *Who Was Who* 1929-1940.

See also DRYSDALE Charles Robert.

MITCHELL Hannah Maria 1871-1956

Hannah Mitchell, a suffragette, was born Hannah Webster, the daughter of a small farmer in the Peak District of Derbyshire. There were six children in the family, three boys and three girls, and Hannah was the fourth to be born. She had a hard childhood, kept busy on both farm and domestic work which the boys, to Hannah's bitterness, were spared. She was given almost no formal schooling and, although taught to read by her father and an uncle, had to pick up what learning she acquired by herself. Her childhood was also soured by the hostility which sprang up between herself and her mother, and which to some degree lasted all her life. Her mother indeed was herself deeply unhappy since she hated her isolated life on the farm. This expressed itself in violent rages which her gentle and kindly husband was unable to handle.

Eventually, in 1885, after a particularly bad quarrel in which Hannah snatched the stick her mother was beating her with, and threatened to retaliate, it was agreed that she would be better off away from home, and she was sent to live with her eldest brother who was newly married. When she was a little older she moved to Bolton, where she lived in lodgings. During these years she had a variety of jobs, some in dressmaking, some in domestic work. A short love affair with a young teacher came to nothing, but later on a friendship with a fellow boarder led to her introduction to socialism, and, in 1895, to marriage.

Gibbon Mitchell, already a convinced socialist, was the son of a widow left to bring up eight children. He had started work at ten as an apprentice draughtsman, and later he designed and made clothes. Finally he became a manager for a firm of ready-made tailors. Committed to the same causes as Hannah, he undoubtedly supported her in all her undertakings. Yet Hannah herself was never entirely happy in the marriage. Domestic life did not suit her, and she took no pleasure in the endless treadmill of housework and cooking. Moreover, at first the couple were very poor and she had to take in dressmaking to make ends meet, so that she had no time for any life of her own. Even Sundays, she found, meant only the same domestic round. The birth of a son, later dearly-loved, was at first the source only of tears, and indeed thereafter the couple made use of birth control to avoid any further increase in the family.

In 1897 her husband obtained a better-paid situation, and once her son started school she had more time for herself. She began to take an active part both in the Independent Labour Party and later in the women's suffrage movement. Indeed her first address to a meeting was on the 'Woman's Cause'. During the winter of 1904–5 she began to help the Pankhursts in their work, visiting trades councils, debating societies, and women's guilds. The local ILP was also involved at this stage, its members, including her husband, acting as bodyguards at their meetings.

As her involvement grew, she began to interrupt political meetings and on one occasion was arrested but was released when her husband, somewhat to her annoyance, paid her fine. Eventually she became a Women's Social and Political Union organiser, while a niece acted as housekeeper. Overwork, and possibly the strain of the ever-present threat of violence, led in 1907 to a breakdown which interrupted her participation in the movement for more than a year. There was also a breach with the Pankhursts, who had ignored her illness. She came, too, to disagree with some aspects of their policy. Instead she worked for a time for the Women's Freedom League, partly as a gesture of gratitude to Charlotte Despard who had been very kind to her. Her breakdown had left her weak, however, and she was never again so active as in the early years of the suffrage movement.

After the war, during which she was a pacifist, she continued to work for the ILP, and in 1924 was elected to the Manchester City Council. In 1926 she also became a magistrate. Her first public service had been in 1904, when she had served for a time on the Board of Guardians, and it is clear that she both enjoyed it and had a talent for it. During the 1920s and 1930s she became an established figure in Manchester, devoting herself to the needs of the poor of the community. She continued to be a feminist, however, and condemned the anti-feminism which she found on many public bodies and also within the Labour movement.

Hannah Mitchell is an example of a working-class feminist whose life reveals not only the particular appeal that feminism made to such a woman, but, even more strikingly, the obstacles she and others like her had to face in serving the feminist cause. Hannah had a powerful desire for independence, which expressed itself as a child in rebellion against her mother, and as a young woman in a frustrated desire for self-expression and self-improvement. In later life she was able to channel it largely into public service, but always it had to take second place to her domestic commitments which could rarely be delegated. Her struggles, however, demonstrate quite clearly that the feminist desire for autonomy and freedom was by no means confined to women of the middle classes.

The source for Hannah Mitchell's life is her autobiography. Written during her seventies, it was edited after her death by her grandson Geoffrey Mitchell and published as *The Hard Way Up. The Autobiography of Hannah Mitchell. Suffragette and Rebel*, Hannah Mitchell (London, Virago, 1968).

MONTEFIORE Dora 1851-1927

Dora Montefiore, suffragette, was the eighth child and fifth daughter of Francis and Mary Ann Fuller. Her father was a land surveyor and estate agent who had been the initiator of the Great Exhibition of 1851. There was a deeply affectionate relationship between father and daughter, and he obviously made great efforts to stimulate her intelligence. After attending a good school at Brighton, she became his amanuensis, travelling with him and helping him prepare papers for the British Association and Social Science Congresses.

On a visit to Australia to see an elder brother, she met George Borrow Montefiore, a wealthy Australian businessman, and they were married in 1879. Ten years later her husband died, leaving her with a daughter of five and a two-year-old son. She then realised, for the first time, the state of the law with regard to widows and, although she had no personal grievances, she began to take an interest in the Australian women's movement. The British movement was, of course, well under way before she left for Australia, but at that stage in her life it had failed to arouse her interest. With the assistance of a friend, Sir George Grey, himself a keen supporter of women's suffrage, she founded in 1891 the Womanhood Suffrage League of New South Wales with a policy of adult suffrage.

On returning to England in 1892 she worked for a time under the leadership of Millicent Fawcett, but felt depressed by the lack of progress of the suffrage campaign. She formed the League of Practical Suffragists which pledged itself not to work for any parliamentary candidate who would not pledge his support for women's suffrage. During this period she became close friends with Elizabeth Wolstenholme-Elmy who had also become profoundly dissatisfied with the stagnation which, in her view, had overtaken the suffrage movement. Consequently they both greeted the rise of the Women's Social and Political Union with enthusiasm, and Dora Montefiore, then living in London, worked energetically in the early days of the London campaign alongside Sylvia Pankhurst and Annie Kenney.

At the same time she was moving steadily to the left in politics. At first, on returning to England, she worked for the Liberal Party but, disillusioned with their attitude to women's suffrage, she turned to socialism, joining the Social Democratic Federation and eventually serving on the executive. In 1907 she attended, as SDF delegate, the Socialist International Conference at Stuttgart. She also became friendly with exiles from Russia, and was to remain deeply involved with international socialism for the rest of her life.

For a time Dora Montefiore was a prominent figure in the WSPU, organising meetings, joining in deputations and contributing to its funds. In 1906 she spent a period in prison. Her own particular contribution to militant tactics was her refusal to pay taxes, and this obtained publicity for the movement and was later to become a major plank in the Women's Freedom League. Very soon, however, there were disagreements between Dora Montefiore and Christabel and Emmeline Pankhurst, and in 1906 Dora left the WSPU and joined the

Adult Suffrage Society, for whom she worked until the vote was eventually won for women over thirty in 1918.

After the war Dora Montefiore joined the communist party, and after her son's death in 1921, she joined his widow and children in Australia. Her health was now failing but she spent her remaining years travelling the world to various communist conferences, and in 1924 for example, although over seventy, representing the Australian communist party at the Moscow International Conference.

Dora Montefiore was an important figure in the suffrage movement, rebelling, like Emmeline Pankhurst, against Millicent Fawcett's leadership and taking the initiative, even before the WSPU was formed, in formulating a more active policy. Like Charlotte Despard, whom in some ways she resembled, she was not able to accept either the Pankhurst style of leadership or some aspects of their militant campaign. Her ardent socialism was also a problem in her relationship with the WSPU as indeed it was for Sylvia Pankhurst, with whom Dora Montefiore had much more affinity than with either Emmeline or Christabel. A courageous and unconventional woman, she has been undeservedly neglected.

Our knowledge of Dora Montefiore comes from her autobiography *From a Victorian to a Modern* (London, Archer, 1927). Her contribution to the women's suffrage movement is discussed briefly in *Queen Christabel*, David Mitchell (London, Macdonald and Jane's, 1977). There are also a few references in *The Suffragette Movement*, Sylvia Pankhurst (London, Longmans, 1931; Virago, 1977).

MORRISON Frances 1807–1898

Frances Morrison, an Owenite socialist, was born Frances Cooper, the illegitimate daughter of a Surrey farm-girl. At the age of fifteen she fell in love with a house-painter, James Morrison, and went away with him to his native Birmingham. For a time they remained unmarried, but four or five years later, when she became pregnant, they married. Four daughters were born during the next few years, and meanwhile Frances ran a small newspaper shop and, encouraged by her husband, began to take an interest in politics. James Morrison himself had been involved in the parliamentary reform movement and was later active in the Owenite Operative Builders' Union.

He had been for a time the editor of a short-lived Radical paper *The Artisan*, and in 1833 became editor of *The Pioneer*, a paper which, under his leadership, became the principal organ of the Owenite-inspired general unionism and the second most widely read newspaper of the period. *The Pioneer* ran a Woman's Page through which women workers could make known their grievances, and Frances herself contributed articles under the pseudonym, 'The Bondswoman'. An intensely optimistic reformer, James shared his wife's ideas. He supported women's efforts to join the trade-union movement, and argued against those men who wished to keep them out. He also denounced the way in which husbands used their position as wage-earners to maintain control over their wives. In collaboration with Frances he produced editorials on a variety of feminist themes ranging from the inequality of the marriage laws to the demand for equal pay.

In 1838 Frances published 'The Influence of the Present Marriage system upon the Character and Interests of Females, contrasted with that proposed by Robert Owen Esq. A Lecture delivered in the Social Institution, Manchester, 2nd September 1838'. In it she argued for the strict enforcement of the marriage laws to combat what she saw as the licentiousness of the age. Even in the egalitarian socialist communes of the future there would, she argued, be no 'indiscriminate wantonness'. Marriages of convenience would, however, be ended and would be replaced by permanent partnerships based on monogamous affection.

In the late 1830s James Morrison died in an accidental fall. A fund was raised within

Owenite circles to provide his widow with a small shop, but this did not, apparently, meet her needs and those of her four young daughters. She moved to Salford and was employed for a time as a 'hostess' at an Owenite social institution. Later she became a travelling lecturer, speaking mainly on the rights of women and the marriage laws, and then with the help of Robert Owen obtained a teaching post at Hulme. Eventually she married a pastry-cook named Robert Sutton, by whom she had another daughter. Nothing is known of her later life, although there were rumours, quite possibly false, that in the 1840s she abandoned her socialist beliefs.

Frances Morrison was one of the small band of socialist feminists inspired by communitarian socialism to develop a new view of marriage and of the relationship between men and women. She seems to have been encouraged by her husband to express her ideas, and their relationship, which began when she was only fifteen years of age, seems to have been an important fact in her development. She was aided by her access, through him, to the socialist press, and later by the Owenite lecture circuit, which enabled her to bring her ideas before a wider public. In common with other socialist feminists she represents an early tradition of British feminism which has, until recently, been neglected.

The source for what little we know of Frances Morrison's life is *Eve and the New Jerusalem*, Barbara Taylor (London, Virago, 1983).

N

NEVINSON Henry Woodd 1856–1941

Henry Nevinson, a journalist, was the second son of George Nevinson, a solicitor, and his wife Mary Basil Woodd. Born in Leicester, he attended Shrewsbury School and Christ Church Oxford, where he came under the influence of the Christian Socialists. He spent a short time teaching Greek at Westminster School, and then studied German literature in Germany. In 1884 he married Margaret Wynne Jones and, after a year in Germany, they settled down in Whitechapel where he worked at Toynbee Hall and lectured on history at Bedford College. Later they moved to Hampstead, but these were years of poverty and frustration which ended only in 1897 when he became foreign correspondent for the *Daily Chronicle* covering the Greco-Turkish war. Henry Nevinson had no talent for domesticity and his temperament craved a life of adventure which was at last satisfied. For the next thirty years he was largely abroad, not simply as a chronicler of events but as a crusader, seeking actively to help subject people struggling for freedom. Perhaps his most important crusade during these years was that against slavery in Portuguese Angola, which he described in *A Modern Slavery* published in 1906.

He was first drawn into the women's suffrage movement in 1907 and his involvement lasted until 1918, although it was interrupted by visits to India, Spain and Albania and by his work as a war correspondent in Europe between 1914 and 1918. Although his chief value to the movement was as a journalist, whose sympathetic reporting of events could always be relied on, his participation involved very much more than this. He made his first speech in 1907 and the following year heckled Lloyd George at a meeting. The violent manner in which he was treated by the stewards aroused his anger and his protests led to a short suspension from his job with the *Daily News*. In that year, with his friend Henry Brailsford, he founded the Men's League for Women's Suffrage. In 1909, along with Henry Brailsford, he resigned from the *Daily News* when the editor refused to condemn forcible feeding, and was for a time out of work.

During the next few years he spoke at meetings, took part in demonstrations, and was involved in several deputations especially against the 1913 Cat and Mouse Act. Apart from his extensive writing on women's suffrage as a journalist, he was also responsible for a pamphlet 'Women's Vote and Men' which had originally been an article in *The English Review* and was republished by the Women's Freedom League in 1913. At first he had been captivated by the beauty and eloquence of Christabel Pankhurst, but later he became disillusioned, especially after the break with Emmeline and Henry Pethick-Lawrence in 1912 when they tried to restrain Christabel from further militancy. Indeed he tried hard to bring about a reconciliation between them but Christabel was determined that they must go, and later Nevinson was to describe her as 'pitiless'. For a time he transferred his allegiance to Sylvia Pankhurst, but eventually joined with a number of others, including the Pethick-Lawrences and Evelyn Sharp, in a new organisation, the United Suffragists, which was active throughout the war in pressing for adult suffrage. His own absence as a war correspondent limited his activity but he was by no means inactive. In 1916, for example, he represented the United Suffragists at a meeting in the House of Commons to discuss the possibility of including women in a suffrage Bill. He also acted as chairman of the National Council for Adult Suffrage, and when women's suffrage was partially achieved in 1918 he was present in the lobby of the House of Commons.

After the war Henry Nevinson continued his work as a foreign correspondent, working in the Middle East, in Europe and in Washington. In 1932 his wife died, and the following year he married Evelyn Sharp who had been a friend and fellow suffrage worker for many years. Although by this time his days as an active journalist were over, he maintained his concern for political freedom and in 1939 was president of the Council for the Defence of Civil Liberties.

Henry Nevinson's involvement in women's suffrage was therefore a relatively brief one, but his support and encouragement were important, both during the period of militancy and during the war, when the enthusiasm of many suffrage workers was lost. In many respects his interest in women's suffrage was inspired by much the same motives as his campaigns in other parts of the world. He was moved partly by a hatred of cruelty and oppression, and partly by pity for the sufferings of the victims, which is why forcible feeding and the Cat and Mouse Act aroused in him such horror and indignation. At the same time he obviously admired the courage and determination of the militant leaders. At heart a romantic, his view of women was not without its protective side, and female beauty had a strong appeal to him. On the other hand, his passion for freedom, which inspired so much of his work, gave him sympathy also for women's need for political rights and self-determination. Moreover, once committed to the cause he was determined and courageous in its support.

Henry Nevinson has written his own account of his involvement with the women's suffrage movement in *More Changes, More Chances* (London, Nisbet and Co., 1925). See also *Queen Christabel*, David Mitchell (London, Macdonald and Jane's, 1977), and *The Suffragette Movement*, Sylvia Pankhurst (London, Longmans, 1931; Virago, 1977). *DNB* 1941-1950 pp. 619-21. Nevinson's Diaries are in the Bodleian Library, Oxford.

See also BRAILSFORD Henry Noel, NEVINSON Margaret Wynne, SHARP Evelyn.

NEVINSON Margaret Wynne ?1860-1932

Margaret Nevinson, a writer, was the daughter of the reverend Timothy Jones, a notable classical scholar who was also a Welsh-speaking Welshman and who had been influenced by the Oxford Movement. Margaret was the only daughter in a family of five sons, and her father taught her Latin and Greek with her brothers, but was later upbraided by her mother for encouraging his daughter to be a blue-stocking. Her brothers went away to school but Margaret remained at home except for occasional and unsuccessful periods at inefficient day-schools. Later on she spent two unhappy terms at a High-Church convent school and a short period at a Paris finishing school.

The sudden death of her father left the family in comparative poverty and ended her formal education, and she remained at home with her conventional mother who believed that a bad marriage was better than no marriage at all. Shortly after this, pressure to accept a proposal from an elderly but wealthy bachelor produced in Margaret a revulsion against marriage itself. She determined to leave home and with the help of a friend of her father obtained a post as a governess. Later she taught for a period in Germany. An ambition to go to Girton was frustrated by lack of money, but the good classical education she had received from her father enabled her to obtain in 1880, a post at South Hampstead High School for Girls. She also started work for a degree at St Andrews, which she eventually obtained.

In the meantime she began to be drawn into the women's movement and collected signatures for the Married Women's Property Act of 1882. In 1884 she married Henry Nevinson, whom she had known as a child. The couple spent twelve months in Germany and returned to live in Whitechapel where her first child, a daughter, was born. She was not, even from the start, content with a life of domesticity, but they were very poor and unable to afford the domestic help which would have freed her. She did, however, do some work for Toynbee Hall, where the warden encouraged her, and later found some paid employment as a rent collector. She also persisted, whenever she had the time, in an early ambition to be a writer. In 1887 there was a move to more satisfactory accommodation in Hampstead and their second child, a son, was born. Not until 1897, however, when Henry Nevinson took up a post on the *Daily Chronicle*, were they removed from the grinding poverty of the early years of their marriage. As foreign correspondent he now found his thwarted desire for adventure at last satisfied, and for the next thirty years was at home only for short periods between assignments overseas.

At first Margaret Nevinson was occupied with the management of the house and the care of her two young children but gradually, as they grew older, she began to find more time for her own life. She wrote articles, served as a school manager, and was later elected as a Poor Law Guardian. In 1905 she was attracted to the recently formed Women's Social and Political Union and became one of the first members of the Hampstead committee. After the split in the organisation in 1907, she joined the breakaway Women's Freedom League, horrified by the autocratic attitudes displayed by Emmeline Pankhurst. She was also an early member of the Women Writers' Suffrage League.

Although at first Margaret Nevinson found the prospect of speaking at open-air meetings terrifying, she overcame her fears and made her first speech in 1906. She was also active on deputations and processions, and as a tax-resister, the policy adopted by the Women's Freedom League in place of the more violent tactics of the Women's Social and Political Union. During her involvement with the suffrage campaign she had the willing support of her children. Her son marched with her, and her daughter, who married in 1911, omitted the word 'obey' from the marriage service. Her husband was also active in the suffrage movement, but, unlike her, supported Christabel Pankhurst, whom he admired exceedingly, although later he too became disillusioned with her policy.

It was as a writer, however, that Margaret Nevinson probably made her greatest personal contribution. She wrote several pamphlets which were published by the Women's Freedom League and included *Five Years Struggle for Freedom. A History of the Suffrage Movement from 1908 to 1912* (1912); *Ancient Suffragettes* (1913) and *The Spoilt Child of the Law* (1913). She also contributed articles to the journal *The Vote*. Her concern was wider than suffrage and she took a particular interest in workhouse reform, making use of the knowledge she had gained as a Poor Law Guardian. She contributed an important series of articles 'Workhouse Characters' to the *Westminster Gazette*, which were later published in book form, appearing in 1918. Most significant of all, however, was her one-act play *In the Workhouse*. This was written to illustrate an actual case, in which it was found that a husband had the authority to detain his wife in the workhouse. It appeared originally in the *Westminster Gazette* but was later dramatised and put on at the Kingsway Theatre. The play was published by International Suffrage Shops, London, in 1911. Although the play was attacked for its plain speaking, the law was changed the following year.

The war was a lonely and anxious time for Margaret Nevinson, particularly on behalf of her son, to whom she was very close, and the final success of the suffrage campaign was clouded, for her, by depression and anxiety. After the war was over, however, she campaigned with the Women's Freedom League for women to be accepted as magistrates and, once this appeal was granted, she was herself appointed as a JP in 1920. She was also asked twice to stand for Parliament, but each time refused, although she maintained her interest in politics, working in elections on behalf of her feminist friends. She also kept up her writing, publishing *Fragments of Life. Tales and Sketches* (London, Allen and Unwin, 1922) and a pamphlet *The Legal Wrongs of Married Women*, published by the Women's Freedom League in 1923. In 1926 she was present at the Women's Freedom League's silver wedding presentation to Emmeline and Frederick Pethick-Lawrence. The year 1926 also saw the publication of her autobiography, only six years before her death in 1932.

Margaret Nevinson's feminism was bound up very closely with her own experiences. The only daughter in a family of sons, she experienced at first hand the educational discrimination which most girls still suffered even in the 1870s. Moreover, she was probably sensitised to this as an injustice by the contrast between the encouragement she received from her intellectual father and the extreme conventionality of her mother's attitude. Her desire to make a life of her own was hampered by her family circumstances and later, after she had with difficulty achieved some degree of independence, she was caught in a marriage which, as her autobiography reveals, brought her a great deal of loneliness and frustration. Only in middle age did she succeed in breaking out of the confines of domesticity to achieve in a small way her early ambition to succeed as a writer. She had a strong resemblance to her father, for whom she always felt a special affinity, and in some respects his influence may be said to have remained with her all her life. Sensitive, independent and courageous, she illustrates the extent to which equal-rights feminism represented for some women a desire for self-expression and personal achievement which family claims often denied.

For Margaret Nevinson's autobiography see *Life's Fitful Fever. A Volume of Memories* (London, A.C. Black, 1926).

See also NEVINSON Henry Woodd.

NICHOLL Elizabeth Pease 1807–1897

Elizabeth Pease Nicholl, an early suffragist, was the daughter of Joseph Pease, a Quaker manufacturer who was instrumental in founding the British India Society and in promoting work for the abolition of slavery in India. He drew his daughter into the anti-slavery movement and she became the most influential woman in the British abolitionist circle. She corresponded with many of the American anti-slavery leaders, including the Grimké sisters, and it was Sarah Grimké who, in 1842, urged her to examine the subject of women's rights. Although sympathetic, she does not appear to have taken any action at this time. Some time during the 1850s she married Professor John Nicholl of the University of Glasgow and moved to Scotland. This caused a breach with the Society of Friends, since she had married outside the Quaker circle.

In the late 1860s, now known as Elizabeth Pease Nicholl, she took part in the campaign for women's suffrage, and remained active at least until 1880 when she attended a woman's suffrage demonstration. During the 1870s she worked for the repeal of the Contagious Diseases Acts which required the compulsory medical examination and treatment of women believed to be prostitutes, and for the medical education of women. Like Anne Knight she represents the link between the Society of Friends, the anti-slavery movement and women's rights. Her feminism was only one aspect of a more general concern for human rights and she was involved, during her life-time, in such apparently disparate causes as Chartism, the Anti-Corn Law League, Italian unification and the RSPCA, all of which have links with feminism. She illustrates the extent to which much of the nineteenth-century feminist movement was bound up with a wider movement for social reform which was essentially humanitarian and frequently also religious in its inspiration.

There is little biographical information available on Elizabeth Pease Nicholl. The best source is *British and American Abolitionists. An Episode in Transatlantic Understanding*, Clare Taylor, Edinburgh, Edinburgh University Press, 1974. There are brief references in *Politics and the Public Conscience*.

Slave Emancipation and Abolitionist Movements in Britain, Edith Hurwitz (London, Allen and Unwin, 1973); 'A genealogy of Reform' by Brian Harrison in *Anti-Slavery. Religion and Reform* ed. Christine Boult and Seymour Drescher (Folkestone and Hamden Connecticut, Dawson-Archer, 1980); *Prostitution and Victorian Social Reform*, Paul McHugh (New York, St Martin's, 1980).

NIGHTINGALE Florence 1820–1910

Florence Nightingale, social and sanitary reformer, was the second of the two daughters of William Edward Nightingale, a wealthy landowner, and his wife Fanny Smith. On her mother's side she was related to William Smith, a Unitarian and a friend of Wilberforce who was prominent in the abolitionist movement. In spite of this background, however, her mother was a worldly and conventional person who wanted nothing more from her daughter than a brilliant marriage. Her father, a Unitarian and a Whig, was scholarly and serious-minded but weak and indolent so that it was largely his wife who dominated the family. During Florence's childhood she was very close to her father who, lacking a son, made her his companion and friend, but later, as she recognised the weakness in his character, she became ambivalent towards him. At no time, however, could she come to terms with her worldly and dominating mother, nor with her sister Parthenope.

Florence as a young woman was charming and clever as well as wealthy and she had no lack of admirers, but neither then, nor later, did she ever respond wholeheartedly to any offer of marriage. Indeed, her earliest passion was for her cousin Marianne Nicholson and throughout her life it was women who aroused romantic longings in her. She rejected her suitors, therefore, and already by 1844 she had proposed to her family her scheme to train as a nurse. Her mother in particular had by no means given up hope of marriage for her daughter and was horrified at the idea of nursing, largely because of the immorality then associated with nurses who were normally ignorant women from the lowest social class.

The next years were desperately unhappy ones for Florence Nightingale. Her restless nature and high intelligence left her bored with the trivialities of a fashionable life, and she longed to have been born a boy. Yet she was not naturally a rebel and found it hard to go against the wishes of her family. Moreover she recognised in herself a need for affection and did not find it altogether easy to make the final sacrifice of husband and children. During these years Richard Monkton Milnes, later Lord Houghton, proved himself the most patient of suitors and she was clearly drawn to him, but the knowledge that marriage would mean only a continuation of her present life always came between them. Eventually, in 1851, he became engaged to someone else and this freed her from the indecision in which she had been trapped.

She now began to press her claims with more persistence, and with the support of friends paid a visit to the hospital at Kaiserworth, which fired her with fresh enthusiasm. In 1853, she was appointed resident lady superintendent at the Invalid Gentlewoman's Institution in Harley Street and her career may be said to have begun. Then, in 1854, mainly through her friendship with Elizabeth Herbert, the wife of Sidney Herbert, the opportunity came to take on the leadership of a group of nurses in the Crimea.

The period during 1854 and 1855 that she spent in the Crimea was the turning point in her life. As a popular heroine it gave her respect which she could use to her own advantage. It also freed her finally from her subordination to her mother. Most importantly of all, it provided her with the great cause for which she had been seeking. Horrified at the waste of life, not through the war itself, which she never queried, but through the lack of hygiene and elementary care, she resolved to spend her remaining strength in improving the health and conditions of the soldiers in the British Army.

On her return to England she was still very

ill as a consequence of her experiences in the Crimea but she refused to rest. Believing that she was soon to die, she drove herself and those about her remorselessly, haunted by the memory of the men who had died. During the next few years she worked for Army reform, using whatever human tools came to hand. Her Aunt Mai became her guardian angel, taking the place of the mother she now rejected. Aunt Mai's son-in-law, Arthur Hugh Clough, became a kind of secretary, and Sidney Herbert was given the task of carrying out the reform that she devised. Others who were important included Dr John Sutherland who met her in the Crimea and for thirty-six years afterwards acted as her trusted advisor.

Reform came slowly, largely due to opposition from the War Office. Moreover, the death of Sidney Herbert in 1861 and Arthur Hugh Clough shortly afterwards were blows from which she found it hard to recover. Nevertheless her efforts were by no means without success, although her own mood, often enough, was one of despair. The Sanitary Commission of 1857 resulted in improvements in Army conditions, and it was largely due to her efforts that the Army Medical College was founded. She was also the main agency behind the Royal Sanitary Commission on India and its report in 1863 was written mainly by her.

During these years Florence Nightingale developed the life-style that she was to follow until she died. Living in seclusion, she maintained the habits of an invalid, rarely leaving her room and accepting visitors only on her own terms. Adopted at first out of necessity on her return exhausted from the Crimea, she maintained this life-style as a defence against those, including her family, who might otherwise have frittered away her time and energy. Work remained her passion and she lived for nothing else.

The reform of the Army was not, however, her only preoccupation. She retained her interest in nursing and in 1859 published *Notes on Hospitals*, followed by *Notes on Nursing*. She then turned her attention to the training of nurses. A training school was established in 1860, which enabled her to develop her ideas on nursing as a profession. Based closely on religious sisterhoods, the emphasis was as much moral as physical. She also took a great deal of interest in the work of William Rathbone, Eleanor Rathbone's father, in the training of nurses for workhouses.

By the 1870s some of the drive which consumed her began to lessen and her personality gradually softened. Her activities in the cause of reform decreased, but by no means ceased, and she involved herself both in reform in India and in the training of nurses, right up until almost the end of her life. By 1895 however she was blind, and soon afterwards the loss of other faculties left her helpless, although she did not die until 1910.

During her life-time Florence Nightingale was inevitably drawn into relationships, almost in spite of herself, with the growing women's movement. In some respects indeed she was one of the outstanding feminists of her generation, her whole life a passionate declaration of the rights of women to an independent life. As early as 1852 she had put down her thoughts on this subject, and in 1859 they were privately printed as part of *Suggestions for Thought to Searchers after Religious Truths*. A moving plea for the emancipation of women from the restrictions that hedged their lives, it sufficiently impressed John Stuart Mill for him to use some of its examples in his *Subjection of Women*, published in 1869. Although privately printed and circulated, *Suggestions for Thought* was never published, so that her arguments were probably not widely known at the time. In 1928, however, Ray Strachey included a section under the title 'Cassandra' as an appendix to her history of the women's movement, *The Cause* (London, Bell and Sons) and it is now well known as an example of early feminist writing.

Nevertheless, there is no doubt that Florence Nightingale was unsympathetic to some of the causes that occupied the women's movement. She was, for example, sceptical at first about the demand for women's suffrage, not because she opposed it, but because she feared that women, like men, would not use the vote wisely. Moreover, other issues, like married women's property, seemed to her more important. She was also inclined at first to doubt the need for women doctors, believing that the need for better nurses was more urgent. Even when she accepted a cause as just, she was not necessarily prepared to join enthusiastically in the campaign. A good example is her attitude to the initial proposals for the Contagious Diseases legislation, which suggested that, in order to protect the Armed Forces against veneral disease, women suspected of prostitution should be compulsorily medically examined and if necessary treated. Uncompromisingly hostile, she did everything in her power to see that this idea was dropped, although she was ultimately unsuccessful and the legislation was passed. Her arguments were wide-ranging but depended in large part on the feminist viewpoint that the Act penalised women and exonerated men.

Nevertheless, when the campaign against the Acts started in earnest in 1870, she was cautious in lending her support. This was in large part, however, a question of style. Florence Nightingale always preferred to work behind the scenes, often anonymously, and Josephine Butler's passionate and charismatic leadership was the exact opposite of her own approach. Undoubtedly, too, her attitude to the women's movement was influenced by her attitude to women. Her resentment against her mother and sister never left her and was undoubtedly, if unconsciously, behind many of her outbursts against women in general, and she always found it easier to work with and through men, although she also needed the affection of women.

Many of the problems faced by Florence Nightingale throughout her reforming career were due to her position as a woman in a man's world. She had to learn how to gain her ends without arousing the antagonism of men who were hostile to the idea of a woman in command, and she soon learned to stay in the background, making use of able and powerful men who were prepared to act on her behalf. Moreover, it says a great deal for her ability in this direction that such men were usually to be found when she needed them. She had, it is true, a great need for domination but she seems to have used it mainly in the service of others. Although she earned her reputation as the 'Lady of the Lamp' in the Crimea, it was as a social reformer that she excelled, and she had extraordinary abilities in the collecting, assembling and reporting of the background material a reformer needs. Not all her ideas were sound, and she failed to keep up with new medical knowledge during her life-time, but in other respects, especially in her concern for hygiene, she was ahead of her time.

A complex and strongly individual personality, her feminism too is not easy to define. She earnestly desired the emancipation of women but as a means to service rather than as an end in itself, and she had no belief in any abstract doctrine of women's rights. Her religious feelings were deep, if highy unorthodox, and she wanted to free women so that they could better share in God's purpose for the world. Her feminism was as much a matter of instinct as of reason and reflects her own desperate desire as a young woman for a sense of destiny and purpose, and it provided an inspiration to future generations of women.

The official biography of Florence Nightingale is *The Life of Florence Nightingale*, Sir Edward Cook (London, Macmillan, 1913). This forms the basis for most later biographies including the well-known but somewhat controversial *Florence Nightingale 1820–1910*, Cecil Woodham-Smith (Harmondsworth, Penguin, 1951). A different approach is taken in *Florence Nightingale and the Doctors*, Zachary Cope (London, Museum Press, 1958). A recent analysis which, however, underplays her feminism, is *Florence Nightingale. Reputation and Power*, F.B. Smith (London, Croom Helm, 1982). A good account of the relationship between her religion and her feminism is in *Josephine Butler, Octavia Hill, Florence Nightingale. Three Victorian Women who changed their World*, Nancy Boyd (London, Macmillan,

1982). See also *DNB* 1901-1911 pp.15-19. A new assessment of her as a feminist is given in *Significant Sisters*, Margaret Forster (London, Secker and Warburg, 1984).

NORTON Caroline 1808-1877

Caroline Norton was a successful poet and novelist. Her father, Thomas Sheridan, was the only son of Richard Brinsley Sheridan, the dramatist and his first wife, Elizabeth Linley, and her mother was Caroline Henrietta Callandar. There were six children of the marriage, three sons and three daughters. Caroline's father died when she was eight years old, leaving the family in straitened financial circumstances. At the age of sixteen, when she was still at school, Caroline met George Norton, the younger brother of Lord Grantley of Womersh who fell in love with her and proposed marriage. No decision was taken at the time but two years later he repeated the proposal and was accepted. Although she did not love him, it must have seemed a good match, for Caroline was almost penniless, and the marriage took place in 1827 when Caroline was nineteen.

In fact, however, the marriage proved disastrous. Beautiful, clever, but passionate and self-willed, Caroline was speedily bored by her husband, who was dull and indolent, and she took little pains to hide her feelings. George Norton responded to her sarcasm with physical violence and matters were made worse by the undisguised hostility of his family, who disapproved of the marriage. Discontented with her husband, Caroline found solace in her sons, Fletcher, born in 1829, Brinsley in 1831 and William in 1833, and in her friends in London society.

Young as she was, Caroline Norton was already making a name for herself as a writer, having published in 1829 a long poem *The Sorrows of Rosalie*, and in 1830 another poem *The Undying One*. In 1832, she also took on the editorship of *La Belle Assemblée and Court Magazine*. These literary successes were important not only in giving her a reputation, but financially, since George was constantly in financial difficulties. It was, indeed, in the hope of obtaining some advantage for her husband that Caroline in 1831 first made the acquaintance of Lord Melbourne who found him an appointment as a magistrate. The friendship between Caroline Norton and Lord Melbourne developed swiftly however. He was fascinated by her beauty and wit, and she found in him a brilliant contrast to her plodding husband. Moreover, although their relationship provoked a certain amount of scandal, George Norton acquiesced in it in the hope of further advantage to himself.

Nevertheless, the marriage was under increasing strain and on one occasion his violence had to be curbed by the servants. She even left him once, but returned for the sake of the children. Eventually, in 1835, Caroline, who had been visiting her relatives, was refused entry to the house or access to the children, who were sent away and, as a first step towards a divorce, George Norton brought a suit against Lord Melbourne for alienating his wife's affections. There is still speculation as to George Norton's reasons for doing this, since he had previously encouraged the relationship, and it has been suggested that he hoped to receive a substantial sum of money in damages. Whatever his motives, however, he had no real evidence of the adultery which the suit required, and the case was dismissed. Indeed it seems possible that George Norton did not himself really believe his accusation. Lord Melbourne would undoubtedly like to have made Caroline his mistress, and she on her part was fascinated by him and enjoyed the contact with the powerful world of politics that he represented but the bitterness that was to engulf her whole life was a consequence, it seems certain, of the knowledge that she had not in fact yielded.

The acquittal of Lord Melbourne ended George Norton's hopes of divorce, but the two remained apart and Caroline continued to be separated from her children. Moreover, in spite of the court decision, her reputation was damaged since there were many who continued to believe in her guilt. Lord

Melbourne too refused to see her and she felt deserted and betrayed by the man who had seemed to love her. It was the loss of her sons, however, that caused her the greatest anguish, and she tried desperately to see them, even, on one occasion, trying to kidnap them.

It was in this state of mind that in 1836, just after the trial, she wrote her pamphlet *The Natural Claim of a Mother to the Custody of her Children as affected by the Common Law Rights of the Father*. According to the law a father had absolute rights and a mother no rights at all, whatever the behaviour of the husband, who was permitted indeed to desert his wife and hand her children over to his mistress if he so desired. She found support for her views from a member of Parliament, Sergeant-at-Law Talfourd, who in his own professional career had twice won the case for fathers to the outrage of his own conscience. He introduced a Bill into the House of Commons which allowed mothers, against whom adultery had not been proved, to have the custody of children under seven, with rights of access to older children.

In 1838 the Bill was passed by the House of Commons but rejected by the Lords, and Caroline Norton wrote another pamphlet *A Plain Letter to the Lord Chancellor on the Law of Custody of Infants*, using the male pseudonym 'Pearce Stevens', which was sent to every member of Parliament and every peer. The interest it aroused eventually carried the Bill and in 1839 the first piece of feminist legislation passed into law. It was not until 1842, however, that Caroline was able to break down the obstinacy of her husband, and indeed he did not yield until the death of William, the youngest boy, as a result of a neglected accident.

During the 1840s Caroline Norton knew a period of greater happiness. No longer parted from her children, she also enjoyed a growing literary reputation and, to a certain extent, a re-acceptance into society. In 1840, for example, *Dreams and Other Poems* was received very favourably, and Hartley Coleridge described her as the 'Byron of modern poetesses'. In 1845 she published her most ambitious poem *The Child of the Islands*. Her first novel, published in 1835, did not meet with much success but in 1851 a second novel, *Stuart of Dunleath*, which drew heavily on her own experiences, was very favourably received. Less happy was her relationship with Sidney Herbert. Deeply attracted to each other, marriage was out of the question and their close friendship came to an end with his own marriage in 1846. Undoubtedly the episode underlined for her the sadness and vulnerability of her position.

The 1840s had also seen something of a truce with George Norton, but in 1851 the death of Caroline's mother precipitated a new crisis. Her mother left her a small legacy, and her husband took the opportunity to reduce her allowance. She disputed his right to do this and in the ensuing battle he discovered that in 1848, without his knowledge, she had received a legacy from Lord Melbourne. This appears to have revived all his old suspicions, and in a fury he again accused her, in *The Times*, of adultery. She responded, and soon all the old bitterness was revived between them. For three years she received no money from him, although she was faced with heavy expenses arising from the illness of her eldest son. It was then that she discovered that she had no legal claim to her legacies, or indeed her earnings, and that George Norton was entitled to everything she owned.

Once more, in her anger and frustration, Caroline Norton turned to an attempt to amend the law, publishing in 1854 *English Laws for Women in the Nineteenth Century* which was largely an account of her own experiences with the law. At the same time, the whole issue of divorce was before Parliament in the shape of a Bill introduced by Lord Cranworth which actually made things worse for women. In 1855, therefore, she published another pamphlet, *A Letter to the Queen on Lord Cranworth's Marriage and Divorce Bill* which pleaded the case of divorced and separated wives. This brought her into direct opposition to the attempts by Barbara Leigh Smith and her allies to amend the law on property for all married women. In the event it was Caroline's more limited position which won the day, and the Marriage and Divorce Act of 1857 incorporated several of her suggestions, which gave divorced and separated women rights to property and earnings acquired after the marriage breakdown, as well as the right to sue. This was an important issue for her, since, in 1837 when she was libelled in the *British and Foreign Review*, she learned that as a married woman she had no legal redress since she had no standing in the law. These reforms, by eliminating the worst cases of hardship, put back the wider cause of married women's property for nearly thirty years.

Although the breach with George Norton was never healed Caroline remained on good terms with her sons. The eldest entered the diplomatic service in 1847 and she travelled abroad with him several times until his death in 1859. Her second son was also delicate, and eventually became a permanent invalid. He settled in Italy and she undertook the education of his children in England. She also enjoyed the companionship of William Stirling, a man ten years her junior, whom she had first met in 1850. He was a constant and attentive friend and their relationship, which persisted even after his own marriage in 1865, was a great comfort to her as she grew older. She still maintained her literary output well into the 1860s, publishing two more novels, *Lost and Saved* (1863) and *Old Sir Douglas* (1867). In 1875 George Norton died, and in 1877 she married William Stirling, now Sir William Stirling Maxwell, whose own wife had died in 1874. She now had the security and protection she had so longed for, but it was not to last, and within a few months she was dead.

By no means a conventional feminist, Caroline Norton took pains to distinguish herself from those women who claimed equal rights with men. She had none of the drive for independence which characterised Harriet Martineau and Barbara Leigh-Smith, and her greatest happiness was to be courted and admired. It was her mistaken marriage and its consequences which forced her to take a feminist attitude as she gradually came to realise how little protection the law gave to a woman faced with the breakdown of her marriage.

She has been criticised because so much of her writing was so intensely personal and because of her persistent harping on her own wrongs. Nevertheless, credit must be given to the fact that she did not simply bemoan her fate but set out to challenge and ultimately to change the laws which wronged her. Moreover, her indignation at the comparison between her own tarnished reputation and the position of Lord Melbourne as the trusted confidant of the young Queen spilled over into a bitter denunciation of the double standard of sexual morality. In her novel *Lost and Saved* she commented 'for though the faults of women are visited as sins, the sins of men are not even visited as faults', a position not very different from that taken up by Josephine Butler. This suggests that Caroline Norton was more of an equal-rights feminist than she herself realised. Driven by circumstances rather than principle to take a feminist stand, she did not hesitate to use whatever means were within her power. Her natural instinct was to seek allies amongst men and she had no sympathy at all with the idea of a woman's movement. She remains, therefore, one of the most unusual and individual feminists of her generation.

The most recent biography is *Caroline Norton*, Alicia Acland (London, Constable, 1948). There is also an earlier biography *The Life of Mrs Norton*, Jane Gray Perkins (London, John Murray, 1909). For her relationship with Lord Melbourne see *The Letters of Caroline Norton to Lord Melbourne*, James O. Hoge and Clark Olney (Ohio State University Press, 1974). See also *Wives and Property*, Lee Holcombe (Oxford, Martin Robertson, 1983) and *DNB* Vol. XII, pp. 206–8. A new assessment of her life and work is in *Significant Sisters*, Margaret Forster (London, Secker and Warburg, 1984).

P

PANKHURST Christabel 1880–1958

Christabel Pankhurst, one of the leading suffragettes, was the eldest of the five children of Richard Pankhurst, a reforming lawyer well known as a suffrage supporter, and his wife Emmeline Goulden. Christabel grew up in an atmosphere in which women's rights were taken for granted, not only by her parents but by the other feminists who visited them. Moreover, the Pankhurst home was a centre not only for feminism but also for socialism as Richard and Emmeline moved away from their adherence to the Liberal Party and joined first the Fabians and later the Independent Labour Party. Although she had been born in Manchester, the Pankhursts moved to London in 1885, returning to Manchester in 1893 where Christabel and her younger sister Sylvia attended Manchester High School. Christabel's ambitions were not of a scholarly kind and she hoped to become a dancer. In 1898 these hopes were dashed when her father died suddenly from a perforated ulcer and her mother had to become the breadwinner for her four surviving children, the youngest a boy of nine. A post was found for her as registrar of births and deaths and this provided a small but regular income, but in addition she opened a shop, with Christabel as her assistant, and for the next two years Christabel lived a rather aimless existence. She hated the shop and spent most of her time daydreaming and reading novels.

In spite of her background Christabel had not so far been drawn to politics. In 1901, however, she met Eva Gore-Booth and Esther Roper, then active in Manchester in promoting the organisation of women's trade unions and encouraging working women to campaign for women's suffrage. Christabel fell deeply under their spell, even arousing the jealousy of her mother to whom Christabel would always be the best loved of her children. She became actively involved with them in their work, lecturing on women's suffrage to working-class audiences. Meanwhile her mother was becoming increasingly dissatisfied with the ILP and when, in 1903, she found that a Memorial Hall to her husband was not open to women she founded the Women's Social and Political Union to promote women's suffrage within the ILP.

By 1904 Christabel too was becoming dissatisfied with the slow progress of the suffrage campaign. Determined to try new methods, she heckled Churchill at the Free Trade League rally in an attempt to inject more spirit into the movement. The following year she took the first real step into militancy when she and Annie Kenney disrupted a Liberal Party meeting in Manchester and, in the commotion that followed, deliberately got themselves arrested and then went to prison rather than pay the fine. Their aim was publicity for the cause, and in this respect their tactic was a brilliant success since it made women's suffrage news. Moreover, it came at just the right time, when many long-term suffrage workers were dissatisfied with the slow progress of constitutional methods, and soon there were plenty of lively recruits to the new organisation.

For a time, however, neither Christabel nor Emmeline were at the forefront of the action which now gradually moved from Manchester to London. Sylvia Pankhurst headed the London campaign, along with Dora Montefiore. Later they were joined by Annie Kenney, Flora Drummond and Teresa Billington. Meanwhile Emmeline was trying to hold down her job as registrar and Christabel was studying for a degree in law which she had started at Owens College, Manchester, in 1903. Consequently the first group of suffragists to go to Holloway in 1906 did not include either Christabel or Emmeline.

By 1907, however, Emmeline had given up her job and Christabel had obtained a first-class degree in law. Her realisation that as a woman, a career in law was closed to her was a further impetus to her feminism. Together the two women moved to London and virtually took over the campaign. Their first step was to discourage the involvement of East End women and then they began a serious attempt to disengage the militant movement from the ILP. This brought them into serious conflict with a number of committed socialists within the WSPU and in the ensuing struggle for supremacy Dora Montefiore and Charlotte Despard were pushed out of the organisation, together with Teresa Billington, now Billington-Greig. Sylvia Pankhurst, although she retained her socialist beliefs, remained within the WSPU out of loyalty to her mother and sister. Teresa Billington-Greig and Charlotte Despard founded the Women's Freedom League which based itself on democratic principles. Within the WSPU, however, there was no longer any pretence at democracy. It was run by Christabel and Emmeline in association with Emmeline and Frederick Pethick-Lawrence who had been recruited by Christabel and Annie Kenney in 1906. To justify their position Emmeline and Christabel used the analogy of a war, in which they were the generals commanding an army of troops.

Although there were some even at this stage who, like Teresa Billington-Greig, had no time for Christabel's autocratic style, she was at this time a most potent advocate of her cause. She was a clever and persuasive speaker who fascinated men and women alike by her personal magnetism and physical beauty. During the next few years, in particular, her brilliant advocacy of women's suffrage impressed even some of her opponents and drew many women into the WSPU which from its small beginnings quickly became a large and wealthy organisation. Its advocacy of a limited suffrage attracted many wealthy women, and it was accused by its socialist opponents of being a bourgeois organisation. But neither Christabel nor Emmeline accepted this charge since they believed that even the most limited extension of the suffrage to women would establish the principle of women's right to vote. Moreover, they never accepted the sincerity of the adult suffrage movement, believing it an excuse to prevent any extension of the suffrage to women.

By 1910 the militant movement had entered a new phase. In prison the use by the women of the hunger-strike had provoked the authorities into forcible feeding which caused not only great suffering but, in some cases, permanent harm. The so-called Black Friday in 1910 in which both the police and the crowd used extreme violence against the demonstrators also did much to harden the mood of the women involved. Passive resistance and token violence began to give way to stone-throwing and, later, the destruction of property by fire. It is necessary to acknowledge that these changes were not initiated by Christabel herself. Although imprisoned in 1908 she afterwards held herself aloof from the danger of arrest in order to direct operations in safety, and it was Emmeline Pankhurst who bore the brunt of the front line. In 1912 Christabel, threatened with arrest, fled to Paris where she remained in hiding for the rest of the militant campaign. If, however, the increasing violence of the movement reflected the mood of the women actively involved in the struggle who, out of recklessness or despair or anger, pushed even deeper into violence either against themselves or against others, there is no doubt that Christabel encouraged it. In 1912, when the Pethick-Lawrences tried to stem the violence, Christabel, with Emmeline Pankhurst's support, virtually banished them. Nor were the Pethick-Lawrences the only ones to be made anxious by the policy, and the years 1912 to 1914 saw a number of leading militants leave the organisation while others, like Annie Kenney, found their loyalty severely taxed.

Christabel used her exile in Paris to write a remarkable series of articles for *The Suffragette* which were later published as *The Great Scourge and how to End It*. The main theme of the articles was veneral disease, and although she weakened her argument by grossly exaggerating its extent the articles as a whole were a powerful indictment of the way in which women's economic dependence and lack of political power kept them in both economic and sexual subjection to men. Men's denial of the vote to women was, therefore, presented not in terms of abstract justice but as a direct cause of such social evils as prostitution and venereal disease. In effect, she argued, women would use their political power to enforce purity amongst men.

It is all the more striking, therefore, that a year after these articles were published both Christabel and her mother abandoned the struggle for the vote and entered with enthusiasm into a campaign of support for the government in its prosecution of the war. They had not, however, abandoned their feminism and in 1917 founded a Women's Party as a curious mixture of feminist policies, including equal pay, equal marriage laws and maternity and infant care, alongside such anti-socialist policies as the abolition of trade unions. Both Emmeline and Christabel took no part in the lengthy negotiations for the vote, but in 1918 Christabel, strongly supported by her mother, stood for Parliament as the leader of the new Women's Party. Unsuccessful, she tried again in 1919, but her support was dwindling and by the end of the year the new party had folded.

While Emmeline sailed for Canada, where she was to remain until 1925, Christabel stayed in England, discontented and idle, but in a short while she had found a new cause in the Second Adventist movement. In 1921 she went to the United States where, for several years, she lectured on the Second Coming. Her lectures were successful, the books she wrote sold well, and she was able to support herself in comfort. For most of the period 1932–39 she was in England, but returned to the United States in 1939 where she lived until her death in 1958.

During her years as a Second Adventist Christabel Pankhurst moved away from feminism which she now regarded as largely irrelevant as a cure for the ills of the world. Although she still chafed at the evidence of sexual immorality, she now sought a religious rather than a political solution. She was entirely out of sympathy with the feminism of the 1920s and 30s with its emphasis on political reforms and its growing sexual permissiveness. Christabel's own brand of feminism had always been religious in its absolute faith and passionate intensity, and this was the secret of its appeal. She convinced her followers not only that her tactics were the only way to success, but that success would open the way to a veritable millennium for women. This supreme faith both in herself and in her cause was sustained by Emmeline Pankhurst, whose faith in her daughter never wavered, but was also part of Christabel's tendency to see the world in messianic terms which was to lead her eventually into the messianic movement.

Christabel Pankhurst had great personal charm and this was an enormous asset in keeping the loyalty and affection of her followers. For her own part, however, she seems rarely to have returned the affection she was given. Men did not appear to interest her, and indeed there are indications in her treatment of them that she tended to despise them. There is no indication, either, that she shared her sister Sylvia's devotion to their father. Her ties with women were stronger and this may be the justification for calling her lesbian, although there is no real evidence for that either. Her relationship with her mother was deeply significant but was certainly much stronger on her mother's side. Indeed the impression gained is of someone whose emotions were more deeply involved in causes than people.

This aspect of her personality, which underlies much of her coldness to individuals, has led to a generally unsympathetic assessment of Christabel both by many of her contemporaries, including Sylvia Pankhurst, and by recent commentaries on her life and work. Her biographer David Mitchell has also been influenced by his disapproval of her type of feminism, and many socialist feminists dislike her because of her anti-socialism. She has also been charged with being motivated solely by personal ambition although her feminism was certainly sincere. It should be remembered in her defence, however, that it was Christabel Pankhurst who revitalised the suffrage cause, and her energy and determination first turned it from a political pressure group into a movement. During the early years of militancy she was a heroine to the constitutionalists and militants alike. Later, however, she became a controversial figure, when the increased violence which she justified if she did not originate, alienated some of her supporters. Moreover, her articles on venereal disease aroused fears of a sex war which alarmed those who placed their emphasis on co-operation between men and women. This should not, however, be allowed to detract from the very real significance of her contribution to the suffrage movement in the decade before the first world war.

Most important of all perhaps was her attempt to construct a theory of militancy which would justify both the policy and the tactics of the militant movement. The subjection of women by men was, of course, fundamental to feminist ideas throughout the nineteenth century, but earlier feminism had worked on the principle that the system could be changed in co-operation with men by the use of reason. Christabel denied that men would ever give up their power voluntarily and urged that women must use force, not persuasion. In pursuit of this idea, which turned all men into potential enemies, she developed concepts which come very close to the modern feminist slogan, 'Sisterhood is Powerful', and she saw in militancy a weapon to only to intimidate men, but to raise the consciousness of women. Indeed her advice to women not to marry, by which she meant the avoidance of all sexual relationships with men, placed her close to the separatist tendencies of radical feminism today. Her stand on socialism also anticipated many contemporary arguments between socialists and feminists, and was a challenge to those who believed that socialism must take priority. She argued tenaciously that, while men retained their monopoly of political power, socialism would be as injurious to women as capitalism. In this respect, therefore, Christabel must be seen as pioneering a position within feminism which, if out of tune with feminism in the 1920s and 1930s, has nevertheless become a matter of profound importance to modern feminists and in this respect her contribution to feminist ideology cannot be ignored.

The biography *Queen Christabel*, David Mitchell (London, Macdonald and Jane, 1977) is biased by Mitchell's failure to understand feminism, but gives a very full account of the facts of her life. 'Christabel Pankhurst: Reclaiming her Power' by Elizabeth Sarah in *Feminist Theorists*, ed. Dale Spender (London, The Women's Press, 1983) is a feminist reassessment which includes a critique of Mitchell. For her role in the suffrage movement see *Rise up Women*, Andrew Rosen (London, Routledge and Kegan Paul, 1974) and *The Suffragette Movement*, Sylvia Pankhurst (London, Longmans, 1931; Virago, 1977). For Christabel's own account see *The Unshackled*, Christabel Pankhurst (London, Hutchinson, 1959). See also *DNB* 1951–1960 pp. 789–91.

See also PANKHURST Emmeline, PANKHURST Richard Marsden, PANKHURST Sylvia.

PANKHURST Emmeline 1858–1928

Emmeline Pankhurst, a leading suffragette, was the eldest daughter and third child of Robert Goulden, a self-made manufacturer, and his wife Sophia Jane Crane. Her father came from a Radical family and had himself supported both the anti-slavery campaign and the Anti-Corn Law League. As a small child she had taken part in anti-slavery meetings, handing round a bag to collect funds for the relief of slaves, and later, at the age of fourteen, she began to attend suffrage meetings with her mother. She was educated at a rather inefficient school in Manchester and at the age of fifteen was sent to a finishing school in Paris. During this period she received a proposal of marriage from a young artist, but he demanded a dowry which her father refused. It is doubtful, however, how far she herself was serious about his offer. Returning to England in 1878, she met Richard Pankhurst, a lawyer who had already made a reputation for himself as a reformer, and an advocate of women's suffrage. He quickly fell in love with the beautiful and lively girl, and, although he was more than twice her age, she responded eagerly to his proposal of marriage, which took place in 1879 when she was twenty and he was forty-four.

The couple settled in Manchester where Emmeline joined in suffrage work, and in the campaign for married women's property and earnings rights. In 1880 Christabel was born, followed by Sylvia in 1882, Frank in 1884 and Adela in 1885. During these years Richard tried unsuccessfully to enter Parliament as an Independent, firstly at Manchester than at Rotherhithe. In spite of his record of service to the suffrage movement, Lydia Becker refused him the support of the suffrage organisation on the grounds that he was a firebrand and this action, which angered Emmeline greatly, may have contributed to her disillusion with the existing suffrage movement. During these years too they moved further to the Left in politics, leaving the Liberal Party when Gladstone refused to put women's suffrage in the Reform Bill of 1884, and joining the Fabian Society.

In 1885 the Pankhursts moved to London with the aim of furthering Richard's parliamentary career. This move, however, created financial problems which Emmeline tried to solve with a disastrous attempt to run a fancy-goods shop. There were, nevertheless, many satisfactions in London for Emmeline, especially in their growing circle of Radical and socialist friends, and she gained a reputation as a political hostess. In 1889 she and Richard were instrumental in the formation of the Women's Franchise League, a ginger group which emphasised married women's rights but which functioned only for a few years. In 1889 tragedy struck the family with the death of Frank from diphtheria, although that year also saw the birth of Harry, their last child.

In 1893 the Pankhursts returned to Manchester and became increasingly absorbed in the Independent Labour Party, which they joined in 1894. In 1895 Richard made his last attempt to enter Parliament, this time as an ILP candidate, but was again unsuccessful. Emmeline, however, became a Poor Law Guardian and her observations of the sufferings of women, particularly widows, mothers of illegitimate children, and women driven into prostitution by poverty, were to form a significant element in her passionate belief in the need for women's suffrage. The Boggart Hole Clough incident also revealed that she had the temperament for direct action. Banned by the City Council, who owned it, from using this site for open-air meetings, the ILP disobeyed this order, and Emmeline, when arrested, threatened to go to prison rather than pay the fine. The case against her was dismissed, although three ILP members did in fact go to prison, and eventually the City Council was forced to withdraw from the fight. The ultimate victory for the ILP may well have been a lesson in militancy for both Emmeline and Christabel.

In 1898 Richard Pankhurst, who had been in poor health for some time, died suddenly from a perforated ulcer leaving nothing behind but debts, and Emmeline was faced with the prospect of supporting her four children. She determined once again on a small shop, but the business was never a success and eventually had to be given up. Fortunately she was offered a registrarship of births and deaths which fell vacant at that time, and this she accepted, giving part of the day to her duties as registrar and part to the shop. Meanwhile she was becoming disillusioned with the failure of the ILP to give more than lukewarm support to the issue of women's suffrage, and in 1903 she founded the Women's Social and Political Union as an offshoot of the ILP focussing specifically on working-class women.

It was Christabel, however, who set the organisation on the path of militancy when, in 1905, she and Annie Kenney disrupted a major Liberal Party meeting in Manchester and, arrested in the commotion that followed, opted to go to prison rather than pay their fines. But if the first step in militancy must be credited to Christabel, Emmeline was not far behind. By 1907 the shop had been closed, she had resigned her position as registrar, forfeiting her pension, and had left Manchester to take her place beside Christabel as one of the leaders of the growing militant movement. From this time forward she threw herself into the struggle with an intensity that left no room for anything else in her life.

Emmeline did not go to prison until 1908, but during the next six years she was imprisoned repeatedly, emerging to take her place in demonstrations, deputations and processions, even when she was so weak that she could not stand. When she was too ill to carry on she was nursed back to some semblance of health and the struggle was resumed again. She spared herself nothing, suffering with other militants in every painful and humiliating experience, believing that even if she died—as she sometimes believed she would—the cause was worth the sacrifice. Certainly she inspired many other women to follow her example, and was a potent source of recruits to the cause.

On the outbreak of war both Emmeline and Christabel were swept by an emotion of patriotism which left no room for opposition to the government. Instead they, and a number of their loyal supporters, turned all their energies to help the war effort. In 1917 they formed the Women's Party, a queer mixture of feminist and fascist policies in which equal pay and equal marriage and divorce laws stood side by side with racial purity and the abolition of trade unions. When the issue of suffrage was raised during the war neither Emmeline nor Christabel took much interest, and negotiations with the government were left to the non-militant groups.

In 1918 Emmeline, now sixty years of age, visited Canada on a lecture tour, one of a number she had made to both Canada and the United States both before and during the war. On this occasion she became involved in the campaign of the National Council for Combating Venereal Disease and stayed on for several years as one of their lecturers. Eventually, however, the work exhausted her, and in 1925, still needing to earn her living, she opened a tea shop in Juan-les-Pins. Like her other business ventures this also failed and she returned to England, where she joined the Conservative Party and determined to enter Parliament. She was adopted as a candidate in the East End, much to the distress of her daughter Sylvia who had never moved away from her socialist beginnings. The breach between Emmeline and Sylvia was further widened by the news of Sylvia's baby, a product of a free love union, which shocked Emmeline to such an extent that she refused to see her daughter. By this time her health was failing rapidly and she did not live to fight the election. After her death in 1928 a bronze memorial statue was erected in Victoria Tower Gardens in memory of her service to women's suffrage. By this time she had become a symbol not only of militancy but of the whole suffrage movement.

Emmeline Pankhurst brought to the suffrage issue a will to succeed that amounted to fanaticism and which could not even for a moment accept the possibility of failure. To this extent it made of militancy a religious rather than a political struggle. Seeing it in many respects as a holy war, Emmeline and Christabel, in their joint leadership, demanded of their followers total obedience and unquestioning loyalty, and there was no room for dissension in their ranks. There were two serious splits over this issue, the first in 1907 when the Women's Freedom League was founded to follow more democratic principles, and the second in 1912 when the Pethick-Lawrences were expelled for their doubts on an extension of militancy. The year 1907 also saw the final rejection by both Emmeline and Christabel of the ILP, which was to lead eventually to their abandonment of socialism itself.

The strength of purpose with which Emmeline pursued her goals had always been a characteristic of her personality. Married to a much older man, she might have been submerged by the weight of his knowledge and experience. In fact she was in many ways the more active and ambitious of the partnership, although she never lost her admiration for him and, even after her widowhood, seems never to have been attracted by another man. Later, under the stress of the militant struggle and her own sufferings, her intensity of purpose began to verge on ruthlessness and she was ready to sacrifice not only friends like Keir Hardie but even, when she deemed it necessary, her own children. Both Adela and Sylvia earned her displeasure by refusing to give up their socialism and both were eventually rejected by her, although Sylvia certainly never ceased to love her. But it was her son Harry who suffered most greatly. Still a child when his father died, he was subsequently neglected by his mother who refused to recognise that his health needed special care. His death from poliomyelitis in 1910 was the tragic consequence.

It was Emmeline Pankhurst's intensity of purpose which enabled her to play the role she did in the militant suffrage movement. Between 1906 and 1914 she was the inspiration and hope of countless women who were drawn into the battle by her example. Perhaps what appealed most to her contemporaries was her superb physical courage, which provided a model that others could follow and which helped to give militancy a heroic quality which moved even those who disagreed with it. Today the precise part played by militancy in the struggle for the vote is debatable but, irrespective of the final verdict, Emmeline Pankhurst has earned herself an enduring place in women's history.

The best source on Emmeline Pankhurst's life is her daughter's account in *The Suffragette Movement*, Sylvia Pankhurst (London, Longmans, 1931; Virago, 1977) and *The Life of Emmeline Pankhurst*, Sylvia Pankhurst (London, Laurie, 1935). There is also an autobiography, *My Own Story*, Emmeline Pankhurst (London, Eveleigh Nash, 1914; Virago, 1979) which was in fact dictated to Rheta Child Dorr during a tour to the US in 1913 and which is mainly significant in revealing her state of mind at that time. *The Fighting Pankhursts*, David Mitchell (London, Jonathan Cape, 1967) is the main source for her later years. There is also a brief memoir *Female Pipings in Eden*, Ethel Smyth, (London, Peter Davies, 1933). See also *DNB* 1922-1930 pp. 652-4.

See also PANKHURST Christabel, PANKHURST Richard Marsden, PANKHURST Sylvia.

PANKHURST Richard Marsden 1835-1898

Richard Pankhurst, a lawyer, was called to the bar in 1867, and in that same year became a member of the executive of the newly-formed Manchester Suffrage Society. We know little of his early life or of his family background, but as a friend of the Chartist, Ernest Jones, and also of John Stuart Mill, he was already known for his Radical sympathies. He was also a convinced supporter of women's rights. During the next few years he devoted a good deal of attention to the suffrage cause, developing a close association with the suffrage leader Lydia Becker. In 1869 he acted as counsel in a suit in which women's enfranchisement was claimed on the basis of ancient statutes. In the following year he drafted the Women's Disabilities Removal Bill, introduced into the House of Commons by Jacob Bright. It was his amendment to the Municipal Corporation Bill of 1869, also moved by Jacob Bright, which resulted in the inclusion of unmarried women householders on the register of local electors.

A permanent breach with Lydia Becker occurred in 1874 when he, along with the Brights, refused to sanction an attempt to exclude married women from a proposed suffrage Bill. In 1878, already over forty years of age, he met the twenty-year-old Emmeline Goulden and a year later they were married. Perhaps stimulated by her encouragement, he now began to entertain parliamentary aspirations of his own, and in 1883 stood unsuccessfully for election as an

Independent in Manchester, making women's suffrage one of the planks in his campaign. He made a second attempt, also unsuccessful, two years later at Rotherhithe.

In 1885 the Pankhurst family moved to London where they became increasingly involved in the London Radical world. In 1889 he and Emmeline were instrumental in the formation of the Women's Franchise League, a ginger group emphasising married women's rights, which included in its programme such issues as equal rights in divorce and inheritance. It was never a very powerful or influential group however, and in the early 1890s was disbanded partly due to Richard's ill-health and the return of the family to Manchester. Both Richard and Emmeline, moreover, were increasingly absorbed in the Independent Labour Party, which they joined in 1894. Richard stood, again unsuccessfully, as an ILP candidate in the 1895 parliamentary election at Gorton, and Emmeline became a Poor Law Guardian. Richard's health, however, continued to worsen, and he died in 1898.

Apart from his work for women's suffrage, Richard Pankhurst was also of great service to the married women's property campaign. He served on the Married Women's Property Committee from its foundation in 1868, and was responsible for drafting a women's property Bill in that year, which eventually, much changed, produced a compromise Act in 1870. He also drafted the unsuccessful Bill of 1873.

Richard Pankhurst was a profoundly idealistic man who frequently gave his legal services free and whose opinions, which he never tried to hide, lost him many briefs. Although he seems to have held the love and admiration of his wife, and secured the lifelong devotion of his daughter Sylvia, his married life was clouded by financial insecurity and later by poor health. The much greater fame which their leadership of the militant movement gave to his wife, and to his daughters Christabel and Sylvia, has to a large extent obscured his own importance. Yet he was an important feminist in his own right, contributing both to the extension of women's suffrage in local government and the extension of married women's property rights.

For an account of Richard Pankhurst's contribution to the women's movement see *Rise up Women! The Militant Campaign of the Women's Social and Political Union*, Andrew Rosen (London, Routledge and Kegan Paul, 1974). For a more detailed and more personal account see *The Suffragette Movement*, Sylvia Pankhurst (London, Longmans, 1931; Virago, 1977). See also *Wives and Property*, Lee Holcombe (Oxford, Martin Robertson, 1983).

See also BECKER Lydia Ernestine, PANKHURST Christabel, PANKHURST Emmeline, PANKHURST Sylvia.

PANKHURST Sylvia 1882–1960

Sylvia Pankhurst, a leading suffragette, was the second of the five children of Richard Pankhurst, a reforming lawyer and active feminist, and his wife, Emmeline Goulden. Although she was born in Manchester, the Pankhursts moved to London in 1885 where they became involved in socialist as well as feminist circles, and Sylvia grew up in an atmosphere of Radical political discussion. The family moved back to Manchester in 1893 and for a time Sylvia attended Manchester High School. Of all the children, Sylvia was the closest to her father, and his death in 1898 from a perforated ulcer, while both her mother and her elder sister Christabel were abroad, affected her very deeply. She not only missed his constant love and encouragement but was haunted by a wholly unjustified but very real sense of guilt. Emmeline Pankhurst was left as the breadwinner with her four surviving children to support but Sylvia was enabled to continue her studies when she won a scholarship to an art school. Soon she developed into a highly talented artist, winning a travelling award to Venice and afterwards a scholarship to the Royal College of Art at South Kensington.

Meanwhile Christabel and her mother had founded the Women's Social and Political Union, and Sylvia was torn between her own strong belief in the suffrage cause and her sense of commitment as an artist. She began to take an increasing share in the affairs of the WSPU and, because she was living in London, took a leading part in the early stages of militancy while Christabel and her mother were in Manchester. From 1905, too, there was a growing attachment between Sylvia and Keir Hardie. An old friend of the family, she had known him since she was a child but, once she moved to London, he became for a number of years the most important person in her life. There was a strong physical attraction between them as well as deep affection, and his sympathy and encouragement did a great deal to help her through her increasing estrangement from her mother and Christabel.

In 1906, after two years at the Royal College of Art, Sylvia Pankhurst gave up her studies, supporting herself as best she could by various artistic commissions and giving most of her time to the suffrage cause. Her first imprisonment came in that year, when she protested in court at a trial in which women had not been allowed to speak in their defence. This was only the first of many periods in prison, which included successive hunger and thirst strikes under the provisions of the Cat and Mouse Act. Indeed Sylvia was hardly less heroic than her mother Emmeline in determining to endure with courage whatever suffering her frequent imprisonments forced upon her. These years also saw the publication, in 1911, of her first book *The History of the Women's Suffrage Movement.* There was also a propaganda tour of the United States.

Increasingly, however, she became disillusioned with many aspects of militant policy, and especially its total abandonment of its original socialism. She had never, like her mother and sister, rejected her membership of the Independent Labour Party, and she had tried from the start to involve working-class women in the East End in order to broaden the base of the suffrage movement. She also began a weekly paper for working-class women, *The Woman's Dreadnought.* Yet she tried to remain loyal to her mother and Christabel, and the final break did not come until the militants adopted a policy of widespread arson in 1912. Still convinced of the need for women's suffrage, she continued to work through her East End women's groups, leading a deputation to Asquith in 1914 which was a significant milestone in his conversion to the necessity for adult suffrage.

During the war Sylvia Pankhurst's break with her mother and sister was complete. She was strongly pacifist, in contrast to their wholehearted support for the war and, with Charlotte Despard, formed the Women's Peace Army, which demanded a negotiated peace. Her chief friend at this time was Norah Smyth, the daughter of a wealthy Liverpool merchant who had joined her in her work in the East End before the war and who, with Sylvia, pioneered social services for women in Bow. After the war they moved apart as Nora Smyth came to feel that Sylvia was becoming too idealistic and too isolated.

By this time Sylvia's commitment to socialism was greater than her commitment to women's suffrage. She changed the name of her paper to *The Workers' Dreadnought* and, in 1917, welcomed the news of the Russian revolution with passionate enthusiasm. Soon she was completely involved in the Hands off Russia campaign. At the end of the war she visited Russia where she met and argued with Lenin. An enthusiastic article from her pen in the *Dreadnought* led to a trial for sedition and a period of five months in prison. In 1921 she published her impressions in *Soviet Russia as I saw it.* She also joined the British communist party but could not work within it peacefully for long and was eventually expelled because of her insistence on freedom of expression.

At the end of the war she met Silvio Erasmus Corio, an Italian left-wing exile, eight years older than herself. They collaborated on a number of journalistic ventures and in 1924 she gave up the *Dreadnought* and they opened up a small café together. In 1927 their only child, Richard, was born. She refused to marry however, declaring in an article in 1928 that she was opposed to marriage as a legal contract. Nor did she, or Richard, take Silvio Corio's name.

But her change of circumstances did not stem her output of books and articles. Nor did her sense of political commitment which remained with her all her life. In 1926 she published *India and the Earthly Paradise* and in 1930 *Save the Mothers*, inspired by the birth of her son and urging the need for better maternal care. She also turned to memories of the past, influenced perhaps by the death of her mother in 1928. In 1931 she published *The Suffragette Movement*, a vivid personal account of people and events followed, in 1932, by *The Home Front* which described her activities during the war. finally, in 1936, she published her biography of her mother, *The Life of Emmeline Pankhurst*.

Meanwhile, under Corio's influence her attention had moved increasingly towards opposition to fascism and especially the fascist regime in Italy. During the 1920s she had been actively engaged in assisting Italian refugees and in the 1930s this was extended to Jews and to support for the republican cause in Spain. In 1936, in protest at Italian activity in Ethiopia, she founded the *New Times and Ethiopia News*, and the cause of Ethiopia was to remain at the centre of her life. She wrote and campaigned ceaselessly until 1954 when Corio died. Then she moved permanently to Ethiopia, where she was deeply and even reverently honoured, until her death in 1960.

Feminism was only one of Sylvia Pankhurst's interests, and by no means the most important one. For some ten years, however, she gave to the women's suffrage movement all her time and energy, serving it devotedly at the cost of great physical, and indeed mental, hardship. Moreover, by choosing to work with women from the East End she not only widened the base of the movement but helped to politicise many of the working-class women who were influenced by her example. Undoubtedly, too, her friendship with Keir Hardie was an important influence on his loyalty to women's suffrage at a time when to do so seriously strained his relationship with the Labour Party. She must also be considered one of the important chroniclers of the movement. Later her interests moved away from women's suffrage and, influenced by left-wing socialism, she came to believe that the vote itself was not important. She did not lose her feminist principles and tried to act them out in her own relationships, but after 1914 other issues captured her allegiance. Even before 1914, however, Sylvia, unlike her mother Emmeline and her sister Christabel, struggled to reconcile feminism and socialism, and she was never prepared to give issues of gender the primacy which characterised the attitudes of Emmeline and Christabel.

It seems certain that the key to Sylvia's personality lies in her relationship with her father. Christabel, the eldest sister, was her mother's favourite, but Sylvia was deeply influenced both emotionally and ideologically by her father's passionate moral commitment. For her both feminism and socialism were beliefs she had learned from her father's lips and she refused to give up socialism in favour of feminism, even if this meant the loss of her mother's affection. The decision by Emmeline at the end of her life to stand for Parliament as a Conservative candidate was a terrible betrayal to Sylvia, just as Sylvia's illegitimate child was a fatal blow to the conventional Emmeline, and the two were never reconciled. Perhaps it was the loss of her father and the estrangement from her mother which made Sylvia much more dependent on personal relationships than either Emmeline, who after her husband's death was totally absorbed by Christabel, or Christabel herself, for whom personal relationships were always secondary to her own sense of her mission. Idealistic, loyal, and tender-hearted, Sylvia's politics, too, were very much a matter of personal commitment and a matter much more of her heart than her head. She shared with all the Pankhursts, however, a fighting spirit and a tenacity of purpose which have guaranteed them a place in history.

There has been a recent biography of Sylvia

Pankhurst by her son, *Sylvia Pankhurst, Artist and Crusader. An Intimate Portrait*, Richard Pankhurst (New York and London, Paddington Press, 1979). See also *The Fighting Pankhursts. A Study in Tenacity*, David Mitchell (London, Jonathan Cape, 1967); *Queen Christabel*, David Mitchell (London, Macdonald and Jane's, 1977); *The Suffragette Movement*, Sylvia Pankhurst (London, Longmans, 1931; Virago, 1977).

See also BARNES Annie, HARDIE Keir, PANKHURST Christabel, PANKHURST Emmeline, PANKHURST Richard Marsden.

PATERSON Emma Anne 1848–1886

Emma Paterson, founder of the Women's Trade Union League, was born Emma Smith, the only daughter of Henry Smith, headmaster of St George's Parish School in Hanover Square, and his wife Emma Dockerill. She was educated by her father, whom she loved greatly, but when she was only sixteen he died, leaving the family in poverty and forcing Emma to give up her apprenticeship to a bookbinder. Her mother made two unsuccessful ventures at founding a school, in one of which Emma taught. Then in 1866 Emma began work for the Workingmen's Club and Institute Union, and in 1867 was made its assistant secretary. It was during this period that she met Thomas Paterson, a cabinet maker, who was one of three joint honorary secretaries and one of the first working-class men to get on the club's council.

After a period of five years Emma, who presumably had by this time become a convinced suffrage supporter, left her job to become secretary of the Women's Suffrage Association. It was an unfortunate move, however, since after only a year she was asked to leave. Although the reasons are not altogether clear, it seems that the association did not regard her as a sufficiently effective speaker. Shortly afterwards, in 1873, she married Thomas Paterson, who was then thirty-nine years of age, and together they went on a honeymoon visit to the United States where they made a study of the American trade-union movement. On her return Emma wrote an article in *Labour News* in April 1874 setting out her views on the need to encourage trade unions amongst women workers and followed this up, in July, by organising a conference on the subject. One of those she approached was Emilie Pattison, later Emilie Dilke, a member of the Women's Suffrage Association, and with her help the Women's Protective and Provident Committee was founded. The purpose of the committee, later the Women's Protective and Provident League, was to assist women workers to form trade unions, and Emma was the driving force behind it, being both its secretary and its chief organiser. The first women to be organised were the bookbinders, and during Emma's period of leadership between thirty and forty unions were established. They were, however, small, and frequently short-lived.

In 1875 Emma was the first woman to attend the Trades Union Congress, where she became a constant attender with a break only in the year of her husband's death. Her most important campaign was for women factory inspectors and, as a result of her efforts, this became TUC policy in 1878, although it was not accepted by Parliament until 1893. From the first she had opposed the regulation of women's hours of work and had argued against it in her evidence to the Royal Commission on the Factory and Workshop Acts in 1875. Her main opponent within the TUC was Henry Broadbent, a member of the TUC parliamentary committee, who believed that married women's place was in the home so that they would not compete with men in the labour force and lower men's wages. Emma Paterson was not against protective legislation as such, only its application solely to women. In 1884, for example, she opposed a TUC resolution banning girls under fourteen from factories making nails, chains and bolts, arguing that it should apply to both sexes. The Women's Protection and Provident League accepted her views, but after her death its policy gradually changed. In time, renamed the

Women's Trade Union League, it became one of the most powerful advocates of protective legislation.

In 1876 Emma, in association with her friend Emily Faithfull, founded the Women's Printing Society and in the same year started the *Women's Union Journal*. Its policy was strongly feminist and it tried to encourage women to take a more active part in the world. They were urged, for example, to learn to swim and to adopt a more practical mode of dress. Although Emma's main work was chiefly within the trade-union movement, she supported women's suffrage, although she did not think it the panacea that some of its adherents claimed it to be. She was also strongly in favour of the election of women to school boards and other public bodies.

In 1882 Thomas Paterson died at the age of forty-seven. He had from the first encouraged his wife in her work, and had very liberal views on the position of women. The son of a cabinet-maker, he had an intense love of books and an enthusiasm for debate. A keen supporter of the working men's club movement, he was also instrumental in paving the way for legislation which assisted non-wealthy inventors. His many other interests included land tenure reform and free libraries. His affectionate support made it possible for Emma to combine her very active public life with marriage, and so did the assistance of her mother who acted as housekeeper. The fact that there were no children must also have made it easier, since there could not have been a great deal of money for domestic help. After his death, which was a serious blow to her, she tried to resume her work but her own health began to fail and she died in 1886 from diabetes.

Emma Paterson started out with few advantages and it was her own initiative and determination which drove her forward. It was only after her marriage, however, that she was able to take full advantage of her abilities, and it is likely that her husband provided her with a secure emotional and financial base from which to start. During the brief period between her marriage in 1874 and her death in 1886 her success was remarkable, not least her achievement in making a woman's voice heard in the hitherto male stronghold of the TUC. Her early death removed from the feminist movement an original talent which spoke with a different voice from most feminists of her generation.

There is a short biography *Emma Paterson. She Led Women into a Man's World*, Harold Goldman (London, Lawrence and Wishart, 1974). See also *DLB* Vol. V, pp. 167-70 and *DNB* Vol. XLIV, p. 17. Emma Paterson wrote a brief memoir of her husband as a preface to his book *New Methods of Science* published in 1886. This was reprinted in *Our Fifty Years. The Story of the Working Men's Club and Institute Union*, B.T. Hall (London, Working Men's Club and Institute Union, 1912).

PETHICK-LAWRENCE Emmeline 1867-1954

Emmeline Pethick, a suffragette, was born in the West Country, the daughter of a well-to-do businessman. Of considerable force of character, his passionate love of justice was to be a formative influence on her life. The second of thirteen children, five of whom died in infancy, her mother's almost yearly childbearing meant that Emmeline received little of her attention, but was consigned to the care of a succession of indifferent and inefficient nursemaids. Her father, too, at this stage in her life, was a distant and somewhat forbidding figure for whom she felt awe rather than love. At the age of eight she was sent to a harsh boarding school, where she spent two unhappy years. A high-spirited independent child, she was not only frequently in trouble with her teachers, but an unjust accusation meant that she spent a whole term in Coventry. A severe illness brought this ordeal to an end, but later school experiences were not much happier, and at a Quaker boarding school an innocent discussion with another child about sex led to the charge that she was a corrupting influence on the other children.

By seventeen she had finished her education and was living at home as the eldest daughter, her mother still occupied with the younger children of whom the last to be born was still only a baby. Emmeline was dissatisfied and longed for wider experiences, but she lacked confidence in herself and did not have the courage to break away, although occasional visits to London kept her discontented. In the end it was a love affair which eventually gave her the motivation to change her life. Less pretty than her sisters, she had believed herself unattractive to men, when she met a young naval officer on leave in England before taking up service overseas. He was strongly attracted to her, and clearly she responded, but because of his financial position marriage was out of the question and at the end of his leave they parted, never to meet again. The episode, short as it was, provided the spur for a complete change in her life.

In 1887 the West London Mission had been founded by Mark Guy Pearse, a Methodist preacher of her father's generation whom she had loved and admired since she was a child. She now wrote to the mission offering her services, which were accepted, and in 1891, at twenty-four years of age, she became the 'sister' or leader of a club for working-class girls. In the course of this work she was able not only to gain confidence in herself and her abilities, but to get first-hand knowledge of working-class life, which turned her from the Liberalism of her father towards socialism.

In 1895 she left the mission to establish the Esperance Girls' Club and, as an extension of its work, a holiday home for girls and a cooperative dressmaking business. By this time she had ceased completely to think of marriage and, indeed, the group of middle-class girls she associated with all thought of themselves as dedicated to their work. But in 1899 she met Frederick Lawrence, a well-to-do young man four years her junior, who was acting as treasurer at the Mansfield House University Settlement while reading for the bar. Almost immediately he fell deeply in love, but she refused his first offer of marriage, since she felt that she could not marry someone who did not share her socialist beliefs. They were also deeply divided on the issue of the Boer War. Later, however, Frederick Lawrence changed his mind about the war and this, with his growing sympathy for socialism, eventually overcame her doubts. She also became convinced that he would respect her rights as a person. They were finally married in 1901, three weeks before Emmeline's thirty-fourth birthday, and took the name Pethick-Lawrence.

After her marriage Emmeline Pethick-Lawrence continued her work for the Esperance Girls' Club, supported now by her husband, whose wealth enabled her activities to be considerably extended. At this time she was not particularly interested in the suffrage issue. Although she certainly believed that women ought to have the vote her imagination was completely occupied by her involvement in the developing fortunes of the Labour Party. In 1905 she and her husband went on a visit to South Africa, where they read about the arrest and imprisonment of Annie Kenney and Christabel Pankhurst, and this aroused Emmeline Pethick-Lawrence's interest, but when she was approached on her return to England, by Emmeline Pankhurst herself, she refused to become involved. It was the simplicity and enthusiasm of Annie Kenney, who made a second appeal, which gradually drew her deeper and deeper into the affairs of the Women's Social and Political Union.

At first her commitment was simply as treasurer, but in 1906 she was arrested when she tried to speak at a demonstration in the lobby of the House of Commons, and this event drew her husband into the affairs of the militants. When she was sent to prison he took over as treasurer and continued to give his services in this and other capacities for the next six years. On this occasion Emmeline did not serve her sentence, as she was released after a few days for health reasons, although later she was to overcome her weakness and was able to survive five more imprisonments over the next six years.

In 1907 she and her husband launched *Votes for Women*, and this remained the journal of the WSPU until 1912. At the end of 1907, when the split occurred within the WSPU which led to the formation of the Women's Freedom League, both the Pethick-Lawrences remained completely loyal to the Pankhursts and their policy. Indeed for several years day-to-day control of the WSPU was largely in the hands of Christabel Pankhurst and the two Pethick-Lawrences. The office of the organisation was in their London house and for five years Christabel herself lodged with them and was part of their household. Emmeline Pethick-Lawrence was particularly valuable as a fund-raiser, her appeals for funds exerting an almost hypnotic effect on her audiences. She also wrote several short pamphlets, although her skill was always as a public speaker rather than a writer. Both she and her husband also used their resources freely to give hospitality and refreshment to those militants who had been weakened by their prison experiences, and Annie Kenney in particular, was, in her own words, 'like an adopted daughter'.

By 1912 the old-style militancy which had involved chiefly the interruption of meetings and the occasional almost ritualistic act of violence had given way to a new phase heralded by the wholesale smashing of shop windows. In retaliation, the WSPU leaders were arrested, although Christabel escaped to France. The Pethick-Lawrences were brought to trial in 1912 and sentenced to nine months imprisonment although, as a result of public protests, they served only a short part of it. More seriously, they were also made liable for the costs, and subsequently were sued successfully for the damage to the shop windows. This worried Christabel who could see that, with the increased violence to property she had in mind, the Pethick-Lawrences would speedily be ruined. At first she simply tried to persuade them to withdraw from the movement by staying in Canada, where they were visiting a brother of Emmeline's, but the Pethick-Lawrences refused. They had seen militancy as a way of rousing public opinion and feared that the new policy would alienate many supporters. Christabel, however, refused to accept their arguments and they were expelled from the WSPU. Unwilling to divide the movement, they accepted their dismissal quietly, if not without private bitterness. *Votes for Women* remained their property and continued its work for suffrage but no longer represented WSPU policy.

In 1914 the Pethick-Lawrences joined the United Suffragists, an organisation of both men and women to work for suffrage. But on the outbreak of war Emmeline's interest turned largely to the peace movement and she became a prominent member of the Women's International League for Peace and Freedom. At the end of the war she stood unsuccessfully for Parliament as a pacifist candidate, but subsequently left this kind of politics to her husband. Instead she worked for peace within the Women's International League.

During the 1920s and the 1930s she also kept intact her commitment to feminism. In 1923 she supported those women in the Labour movement who were campaigning for the provision of birth-control information to working-class women. In 1926 she became president of the feminist Women's Freedom league, succeeding Charlotte Despard, and held this position for the next nine years. She was also vice-president of the Six Points Group, an influential pressure group concerned to extend women's legal rights and strongly opposed, also, to the marriage bar and other practices which restricted the employment of women. She served too on the executive of the Open Door Council, another equal-rights pressure group concerned in particular with the effect of protective legislation on the employment rights of women.

The outbreak of war in 1939 left her long-standing pacifism shaken as her horror of war struggled with a recognition of its necessity. At seventy-three she was increasingly handicapped by deafness, and her public life was now virtually at an end. In 1950 a fractured leg left her partially immobilised although she was able to enjoy her golden wedding celebrations in 1951. A series of heart attacks followed, and she died in 1954 at the age of eighty-six.

Emmeline Pethick-Lawrence was one of the few militant leaders whose commitment to feminism continued after the end of the first world war, and she realised that even after the vote had been granted to women much still remained to be done. Nor did she find it difficult, like some women, to reconcile her socialism and her feminism, believing that both were necessary, since without feminism socialism 'would not touch some of the worst evils'. She was never totally committed to militancy and, although she accepted its necessity, it was to some extent outside her own nature. Nor was she ever able to see the militant movement in terms of a war against men, and she was always deeply conscious of the sacrifices made not only by her own husband but by a number of other men who served the suffrage movement.

Her own feminism sprang originally from her sympathy for the working-class women she met as a voluntary social worker during the 1890s, and her first feminist commitment was to the cause of widows' pensions. It was this early experience, too, which helps to explain her support for the birth-control campaign in the 1920s. Unlike some other socialist women, however, her concern for the plight of working-class mothers did not lead her to ignore the needs of women in employment for equal pay and equal opportunities, and her feminism therefore extended over an unusually broad front. She was never primarily an intellectual, and, as she herself recognised in her autobiography, she shared with her father a passionate desire for justice which was at the root of both her socialism and her feminism.

There is an autobiography, *My Part in a Changing World*, Emmeline Pethick-Lawrence (London, Gollancz, 1938). See also *Pethick-Lawrence. A Portrait*, Vera Brittain (London, Allen and Unwin, 1963); *Memories of a Militant*, Annie Kenney (London, Arnold, 1924); *A New World for Women*, Sheila Rowbotham (London, Pluto, 1977).

See also KENNEY Annie, PANKHURST Christabel, PETHICK-LAWRENCE Frederick William.

PETHICK-LAWRENCE Frederick William 1871–1961

Frederick Lawrence, a Labour politician, was the son of Alfred Lawrence and his wife Mary Elizabeth Ridge. The youngest of a family of two boys and three girls, his father died when he was only three years old. His father's younger brother Edwin became his guardian and encouraged his interest in mathematics. At thirteen years of age he was sent to Eton, and this was followed by six academically successful years at Cambridge where he was president of the union and later a Fellow at Trinity. His studies included not only mathematics, at which he was brilliant, but also natural science and economics. The academic life did not, however, attract him and he left Cambridge and travelled around the world for two years. On his return in 1899 he joined Mansfield House University Settlement where he acted as treasurer while reading for the bar. He also, at his uncle's suggestion, became a parliamentary candidate as a Liberal-Unionist.

Soon after joining the settlement he met and fell in love with Emmeline Pethick, a young voluntary social worker four years his senior who had developed strong socialist sympathies as a result of her eight years spent amongst girls and women of the working classes. She, however, was dedicated to her work and refused to marry him, largely because of his lack of sympathy for socialism, and especially his support for the Boer War. Forced by her refusal to re-think his position, Frederick Lawrence visited South Africa and in consequence changed his mind about the war and was forced to withdraw his parliamentary candidature. His gradual move to the Left in politics which followed reconciled Emmeline to the prospect of marriage, and the wedding took place in 1901. Knowing her need for independence, he took the name of Pethick-Lawrence.

During the next few years he maintained his interest in politics by editing a political journal *The Echo*. They also travelled, and in 1905 he and Emmeline made a lengthy visit to South Africa.

Previously, although approving in principle, neither Emmeline nor Frederick had taken much interest in the suffrage movement but in 1906, cajoled by Annie Kenney, Emmeline accepted the post of treasurer to the Women's Social and Political Union, realising their lack of organisational experience. Soon afterwards, however, in the course of a demonstration in the lobby of the House of Commons, she and several other women were arrested and this event drew Frederick Pethick-Lawrence into the movement. He not only took over Emmeline's work as treasurer but made use of his legal training to give what help he could to the prisoners. From this time, as he put it, the suffragettes 'surged into my life'. Recognising the need of the movement for organisation, he took over this side of the WSPU completely and the Pethick-Lawrences' London home, where Christabel Pankhurst was also living, became the headquarters of the militant movement. A wealthy man, he also financed a journal, *Votes for Women*, with he and his wife as co-editors, and this became the official journal of the WSPU.

In 1907, when the WSPU split and the Women's Freedom League was founded, largely in protest at the autocratic methods of the Pankhursts, the Pethick-Lawrences stayed completely loyal to Emmeline and Christabel Pankhurst and supported them in every respect. Indeed Frederick, in particular, had a tremendous admiration for Christabel, and gradually he became her devoted henchman. For five years the two Pethick-Lawrences in association with Christabel were virtually in control of WSPU affairs. Moreover, as treasurer, Frederick was the only man to have an official place in the militant movement. During these years, apart from his role as co-editor of the journal, he published *Women's Fight for the Vote* (London, 1910).

In 1912, however, his association with the WSPU came to an abrupt end. The growing bitterness amongst the militants had resulted in a gradual increase in violence over the years, but this had normally taken the form of isolated incidents, often symbolic in nature, such as a single stone through a window. Now the policy changed to one of violence against property designed to inflict considerable damage with the intention of forcing the government to give way. In retaliation the leaders of the WSPU were arrested on a charge of incitement to violence and, although Christabel escaped to France, the Pethick-Lawrences were sentenced to nine months imprisonment. This was the first time Frederick had been imprisoned and he was exhilarated at being in the front line at last. But although he was forcibly fed on a number of occasions, he was soon released. More serious was the imposition not only of the costs of the trial but a successful claim against him for the broken windows.

Although, up to this point both the Pethick-Lawrences had served Christabel faithfully, they were never altogether happy when militancy turned into actual violence, and in *Women's Fight for the Vote* Frederick had declared his belief that militant methods must be restricted to 'the absolute necessities of the situation'. Accordingly he tried to oppose the new policy, arguing that it would be likely to turn public opinion against them. Christabel, however, would brook no opposition and, when the Pethick-Lawrences refused to remove themselves voluntarily from the scene, they were summarily dismissed. Christabel was always severe when faced with what she considered disloyalty, and in the Pethick-Lawrences' case she also had to face the fact that to involve them in the new policy would undoubtedly mean further attacks on Frederick's private fortune. Although both Emmeline and Frederick accepted their dismissal quietly, there is no doubt that Frederick in particular felt it deeply since he was half in love with the fascinating Christabel.

The journal *Votes for Women* was financed by Frederick Pethick-Lawrence and remained in his possession until 1914, when he handed it over to the United Suffragists, a group of men and women committed to women's suffrage, which both Emmeline and Frederick now joined. Once the war had started he turned his attention to the Union of Democratic Control, a group working for a negotiated peace. Eventually, when called up for military service, he became a conscientious objector. In 1917 he fought an election on the principle of peace by negotiation but obtained only 333 votes. In 1921 he tried again for Parliament, this time as a Labour candidate, but was again unsuccessful. Finally, in 1923, he defeated Winston Churchill at West Leicester and his long parliamentary career had begun.

Once in the House of Commons, Frederick Pethick-Lawrence showed clearly that he had not forgotten his feminism. His maiden speech, prepared with the assistance of Emmeline, was on pensions for widowed mothers and it was his question which led the Prime Minister to announce a new suffrage Bill to enfranchise all adult women. In 1936 he supported Ellen Wilkinson when she introduced a motion giving women equal pay with men in the Civil Service.

But by this time his feminism was certainly subsidiary to his interest in economics and financial affairs. In 1929 he was appointed financial secretary to Philip Snowden, the new Chancellor of the Exchequer, and later he became chairman of the Public Accounts Committee. In 1945 he was awarded a peerage and, now a member of the House of Lords, became Secretary of State for India and Burma, and as such played an important part in the negotiations which led to Indian independence. In 1951 he and Emmeline celebrated their golden wedding, three years before her death in 1954. In 1957 he married Helen Craggs, a former suffragette, twenty years his junior. One of his last acts was to help in the publication of Christabel Pankhurst's *Unshackled*, an account of the militant movement. His bitterness now forgotten, he insisted in rejecting all photographs of her in later life, and chose for a frontispiece a picture of her in a flower-decked hat he himself had given to her. A few years later, in 1961, he died.

Frederick Pethick-Lawrence, in spite of his long career as a politician, was not a passionate or rhetorical speaker although he was always clear and logical. His gifts were largely in the field of organisation and finance, and he showed these to good effect during his association with the militant suffrage campaign. Yet, in spite of his reputation for logic, he was essentially a romantic in his approach to women, both in his personal relationships and in his feminism. A firm upholder of equal rights for women, he nevertheless perceived women as having a greater concern than men for the future of the race and humanity at large. Consequently he anticipated that their effect on public life would be a humanising one, essentially because through the role of mother they were more caring of others.

It is also possible that in some respects he felt closer to women than to men, and it is perhaps not without significance that at Eton he found it difficult to get on with the other boys. Certainly his long and loving partnership with Emmeline was much the most important relationship in his life, drawing him into socialism and later into feminism. His position within the militant hierarchy also testifies to his ability to work closely with women. Few men have been prepared to give so much as Frederick Pethick-Lawrence did for the feminist cause, and he deserves, therefore, a rather special place in the history of the feminist movement.

There is a biography, *Pethick-Lawrence. A Portrait*, Vera Brittain (London, Allen and Unwin, 1963). See also his autobiography, *Fate has been kind*, F.W. Pethick-Lawrence (London, Hutchinson, 1943); *DNB* 1961–70, pp. 835 –7.

See also PANKHURST Christabel, PETHICK-LAWRENCE Emmeline.

PHILLIPS Marion 1881–1932

Marion Phillips, the chief woman officer for the Labour Party, was born in Australia, the youngest of seven children, three boys and four girls, born to Philip David Phillips and his New Zealand wife Rose Asher. Marion's father was a well-to-do Australian-born lawyer and she was brought up in comfortable surroundings and given a remarkably good education for a girl of her period. After spending two years at the Presbyterian Ladies' College, one of the most advanced girls' schools of its time, she completed a BA degree in history at Melbourne University in 1903. The following year she came to London and won a research scholarship at the London School of Economics, where she completed a DSc and won a Hutchinson medal for her work, which was later published as *A Colonial Autocracy* (1909).

In 1906 she began work for Beatrice Webb on an enquiry into the conditions of children and widows at Derby as part of the commission into the working of the Poor Law. She was also turning to the Left in politics, and in 1907 joined both the Fabian Society and the Independent Labour Party. In 1909 she set up house with two women friends, Mary Longman and Ethel Bentham, a doctor from the London School of Medicine and a member of the Women's Labour League. For the next ten years their house in Holland Park served as a centre for feminist socialist activity until the group was broken up by the marriage of first Ethel Bentham and then Mary Longman.

It may have been the influence of these friends which turned Marion's ambitions away from an academic career. Although she was a lecturer at the London School of Economics in 1911 and between 1918 and 1920, her interests turned increasingly towards politics. In 1911, after her work for Beatrice Webb was over, she was for a time an organising secretary to the Women's Trade Union League, assisting Mary Macarthur in the legislation following the introduction of the National Insurance Bill. In 1908 she had joined the Women's Labour League and in 1909 was on its executive committee. In 1911 she took over as temporary secretary, being made a full-time secretary in 1912.

Although she supported women's suffrage, she was far from being a militant and indeed her socialist principles would have made it impossible for her to support the anti-socialism of the Women's Social and Political Union. She did, however, act as secretary to the National Union of Women's Suffrage Societies for a time in 1910, although the suffrage issue itself does not seem to have been of central concern to her.

During the war she served on several important committees, including the War Emergency Workers' Material Committee and the Queen's Work for Women Fund Committee. In 1917 she was made secretary of the newly-formed Standing Joint Committee of Industrial Women's Organisations which represented women in trade unions, the Co-operative movement and the Women's Labour League.

At the end of the war Marion Phillips became chief woman officer for the Labour Party, and as such was engaged in a wide variety of activities, all concerned with what may be broadly described as the political education of women. She was particularly influential as editor of *Labour Woman*, in which she tried to prepare women for their new role as citizens, emphasising such issues as food, housing and children. She also tried to encourage them to take an interest in elections. In 1918 she had edited a volume of essays, *Women and the Labour Party* (London, Gollancz, 1918) and she was also responsible for an instructional manual for women who wished to be active in the Labour Party. Apart from her writing she also spent a great deal of time travelling about the country visiting local branches. At the same time she played a prominent part in the formation of the International Federation of Working Women and in the campaign for women's greater involvement in the League of Nations.

She had always maintained close contact with the ILP, and in 1926 she became an ILP candidate in Sunderland. She was successful in the 1929 election but in 1931 she developed cancer of the stomach and died in 1932 after only a very brief parliamentary career, marred by her own ill-health and by tensions within the constituency.

Marion Phillips spent a great part of her life working for women in one way or another, her chief concern being for women of the working classes and especially working-class wives and mothers. She wanted their voice to be heard in politics because she believed both that they had special needs which might well be overlooked if men kept control of political life and also that their special experience in the home gave them knowledge which deserved to be made available to all. Her conception of the needs of working-class wives was, however, curiously limited and she deliberately avoided the issues not only of venereal disease and abortion but even of contraception at a time when women in the Labour movement were running a campaign within the Labour Party to make birth-control information more easily available to working-class women. Marion Phillips strongly opposed their efforts to bring this issue before the Labour Party Conference, believing that to do so would have a divisive effect within the movement. How far there were more personal motives is difficult to judge, but the fact that she was unmarried may have led her to minimise the significance of birth-control information to working-class women.

In the last resort the impression remains that Marion Phillips was a socialist first and a feminist only second. Although she was completely sincere in wanting to see working-class women take a greater share in politics, and recognised indeed that they had a special contribution to make as women, the issues which concerned her were those raised by socialism rather than feminism. Consequently she placed little emphasis on those hardships which women suffered as a result of gender rather than class, and this may be why she believed that sex should be kept out of politics. In this respect she contrasts sharply with Eleanor Rathbone, also unmarried, who placed considerable emphasis on the subordination of working-class women within the family. Marion Phillips is a good example of the way in which many women in the Labour movement gradually subordinated their feminism to the needs of the Labour Party.

For Marion Phillips' biography see *DLB* Vol. V, pp. 173–9.

PROCTOR Adelaide Anne 1825–1864

Adelaide Proctor, a popular poet, was the daughter of Bryan Walter Proctor and Anne Skepper. Her father was a barrister and later worked in a government office, but was better known as Barry Cornwall, a popular poet and a friend of both Dickens and Thackeray. Indeed he and his charming and witty wife entertained almost everyone in the contemporary literary world. Her parents were deeply attached to each other and to Adelaide who was the first-born of their six children. Her own talent as a poet was revealed in 1853 when she sent Dickens several poems under the pseudonym 'Mary Berwick'. He published them and asked for more, and a few years later, in 1858, she published a collection of her verses under her own name, which gained immediate success. The author of the verses of 'The Lost Chord', she was Queen Victoria's favourite poet, and it has been claimed that her poems sold more editions than those of any other contemporary English poet with the exception of Tennyson.

In 1850 she had been converted to Roman Catholicism, probably as a result of a year-long visit to a Roman Catholic aunt in Italy. Later her two sisters followed her example, and one of them joined the Order of the Irish Sisters of Mercy. Although this grieved her father it does not seem to have caused any rift in the family, nor any breach with her friends.

It is not clear when or indeed how she developed an interest in the position of women, but it may well have been under the influence of Anna Jameson, who was a friend of the family. Her mother had also known the mother of Bessie Rayner Parkes since childhood and, although Adelaide was older by several years, she and Bessie eventually became close friends. By the end of the 1850s Adelaide was firmly established as one of the little band of women who between them founded both *The Englishwoman's Journal* in 1858 and the Society for the Promotion of the Employment of Women in 1859. In 1861 she edited a volume of poetry and prose which was set up by women compositors at the Victoria Press. However, this was virtually the end of her period of involvement since, never robust, her health began to fail, and she died, still a comparatively young woman, in 1864.

Although Adelaide Proctor never married she had two unhappy love affairs which were kept secret during her life-time. This does not appear to have been a factor in her feminism although it may have encouraged a tendency to melancholy in her verses which exactly appealed to the taste of the Victorians. She was deeply loved by her family and friends, especially by Bessie Rayner Parkes who was seriously ill for a time after her death. Contemporary accounts stress especially her courage and gaiety and her sense of humour. Her feminism seems to have sprung mainly from her involvement in philanthropy, and her particular concern was the need of women for greater opportunities for employment. Indeed she was sufficiently conventional in her attitudes to regret that her own reputation as a poet outstripped that of her father. Nevertheless, for a brief spell, she was an important part of the small group of women who pioneered feminism as an organised social movement.

There is no biography of Adelaide Proctor and our knowledge of her life is scanty. Bessie Belloc, formerly Bessie Rayner Parkes, wrote her recollections of her friend in a volume of essays, *In a Walled Garden* (London, Ward and Downey, 1895). There is also an interesting account of her as a poet in 'Queen Victoria's Favourite Poet' by Margaret Maison in *The Listener* 29 April 1965, pp. 636–7. See also *DNB* Vol. XLVI, pp. 416–7.

See also BELLOC Bessie Rayner.

R

RATHBONE Eleanor 1872–1946

Eleanor Rathbone, the moving spirit behind the campaign for family allowances, was the daughter of William Rathbone and his second wife, Emily Acheson Lyle. On her father's side she came from a Quaker and Unitarian background which, for six generations, had represented Lancashire Liberalism and Quaker philanthropy. Her father's two marriages had brought him ten children, and Eleanor was the second youngest. A prosperous merchant and shipowner, William Rathbone displayed all his forebears' concern for public work; his chief interest, embarked on at the time of the death of his first wife, being the development of a system of district nursing. Later, in association with Florence Nightingale, he sought to improve workhouse nursing in Liverpool. In 1869, at the age of fifty, he entered Parliament, where his special concern was the reform of local government.

Eleanor was educated mainly by governesses and tutors although she also spent a short period at Kensington High School. In 1893 she entered Somerville College, Oxford, leaving in 1896 with a second-class degree in philosophy. Gradually, however, she moved away from an interest in philosophical issues towards more practical affairs. She became a visitor for the Liverpool Central Relief Society and honorary secretary of the Liverpool Women's Industrial Council. Meanwhile her father, who had retired from Parliament in 1895, died in 1902 and she wrote an account of his life and work which reveals her love and admiration. In many respects she set out to follow in his footsteps, and in 1909 was elected the first woman member of the Liverpool City Council. During the next few years she also did a good deal of social research, starting with a study of dock labour, but perhaps of more significance for her later development was *The Condition of Widows under the Poor Law*, which she published in 1913. In it she revealed her growing perception of motherhood as a service to the community, a view which was soon to lead her to the conception of family allowances.

Her other interest during this period was women's suffrage. A committed feminist in her college days, in 1897 she became parliamentary secretary to the Liverpool Women's Suffrage Society and was soon one of its leading spirits. At no time was she attracted to the militant wing of the movement, remaining always within the constitutional National Union of Women's Suffrage Societies and eventually being elected to its executive committee. In 1912, when the executive decided to give its support to the Labour Party which, by this time, was committed to a policy of adult suffrage, she disagreed and tried to organise an opposition to the decision. Seen by the executive as disloyal, she was censured, and resigned, but shortly afterwards was reinstated.

The outbreak of war found her in support of Millicent Fawcett's pro-war stand and she became increasingly involved in NUWSS affairs. She was particularly concerned with the various problems arising out of the separation allowances paid to the Armed Forces, and this experience further strengthened her increasing belief in family allowances, since separation allowances, unlike earnings, worked on the principle of payments according to the size of the family. In 1917 she called together a small committee of seven members, including several colleagues from the NUWSS as well as the socialist Henry Brailsford. The committee produced a pamphlet, *Equal Pay and the Family. A Proposal for the National Endowment of Motherhood*, and so initiated the campaign for family allowances which was to be Eleanor Rathbone's major contribution to feminism.

In 1919, on the resignation of Millicent Fawcett, Eleanor Rathbone became president of the National Union of Societies for Equal Citizenship, the new identity of NUWSS, a position which she held until 1928. During this period she worked closely with Eva Hubback and Mary Stocks on a number of equal-rights issues, but her main endeavour was to make family allowances a major plank in the NUSEC programme of reform. In 1924 she produced her most important book, *The Disinherited Family*, in which she presented a case for family allowances on mainly feminist grounds, arguing forcefully that such a system would divorce maternity from the 'economic conditions of a glorified serfdom'. She clearly saw such allowances as a way to end the economic dependence of a wife on a husband which left her at his mercy and encouraged in him that 'instinct of domination' which fed his selfishness and at times even his brutality. For this reason it was an essential part of the proposal that the money should be paid direct to the mother. It was also argued that such a scheme would make equal pay a more feasible proposition since the state, not the father, would now be responsible for the upkeep of children.

By 1925 NUSEC was ready to accept family allowances as part of its policy, swayed in large part by Eleanor's presidential address in which she argued for the adoption of a 'new feminism' which sought not simply to imitate men but to give women what they needed to fulfil their own lives. The Independent Labour Party also accepted family allowances in principle in 1926. In general, however, the idea made little headway during this period, since it was seen as a threat to parental responsibility. Within the trade-union movement there was also a great deal of suspicion since it was seen as a challenge to the family wage.

In 1927 Eleanor Rathbone read Katherine Mayo's *Mother India* and was appalled at its revelations, especially on child marriage. Anxious to do something herself, she resolved to seek election to Parliament. She had previously failed to gain the seat at Toxteth as an Independent in 1922, but in 1929 was returned as the Independent Member for the Combined British Universities. Her efforts for the Indian women were to some extent frustrated by opposition from those who feared that such a campaign might strengthen distrust of Indian self-government, but she became actively involved in the campaign for women's suffrage in India. She also took up a number of other issues concerning women in the colonies, including female circumcision in colonial Africa and forced marriage of Arab girls in Palestine. An advocate of a militant League of Nations, she also became deeply involved in the rescue and support of European refugees. In British politics she was largely responsible for the Inheritance Family Provision Act of 1938 concerned with ending the capricious disinheritance of spouses and children.

Family allowances still, however, remained her major concern and during the 1930s opinion slowly moved in their favour, particularly within the Labour movement which came to see them as a way of alleviating poverty in large families. Concern at the falling birth rate provided another argument in their favour, especially when it was combined with fears for the future of the Anglo-Saxon 'race'. Eleanor Rathbone herself exploited all these arguments, so that in time the feminist case for family allowances was almost lost to sight. By the end of the war the way had at last been prepared for the acceptance of the scheme, but by that time the feminist argument had been so overlaid with other issues that the Bill at first proposed that the allowance should be paid to the father. Such a proposal completely negated any feminist implications, and Eleanor Rathbone was so horrified that she threatened to vote against the Bill. A number of women's organisations added their voice to hers and eventually the government capitulated. But this was to be her last battle, and in January 1946 she died, very suddenly, from a heart attack.

Although Eleanor Rathbone never married, she shared her life completely with a woman friend, Elizabeth Macadam. They met soon after the death of Eleanor's father in 1902, when Elizabeth Macadam became warden of Victoria Women's Settlement in Liverpool, and soon became close friends. After the war Elizabeth moved to London and became honorary secretary of NUSEC and joint editor of its journal, the *Woman's Leader*. She and Eleanor Rathbone took a house together and remained close companions until Eleanor's death in 1946. Another friend was Mary Stocks who later became her biographer. Although Eleanor Rathbone was able to work with men, the only man who seems to have come close to her was her father who, in some respects, was the most important influence on her life.

Eleanor Rathbone was one of the most significant of the post-war generation of feminists since she tried, if not altogether successfully, to develop a feminist ideology which went beyond equal rights to explore some of the problems associated with women's own particular needs, especially as mothers. Her ideas went beyond simple welfare provisions, beneficial as these might be, and her scheme of family allowances was clearly intended as a measure to actually change the balance of power within the family. She also saw women as different from men, largely because of their maternal function, and she believed, in consequence, that an increase in women's political power would mean a greater emphasis on the avoidance of suffering, especially on the part of the less powerful and articulate members of society. She was, therefore, amongst that group of feminists who saw the political emancipation of women as a way to reform the world.

On the other hand it is clear that although Eleanor Rathbone herself did not desert her feminist principles, the eventual success of her scheme owed very little to feminism. Moreover, she herself contributed to this state of affairs by allowing other arguments to dominate the campaign. At the same time, in spite of her outspokenness on male domination, she was very traditional in some of her views on both the family and motherhood. Although she accepted that women should be free to follow their own inclinations, she clearly believed that most women would find their destiny in motherhood. She supported the NUSEC line on birth control but she was never very closely involved in the issue, and believed that the fall in the birth rate was a revolt against the conditions of maternity rather than a real desire for fewer children. Indeed, at the end of her life she was pressing for an end to the prejudice against large families. There was also a strain of puritanism in her thinking which may have made for orthodoxy in her attitude towards the family. For example, she argued that family allowances should not be paid to unmarried mothers in case this led to an increase in illegitimacy. Her sympathy for eugenic arguments also revealed itself in her concern for the effect of the differential birth rate and in her suggestion that it might be necessary to check the marriage of the mentally deficient or diseased.

To a large extent Eleanor Rathbone's feminism was part of a humanitarianism rooted in a profound compassion for the suffering of others. She was moved particularly by physical cruelty and physical hardship, and this was why the abuse of female children in the colonies aroused her to such anger. Behind her advocacy of family allowances, too, was her desire to check masculine brutality and self-indulgence. Yet this compassion could lead her into intellectual and moral arrogance, and this left her open to eugenic arguments which distracted her and her followers from feminism. A complex and intriguing figure, Eleanor Rathbone illustrates both the strengths and the weaknesses of feminism in the years after 1918.

There is a biography *Eleanor Rathbone*, Mary Stocks (London, Gollancz, 1949). Jane Lewis has analysed her contribution to the 'new feminism' in 'Beyond Suffrage', *Maryland Historian* Vol. VI (1), 1973, pp. 1–17. For an account of the family allowance movement see *The Movement for Family Allowances 1918–45*, John Macnicol (London, Heinemann, 1980). See also *DNB* 1941–50 pp. 711–13. For Eleanor Rathbone's main writings see her 'Changes in Public Life' in

Our Freedom and its Results ed. Ray Strachey (London, Hogarth Press, 1936) and the *Disinherited Family,* originally published in 1924 but re-issued in 1949 (London, Allen and Unwin).

See also BRAILSFORD Henry Noel, HUBBACK Eva Marian, STOCKS Mary Danvers.

REDDISH Sarah 1850-1925

Sarah Reddish, a suffragist, was born into a Bolton working-class family where Co-operation was almost a way of life. Her father later became an active member of the Bolton Education Committee. She herself started life as a cotton-mill worker, but in 1893 was appointed as a regional organiser for the Women's Co-operative Guild in the north of England. She served two years in the post and, with her clear, logical and convincing speeches, was responsible for a considerable increase in membership. Although nothing is known of her early life, it is likely that her speaking skills were developed in the trade-union movement. She was also a keen guildswoman and was made president of her local branch in Bolton in 1886. In 1889 she was first elected to the central committee of the guild and in 1897 was its national president. As a guildswoman she took an active part in the campaign for the extension of co-operative membership to women. She was also involved in the guild campaign to improve the wages of female Co-operative employees.

A keen supporter of the suffrage movement, the Bolton Guild, under her leadership, became a place where suffrage speakers were always welcome. She was also active in the collection of signatures for the textile workers' petition to Parliament asking for women's suffrage, and in 1902 was one of the deputation which presented the petition to Parliament. Between 1903 and 1905 she acted as an organiser for the North of England Society for Women's Suffrage.

She had always strongly supported the need for women to stand for local government, setting out her views in 'Women and County Borough Councils: a claim for Eligibility', and in 1898 had been elected to the Bolton School Board. In 1905 she became a member of the Bolton Poor Law Guardians, serving in this capacity until 1921, by which time she was over seventy years of age. She always maintained her interest in women's affairs, and in 1919, after the first instalment of women's suffrage, she organised the Bolton Women's Citizens Association.

Little is known about Sarah Reddish, although she clearly emerges as a woman of energy and determination who employed her considerable talents in the service of a variety of causes of importance to women. She stands out particularly by reason of her working-class origin, at a time when few such women rose into positions of leadership even within organisations serving the needs of working-class women.

The main source on Sarah Reddish is *One Hand Tied Behind Us. The Rise of the Women's Suffrage Movement*, Jill Liddington and Jill Morris (London, Virago, 1978). For her involvement in the Co-operative Women's Guild see *Caring and Sharing. The Centenary History of the Co-operative Women's Guild*, Jean Gaffin and David Thoms (Manchester Co-operative Union Ltd., 1983).

RIGBY Edith Rayner 1872-1949

Edith Rigby, a suffragette, was the daughter of Alexander Clement Rayner and his wife Mary Pilkington Sharples. The second of seven children, four of them girls, she was born in Preston where her father practised as a doctor. She was educated at a boarding school, Penthos College in North Wales, an area which so impressed her that in 1926 she returned to spend the rest of her life there. From an early age she began to show the drive for independence and adventure which was perhaps the main feature of her personality. At the age of sixteen she acquired the first ladies' bicycle to be seen in Preston, and at eighteen, in spite of her parents' protests, cycled alone to Leicester to visit a school friend. With this same friend, while still at school, she had already discussed the inferior position of women in society.

Edith was a very beautiful girl with blue eyes and golden hair and she attracted many proposals of marriage. In 1893, just before her twenty-first birthday, she married Charles Rigby, a thirty-four year old doctor who had been a particularly persistent suitor. Devoted to his wife, Charles Rigby was a gentle, tolerant and indeed easy-going man who allowed his wife the freedom her nature demanded and without which the marriage would have foundered. From the start she continued to pursue her own interests, which were many and varied, including an enquiry into the working conditions of mill girls in the area. She also started a night school and a recreation club for working girls. More unusually, feeling the need for more freedom and perhaps more solitude than married life allowed, she took a plot of land with a bungalow some miles away to which she could retreat. At one time during the early years of their marriage her husband protested at her neglect of her household responsibilities. Without any argument she simply disappeared and was eventually discovered, by a hired detective, acting as housemaid to a titled family in London. This was apparently the last protest he ever made.

After twelve years of childless marriage she made the decision to adopt a baby. Her husband opposed the idea but she went ahead and in 1905 adopted Sandy who had been born in 1903. It is not clear why she wanted this child so much, since a domestic existence had no charms for her at all and a small child would inevitably have increased her domestic responsibilities, a fact which must have been behind the opposition of her husband. Certainly, if only temporarily, she must have felt the urge for a child of her own and this overruled more prudent considerations. In fact, however, scarcely more than a year later her involvement in the affairs of the Women's Social and Political Union drew her out of the home to a greater extent than ever.

Driven by admiration for Christabel Pankhurst, she formed a branch of the WSPU in Preston and worked almost without respite, holding meetings indoors and out, and collecting signatures for petitions. Nor were her activities confined to Preston. In 1907 she took part in a suffrage procession from Hyde Park, and her first imprisonment followed. In 1908 she was imprisoned again when she was at the head of an attempt to deliver a petition to the House of Commons. On another occasion she was one of those who chained themselves to the railings in Downing Street. She remained with the WSPU even after the breach which led Charlotte Despard, a close friend of Edith's, and Theresa Billington to form the Women's Freedom League.

As the years went by Edith was frequently in prison where she regularly went on hunger strikes and was forcibly fed. Later, when the Cat and Mouse Act came into force, she was often in hiding when not actually imprisoned. Her escapades grew more outrageous, although often marked by a sense of humour. During 1913, for example, she pelted J.H. Thomas, the Labour MP, with black puddings, and organised the tarring of a statue of Lord Derby in a Preston park. Perhaps her most violent act was the burning down of a wooden bungalow in the grounds of Sir William Lever, later Lord Leverhulme. She also planned to plant a bomb in the Liverpool Corn Exchange, and the bomb was indeed prepared, but she was arrested before the scheme could be carried out.

Meanwhile her husband was left alone for long periods, sometimes not even knowing where his wife was, and caring as best he could for the adopted child. Although he felt the disadvantage of his own position strongly, and was besides anxious on behalf of Edith's health which had been weakened by her hunger strikes, he was himself in support of women's suffrage and strongly defended her when she was attacked. Indeed, he was proud of his wife and especially of her courage, and seems to have shared the militant view that their sacrifices would in the end bring about victory.

At the outbreak of war in 1914 Emmeline and Christabel Pankhurst called a truce to militancy and themselves became strong supporters of the government and the war. Edith Rigby was one of those who resented this arbitrary decision and helped to form an independent branch of the WSPU in Preston which continued to work for suffrage using non-militant means. For Edith herself, however, women's suffrage was no longer an issue which could hold her attention. In 1915 she moved from Preston to a small-holding where she grew fruit and vegetables and kept animals, joined by her husband whenever he could spare the time from his practice. She developed an interest in natural foods and, more importantly, in the writings of Rudolf Steiner which eventually became the main focus of her life.

Once the war was over she lost interest in the small-holding, her whole attention now on Rudolf Steiner and his message, and she began to translate Dr Friedrich Rittelmeyer's *Rudolf Steiner Enters my Life*. Eventually, when her husband retired, she decided to move to North Wales, but before the house was built her husband died suddenly from pneumonia. Between 1926 and her death in 1949 she lived a happy and active life, still a disciple of Rudolf Steiner but taking up many new interests including archaeological field work.

Although during the years of Sandy's childhood she had been absorbed completely in the militant campaign, in later life she enjoyed a close relationship with him and with his family. She also entered into a very warm relationship with her nephew Herbert who lived with her for a time in his early teens. She was, therefore, fully capable of forming both affectionate and lasting relationships. Marriage, however, even to a husband as accommodating as Charles Rigby, was a relationship that her independent nature could not endure, and she constantly found reasons to escape its pressures and to enter into a life of her own.

Edith Rigby's feminism, therefore, may be seen as a reflection of her own desire for independence, but this is by no means the whole of the picture. For most of her life feminism was distinctly subordinate to other interests, and indeed in old age she came to regret her involvement in the suffrage movement. During her early married life her interest in working-class girls was more philanthropic than feminist and she was not fully awakened to the suffrage movement until she was inspired by Christabel Pankhurst's example. Militancy attracted her because it appealed to the element of daring in her nature as well as to the fanaticism which in some degree entered into all her enthusiasms. In this respect she is like a number of other militants, including Christabel Pankhurst herself, who, after militancy was over, found another faith in which to believe, and who afterwards had no place in their lives for feminism.

There is a sense, however, in which Edith Rigby's whole life was a rejection of conventional belief about women, in her refusal to wear fashionable shoes and dresses, to take pride in her housekeeping, or to accept the authority of her husband. How far this was seen by her as a specifically feminist revolt is unclear, but her consciousness of women's inferior position was awakened when she was only a schoolgirl and her early life in particular seems to have been determined by a desire to break out of the constraints which then surrounded a young lady. The militant movement gave political direction to this revolt but her conversion to the ideas of Rudolf Steiner turned her energies in a different direction. Moreover, the death of her husband finally freed her from the remaining constraints of her marriage. She has considerable interest for us, therefore, not only as one of the most lively of the militants but as a woman who tried in her own way to make for herself an independent life.

The only source for Edith Rigby's life is *My Aunt Edith*, Phoebe Hesketh (London, Peter Davies, 1966).

ROBINS Elizabeth 1862–1952

Elizabeth Robins, a well-known actress and later a writer, was born in Louisville, Kentucky, and grew up in Ohio. Her mother had been an opera singer but was committed to an insane asylum while Elizabeth was still a child. Her father seems to have been of somewhat advanced views, since he had an interest in Owenite socialism which he combined, somewhat curiously, with a belief in Social Darwinism. Elizabeth was given a superior education and sent to Vassar to study medicine at a time when women doctors were still something of a rarity. But this was not in accord with her own inclinations, and she ran away to go on the stage. After playing hundreds of different roles on tour she married a fellow actor, George Richmond Parker but continued her career as an actress. Not very long afterwards, however, her husband committed suicide by drowning himself in a suit of stage armour. Whether from sorrow or from distaste at her first experience of marriage, Elizabeth Robins rejected in later years not only a number of other offers of marriage but a number of less orthodox proposals, including one from George Bernard Shaw.

After the death of her husband she left the United States, going first to Norway and then to London where she began, in the late 1880s, a very successful career on the stage. She virtually introduced Ibsen to England and, as the first Hedda Gabler, took London by storm. During the 1890s she started a second career as a successful novelist under the pseudonym 'C.E. Raimond'. She not only supported herself during these years but also her mother and helped a younger brother to study medicine. She was obviously deeply attached to her brothers, and in 1900 she made an expedition to Alaska to search for her lost brother Raymond. The novel she later wrote about her experiences, *The Magnetic North*, added to her reputation as a writer.

She herself claimed that the struggle to produce Ibsen in England made her a feminist, and well before her entry into the suffrage movement she struggled to free actresses from the actor-manager system. Although she admired Millicent Fawcett, she was very strongly attracted to the Women's Social and Political Union, and was a member from its start in 1903. Her main asset was her writing and she contributed a whole series of articles both to the journal *Votes for Women* and to other papers. She was also active in both the Actresses' Franchise League, which she helped to organise, and in the Women Writers' League of which she was president in 1908.

She is, however, best known for her play *Votes for Women* which was first produced in 1907 and was later turned into a novel, *The Convert*. This highly passionate defence of the suffrage cause does not hesitate to face the issue of the militants' hostility to men and explores the extent to which this was based on men's sexual exploitation of women. The militant suffragette heroine is represented as a woman who has turned away from men because she was forced into an abortion by her lover who refused to marry her because he feared for his inheritance.

Eliabeth Robins was well aware personally of men's exploitation of women from her earlier position as a successful and highly courted actress. She hated men's philandering and was furious with H.G. Wells when he seduced the young daughter of her friend Maud Pember Reeves and later on denied the paternity of the child. She was sceptical, too, of the lukewarm feminism of men like George Bernard Shaw and believed that women must depend upon one another.

Her own work for women was not confined to the suffrage cause. She helped many women medical students and with her great friend Dr Octavia Wilberforce worked hard for decent medical care for women and children. She also believed firmly that single women should be able to adopt children and did indeed, with the help of Octavia Wilberforce, adopt and bring up a child. Margaret Drier Robins, one of the leaders of the Women's Trade Union League in the

United States, was her sister-in-law and she herself took a keen interest in breaking down class barriers within the women's movement. Other issues that appeared in her articles included the legal disabilities facing married women, and she was a strong opponent of the marriage bar.

The end of the main suffrage struggle in 1918 did not end her commitment to feminism. In the 1920s she was a regular contributor to the feminist *Time and Tide* and a supporter of the Six Points Group which was strongly committed to a continuation of the struggle for sex equality. She also made a further contribution to feminist thinking in *Ancilla's Share. An Indictment of Sex Antagonism*, published anonymously by Hutchinson in 1924. She lived on, however, until 1952, dying at the great age of ninety.

Elizabeth Robins saw the militant suffrage movement as important because it illustrated the power that came from women working together. Although she believed that sex-antagonism had to be faced she denied that the women's movement had caused it, believing that it had done no more than bring it out of hiding. Women, she claimed, had been too silent in the past, their tongues chained not only by their inarticulateness but by the stranglehold of male publishers and critics. Indeed, unlike some feminists of her generation, she would have been quite at home in the modern women's movement, and indeed it is clear that she anticipated some of its most important attitudes. Although a committed equal-rights feminist, she went far beyond the legal and even the political disabilities of women, seeing quite clearly the extent to which men had taken over women's minds. The task of the women's movement as she saw it was to make men, by force if necessary, see things from a woman's point of view. In this light her sex-hostility, so clearly in evidence in *Votes for Women*, is less antagonism against men as such as anger against their treatment of women. She reflected, therefore, a powerful mood which characterised the militant suffrage movement and has emerged even more strongly within radical feminism today. For this reason she is of particular interest to modern feminism.

Elizabeth Robins published her memoirs, *Both Sides of the Curtain* (London, Heinemann, 1940). There is also a biographical sketch of Elizabeth Robins in the reprinted edition of her novel *The Convert* (London, The Women's Press, 1980). See also *A Literature of Their Own*, Eileen Showalter (Princeton, Princeton University Press, 1977); *The Edwardian Turn of Mind*, Samuel Hynes (Princeton, Princeton University Press, 1968); *Women of Ideas*, Dale Spender (London, Routledge and Kegan Paul, 1982). A number of her articles have been reprinted as *Way Stations* (London and Plymouth, The Women's Press, 1913). Another of her feminist writings is *Ancilla's Share. An Indictment of Sex Antagonism* (London, Hutchinson, 1924). The Robins Papers are at the Humanities Research Center, University of Texas, Austin, USA.

ROPER Esther 1868–1938

Esther Roper, a suffragist, was born in Wilmslow, Cheshire, but nothing is known about her early life. In 1891 she graduated from Owens College, Manchester, and in 1893 was appointed secretary of the Manchester National Society for Women's Suffrage, later to become the North of England Society for Women's Suffrage, a post which she held until 1905. From the start it was her decision to organise special suffrage campaigns for working women, and it was reaching out to women in the working classes which was to be her main contribution to the suffrage movement. To this end, working women were visited in their own homes as well as at the factory gate, and two working-class women were appointed as organisers. Apart from her suffrage activity she was keenly interested in Owens College and was a member of its women's debating society. She also took an interest in the university settlement. Her attempt, in 1902, to become what would have been the only woman governor of the college was, however, unsuccessful.

In 1896, while she was on holiday in Italy, she met Eva Gore-Booth and the two women immediately became friends. In 1897 Eva joined Esther Roper in Manchester where she shared a home with her brother Reginald, seven years younger than herself and subsequently to become a master at Eton. From this time forward Eva was to be an equal partner in Esther's work. Esther was one of the principal figures in the petition signed by 67,000 textile workers, which was organised during 1901 and 1902 and presented to Parliament. During 1902 she also spoke at a deputation of women graduates to Westminster. With Eva Gore-Booth she founded and edited the *Women's Labour News* and also contributed articles to *The Common Cause*. Opposed to restrictions on women's right to work, both women took part in 1908 in the efforts of the Manchester Barmaids' Association to protest against efforts to prevent women working in bars. She was also the author of a pamphlet, *The Cotton Trade Unions and the Enfranchisement of Women*.

For a time Esther and particularly Eva were friends of Christabel Pankhurst. At a time when she was at a loose end after the sudden death of her father, they introduced her to political activity and in 1903 persuaded her to start her studies in law. In 1905, however, the friendship came to an end, largely because of a disagreement between them on the issue of militancy.

In 1913 a breakdown in Eva's health led both women to move to London where they became involved during the war in the Women's Peace Crusade. Eva died in 1926 but Esther lived on until 1938. After Eva's death she wrote a biographical introduction to a collection of Eva's poems in 1929, and an introduction to the prison letters of Constance Markievicz, Eva's sister, in 1934. A reflection of her more personal interests was the publication, in 1920, of *Select Extracts illustrating Florentine Life in the Fifteenth Century. Texts for Students*.

An extremely reticent person, Esther Roper remains hidden behind the more colourful personality of Eva Gore-Booth. Yet it was her initiative which led to the approach to working-class women which helped to give the suffrage movement a wider appeal, and in the years between 1893 and 1905 before militancy took the centre of the stage she was one of the most important figures in the women's suffrage movement.

There is no biography of Esther Roper but some information can be found in *One Hand Tied Behind Us. The Rise of the Women's Suffrage Movement*, Jill Liddington and Jill Norris (London, Virago, 1978) and in *Rise up Women! The Militant Campaign of the Women's Social and Political Union 1903-1914*, Andrew Rosen (London, Routledge and Kegan Paul, 1974). See also *Votes for Women. The Story of a Struggle*, Roger Fulford (London, Faber and Faber, 1956). Esther Roper's memoir of Eva Gore-Booth, *Biographical Introduction to the Poems of Eva Gore-Booth* (London, Longmans Green and Co., 1929) also contains information on their joint activities.

See also GORE-BOOTH Eva Selina.

ROYDEN Maude 1876-1956

Maude Royden, a preacher, was the youngest daughter of Sir Thomas Bland Royden, a shipowner, and his wife Alice Elizabeth Dowdall. Because of a dislocated hip she was lame all her life. She was educated at Cheltenham Ladies College and Lady Margaret Hall, Oxford, where she obtained a second-class degree in modern history in 1899. The next three years were spent at the Victoria Women's Settlement in Liverpool, but in 1901 she had met the Reverend George William Hudson Shaw and shortly afterwards he invited her to act as an unpaid curate in his parish. It was not long before they were deeply in love, but the Reverend Hudson Shaw, seventeen years her senior, was already married, although the severe mental illness of his wife Effie denied him both any sexual relationship with her or any real companionship. At the same time her dependence on him meant that he could never leave her. For the rest of his life he and Maude Royden remained on terms of the most intimate friendship in which for most of the time she lived either in the same house or close by but, because of their religious and moral principles, their love was never consummated.

In 1908 Maude Royden decided to devote most of her time and energy to the suffrage cause, and she lectured and wrote extensively on behalf of the National Union of Women's Suffrage Societies, the constitutional wing of the suffrage movement. Between 1912 and 1914 she was editor of *The Common Cause*. She was also one of the contributors to *The Making of Women. Oxford Essays in Feminism* edited by Gollancz (London, Allen and Unwin, 1917). Her essay was a powerful argument against the double standard of sexual morality, but it also recognised the existence and significance of female sexuality, although only within the bounds of married love.

Perhaps her most important contribution, however, was her stand beside Eleanor Rathbone in the demand for a new approach to feminism which emphasised the ways in which women differed from men. For this reason she strongly supported Eleanor Rathbone's plea for family allowances and was a member of the original committee on the subject in 1917. Like Eleanor Rathbone, she defended the scheme because it rendered women to some degree financially independent and because it helped to make equal pay a more practicable proposition. Above all, however, she supported it because of the importance she attached to motherhood. To deny its significance for women was, she argued, to accept masculine standards, and she deplored attempts to reduce motherhood to a mere episode in a woman's life. She was opposed to the widespread development of nurseries and, in a pamphlet 'National Endowment and Motherhood' published in 1917 by the Women's International League, hoped that family endowment would mean the withdrawal of large numbers of married women from the labour market.

Denied marriage and children because of her love for the Reverend Hudson Shaw, her ambitions centred upon becoming a minister herself. As a member of the Church of England she was denied this, but in 1917 she became an assistant preacher at the nonconformist City Temple. In 1920 she acquired an interdenominational pulpit at the Guildhouse and she continued her career as a preacher until 1936, making tours to the United States, Australia, New Zealand, India and China. In 1936 she resigned her position to work for world peace, although she renounced her pacifism during the second world war.

During these years she was no longer active as a feminist, but she remained deeply interested in the issue of maternal and child welfare, and in the 1920s was converted to the necessity of birth control as a means to this end. Indeed, she was one of the original patrons of Marie Stopes' birth-control clinic. Her interest in issues of sexual morality continued and she wrote for the National Council for Combating Venereal Diseases, as well as publishing *Sex and Commonsense* (London, Hurst and Blackett, 1922).

In 1944, shortly after the death of his wife, she and the Reverend Hudson Shaw were married, but it was to be only a very brief happiness. Already desperately ill, he lived for only two months after their marriage. Afterwards, in *A Three-Fold Cord* (London, Gollancz, 1947), she wrote a frank and moving account of their relationship. Her own death occurred in 1956 at the age of eighty.

Maude Royden is chiefly of interest because of her attempt to develop a concept of motherhood that took account of the changing nature of marriage which made a wife a more equal partner in the system. A moralist, both by inclination and profession, she also tried to develop a new approach to marriage which would allow a place to women's sexuality without abandoning the concepts of pre-marital chastity and marital fidelity. To a large extent her ideas were a somewhat uneasy compromise between Victorian and modern values, but she addressed herself to issues neglected by most nineteenth-century feminists and which modern feminism has yet to come to terms with.

There is no biography of Maude Royden and *A Three-Fold Cord* (London, Gollancz, 1947) deals with only a limited aspect of her life and work. There is an account of her 'new feminism' in 'Beyond Suffrage', Jane Lewis, *Maryland Historian* Vol. VI (1), 1973 pp. 1–17. See also *DNB* 1951–1960 pp. 855–6.

S

SCHREINER Olive 1855–1920

Olive Schreiner, a writer, was born in Cape Colony, the fifth daughter of missionary parents. Her mother, Rebecca Lyndall, was herself the product of a deeply puritanical upbringing and tried to raise her children in the same way. Her father, Gottlob Schreiner, a more gentle person whom Olive loved deeply, was a failure as a missionary and later a failure in business so that her childhood was one of great poverty and considerable physical hardship. More damaging still was the acute sense of rejection that coloured her childhood, caused partly by her mother's harsh discipline but partly, too, by her own refusal, while still only a child, to accept the rigid Christianity held by her parents. Instead, entirely self-taught, she began to move towards a secularist morality and a deeply felt sense of the injustices suffered by women. When only seventeen she had a brief relationship, possibly a seduction, with an older man which left her feeling both guilty and betrayed, and which may have contributed to the sense of women's sexual exploitation by men which was so important in all her work.

Between 1874 and 1881 she worked in various families as a governess, an experience which was by no means a happy one, and during these years she began to develop as a writer. In 1881, dissatisfied with her life in South Africa, she travelled to England hoping to train as a nurse. Her asthma, which was to plague her all her life, prevented this and she turned again to her writing. In 1883 her novel *The Story of an African Farm* was published and almost immediately established her reputation as a new and unusual talent. It also brought her into contact with advanced opinion, and she became friends with people like Havelock Ellis, Edward Carpenter and Eleanor Marx. For several years, indeed, she was on terms of the most intimate friendship with Havelock Ellis, although they were never lovers in the conventional sense. Through him she joined the Progressive Association and the Fellowship of the New Life, and was a member of the Men's and Women's Club formed specifically to examine the nature of the relationship between men and women.

During these years Olive Schreiner struggled to come to terms with her feminism and with the needs of her own sexual nature. She was very conscious of the extent to which women's sexuality was used by men to trap and exploit women, and this indeed was perhaps the most dominant theme in her feminism all her life. She saw, therefore, any sexual involvement as a threat to her freedom and for several years tried hard to suppress her sexual needs and to develop a purely intellectual friendship with men. Her resolve to be accepted as a man by men broke down, however, when she fell deeply in love with Karl Pearson. His rejection of her led to a complete breakdown in her health and eventually, in 1889, a return to South Africa.

Nevertheless, although her fears of sexual involvement were very real, she continued to dream of an ideal marriage partner and shortly after her return to South Africa believed she had found him in Samuel Cronwright, a politician and farmer who admired her work greatly and shared some of her views. They married in 1894, taking the name Cronwright-Schreiner, but a year later the death of her newborn daughter was a tragedy from which she never recovered, especially when a series of miscarriages and the fact that she was now in her forties made it plain to her that she would never bear another child. Nor was her marriage the perfect union she had hoped for. There was never any open rift between them, but there were incompatibilities of temperament and she grew increasingly unsettled. After the end of the Boer War she began to long to leave South Africa. Eventually, in 1913, she returned to England alone, and there was only one brief reunion with her husband before her death in South Africa in 1920.

Although her feminism pervades all her writings, her most important feminist statement is in *Women and Labour* published in 1911. This is primarily an attack on women's parasitism, which she believed destroyed their intelligence and vitality. Strongly evolutionary in her thinking, she believed that future development would eventually provide the conditions which would make possible a new fellowship between the sexes, although she nevertheless urged that women must still fight for their freedom. She accepted the necessity for the economic and political enfranchisement of women placing, indeed, a particular emphasis on the need for economic independence if women were to avoid the sexual exploitation both inside and outside marriage which she believed to be particularly characteristic of modern society.

There was, however, no rejection of marriage or the family, and she looked to a future in which marriage would be a freely entered and loving partnership and in which the new woman would be matched by the new man. At the same time, although she thought sexual love had an important part to play in marriage, she had a horror of sexual laxity and was strongly opposed to any move towards the imitation by women of what she called the 'licentious human male'. She was also aware of the extent to which women's self-confidence had been destroyed by their long oppression and, although she opposed some of the more violent aspects of the militant suffrage movement, she deeply admired the physical courage of the militant leaders. Indeed, convinced that the vote was not the panacea it was sometimes claimed to be, she believed that the most important consequence of the suffrage struggle was that it showed that women were willing and able to fight for their rights.

Although feminism always came first with her, Olive Schreiner's strong sense of justice led her to champion other oppressed groups. She became a socialist and later, in South Africa, a powerful opponent of racism. Her pacifism was also of profound significance in her life and she was an important figure in the opposition to the Boer War, during which she was interned. Although deeply influenced by Enlightenment doctrines, there was also a powerful evangelical element in her writing which may have derived from her missionary parents. Her vision of the future relationship between the sexes is indeed essentially a moral one, and this moral vision is an inescapable part of her thinking.

Olive Schreiner is an interesting example of a woman whose feminism was, in origin at least, a direct outcome of her own experience. Until she came to England in 1881 she was isolated from both the feminist movement and feminist literature, and although she was familiar with John Stuart Mill's writing, she had not at that time read his *Subjection of Women*. She saw for herself the limitations placed by society on women's lives, and this is brought out in her fiction, and also in her own longing for the freedom of being a man. The very personal nature of her feminism was to remain to some extent a characteristic of her own association with the women's movement. Although she worked with the suffrage movement in South Africa, she always believed that she could contribute most as a writer, and it is in her writing that her contribution to feminism should be judged. Moreover, her life is itself an eloquent expression of the difficulties facing a woman of her time who tried to put her feminism into practice. Above all, her exploration of the conflict in women's lives between love and freedom bring us to the heart of one of feminism's most central dilemmas.

There are several biographies of Olive Schreiner, but the most recent and very comprehensive account is *Olive Schreiner*, Ruth First and Ann Scott (London, André Deutsch, 1980). See also *Olive Schreiner. Feminism on the Frontier*, Joyce Aurech Berkman (Vermont, Eden Press, 1979); *The Letters of Olive Schreiner 1976–1920* ed. S.C. Cronwright-Schreiner (London, Fisher Unwin, 1924); 'Olive Schreiner. New Women, Free Women, All Women', Liz Stanley in

Feminist Theorists, Dale Spender (London, The Women's Press, 1983); *DNB* 1912–21 pp. 484–5.

SHAEN William 1820–1887

William Shaen, a solicitor, was the youngest son of Samuel Shaen and his wife Rebecca Solly, both of whom came from old nonconformist families. He was educated at Brighton and afterwards at University College, London, where he obtained a BA in classics in 1840. Later he studied philosophy at Edinburgh and achieved an MA in philosophy from London in 1842. Following this he began to read for the bar, and during this period of his life met James Stansfeld, also a noted feminist, and the two became friends. His studies at the bar were, however, interrupted and instead he served his articles as a solicitor under William Ashurst, a well-known Radical who was also a feminist. In 1851 William Shaen married Emily Winkworth, the sister of Susanna and Catherine Winkworth, who later became celebrated for their translations of German religious writings. The Shaens remained on close terms of close intimacy with James Stansfeld, who had married Caroline, William Ashurst's daughter, and with William Ashurst himself, sharing many attitudes in common.

Even as a young man William Shaen took a strong interest in education and in 1848 was active in the foundation of the University of London. He was also closely involved, as was his wife Emily, in F.D. Maurice's Working Men's College. It was, however, the higher education of women which claimed his attention most deeply. In 1848 he assisted in the foundation of Bedford College and later he was closely connected with both Girton College and Newnham College at Cambridge. He was also one of the first to be involved in the campaign for medical education for woman, since he took the chair at a meeting on the subject as early as 1858, when the idea was scarcely off the ground. Later he gave a great deal of assistance to Elizabeth Garrett in her attempts to qualify as a doctor, and afterwards helped in the formation of the London School of Medicine for Women. Women's suffrage was another cause that had his full support and so did the attempt to achieve equality between the sexes with respect both to divorce and the guardianship of children.

It was, however, the campaign for the repeal of the Contagious Diseases Acts which aroused his deepest moral indignation. The Acts attempted to protect the Armed Forces against venereal disease by providing for the compulsory examination and if necessary treatment of women believed to be prostitutes. William Shaen believed firmly that chastity should be a law for both men and women alike, and that an act which was criminal for one sex should be equally criminal for the other. He played a leading part in the campaign against the Acts, and was for many years president of the National Association for their repeal. He also drew up several documents on the legal side of the question. His interest in the issue led him to join in the foundation of the Social Purity Alliance, but he stressed in this connection not only the need for rescue work but also the importance of low wages and bad housing as causes of prostitution.

Apart from his feminism, William Shaen was drawn towards a number of other issues which expressed his deep feeling for the suffering of the oppressed. An active member of the Society of the Friends of Italy, the Italians called him 'L'angelo salvatore'. He also supported the anti-vivisectionist cause, believing that men and women had a special responsibility to those who could not help themselves. He sympathised deeply with the American anti-slavery movement and supported the Aborigines Protection Society and the rights of Kaffirs and Zulus. Like many other feminists he also believed firmly in the temperance cause.

His relationship with his wife was close and affectionate, and they shared many interests. In 1862 however, when only forty years old, she was taken ill with a severe and painful spinal illness just after the birth of her last child, and although her health later improved a little she remained an invalid for the rest of her life. She died shortly after her husband in 1887.

William Shaen's feminism was very much part of his hatred of tyranny and suffering. Josephine Butler wrote of his chivalry towards women and this was perhaps expressed most clearly in his attitude towards the prostitute, whom he saw as a victim of oppression. His chivalry was allied to a very strong sense of justice which led him to support the stand for equal rights, whether in the field of education, employment or sexual morality. As a moralist indeed he could be very stern and uncompromising, upheld in this by a religious faith which owed a great deal to the Unitarian, James Martineau. Although he was outwardly stern and even cold, Josephine Butler, who admired him greatly, wrote of the underlying gentleness and kindness of his nature.

William Shaen's daughter Margaret J. Shaen wrote a brief biography, *William Shaen. A Brief Sketch* (London, Longmans Green and Co., 1912). She also wrote an account of his wife's family in *Memorials of Two Sisters. Susanna and Catherine Winkworth* (London, Longmans Green and Co., 1908). For the recollections of Josephine Butler see her *Personal Reminiscences of a Great Crusade* (London, Horace Marshall, 1898).

See also ASHURST William Henry, STANSFELD James.

SHARP Evelyn 1869-1955

Evelyn Sharp, a journalist, was the ninth of the eleven children of James and Jane Sharp. Her father was a slate merchant by inheritance, but retired early from business to follow his other interests. Both parents were musical, and this ability was inherited by most of their children, especially by the eldest son Cecil Sharp, but not by Evelyn herself. Her mother was a conventional woman, her life bounded by parties and housekeeping, and it was not until she was a very old woman that Evelyn came at all close to her. Evelyn herself was brought up conventionally, and was educated at home until the age of twelve, when she went to school, but was recalled home at the age of sixteen in spite of her own desire to go to college. She continued her studies on her own initiative, passing several university local examinations, and also tried her hand at writing novels and stories most of which were rejected. Her only break during this period was three months in Paris in 1890 with two of her sisters, where she attended lectures at the Collège de France.

Finally, after six or seven unhappy years, she determined to go to London to earn her own living. Her decision was greeted with consternation by her parents who believed that daughters should stay at home and wait to be married, but they did not try to prevent her, and she was aided in her plans by her old headmistress. At first she maintained herself by teaching, but it was not long before she was starting a successful career as a writer, mainly of children's stories. Within a year of leaving home she was attached to the *Yellow Book*'s group of young writers and became acquainted with a wide circle of celebrities. By 1900 she had published four books, including *All the Way to Fairyland* (London, J. Lane, 1898) and *The Other Side of the Sun* (London, J. Lane, 1900). In 1903 she began her career as a journalist. It was during this period, too, that she met Henry Nevinson, and this was the start of a close friendship which led eventually to their marriage in 1933, on the death of Henry Nevinson's wife Margaret.

Her involvement in the suffrage movement did not really begin until 1906, although previously she had been a member of the Anti-Sweating League. Her conversion was effected when, as a journalist, she was sent to cover a lecture by Elizabeth Robins, and soon she herself was a member of the Women's Social and Political Union. She took part in a number of activities including public speaking but, because of a promise made to her mother, did not go to prison until 1911. In 1910 she wrote *Rebel Women* (London, A.C. Fifield, 1910). In 1912, when the split between the Pankhursts and the Pethick-Lawrences occurred, both she and Henry Nevinson were on the Pethick-Lawrence side and she left the WSPU, but her activity for suffrage continued unabated, and she became editor of the journal *Votes for Women*, now taken over by the Pethick-Lawrences. In 1914 she joined the United Suffragists, a group of both men and women, and largely sustained it during the war years when many other active members were away. Part of her policy was a refusal to pay taxes, and in 1917 her belongings were seized by bailiffs, although her furniture was bought back by friends. The day the Suffrage Bill finally received its royal assent was, she declared later, the happiest of her life.

After the war she continued her career as a journalist, frequently working abroad on behalf of the *Daily Herald*. Her biography *Hertha Ayrton. A Memoir* (London, Arnold, 1924) was a record not only of their friendship but of their shared feminism. She had joined the Labour Party in 1918, but rejected the offer to stand for Parliament, as she felt she could contribute more as a writer. After 1923 she was mainly concerned with poverty and other social problems, including unemployment. She was, however, a supporter of the birth-control movement of the 1920s, arguing that such knowledge ought not to be confined to the wealthier and more educated classes. Her eventual marriage to Henry Nevinson in 1933 was, however, to be short-lived since, already a very old man, he died in 1941. She survived him by fourteen years, dying in 1955.

Evelyn Sharp was an important convert to the suffrage movement because of her reputation as a novelist, which enabled her to act as a link between the literary and the suffrage world. Later she was one of those who kept the suffrage cause alive during the war years. Brought into the movement by her memories of the frustrating years when she had been an unmarried daughter at home, denied the education she longed for, she saw feminism in terms of women's need for economic independence and self-expression. It is not surprising, therefore, that she had a great admiration for the distinguished woman scientist Hertha Ayrton with whom she shared a very close friendship and whose biographer she later became. Although a member of WSPU for a number of years, she never seems to have been close to the Pankhursts and had no sympathy with their desire to exclude men from the movement. In later years other issues took precedence with her and she was never an active part of the feminist scene in the 1920s. Nevertheless, she was for a time one of the key figures in the suffrage movement.

The only source on Evelyn Sharp's life is her autobiography, written almost twenty years before her death, *Unfinished Adventure* (London, Bodley Head, 1933). For Henry Nevinson's account of their suffrage activities see *More Changes, More Chances* (London, Nisbet, 1925). The Evelyn Sharp Papers are in the Bodleian Library, Oxford.

See also NEVINSON Henry Woodd.

SHARPLES Elizabeth 1804-1861

Elizabeth Sharples was born in Bolton of middle-class parentage, since her father Richard Sharples was a manufacturer of quilts and counterpanes. Nothing is known about her mother. She was educated in a school for young ladies and grew up with strongly evangelical religious views. Her doubts began to grow however, and in 1829 when Richard Carlile visited Bolton she was interested enough to attend his lectures. Soon afterwards, apparently on the recommendation of a cousin, she began to read his newspaper *The Republican*.

In 1831 Richard Carlile was in prison in London and Elizabeth, who had recently lost her father, persuaded a Mr Hardie, a local free-thinking bookseller, to write to Richard Carlile offering to help. He accepted her offer and in January 1832 she arrived alone in London, a young lady still only twenty-eight years old. Almost immediately she gave her first public lecture at the Rotunda, a lecture hall and meeting place which Richard

Carlile used as a platform. Already, apparently, a convinced feminist, her lectures attracted a lot of attention and soon she was speaking three or four times a week. She also started a journal *The Isis* of which she was editor and which reported her lectures verbatim. To critics opposed to her lectures she asserted a woman's right to speak of politics and proclaimed that she was setting an example of female equality. Fundamentally a free-thinker, her attacks on the Church were sustained and bitter, but she also linked her feminism and her secularism, pointing out the subordinate place Christianity accorded to women. Like some of the Owenite feminists she made use of the Adam and Eve myth, turning it upside down and arguing that Eve's action made the tree of knowledge available to man.

Richard Carlile's release from prison was, however, to mark the end of her independence. Already more than forty years old, Richard Carlile had a wife and three sons but the marriage, contracted in 1813, had been for many years an unhappy one due to incompatibilities of temperament. In 1832 there was a legal separation and he and Elizabeth entered what they termed a 'moral marriage' since it could not be a legal one. In spite of Richard Carlile's views on birth control, his union with Elizabeth produced three children in four years, and this left her no time for public work. In 1843 Richard Carlile, his health broken by years of imprisonment, died, leaving her in poverty, and it was a desperate struggle to keep and educate the three children. In 1849 she took in Charles Bradlaugh when, at the age of sixteen, he had been driven from home for his free-thought views, and he described her as a woman whose enthusiasm had been cooled by suffering and poverty. She herself died in 1861 and the three children emigrated to America.

Elizabeth Sharples' story, which we know only in outline, is another demonstration of the extent to which feminist ideas were actively promulgated in the 1830s by women themselves, as part of both secularism and Owenite socialism. Her own career was tragically brief, cut short in less than a year by the demands of marriage and children in circumstances of acute poverty, but she was clearly a woman of exceptional courage and ability who challenged accepted models of womanhood in both her ideas and her behaviour.

Details of Elizabeth Sharples' life can be found in *Class in English History 1680-1850*, R.S. Neale (Oxford, Basil Blackwell, 1981) and *Richard Carlile: Agitator*, Guy Aldred (London, Pioneer Press, 1923). For her relationship with Charles Bradlaugh see *Charles Bradlaugh. a Record of his Life and Work*, Hypatia Bradlaugh Bonner (London, T. Fisher-Unwin, 1895).

SHIRREFF Emily Anne Elizabeth 1814-1897

Emily Shirreff, a pioneer in the movement for the better education of women, was the eldest daughter of Rear-Admiral William Henry Shirreff and Elizabeth Murray, daughter of the Hon. David Murray. Six children were born, but the two sons died young, and Emily herself suffered a serious illness at the age of seven which left her in fragile health. The family lived in France between 1826 and 1829 and in Gibraltar between 1830 and 1834 when they returned to England. Their mother was conventional in her attitude to the education of girls, and they were left largely in the hands of governesses, but later their father guided their studies and they mixed with a number of intellectual families.

Emily's first literary effort was written jointly with her younger sister Maria. Entitled *Letters from Spain and Barbary*, it was published in 1835 soon after their return from Gibraltar. In 1841 Maria married but, although a severe blow to Emily, it did not put an end to the friendship between the two sisters. They collaborated in *Thoughts on Self Culture addressed to Women*, published in 1850, which was essentially an argument on behalf of women's education, and in 1853 they published a novel, *Passion and Principle*.

In 1853 Emily met Henry Buckle, several years her junior, and then quite unknown. A close friendship developed between them, and he helped her in writing *Intellectual Education and its Influence on the Character and Happiness of Women*, published in 1858. In return she helped him in his first public lecture, 'The Influence of Women on the Progress of Knowledge', delivered in 1858 after the publication of the first volume of his *History of Civilization* had brought him fame. At one stage there seems to have been the possibility of marriage between them, but the friendship seems already to have waned by the time of his death in 1861.

During the 1860s Emily was absorbed almost completely in family nursing, but during the 1870s she, like Maria, became deeply involved in the movement for the better education of women. In 1870, indeed, she served for a time as Mistress of Girton but left after a disagreement with Emily Davies. She remained, however, a staunch supporter of the college. In 1871 she and Maria launched the National Union for the Improvement of the Education of Women of all Classes, better known as the Women's Education Union. Emily became its honorary secretary and the joint-editor of its journal. In 1872 the Girls' Public Day School Company was founded and Emily was an active worker in its service.

In 1874, however, her attention was captured by the Froebel movement, and this became the central focus of her activity for the rest of her life. She wrote a number of pamphlets for the society in which she claimed that nature had given women a special responsibility for the care of children. Mothers, she believed, were the natural educators of young children, and in this particular role women had a special responsibility for the moral progress of society.

Emily's feminism, therefore, was closely bound up with her attitude to woman's role as both mother and educator and, although she supported women's suffrage, her views were, in general, narrower than those of her sister Maria. Although she believed firmly that girls should be freed from dilettantism in education and that their education should be no different from that of boys, her chief emphasis, especially in her work for the Froebel movement, was on women's spiritual and moral role. She illustrates clearly, therefore, some of the contradictions in nineteenth-century feminism, particularly within its educational wing, which often combined a radical educational programme with a traditional view of the female role.

There is a biography of Emily Shirreff and her sister Maria Grey, *Liberators of the Female Mind. The Shirreff Sisters. Educational Reform and the Women's Movement*, Edward W. Ellsworth (London, Greenwood Press, 1979). See also *DNB* Vol. LII pp. 144-5.

See also GREY Maria Georgina.

SIDGWICK Eleanor Mildred (Nora) 1845-1936

Nora Sidgwick, a Principal of Newnham College, was the eldest surviving child of James Balfour and Blanche Cecil, daughter of the Marquis of Salisbury. Her mother, widowed while still a young woman, was a devoted if dominating woman who encouraged her daughter's talent in arithmetic. Herself interested in women's education, she had persuaded her wealthy husband to make provision for his daughters' independence as well as his sons'. Brought up in an atmosphere of profound religious conviction, Nora developed a strong sense of service to others, but the expression of emotion was taboo, and later Nora was to confess to a horrified niece that it was doubtful if she had ever really felt excited in her life.

After her mother's death Nora acted as housekeeper to her brother Arthur, a few years her junior, who was later to achieve eminence as Prime Minister. It was during this period that, in 1875, she met Henry Sidgwick, who had been her brother's tutor at Cambridge, and who had remained a close friend. At this time Henry Sidgwick was deeply involved in the development of what was to become Newnham College and, initially through her brother's interest, Nora too became drawn into the work where her financial acumen was particularly valuable. In 1876 she and Henry Sidgwick were married and they began a partnership in which her intellectual ability and qualities of character played a vital role. Nevertheless there is little doubt that it was Henry Sidgwick who had the drive and initiative so that he led and she followed. If, however, his was the dominant personality, the success of the marriage owed everything to Nora's acceptance of her husband's sexual impotence. It must have been a sorrow to her, more especially since it denied her children, but it did not undermine her love for him. Possessed of a sociable nature and great sweetness of character, Henry was nevertheless subject to moods of deep depression and Nora brought serenity to the partnership.

Although she had no formal educational qualifications, her scientific and mathematical ability was considerable. For a time, indeed, she carried out scientific experiments under her brother-in-law Lord Raleigh's direction at the Cavendish Laboratories, and her name appeared jointly with his on three papers for the Royal Society. This was always the kind of work she liked best, and her increasing involvement in the daily life of Newnham College was a sacrifice on her part, especially since her extreme reserve made it difficult to enjoy the social aspects of college life. Nevertheless, in 1850, when a second Hall was built, she accepted the position as its head, and the Sidgwicks gave up their home and lived for two years in the college. Later, in 1892, when Ann Jemima Clough died, Nora was made principal, a post which she retained until the end of 1910. From the first she had been generous with money as well as time, and her gifts to Newnham over her life-time were calculated at over £30,000.

Just as Nora Sidgwick had been drawn into Newnham largely by the enthusiasm of her husband, so she was involved by him in the affairs of the society for Psychical Research. Founded in 1882, largely on his initiative, its researches depended greatly on her talent. Her first paper for the society, *Phantasms of the Dead*, was published in 1885 and she took a large share in the editorial work of its proceedings. Moreover, she remained closely involved even after her husband's death in 1899 and was president in 1908. Highly sceptical at first, she later became more sympathetic to the idea of communication between the living and the dead. More relevant to the women's movement was her research on students' health, published in 1890, in which she compared the health level of women students with the sister nearest in age who had not been to college. In it she demonstrated that attendance at college had not affected the health of students either for better or worse. The same study also demonstrated that, compared with sisters and cousins, college education did not affect a girl's marriage chances or the size of her family, and that the tendency of college-educated women to marry less often or have fewer children than other women was a consequence of social class rather than education.

Like that of her husband, Nora's feminism developed slowly and when she was first involved with Newnham she had doubted whether women were either intellectually or physically fit for a full university education. These doubts were eventually resolved, and by 1896 she was fully committed to equality in the higher education of men and women. Nevertheless, she continued to believe that marriage and motherhood was the natural career for a woman, and that most women would choose marriage rather than a career if the opportunity came. By the 1880s, however, she was an enthusiastic supporter of women's suffrage and always presided at pro-suffrage lectures given at the college. She was, however, never drawn into sympathy for the militant movement, believing that it damaged women's reputation for good sense.

Nora Sidgwick remained in Cambridge until 1916. Her period as principal of Newnham ended in 1910 but she remained associated with the college as bursar. After leaving Cambridge she lived with her brother Gerald and his wife, dying in 1936 at the age of ninety. Her dedication to Newnham remains her main contribution to the women's movement and as its principal she served the cause of women's higher education to the best of her ability. Her feminism, however, was highly rational and lacked both the passionate and, indeed, the personal commitment of educational pioneers like Emily Davies. Her attitude to marriage was also highly conventional and it is perhaps significant that even after her husband's death she chose to continue her life on lines that he had laid down for her. Emotional commitment and emotional appeals were alike foreign to her nature but the serenity which was one of her most appealing characteristics undoubtedly concealed a highly repressed nature. It is surely significant, for example, that when Josephine Butler appealed to her for help in one of her campaigns against legalised prostitution she not only refused, but argued that it was better not even to think about such subjects. Conservative in politics and feminism alike, she represents, therefore, the opposite extreme from those women whose feminism was a revolutionary creed which would in time, they believed, transform the world.

There is a biography of Nora Sidgwick by her niece, *Mrs Henry Sidgwick. A Memoir*, Ethel Sidgwick (London, Sidgwick and Jackson, 1938). See also *Newnham. An Informal Biography*, Mary Agnes Hamilton (London, Faber and Faber, 1936); *A Life of Arthur James Balfour*, Max Egremont (London, Collins, 1980); *Family Homespun*, Blanche Dugdale (London, John Murray, 1940); *DNB* 1931-1940 pp. 811-12. *Health Statistics of Women Students of Cambridge and Oxford and of their Sisters*, Mrs Henry Sidgwick (Cambridge, 1890).

See also SIDGWICK Henry.

SIDGWICK Henry 1838-1899

Henry Sidgwick, philosopher and political economist, was the third son and fourth child of the Reverend William Sidgwick and his wife Mary Crofts. In 1841 his father died and his mother took the family to live near Bristol, where he went to school. In 1852 he went to Rugby, and later to Cambridge where, at the age of twenty-one, he was elected to a Trinity Fellowship. At first his main interest was philosophy but later, under the influence of John Stuart Mill, he turned to political economy. At this time, too, perhaps also through his admiration for John Stuart Mill, he began to take an interest in the position of women in society. Although he started from a somewhat conservative position in which he found the idea of women voting at the polls 'violently radical', he was soon won over to the cause of women's education, and by 1867 had been drawn into the project set in motion by Josephine Butler and Ann Jemima Clough for special university examinations for women. By 1869, moreover, he had taken the personal initiative of organising special lectures for women in Cambridge, and, partly at his own expense, of providing a house in which the students could lodge. Ann Jemima Clough was asked to take charge and in a few years this enterprise developed into Newnham College.

It was not long, however, before Henry Sidgwick found himself in serious conflict with Emily Davies who was at this time laying the foundations for Girton at Cambridge. Although both Henry Sidgwick and Emily Davies were united in their desire to open Cambridge education to women, the principles under which each operated were entirely different. Emily Davies wanted, from the very first, a higher education for women identical in every respect to that of men, to enable women to compete for employment on equal terms, while Henry Sidgwick was prepared to compromise this principle by making concessions to the inadequate preparation with which most girls entered Cambridge. Consequently, girls at Newnham were allowed longer for their studies, or even allowed to enrol with no intention of taking a degree at all. Perhaps the biggest obstacle to their co-operation, however, was Henry Sidgwick's opposition to the compulsory Greek and Latin which formed a necessary preliminary to a degree at Cambridge. Wanting it abolished for boys, Henry Sidgwick was strongly opposed to its imposition on girls, believing that it would inflict the stranglehold of classics firmly on secondary education for girls, just as it had imposed it on the secondary education of boys. He had no wish, therefore, to see degrees for women following the identical, and to his mind wrong-headed, pattern required from men, and preferred women to design their own degrees on lines which university reformers indeed were already advocating for men. For Henry Sidgwick, therefore, the issue was primarily one of university reform, whereas for Emily Davies it was first and last one of equality between the sexes, and neither came fully to understand the other's point of view.

During these same years, which saw the first steps taken to bring women students into Cambridge, Henry Sidgwick was undergoing a period of serious and painful religious doubt which led him, in 1869, to resign his fellowship. He remained at Cambridge, however, as a lecturer in moral sciences, although with a diminished salary, and continued to maintain his interest in the growing number of women students and the consequent expansion of the original house into Newnham College. In 1875 the publication of his first book, *The Methods of Ethics*, led to his appointment as college praelector of moral and political philosophy, and this was followed by his marriage to Eleanor (Nora) Balfour, the sister of his former student and great friend Arthur Balfour, later to become eminent as a Conservative Prime Minister.

The wedding was in 1876, and the couple at once embarked on what was, for its period, an unusually close partnership in which Nora's considerable intellectual gifts played a highly significant part. It was also a very happy marriage, in spite of Henry Sidgwick's sexual impotence which might well have been a threat to their life together. A man of singular sweetness of temper and great charm, Henry Sidgwick complemented his wife's serenity and personal reserve. He was, however, also prone to periods of severe depression and sleeplessness which reflected an inner unease not normally revealed to the world and which his wife's tranquillity of temperament helped to calm. It is possible too, that his own sense of failure as a sexual partner may have contributed to his sense of dependence on his wife and his admiration for her qualities of mind and character which characterised their relationship.

Nora had been involved in the affairs of Newnham even before her marriage, but once living in Cambridge she soon began to play a much more active part in its development. The rapid increase in the numbers of students and the need for larger premises meant that Nora Sidgwick's abilities, especially in the area of finance, became increasingly important. Between 1880 and 1882 she was vice-principal, and for these two years she and her husband made their home in the college. Then, in 1892, when Ann Jemima Clough died, she became principal, and the college their permanent home. As husband of the principal, Henry Sidgwick was naturally drawn into the daily life of the college, where his outgoing nature made him a considerable asset, especially as a foil to Nora's habitual reserve. During these years he was also involved in various attempts to improve the position of women students, and especially their right to a degree, although he continued to maintain his opposition to compulsory Latin and Greek.

Although their work for Newnham dominated their lives, perhaps even more significant for Henry Sidgwick personally was his partnership with Nora in the cause of psychic research. His interest in this field, one which Nora came to share, originated in his loss of belief in Christian dogma, which destroyed much of his religious faith but left him searching for some evidence of personal immortality. Denied the simplicity of faith he turned to science, and in 1882 was instrumental in founding the Society for Psychical Research, of which he became president. Nora, who was an extremely gifted mathematician and had collaborated with her brother-in-law Lord Raleigh on several papers for the Royal Society, was an invaluable assistant although, to Henry Sidgwick's chagrin, much of their work was in fact concerned with discrediting false claims. By 1899 he was looking forward to his retirement from teaching, but in that year cancer was diagnosed, and he died after a short illness. Nora continued his work both at Newnham and in psychic research, dying in 1936 at the age of ninety.

Unlike a number of other men who played a part in the women's movement, Henry Sidgwick was not drawn into this work by the influence of his wife. Indeed, to a considerable extent it was he who drew Nora into his life and work rather than the other way round. What made Henry Sidgwick a feminist was his own sense of justice and his intellectual honesty which drew him to examine and accept the arguments on women's behalf. Moreover, once convinced of their case, he was not content until he had made his own contribution of time and money to further their cause. Later, when his wife's services were called upon he urged her to accept the call, even though it meant, for him, the sacrifice of his domestic privacy and the loss, even more keenly felt, of her assistance in the work of the Society for Psychical Research.

His feud with Emily Davies does, however, indicate some of the limits of his feminism. He was never able to understand the passionate desire of Emily Davies for equal qualifications for men and women, and failed altogether to realise the dangers inherent in a separate curriculum for girls. Indeed, by temperament, Henry Sidgwick was in many ways a conservative rather than a radical thinker, and certainly had nothing of the revolutionary in his make-up. He found the overthrow of traditional beliefs difficult and even painful, as his equivocal position on Christianity testifies, and he was slow to accept the need for any real change in the position of women. In 1862 he had thought women's suffrage 'violently radical', although he came to accept it later, and, in spite of his eventual belief in equal rights for women in both education and employment, he never seems to have challenged the existing position of women within marriage and the family. In 1884, for example, in a letter to the *Spectator* on women's franchise, he based his argument largely on the needs of unmarried women and widows who have to earn their own living. It is interesting to notice that his wife too shared his somewhat conservative views on women and the family. A strong supporter of the constitutional suffrage movement, she nevertheless believed that marriage and motherhood was the natural career for even the most learned of women. If, however, Henry Sidgwick emerges as a rather faint-hearted feminist, he was also a highly practical one, and his unselfish services to women's higher education in Cambridge deserve to be remembered.

There is a biography, *Henry Sidgwick. A Memoir*, Arthur Sidgwick and Eleanor Mildred Sidgwick (London, Macmillan, 1906). See also *A Life of Arthur James Balfour*, Max Egremont (London, Collins, 1980); *Family Homespun*, Blanche Dugdale (London, John Murray, 1940); *Mrs Henry Sidgwick. A Memoir*, Ethel Sidgwick (London, Sidgwick and Jackson, 1938); *Women at Cambridge. A Men's University–though of a Mixed Type*, Rita McWilliams Tullborg (London, Gollancz, 1975).

See also CLOUGH Ann Jemima, DAVIES Sarah Emily, SIDGWICK Eleanor Mildred.

SMITH Mary 1822–1889

Mary Smith, a school teacher, was the daughter of William Smith, an Oxfordshire boot and shoe maker, and his wife Anne Pride, a farmer's daughter. After the marriage Mary's mother, Anne, opened a grocer's shop in the family home and this was an important economic resource for the family. Mary was the second daughter and the fourth child but the birth of the fifth child, when Mary was two, cost her mother her life. All Mary's affection, therefore, was given to her father, and his subsequent remarriage did nothing to change this. While Mary was still a child he had been converted to nonconformism of a strict kind and for this reason the family were regarded by the villagers as 'queer folk', but his strong principles were accepted and admired by Mary throughout her life and she regarded him always as the best man she had ever known.

Although a studious child, Mary found school disappointing and she appears in fact to have been largely self-taught with a passion for self-improvement that lasted all her life. In her early teens she left school to help manage the family shop, since her father at that time was heavily in debt. Some years later, when she was probably about twenty, she went as a family help to a local nonconformist minister, a Mr Osborn, travelling with his family to Westmorland. The family seriously exploited her, however, and soon afterwards she left their service and opened a small school for girls. Later, when the Osborns moved to Carlisle, she was once more prevailed upon to help them and she gave up her school to go with them. Once more, however, the arrangement failed to work and, far from paying her wages, they borrowed money from her.

She eventually found congenial employment looking after the children of a Quaker family which seems to have encouraged her literary ambitions. By this time she was in her late twenties, but although she had several admirers, she had no inclination for marriage without affection, and none of her suitors had the intellectual interests which she looked for in a husband. Meanwhile the Osborns were in difficulties and appealed once again for her help, this time to teach in a small school they had started. In spite of her previous experiences with Mr Osborn she responded, only to find herself once more seriously overworked and underpaid. Eventually, in 1852, she left the Osborns for the last time, but remained in Carlisle where she started a successful school of her own.

In the years that followed Mary Smith gained some degree of financial security, and in addition some local recognition as a public lecturer. She published poems and little sketches in the *Carlisle Express*, as well as two volumes of her poems, but sales were very slow and she never achieved the wider literary reputation she hoped for. She also began to take an interest in the position of women, believing that many of her own problems were due to her sex. As a young woman struggling for financial independence she had had to endure many hardships, and even insults, especially since many careers open to a young man in her position were totally closed to her as a woman. She also believed that her sex had handicapped her in her literary aspirations.

Her active involvement in the women's movement seems to have occurred when her attention was drawn to the founding of the Manchester Women's Suffrage Society in 1866. She took up the cause enthusiastically and helped to found a suffrage society in Carlisle, although this never proved very successful. Subsequently, during the 1870s, she was drawn into both the campaign for a Bill to safeguard a married woman's property and earnings, and the campaign led by Josephine Butler against the Contagious Diseases Acts. These Acts, by requiring the compulsory examination and if necessary treatment of women believed to be prostitutes, were seen by their opponents as condoning both vice and the double standard of sexual morality. Moreover she was a highly active supporter, giving lectures, writing articles for the press and organising petitions. She also worked on behalf of temperance, lecturing on the evils of drink and the need for the provision of coffee houses. As she approached sixty, however, her health failed and she had to give up public work and, more importantly, her school on which she depended for financial support. She died in 1889 at the age of sixty-seven.

Mary Smith's feminism was clearly rooted in her own experience and she was quick to respond when faced with the emergence of a women's suffrage movement, fully appreciating the necessity of the vote to working women like herself. Her sympathies, however, extended to embrace a wide variety of causes which affected the lives of women, both single and married. Her puritan upbringing had its effect both in her strong sense of duty to others and her support for temperance. It was probably too this strong sense of duty which drew her into the controversial Contagious Diseases campaign, in spite of her vulnerability as an unmarried woman and, besides, the headmistress of a girls' school. Her involvement in the women's movement was limited to her own locality and she never achieved national recognition so that it is not surprising that she is forgotten today. She is, however, one of the small but significant number of women who played their part in the expansion of the women's movement which characterised the 1870s.

Our knowledge of Mary Smith is gained from her autobiography, *The Autobiography of Mary Smith. Schoolmistress and Nonconformist.* Vol. I (London and Carlisle, Bemrose and Sons, 1892). Volume II of the autobiography contains a selection of her poems.

SMYTH Ethel Mary 1858–1944

Ethel Smyth, a composer, was the daughter of Major General John Hall Smyth and his wife Nancy Struth. At the time of their marriage he was a young officer in the Bengal Army, but later he returned to England where he commanded the artillery depot at Woolwich. There were eight children, six of them girls, and Ethel was the fourth to be born. She was a naughty and quarrelsome child and, by her own account, something of a tomboy, in contrast to an older brother who was quiet and orderly. She could beat him at most things, and this may have given her the confidence to compete in a man's world later on. Her education was mainly at home, although she was sent to school for a few years. At the age of twelve a chance-heard Beethoven sonata determined her to give her life to music, but for a long time the opposition of her father made this seem an impossible dream. A strong-willed and obstinate man, her father inspired awe in her throughout her childhood.

In 1875 she was given music lessons for a while but these were stopped on her father's orders and for the next two years she almost gave up hope. Indeed on a visit to Ireland she became secretly engaged, mostly from flattered vanity and perhaps her dissastisfaction with her life at home. After only three weeks however she returned the engagement ring. Then, in 1877, a concert in London introduced her to the music of Brahms and re-awoke all her ambitions. This time she rebelled passionately and determinedly, facing her father with a will as strong as his own. She refused to go to church and to sing at dinner parties, and finally locked herself in her room. By this time her mother was on her side and eventually, in 1887, when she was just nineteen, she got her way.

For the next seven years Ethel Smyth studied music at Leipzig with the aid of a small allowance from her father. Soon after her arrival she was befriended by Elizabeth (Lisl) Herzogenberg, herself a talented musician and a friend of Brahms. A young married woman who longed hopelessly for children, she came to accept Ethel as her own child and Ethel, for her part, came to look on her as a mother. Her relationship with her own mother was a difficult one, especially at this time. Dominated by her husband, her mother was deeply unhappy, especially after the death of her eldest son Johnny, and she took refuge in stormy scenes. Ethel loved her mother deeply, but they were unable to remain in the same house without incessant quarrels, and her life with Lisl gave her the kind of tranquil mother-daughter relationship she craved.

During her seven years at Leipzig Ethel Smyth was supremely happy. This happiness ended when she met Harry Brewster, an American who had been brought up in France and who was married to Lisl's sister Julia. It was not long before Harry and Ethel were deeply in love, and the next few years were for Ethel the most unhappy in her life. Harry Brewster was torn between his love for Ethel Smyth and his concern for his wife who was broken-hearted. For her part, too, Ethel was loth to enter into a relationship which she believed to be immoral. Most wounding of all was the anger of Lisl, who blamed Ethel entirely, and a complete rupture followed which lasted the rest of Lisl's life, leaving Ethel, who loved Lisl more than anyone else throughout the whole of her life, heartbroken.

In the years that followed Ethel Smyth tried to break off completely from Harry Brewster and once, for over a year, burned all his letters unopened. Her love could not be denied however, and from 1890 they exchanged letters openly and even met secretly from time to time, although in spite of Harry Brewster's pleas Ethel would not allow any sexual relationship. Finally, in 1895, Julia died and marriage at last became possible. Ethel however found she did not want to give up her freedom, although now that Julia no longer stood between them, she agreed that they should become lovers. The liaison, discreetly maintained, lasted until Harry Brewster's death in 1908 and brought her considerable happiness. There is no doubt indeed of Harry Brewster's enduring importance in her life, and it is entirely possible that if he had been free when she first met him, they would have married. By 1895, however, she was too accustomed to her independence to want to yield it to anyone, however dearly loved.

By 1895 moreover, now thirty-seven years old, Ethel Smyth was beginning to make a name for herself as a composer, with the first performance in 1893 of her mass at the Albert Hall. During the next few years she composed several operas, including her most famous work, *The Wreckers*, completed in 1904 and first performed in 1909. Then, in 1910, her life changed dramatically in a most unexpected way. Previously, in spite of a much earlier friendship with Rhoda Garrett, she had been totally indifferent to the women's movement and even treated it with a certain amount of ridicule. In 1910 however, reproached by a friend in Austria for her lack of interest, she went to hear Emmeline Pankhurst and was completely swept off her feet. Impulsively, she decided to give up music for two years to devote herself to the suffrage cause.

During those two years she threw herself into the militant movement with the enthusiasm that characterised all her doings. Determined to go to prison, she broke the window of a Cabinet minister's house and was given a two months' sentence. The *March of Women* which she specially composed became a significant rallying cry, while her reputation as a musician gave an important propaganda value to all her activities. Moreover, she found militancy a thrilling experience revelling, like other women before her, in the fellowship that prison brought and which was a totally new experience to her. Her involvement, too, had a profound long-term effect. Previously she had resented any attempt to snub her as a musician because of her sex, but this personal resentment turned into a strongly feminist consciousness which survived long after the militant movement itself was at an end.

In 1912 she returned to her music and during the next ten to fifteen years composed several more operas. She also embarked on a new career as a writer, producing several lively and highly successful books, chiefly of reminiscences. During the 1920s too she began what was virtually a one-woman campaign in support of women orchestra players. This was first sparked off in 1920 when all the women players in the Hallé orchestra were sacked, and she continued to attack the prejudice of many conductors against women players for the rest of her active life, enlisting, in 1929, the help of Nancy Astor in the cause.

During these years she also came to believe firmly that sex prejudice had harmed her own career as a composer, and turned her attack into a feminist analysis of the general position of women in music. Moreover, her approach was a decidedly modern one in that she saw clearly how deeply sex prejudice was built into the whole structure of the music profession. She blamed men for their clannishness and their resistance to women breaking into what they had always regarded as their private sphere, and she was also aware of the limitations placed on women by their exclusion both from musical education and from the whole system of patronage in music. At the same time she pointed out that women themselves must stop the practice of allowing men to do their thinking for them, a consequence, as she also perceived, of their long history of subjection. On the other hand, men must cease to judge women by masculine standards and must face up to the fact that it was necessary to understand what women were trying to say. Indeed she expressly rejected the view that men and women were basically the same, and argued that women must come to understand and explore their differences.

Ethel Smyth's feminism was rooted in the independence of mind which had enabled her not only to defy her father but to break into the very masculine world of music. At first all her energy went into her own personal struggle and she came late to the women's movement, but once awakened her feminism lasted well beyond the suffrage movement which brought it to light. Her independence of mind extended to her views on men and marriage and, indeed, throughout her life she found friendship with women easier, and certainly much less threatening than with men, although her sexual feelings, which were quite strong, appear to have been aroused by men rather than women. A remarkable woman by any standards, her feminism was only a small part of her extraordinary life, but it was a vital part which has too often been ignored.

The main source is *Ethel Smyth. A Biography*, Christopher St John (London, Longmans, 1959). See also her own writings, especially *Impressions that Remained* (Two Vols.) (London, Longmans, 1936) and *As Time Went On* (London, Longmans, 1936). For her attitude to women and music see especially *Female Pipings in Eden* (London, Peter Davies, 1933). *DNB* 1941–50 pp. 804–5.

SNOWDEN Ethel Annakin 1880–1951

Ethel Snowden, a suffragist, was born Ethel Annakin, the daughter of a Harrogate building contractor, but this is all we know about her early life. She had insisted on leaving home to become a teacher, and had trained at Edge Hill College, where she had come under the influence of the Reverend Dr C.F. Aked, a Radical preacher. He converted her to socialism and she went into the slums of Liverpool to preach teetotalism. Later she started lecturing for the Independent Labour Party, where she made a big impression with her powerful delivery and graceful appearance. Indeed, she was described by one listener as a second Annie Besant. In 1904 she took up a teaching post at Nelson near Cowling and soon became a frequent visitor to Philip Snowden's home. It was widely believed at the time that she was the one who proposed marriage, perhaps because Philip was diffident, and the wedding took place in secret in 1905.

At this time Philip Snowden was already forty-one years of age. Born in 1864, the son of a weaver, Philip was both clever and ambitious. He had trained for a time as a pupil teacher, and eventually became a civil servant. In 1891 an attack of what was probably spinal tuberculosis left his spine permanently damaged and for some time he was in fact paralysed. His career as a civil servant over, he turned to politics, and in 1896 began to work as a travelling socialist preacher in the ILP. Eventually he became the ILP expert on taxation and public finance and in 1903, the year he met Ethel, he became its chairman. He and his widowed mother were exceptionally close and from the start she had opposed his friendship with Ethel, and it was mainly for this reason that the marriage was kept secret, his mother being told only when the wedding was over. The only witnesses were the couple's joint friends Isabella and Bessie Ford.

Although it was suggested that Ethel had married him to further her own political ambitions, in fact she proved a devoted wife who watched over his health carefully. There were no children, and it was widely suggested that Philip was impotent, although this may not necessarily have been true. In any event the marriage seems to have been a successful one for both partners. Ethel left her career as a teacher but continued to lecture, concentrating on the issue of suffrage, which increasingly claimed her attention. In 1907 she went to the United States on a lecture tour and was so successful that she was invited back nine times altogether over the next twenty years, lecturing on both women's suffrage and temperance.

Her growing commitment to suffrage led her to join the National Union of Women's Suffrage Societies, and in time she became one of their most active speakers. With the help of Isabella Ford she also converted Philip who, before their marriage, had been actively opposed to the issue. He became one of the most sympathetic of the Labour leaders, arguing the case consistently and persuasively both inside and outside Parliament. By accepting the NUWSS argument for a limited suffrage Bill both he and Ethel disagreed with those in the Labour movement who were only prepared to support women's suffrage as part of an adult suffrage measure. Ethel never wavered on this issue and even went so far as to resign from the ILP so that she could be untrammelled by party loyalty. On the other hand, both she and Philip were opposed to the tactics of the militants, and were themselves attacked by the militants and their meetings interrupted.

During this period Ethel wrote numerous articles and pamphlets on the subject of women. She also published two books, *The Woman Socialist* in 1907, and *The Feminist Movement* in 1913. At this time of her life her views on marriage and the family were decidedly radical, and represented a genuine attempt to reconcile feminist and socialist ideas. For example, she advocated co-operative housekeeping and child-minding, and wanted mothers to have salaries paid by the state, and wives to have joint title with their husbands to the housekeeping money. She also wished to abolish marriage in church, and to make divorce easier. At the same time she was influenced by eugenic arguments and wanted strict state control of marriage, to forbid it to the mentally weak and to anyone under the age of twenty-six. Moreover, at a time when some socialist feminists were keen to advocate greater sexual freedom for women, she was involved in the campaign to abolish barmaids on the grounds that it was immoral for young girls to sell drinks to men.

During the war she maintained a strong pacifist position, actively supporting the Women's Peace Crusade. With the end of the war she returned to Labour Party politics and did not become involved in the feminist activities which the NUWSS, now the National Union of Societies for Equal Citizenship, was actively promoting during the 1920s. She was, however, elected to the women's section of the national executive of the Labour Party and also travelled extensively in Europe in various attempts to re-establish a United Socialist International. She also visited Russia as a member of the official TUC-Labour Party Committee of Enquiry, but her critical report, published as *Through Bolshevik Russia* (1920) was received so badly by the Labour Party that when she stood again for the national executive she was defeated, and never again held any official position within the party.

In 1922 she was asked to oppose Nancy Astor, but refused on the grounds of Nancy Astor's work for women and children. She was then invited to stand for South-East Leicester but decided instead to devote her energies to Philip, who was a candidate for Colne Valley. It is not clear, however, whether this decision was made because of Philip's health or her own growing lack of popularity within the Labour Party. Beatrice Webb, who hated her, called her the worst sort of social climber, and even went so far as to allege that Philip Snowden's career had been hampered because of Ethel's unpopularity. The charge made by Beatrice Webb, that Ethel was no longer a socialist, may also have some considerable truth in it, since in the years that followed she turned to other things.

In 1926 she was made a member of the Board of Governors of the newly established BBC, representing the interests of both women and labour. There she soon quarrelled with the dictatorial John Reith. She also took a leading part, during these years, in the revival of Covent Garden Opera. In 1932 she was not re-appointed to the BBC and her last official appointment came to an end.

After her husband's death in 1937 she continued to speak and write, but her main activity was now propaganda for temperance. During the war she became deeply worried about declining moral standards, especially among girls in the Armed Services. She also disliked the loose attitudes in the BBC towards drinking, marital unfaithfulness and swearing. In 1947 she suffered a stroke and was permanently disabled until her death in 1951.

In spite of Ethel Snowden's popularity as a lecturer, she was always a controversial figure, perhaps because tact and discretion seemed foreign to her nature. After the war her unpopularity increased and she was criticised for her patronising manner and her social climbing. Her feminism, too, was always somewhat unorthodox, combining radical views on the family with a traditional outlook on morality. Her main contribution to feminism was made between 1905 and 1914 when she became one of the leading speakers for the constitutional movement. Her influence on Philip Snowden was considerable, and under her guidance he emerged as one of Labour's most consistent feminists.

There is no biography of Ethel Snowden and the information we have is derived from the biography of her husband, *Philip Snowden*, Colin Cross (London, Bassie and Rockliff, 1966). For Beatrice Webb's views see *Beatrice Webb's Diaries 1924–1932* (London, Longmans Green and Co., 1956).

See also FORD Isabella Ormston, SNOWDEN Philip.

SNOWDEN Philip 1864–1937

Born in Cowling, West Riding, the son of a highly intellectual weaver and a strong-willed mother, Philip Snowden was both clever and ambitious. He trained for a time as a pupil-teacher, was then an insurance clerk and finally a civil servant in the excise department of the Inland Revenue. In 1891 an attack of what was probably spinal tuberculosis left his spine permanently damaged, and for a time he was in fact paralysed from the waist down.

His career as a civil servant over, he turned to writing, then to politics, and in 1896 began his work at a travelling socialist preacher. At this time he was living at home with his mother, now a widow. In 1903 he became chairman of the Independent Labour Party and in the same year met Ethel Annakin who, in 1905, in spite of the opposition of his mother, become his wife. In 1906, after two unsuccessful tries, he entered Parliament as the member for Blackburn.

Philip Snowden's main interest in Parliament was finance, and his maiden speech was on free trade. His general principles were frugal government, direct rather than indirect taxation, and non-contributory social services. Under the influence of Ethel, however, his previously unsympathetic attitude to women's suffrage was changed into enthusiastic support. Moreover, unlike many of his Labour Party colleagues, he was prepared to accept the arguments in favour of a limited suffrage Bill, claiming that many of those enfranchised would be working-class householders.

During the next few years Philip Snowden argued the suffrage case at every opportunity both inside and outside Parliament. For example, he was always an ardent advocate at party conferences and helped gradually to swing opinion in the women's favour. He also spoke willingly on suffrage platforms. In 1910 he became joint secretary of the ill-fated Conciliation Committee which sponsored a Bill designed to secure the co-operation of all parties to a limited suffrage Bill. In 1913 he published a women's suffrage pamphlet, *The Dominant Issue*. Like Ethel, he could not support militant tactics, and this led to several confrontations with the militants during 1913 and 1914. Nevertheless, he was prepared to collaborate in a suffrage attempt to petition the King as he walked in procession to open Parliament.

Nor were his efforts for women confined to the issue of suffrage. During a debate on the People's Budget in 1907 he moved an amendment which attempted to separate the incomes of husbands and wives for tax purposes. In 1913, when the question of paying maternity benefits to wives was under debate, the Labour Party was opposed, believing that it should go to the husbands, but Philip Snowden defied the party and voted for the measure.

In 1914 he made clear his anti-war views and his opposition to conscription. He joined the Union of Democratic Control and in 1916 began to campaign for a negotiated peace. In 1918, like all anti-war MPs, he lost his seat but was returned to Parliament in 1922, and in 1924 in the first Labour government he became Chancellor of the Exchequer. Later, from 1924–9, he was Shadow Chancellor. In 1929 he was again Chancellor and, alarmed at the increasing crisis, accepted MacDonald's invitation to form a national government. During these years he was dominated in one form or the other by financial issues and by his attempt to solve the problem of unemployment. He continued to maintain his faith in traditional economic policies and to move to the Right politically. The position of women was no longer of particular interest to him, although in 1928 he was the principal opposition speaker on the Franchise Bill which finally gave women the vote on the same terms as men. In his speech he referred to the fears which had dominated the struggle for women's suffrage and which experience since 1918 had completely falsified.

His last years were made unhappy by his increasing ill health and by the bitterness of his expulsion from the Labour Party when he joined the national government. Without a seat in Parliament he accepted a position in the House of Lords, but in 1932 he resigned from the Cabinet. By 1936 he was almost entirely unable to walk and totally out of touch with the younger generation in the Labour movement. His death occurred in 1937 as the result of a heart attack.

Philip Snowden's later unpopularity and his reputation as a traditionalist in economic matters has obscured the extent to which his thinking on the position of women was more radical than that of most men in the Labour movement. Although, initially at least, influenced by his wife Ethel to whom he was devoted, his conversion, when it came, was complete and his advocacy passionate and sincere. His main interest was in women's suffrage which, he believed, would raise the whole standard of national life, but he took up a number of other women's issues, and his willingness on more than one occasion to defy the party whips is evidence of both his courage and his conviction.

There is a biography, *Philip Snowden*, Colin Cross (London, Barrie and Rockliff, 1966). See also *An Autobiography*, Philip Snowden (London, Nicholson and Watson, 1934). Also *DNB* 1931–1940, pp. 822–5.

See also SNOWDEN Ethel Annakin.

STACEY Enid ?–1903

Enid Stacey was one of the first of the women lecturers employed by the Independent Labour Party. Nothing is known of her early life, but she almost certainly came from a middle-class family. A graduate of Cambridge, she worked for a time as a high-school mistress in Bristol and became both a socialist and a feminist. She lost her job when her name was taken by the police while speaking at a prohibited meeting, and by 1894 was a travelling woman lecturer for the ILP. From the first she seems to have tried to draw together socialism and feminism, and was an important influence in bringing the issue of women's suffrage to the attention of the ILP. A friend of Esther Roper, she became involved in the women's suffrage movement and in 1898 lectured to the National Union of Women's Suffrage Societies in Manchester. In 1903 she joined in the suffrage deputation of women graduates to Westminster.

She wrote frequently for the socialist journal the *Clarion* and also contributed 'A Century of Women's Rights' to Edward Carpenter's *Forecasts of the Coming Century* (Manchester, Labour Press, 1897). Her views were somewhat in advance of her time since, as well as claiming equal rights within marriage and fairer divorce laws, she wanted women to have the right to choose whether to have children. Like many women socialists, she was in favour of protective legislation but wanted it as far as possible to apply to both men and women. In 1903 she married a clergyman of the Church of England, but died shortly afterwards worn out, Sylvia Pankhurst believed, by the exhausting routine of open-air speaking. It is not known when she was born but it was probably some time in the 1860s.

Very little information is available on Enid Stacey, but the most important source is *One Hand Tied Behind Us. The Rise of the Women's Suffrage Movement*, Jill Liddington and Jill Norris (London, Virago, 1978). See also 'Women in Labour Politics' in *Women in the Labour Movement. The British Experience*, ed. Lucy Middleton (London, Croom Helm, 1977); *Philip Snowden*, Colin Cross (London, Barrie and Rockliff, 1966); and *An Autobiography*, Philip Snowden (London, Nicholson and Watson, 1934).

STANSFELD James 1820-1898

James Stansfeld, Parliamentary leader of the campaign against the Contagious Diseases Acts, came from an old Yorkshire family which had long been non-conformist. He was the only son of James Stansfeld, a solicitor's clerk who became a county court judge, and his wife Emma Ralph who was herself the daughter of a non-conformist minister. After attending school in Liverpool he became, in 1836, a student at University College, London where he obtained a pass degree in 1840. At this time he made the acquaintance of William Ashurst, a Radical solicitor, whose home was a centre where refugees from all countries received help and encouragement. James' own Radical sympathies were already well advanced and he became not only a close friend of the family but a son-in-law, when he married Caroline Ashurst in 1844. There was one child, a son, born in 1852.

In 1849 James Stansfeld was called to the bar but, finding the practice of law unprofitable he and his brother-in-law, Sidney Hawkes, the husband of Emilie Ashurst, started a brewery. Sidney Hawkes, however, proved a somewhat unsatisfactory partner and James Stansfeld continued the brewery on his own. During these years his chief interest was in the cause of Italian unity. Mazzini was an intimate friend of the Ashursts, deeply admired by Caroline, and soon became a welcome visitor to the Stansfeld home. James himself was strongly drawn to the Italian cause and soon became an active member of the Friends of Italy movement.

In 1859 he entered Parliament, representing Halifax as a Radical, and his obvious ability soon attracted notice. He was appointed as a Junior Lord of the Admiralty in 1863 and seemed set for early promotion when his enthusiasm for the Italian cause implicated him in a scandal concerning an attempt on the life of Napoleon III. Although not directly involved, his close friendship with Mazzini went against him and he was forced to resign his appointment at the Admiralty. The set-back was, however, only temporary and he was back in office in 1866 as under-secretary for India. In 1869 he became financial secretary to the Treasury, and in 1871 he entered the Cabinet as president of the Poor Law Board, where he embarked on plans for reform.

Soon, however, and almost in spite of himself, James Stansfeld found himself drawn into the campaign against the Contagious Diseases Acts which required the compulsory examination and if necessary treatment of women believed to be prostitutes. Originally he had seen these Acts as a necessary consequence of enforced celibacy in the Armed Forces, but was attacked by some of his most active supporters and, in trying to answer them, he came gradually to see the Acts as approaching the state sanction of prostitution. In 1874, when the fall of the Liberal government released him from office, he determined to devote himself wholeheartedly to the repeal movement. He understood that if repeal was to be achieved the Liberal Party must be converted, and set himself to achieve this end. The decision, however, put an end permanently to his hopes of office since when the Liberals were returned to power in 1880 he was given no place in Gladstone's Cabinet. This was a grave personal disappointment but it enabled him to act as the parliamentary leader of the campaign and to steer it to a successful conclusion in 1884. As a repealer, he differed from some of the religious opponents of the Acts who believed that venereal disease helped to prevent immorality. He wanted scientific and medical knowledge to bring about a cure, but he objected to the compulsion inherent in the Acts and to the necessity of prostitution which they implied. This more moderate view helped him to overcome some of the opposition to repeal within the medical profession.

Although best known for his part in the repeal movement, James Stansfeld was also a persistent and hard-working campaigner for women's rights. He himself dated his conversion to his shame when women delegates from the United States were excluded from the World Anti-Slavery Convention in 1840, and these feelings were reinforced by his acceptance into the strongly feminist Ashurst family. A consistent supporter of women's suffrage, he was one of the speakers at the first public meeting in London in 1869. As president of the Poor Law Board he was able to give even more concrete proof of his feminist sympathies when in 1872, against the views of his officials, he appointed Mrs Nassau Senior as the first woman Poor Law inspector. But it was in the field of medical education that he was able to act most effectively, both inside and outside Parliament. He was, for example, influential in the passage of the important Enabling Bill of 1876 which made it easier for universities to admit women to medical degrees. He also supported a number of measures to improve the medical training available to women. In 1876, for example, he tried to obtain the admission of women students to some of the wards of London Hospital. He was also closely associated with the London School of Medicine for Women from its foundation until his retirement from active life in 1895.

In 1881 his wife Caroline became seriously ill and the next few years were shadowed by his grief at her suffering, and her death in 1885. In 1887 he married Frances Severn, the widow of Henry Severn. In 1892 he was given a peerage, although he was still denied the place in the Cabinet which his involvement in the repeal campaign had cost him. His own health was failing and in 1895 he retired from politics. On his retirement the leaders of the women's movement presented him with a memorial to signify their gratitude for his services to their cause. After his death in 1898 a fund was raised to set up the Stansfeld Trust to examine future legislation from a feminist standpoint.

James Stansfeld's contribution to the women's movement was largely through his position in Parliament. His political skills enabled him to intervene successfully in both the campaign against the Contagious Diseases Acts and the movement for the medical education of women, while as president of the Poor Law Board he was able to break new ground by establishing a woman inspector. In all the causes which he embraced throughout his life, feminism included, he was motivated by a strong sense of justice and a deep compassion for those he believed to be oppressed. Moreover, once his support was enlisted he proved himself a loyal and unselfish friend. There is no doubt that he felt deeply the loss to his political career that his leadership of the campaign against the Contagious Diseases Acts brought about, but, once convinced, he could not turn aside from what he saw as his sacred duty. His courage and integrity, therefore, made him particularly valuable as a friend and ally of the feminist cause.

There is a biography, *James Stansfeld. A Victorian Champion of Sex Equality*, J.L. and Barbara Hammond (London, Longmans, 1932). His work for medical education is also described in *The Life of Sophia Jex-Blake*, Margaret Todd (London, Macmillan, 1918). For two recent assessments of his part in the campaign against the Contagious Diseases Acts see *Prostitution and Victorian Social Reform*, Paul McHugh (New York, St

Martin's Press, 1980) and *Prostitution and Victorian Society*, Judith R. Walkowitz (Cambridge, Cambridge University Press, 1980). See also *DNB* Supplement Vol. III, pp. 352-3.

See also ASHURST William Henry, BUTLER Josephine, JEX-BLAKE Sophia, VENTURI Emilie Ashurst.

STOCKS Mary Danvers 1891-1975

Mary Stocks, a birth control campaigner, was the eldest of three children, one boy and two girls, of Roland Danvers Brinton, a London general practitioner. On her mother's side she was part of the wealthy Rendel family, headed by her grandparents Sir Alexander and Lady Rendel, and her childhood seems to have reflected this background. It was orderly, comfortable and secure, with a devoted nurse, loving parents and a closely-knit extended family of Rendels known as the 'connection'. Through the Rendels she also made close links with the Strachey family since one of her uncles married Eleanor Strachey, and another loved Philippa or Pippa Strachey devotedly but unsuccessfully for many years.

Mary Brinton attended St Paul's Girls' School, but disliked it, and left at the age of seventeen. For a time she was attracted to social work, influenced by the many philanthropic interests of the Rendel family. She met both Beatrice Webb and Octavia Hill, but eventually became a voluntary worker concerned with the administration of school meals. Inevitably, too, she was drawn into the suffrage movement, since the Rendels were deeply involved, some in the Women's Social and Political Union and others in the National Union of Women's Suffrage Societies. The Strachey family were ardent supporters of NUWSS, especially Philippa, who was its full-time secretary and organised all its processions. Another friend, Ray Costelloe, later to become Ray Strachey, was also active in the movement. Mary was spellbound by Emmeline Pankhurst but disliked the dictatorial elements in WSPU and remained firmly committed to NUWSS, for whom she carried a banner in 1907 while still a schoolgirl. Later she stewarded at meetings, distributed literature, and acted as crowd whipper-in at open-air meetings. She also tried her hand at public speaking but this venture was opposed by her mother.

Although Mary had disliked school, she was attracted by the idea of further study and in 1910 entered the newly opened London School of Economics where she achieved a first in economic history. While a student, she met John Stocks, then twenty-eight years old, a fellow of St John's College, Oxford, and the son of the Archdeacon of Leicester. He was a socialist, a keen member of Oxford Women's Suffrage Society and a firm supporter of higher education for women. Their attraction was mutual and within a few weeks of meeting they were engaged, although they deferred their marriage until 1913, when she had completed her studies.

After their marriage they settled in Oxford, where she gave tutorials in economics, but this life was interrupted when John Stocks joined the Army. In the years that followed Mary Stocks continued her teaching in London, partly at the London School of Economics, partly at Kings College. She also served on the executive committee of NUWSS and played a part in their campaign for the suffrage Bill in 1918. She was also involved from the start in Eleanor Rathbone's struggle for family allowances, serving with Maude Royden and Henry Brailsford on the small committee which produced a pamphlet, *Equal Pay and the Family*, in 1918. A daughter was born in 1915 and a son early in 1918 but a competent children's nurse allowed her to continue her work with only brief temporary interruptions.

When her husband, who had been seriously wounded, left the Army they settled down again in Oxford, where she continued to take part in some teaching. In 1920 their last child, a daughter, was born. In 1924 her husband was appointed professor of philosophy at Manchester University, and this began a very happy and fruitful period in her life. It revolved largely around the Manchester

University Settlement, with which her husband was closely involved, and her own work for birth control. In 1925 she opened the first provincial birth-control clinic in Manchester and was soon fully occupied not only in the work of the clinic but in lecturing on the subject at women's meetings. In 1930 she was made a JP and this became another absorbing interest.

Meanwhile she had maintained her activity in NUWSS, now the National Union of Societies for Equal Citizenship, and during the early part of the 1920s was joint editor of their journal the *Woman's Leader*. She also spearheaded the campaign to get NUSEC to include birth control in its policy, and in 1925 was the author of a NUSEC pamphlet *Family Limitation and Women's Organizations*. In it she expressed her view that feminism involved more than identity of treatment with men, and also required greater control by women of their own needs, especially the needs of mothers. Although advocating that contraceptive advice should be made available to mothers of all classes, she was careful also to express her disapproval of abortion.

This attention by Mary Stocks to the need to widen the conception of feminism did not mean that she wanted to abandon the struggle for equal rights. After full suffrage was achieved in 1928 she was one of the very few NUSEC leaders who wanted to maintain the organisation as a feminist pressure group. She spoke of the antagonism to women doctors and to married women teachers, and the persistence of unequal pay and the barriers to promotion in the Civil Service. The majority view was expressed by Eva Hubback who wanted the emphasis placed on education for citizenship, and subsequently NUSEC became the Townswomen's Guild with largely educational rather than political aims.

By the 1930s, however, Mary Stocks was turning to a rather different kind of issue. Soon after her appointment as a JP she was placed on a Home Office Committee on Persistent Offenders, and in 1932 was a member of the Royal Commission on Betting and Lotteries. Later government assignments included the Post Office, the BBC, and university grants. On at least one occasion, however, she found the opportunity to press her feminist views, when serving with Beveridge on the Unemployment Committee in 1935. Her recommendation that benefits and contributions should be equalised between men and women was duly recorded, but Beveridge did not try to conceal his annoyance.

In 1936 her husband was appointed vice-chancellor at Liverpool University, but after only six months his sudden death from a heart attack uprooted the family once again, this time to London. After a period as general secretary of the London Council of Social Services, Mary Stocks became, in 1939, principal of Westfield College where she remained till her retirement in 1951. Subsequently she became an active broadcaster and in 1966 was made a member of the House of Lords. During this period she wrote a number of biographies and histories, including a biography of her friend Eleanor Rathbone in 1948, and a history of district nursing in 1960. These all, however, reflect interests other than feminism.

The impression to be gained from her later years is that by the end of the war the active phase of her feminism was largely over. Perhaps her latest direct involvement was in 1947 when she was one of the sponsors of a conference concerned with women's under-representation on public bodies and the lack of scope in their careers. The proceedings were later published as *The Feminine Point of View* ed. Olwen W. Campbell (London, Williams and Norgate, 1947). This move away from feminism was not so much because of any change of heart, but simply because she gradually came to believe that the battle was mainly won. Indeed in her autobiography in 1970 she concluded, 'I am no longer a member of an unprivileged sex' (p. 235).

Undoubtedly her own personal success in penetrating the masculine establishment had influenced her in this view as well as the eventual success, by 1970, of her own particular campaign for the extension of birth-control information to working-class women. The extent to which her feminism was rooted in the philanthropy which was such a significant feature of her family background may also have played a part in the decline in her feminist commitment which coincided with the establishment of the welfare state. Her main contribution to feminism came in the 1920s when she was one of the most active of the women who tried to maintain the commitment to feminist goals when the public enthusiasm which had marked the main suffrage campaign was over. Moreover, alongside her great friend Eleanor Rathbone she tried to extend the concept of feminism beyond equal rights to include a new way of looking at motherhood and the family. These ideas for extending feminism were never full developed and it was left to a new generation of women, in the 1960s and 1970s, to revitalise the women's movement, but the significance of her contribution should not therefore be undervalued.

The main source of information on Mary Stocks is her autobiography *My Common Place Book* (London, Peter Davies, 1970). See also *Organization Woman*, Mary Stott (London, Heinemann, 1978).

See also HUBBACK Eva Marian, RATHBONE Eleanor, STRACHEY Philippa, STRACHEY Rachel.

STOPES Marie Charlotte Carmichael 1880-1958

Marie Stopes, a birth control campaigner, was the first of the two daughters of Henry Stopes and Charlotte Carmichael. Henry Stopes was a well-to-do brewer who was also a distinguished amateur scientist. His wife was both an intelligent and a highly educated woman, and a passionate advocate of women's suffrage, so it must have seemed at first, when they met at the British Association for the Advancement of Science, that they were well-matched, in spite of the fact that she was eleven years his senior. In fact, however, the marriage was an unhappy one. She had a considerable aversion to sexual intercourse, and although a second child was born in 1885, the couple gradually turned away from each other. Indeed Charlotte Stopes seems to have found it as difficult to show love to her children as to her husband. Henry Stopes on the other hand was an affectionate father, and he and Marie had a very close relationship throughout her childhood in which she was allowed to share his scientific interests.

Although she was eventually to become a brilliant scientist, Marie Stopes did not at first seem a particularly able child and her early academic failures, coupled with strong pressure from her parents to succeed, may have produced the insatiable passion for achievement which was to characterise her all her life. At the age of eighteen, however, she won a science scholarship, and, against everyone's advice, chose to take it at University College London because it was a mixed college. There is little doubt that at this stage in her life she identified very strongly with her father and his scientific friends. Working with tremendous concentration, she achieved a double first-class in botany in less than the usual time, although the death of her father at the early age of fifty must have robbed her achievement of some of its satisfaction. Moreover, in his enthusiasm for science he had neglected his business and Marie Stopes was faced with the necessity to support herself.

After a further year in London Marie Stopes was given the financial opportunity to study for a year in Munich. So far she had escaped any serious emotional entanglement and, indeed, did not at this stage find young men attractive, but at Munich she fell very deeply in love with a Japanese professor, Kenjito Fujii, a married man much older than herself. Recognising his unsuitability on so many counts, she tried to forget him and at the end of the year, her PhD achieved, she returned to England and obtained a lecturing post at Manchester. He followed her, however, and eventually they openly accepted their love although, probably because of her conventionality, they did not become lovers. His wife, however, had found another man and was asking for a divorce, and this gave them hope of a marriage in the future.

He returned to Japan and Marie Stopes, whose appetite for work remained unaffected, achieved her DSc in 1905 to become the youngest doctor of Science in Britain. She was also already making a name for herself in the subject of fossils in coal. In 1906 Kenjito Fujii was divorced and Marie Stopes succeeded in obtaining a grant from the Royal Society, the first time such help had been given to a woman, to enable her to study in Japan. By this time, however, Kenjito Fujii's ardour was rapidly cooling. He received her coldly, and kept her at arm's length throughout the whole of her two-year visit, alleging illness as an excuse. Gradually she was forced to accept his rejection, a blow both to her love, and her pride, from which she never completely recovered.

By the time she returned to England Marie Stopes was twenty-eight years old and, although she had succeeded brilliantly in her career, her quest for love had been thwarted. During the next few years her career continued to succeed, and she became established as one of the leading paleo-botanists of her day, moving from Manchester to London. Her efforts to find a husband were, however, unrewarded until, in 1911, at a conference in the United States, she met Reginald Gates. Within a week of meeting he proposed and was accepted, and shortly afterwards he joined her in London and they were married. The marriage, however, was a total disaster. An intelligent man, with a great deal of surface charm, he was weak, jealous and obstinate. He was also sexually impotent.

Although the basic problem in the marriage was his sexual impotence he could not, perhaps because of it, come to terms with Marie Stopes' feminist principles, taking exception to her support for the women's suffrage campaign. Nor could he contain his jealousy at her higher academic position. A further complication was his jealousy of their lodger, Aylmer Maude. Although Maude was almost certainly in love with Marie Stopes, her own feelings were decidedly ambiguous. He was not only twenty-two years older but married, although separated from his wife. Nevertheless he undoubtedly gave Marie support, affection and encouragement at a time when it was desperately needed. It was at his suggestion that she began to read books on sex and sexuality, turning particularly to Edward Carpenter and Havelock Ellis, and these writings, as well as her own sexual frustration, led her to the idea that sexual deprivation was damaging to a woman. Eventually, driven desperate by the unhappiness of her marriage, she obtained, in 1914, a certificate of virginity and walked out on her husband, by doing so forfeiting all her rights to their home, although she paid more than half the rent and bought most of the furniture. Two years later, in 1916, the marriage was annulled.

It was during this painful episode in her life that Marie Stopes wrote *Married Love*, essentially a plea for greater consideration of the woman's side of marriage. She did not decry marriage, extolling it, indeed, as woman's ultimate goal, but she wanted it to be an equal, not an unequal partnership. Essentially romantic, she conceived the sexual side of marriage in ideal terms as a spiritual rather than just a physical union, but the book represents not the actual experience of such a marriage, but the daydreams of a woman who has been denied it. When it was eventually published in 1918 it was a sensational success. Afterwards Marie Stopes, who had been converted to the idea of birth control, completed *Wise Parenthood*, a concise guide to contraception, also published in 1918.

Although she was now free, Marie Stopes had rejected a relationship with Aylmer Maude. She was still looking for the ideal marriage and had begun to long desperately for a child. In 1918, while still looking for a publisher for *Married Love*, she met Humphrey Verdon Roe, then thirty-nine years old. A rich man who had made his money in aeroplanes, he was also handsome and boyish looking in appearance, and they were immediately attracted to each other. She persuaded him to break off his engagement to another woman, and within a short time they were married. Her happiness was, however, cut short when in 1919 her longed-for child was stillborn.

Nevertheless, she was still close to her husband and together they set out on the birth-control campaign for which she is chiefly known. Money was for the first time in her life freely available, both from her husband who gave generously, and from the royalties on her books. In 1921, after a meeting she had organised at Queen's Hall, she founded the Society for Constructive Birth Control and Racial Progress, with herself as president and her husband as honorary secretary, and with their financial backing the first of the Marie Stopes birth-control clinics was founded. In 1922, however, a Dr Halliday Sutherland, a Roman Catholic, launched a vicious attack on her, which received considerable favourable publicity. She retaliated by suing him for libel. Initially the case went against her, but she won an appeal. Then Dr Sutherland took the case to the House of Lords and won. Nevertheless, although painful for her, the trial undoubtedly gave the birth-control campaign considerable publicity which worked as much to its advantage as against it.

By this time Marie Stopes was beginning to show the arrogance and dogmatism which characterised her as she grew older. This showed itself particularly in a growing lack of sympathy with others who were fighting the same cause. She disapproved of birth-control clinics other than her own, believing that only her approach was the right one. Nor, even more surprisingly, would she support Nurse Daniels when she was dismissed by Edmonton district council for giving birth-control advice and she refused to help Guy and Rose Aldred when they were found guilty of selling birth-control literature. Nor, as time went by, did she find the happiness in marriage that she had hoped for. A son, Harry, was born in 1924 but her husband was already experiencing sexual problems, possibly due to a war-time spinal injury. She published *Enduring Passion* in 1928 but already she was growing tired of her husband, and eventually she lost not only affection but even respect for him. By 1933 their sexual relationship was over and by the end of that decade he was an unwelcome visitor in his own house. The problem was exacerbated after 1929 when as a result of unfortunate investments he lost his money so that Marie Stopes provided the income for the household.

Although disappointed in her marriage, Marie Stopes had not lost her belief in a relationship which would combine the spiritual and the sexual. In 1938 she seemed to have found it in a brief but passionate friendship with Keith Briant, a young man just down from Oxford. He admired her greatly and she responded with a set of erotic love poems, *Love Songs for Young Lovers*, published in 1938. By this time birth control was no longer of such great importance in her life. She developed an interest in poetry and cultivated a salon with such writers as H.G. Wells, Hugh Walpole, and Lord Alfred Douglas in attendance. Her husband was banished, and when he died in 1949, at the age of seventy, he was long separated from her and living in seedy lodgings.

Moreover, she had also severed herself from her son Harry. He grew increasingly restive under her possessive management, but the final break came when he married a girl against her wishes. They met occasionally, but she refused to see him when she was dying and cut him out of her will. She was still capable of passion, however, and at the age of seventy-three fell in love with a young man, thirty-seven years her junior, believing that at last, too late, she had found her soulmate. Indeed she had such a yearning for life that she was determined to go on living until she was a hundred years old and, at the very end of her life, still dressed in the flamboyant clothes of her youth. In 1957, however, she discovered that she had cancer of the breast, and by the time she sought advice it was too late.

Although her father was an important influence on Marie Stopes, her feminism was an inheritance from her mother and, indeed, they shared a common enthusiasm for the suffrage campaign. Moreover, her feminism was by no means limited to the cause of suffrage, and in 1920 she helped in the fight against the decision by the Rhondda Valley education authority to sack their married women teachers. She was also a firm supporter of separate taxes for husband and wife. Her demand that consideration should be given to women's sexual needs was also an aspect of her concern for women's rights, as was her campaign for birth control which emphasised that it was necessary both for a woman's health and for her sexual satisfaction.

On the other hand, her conception of married happiness was simplistic and, largely because of her own unfulfilled needs, she over-emphasised the significance of sexual satisfaction and underrated the other problems that could wreck a marriage. Indeed, she almost certainly did not fully appreciate the extent to which sexual satisfaction was related to other aspects of a partnership. Her message that women's needs had been overlooked was, however, important and necessary, and although it did not originate with her, she did a great deal to publicise it. She failed, however, to examine deeply enough the social and economic relationships in which women's sexuality had been both exploited and denied and, like Havelock Ellis, accepted too readily conventional attitudes towards male and female roles. Her contribution was also limited by aspects of her personality, particularly by her inability to work with others, who were always seen as rivals rather than colleagues. She could also be dogmatic and even obsessive in her dislikes. She was, for example, almost fanatical in her attitude to eugenic principles as well as in her hatred of homosexuality. Nevertheless, she was a woman of great brilliance and possessed of extraordinary tenacity of purpose. Many of her attitudes to sex were conventional, but in spite of her limitations—or even perhaps because of them—she did perhaps more than anyone else to change the popular attitude to female sexuality.

The most recent and most thorough biography is *Marie Stopes*, Ruth Hall (London, André Deutsch, 1977). There is also an earlier and much more limited biography by Keith Briant, *Marie Stopes–a Biography*, Keith Briant (London, Hogarth, 1962). For some recollections by Mary Stocks see *Still More Commonplace* (London, Peter Davies, 1973). See also *DNB* 1951–60 pp. 930–1.

STRACHEY Philippa (Pippa) 1872–1968

Pippa Strachey, a suffragist, was the daughter of Richard Strachey, a distinguished Indian administrator, and his wife, Jane Maria Grant. There were ten children of the marriage and Pippa was the fifth child and the third daughter. The best-known of the Strachey children was Lytton Strachey, born in 1880, but Joan Strachey, born in 1876, had a distinguished career in education and became principal of Newnham College. Pippa Strachey's mother was herself an unorthodox woman who was a disciple of John Stuart Mill and an ardent feminist. A friend of Millicent Fawcett, she was active in the suffrage movement and Pippa Strachey, as she grew up, joined her mother in the National Union of Women's Suffrage Societies, becoming eventually its full-time secretary. Although of immense strategic importance, Pippa Strachey remained out of the limelight and was seldom seen on a suffrage platform. A brilliant organiser, she was the genius behind the NUWWS processions, plotting their routes, negotiating with the police, and in general ensuring that all went off without a hitch.

In 1911 Pippa's brother Oliver Strachey had married Ray Costelloe, herself a convinced feminist and, in spite of the fifteen years difference in their ages, the two women became fast friends. During the war they continued to work together, chiefly safeguarding the interests of women at work, and to this end the Women's Service Bureau was set up to help place women in all kinds of jobs previously held by men. From 1917, too, both Ray and Pippa Strachey worked behind the scenes to ensure the smooth passage of the proposed new suffrage Bill which in 1918 granted suffrage to most women over thirty years of age.

After the war the Women's Service Bureau changed its name to the London Society for Women's Service, concentrating its energies on women's work, and Pippa Strachey worked, unsalaried, as its secretary. A Women's Service Library was established, which housed a mass of books and documents accumulated during the suffrage struggle, and a Women's Service House was established to act as a club. The society was renamed the Fawcett Society, in honour of Millicent Fawcett, in 1953, and in 1957 Fawcett House was established which housed both the library and the Fawcett Society for the next twenty years. Pippa Strachey, who had received a CBE for her services in 1951, remained in charge, and was over ninety years of age when she finally retired. She died in 1968 at the great age of ninety-six.

Pippa Strachey never married, although Mary Stocks, who was related by marriage to the Strachey family, recalls that an uncle of hers, Herbert Rendel, long remained a bachelor because of his unrequited love for Pippa Strachey. She remained instead completely devoted to her family and especially to her younger brother Lytton. She nursed him through several early illnesses and was with him during his last few weeks of life in 1932. At this time, according to his biographer, she 'never betrayed her grief or thought of herself'. She was also the close companion of her mother all her life and nursed her night and day during her last illness. Charming, able and unselfish, she was greatly beloved during her life-time, and remembered with affection after her death. Indeed she so much resembles the ideal Victorian sister and daughter in her virtues that her feminism comes as something of a surprise. Whatever the source of her loyalty to the feminist movement, and perhaps this is something we cannot know, there is no doubt that she served it devotedly all her long life, bringing to it those talents for organisation and administration which otherwise, perhaps, would have gone unfulfilled.

There is not very much information on Pippa Strachey's life and work. She is mentioned in *My Common Place Book*, Mary Stocks (London, Peter Davies, 1970); *Lytton Strachey. A Critical Biography*, Michael Holroyd (London, Heinemann, 1967–8); *Remarkable Relations. The Story of the Pearsall Smith Family*, Barbara Strachey (London, Gollancz, 1980).

See also STOCKS Mary Danvers, STRACHEY Rachel.

STRACHEY Rachel (Ray) 1887–1940

Ray Strachey, best known as the author of *The Cause*, was the eldest of the two daughters of Frank Costelloe and Mary Pearsall Smith. The main influence on her life, however, was her grandmother, Hannah Whitall Smith who had custody of the two girls after Frank Costelloe's death in 1899. Hannah Smith was a Philadelphian Quaker who developed strong feminist sympathies and was active in both the temperance and the suffrage movements in the United States. She was a devoted mother, but, in later life especially, became estranged from her husband. Throughout her life, indeed, she had a low opinion of men and was strongly opposed to the idea that they should be the masters in marriage. This was certainly not true in her own case, and the family was in many respects a matriarchy. Her daughter Mary married Frank Costelloe, an Irish Catholic writer, in 1885 and moved to London London, soon afterwards followed by her mother, who settled in England permanently. Two years later Rachel (Ray) was born but already Mary Costelloe was unhappy with her marriage. Another child, Karin, was born in 1889, but in 1890 Mary met and fell in love with Bernard Berenson and shortly afterwards eloped with him. Frank Costelloe successfully claimed the children but, on his death in 1899, custody was given to Hannah Smith.

From this time Ray Costelloe was entirely her grandmother's child. Her own mother Mary was beautiful, gay, romantic, but completely apolitical, and in her visits to her children tried to make Ray more like herself, but this pressure Ray obstinately rejected. A good scholar, she was educated at Kensington High School and later went to Newnham College, Cambridge. While still only a schoolgirl she met the Strachey family and later became great friends with Lady Strachey and her daughter Pippa. Both Lady Strachey and Pippa were deeply committed to the suffrage movement and they soon drew Ray Costelloe into the campaign. She became very active and, while still a college student, organised a group of college friends on a propaganda caravan tour. She was always, however, strictly constitutional in her methods, finding the militants emotional and unscrupulous. In time she became a leading member of the National Union of Women's Suffrage Societies and a friend of Millicent Fawcett. She also embarked on a writing career and in 1912 published a biography of the American feminist and temperance worker Frances Willard.

In 1911 she met Oliver Strachey, a brother of Pippa Strachey. A man of thirty-seven, Oliver Strachey had just left his job in India and was without any prospects for the future. He was also divorced from his wife who had left him some years earlier. Something of a rolling stone, Oliver Strachey had wanted to be a concert pianist but was without the necessary talent and had not, subsequently, been able to settle down to the job he had been found with the East India Railway. Although he did not appear a promising prospect for a husband, the two were married in 1911. For a time Ray Strachey supported them out of her income and they began a joint book on Indian history. In the meantime Ray Strachey had published *A Quaker Grandmother* in 1914 in memory of her grandmother who had died the previous year. In 1914, however, Oliver Strachey found employment with the War Office in the codes and cypher department, and discovered at last the work he had a real talent for and which he was to engage in until his retirement early in the second world war.

Ray Strachey, meanwhile, was soon deeply involved in work on behalf of women war workers and found herself engaged in battles with the War Office over unequal pay and unsuitable conditions of work. Later, in 1917, along with Pippa Strachey, she was closely involved, as Millicent Fawcett's chief lieutenant, in all the behind-the-scenes negotiations which in 1918 resulted in the measure which gave women over thirty the vote at last. By this time there were two children, Barbara and Christopher.

In 1918 Ray Strachey was one of the women who stood unsuccessfully for Parliament. She tried twice more in 1922 and 1923 before she gave up the idea. When, however, Nancy Astor was elected she offered her services without pay as a part-time parliamentary secretary and Nancy Astor accepted. She found Nancy Astor, who had had no dealings with the women's movement, very ignorant but willing to learn, and Ray Strachey prepared briefs for her for a large part of her parliamentary career. She also edited the old suffrage paper, *The Common Cause*, now renamed the *Women's Leader*.

In 1921 she had acquired a house with nine acres of land on Friday Hill and here she spent as much time as her duties allowed. She took to wearing Land Army costume and her neglect of her appearance was, according to her daughter, 'stupendous'. Her relationship with her husband was still friendly, but the marriage gradually became a very detached one in which they went their separate ways. They were totally different in their temperament, since Oliver loved parties and Ray hated them. Oliver Strachey, indeed, had become something of a womaniser but Ray treated this with a complete lack of concern. Indeed she seems to have been perfectly happy with the life she had made for herself and the marriage worked on the basis of a good deal of mutual tolerance.

During these years, apart from her other work, she did a great deal of writing. She completed two novels on American history and then, in 1928, published her most significant contribution to feminism, *The Cause*. This remained almost the only source of the history of the women's movement in Britain until the new wave of feminist writing in the 1970s. It was followed, in 1931, by a biography of Millicent Garrett Fawcett, who had been in many respects both her friend and her mentor.

By the 1930s Oliver and Ray Strachey were in financial difficulties. Oliver did not have a large salary and Ray's private income was falling, while both of them were extravagant with money. Ray was forced to look for the first time for paid work and in 1935 found a congenial post running the Women's Employment Federation which was concerned with finding better jobs for women. The employment of women had always been of particular interest to Ray Strachey and earlier she had worked to open the legal profession to women. In 1936 she contributed an essay 'Changes in Employment' to an important collection of essays, *Our Freedom and its Results*, which she had edited. In it she examined some of the problems associated with the limitations on women's employment, drawing attention in particular to the issues raised by women's biological role as mothers and their sociological function as homemakers. She advocated such necessary changes as a greater share by men in the care of children and, as a corollary, a lessening of intensity and competition in the world of work.

Ray Strachey continued to work specifically on the issue of women's employment. In 1937 she published *Career Openings for Women* and, during the early months of the war in 1939, she was involved in a vigorous effort of women MPs to remedy unemployment amongst professional women. In 1940, however, still only fifty-three years of age, she was taken ill and died after an operation.

A dedicated feminist, Ray Strachey, unlike some women, did not turn away from feminism once the vote was won. She saw clearly that winning the vote was not the end of the war and that a great deal still remained to be done. Moreover, she was far-sighted enough to see that if women were to fulfil their potential, changes were required both in the family and in the nature of work, and she thus anticipated some of the demands of the modern movement. Her feminism had its source not only in her love for her grandmother but also in her rejection of the style of femininity adopted by the mother who had rejected her. This rebellion against her mother's values did not lead her to reject marriage, but she refused to let it govern her life. Nor did she apparently adopt her grandmother's distrust of men, although she does seem to have preferred the company of women. Her very considerable contribution to feminism has tended to be overlooked and she is remembered chiefly as the author of *The Cause*. This, however, was only one part of the services she rendered to the women's movement.

The main source of information on Ray Strachey is *Remarkable Relations. The Story of the Pearsall Smith Family* by her daughter Barbara Strachey (London, Gollancz, 1980). See also *My Commonplace Book*, Mary Stocks (London, Peter Davies, 1970) and *Lytton Strachey. A Critical Biography*, Michael Holroyd (London, Heinemann, 1967).

See also STRACHEY Philippa.

SWANWICK Helena Maria Lucy
1864-1939

Helena Swanwick, a suffragist, was the daughter of Oswald Adalbert Sickert, an artist and cartoonist of Danish origin. Her mother was the illegitimate daughter of a Fellow of Trinity College, Cambridge, and much of her youth was spent abroad where she met her future husband. After their marriage she lived in Munich, where Helena was born. There were six children, with Helena, the only daughter, and this seems to have been a factor in her later feminism, since, growing up something of a tomboy, she resented the greater freedom given to her brothers. Indeed, on the whole, she did not have a happy childhood. Her father was authoritarian and Helena remained afraid of him all his life, while her mother made it plain that she would have preferred a pretty pliable girl who shared her own interest in clothes. Only after she was married did any real friendship grow up between them.

The family moved from Germany in 1868 to settle permanently in England. Helena spent two years at school in France and some years later, at the age of fourteen, four extremely happy years at Notting Hill High School. By this time she had discovered John Stuart Mill's *Subjection of Women* and was pleased to discover that her own personal rebellion was linked to a wider social movement. As her ideas on the subject developed she began to feel a growing sense of estrangement from her mother's efforts to teach her to be a good wife. A more serious dispute arose in 1882, when she wanted to go to Girton College to study economics. Her mother opposed this, wanting her, as the only daughter, to stay at home, and Helena's father, agreeing with her mother, refused to pay the fees. Only the intervention of her godmother, who provided the money, made Girton possible.

It had been Helena's intention to get a job when her studies were over, but the sudden death of her father in 1885, and her mother's grief-stricken reaction, kept her at home even though she was still unhappy there. In 1886, however, she became engaged to Frederick Swanwick, a lecturer in mathematics at Owens College, Manchester, and thirteen years her senior. They had met in 1883, while she was a student at Girton and had immediately been attracted to each other. They were married in 1888 and set up house in Manchester.

After her marriage Helena Swanwick was mainly occupied in keeping house on an income which did not allow for very much domestic help. She earned some money by coaching and by publishing articles and stories from time to time in various magazines, and later began to review and write for *The Guardian*. She was happy in her marriage, which was only marred by her unsatisfied longing for children. In 1900 there was a move to Knutsford, after the death of her husband's crippled mother, and this improved her health and gave her a life-long interest in gardening.

It may, therefore, have been other pre-occupations which kept Helena Swanwick, in spite of her early feminism, from taking any active part in the suffrage movement until 1905, when the example of Christabel Pankhurst and Annie Kenney aroused her conscience. She could not work with the Pankhursts, repelled both by their dictatorial methods and their policy of deliberate martyrdom, but she increased her journalistic work, covering many women's meetings and conferences, and eventually became widely used as a 'moderate' speaker. In 1909 she was made editor of the National Union of Women's Suffrage Societies' weekly journal, *The Common Cause*. In 1911 there was a move to London, made possible by her husband's retirement from his university post at the age of sixty. This enabled her to give more time to the suffrage issue, but her dislike of militancy continued to grow, and in 1912 she resigned her editorship of *The Common Cause* when she was refused permission to take an active stand against the Women's Social and Political Union in its pages. She wanted to oppose not only what she saw as blind partisanship but also the increasing anti-male stance taken up by the Pankhursts. In order to express her own views she wrote *The Future of the Women's Movement*, published in 1913.

With the advent of war however, Helena Swanwick's feminism took second place to her pacifism. For the first time she was glad not to have children of her own. She resigned from the NUWSS on the issue of pacifism, and joined the Union of Democratic Control which was working for a negotiated peace. Later she took a leading part in forming the British section of the Women's International League, and was its chairman for seven years.

After the war she strongly opposed government policy, especially on the Versailles Treaty, the blockade of Germany and intervention in Russia. In 1921 she published *Women in the Socialist State*. She also became deeply involved in the League of Nations Union, and in 1924 and again in 1929 was a member of the British Empire delegation to the League of Nations. Between 1924 and 1927 she was editor of *Foreign Affairs*, the journal of the Union of Democratic Control. By this time, however, she and her husband were both in poor health and his death in 1931 also virtually ended her own public career. She herself died in 1939 from a heart attack, accelerated by an overdose of sleeping tablets, deliberately taken.

Helena Swanwick is probably better known as a pacifist and an internationalist than as a feminist, but for a number of years she was an important propagandist for the constitutional suffrage movement. Rebellious as a young girl, she seems to have found contentment in marriage to a tolerant and unselfish man, and this may have contributed to her strong dislike of any attempt to base feminism on the notion of a sex war. Temperamentally she was repelled by the emotional side of militancy and by its tendency to subjugate the individual to the group. Indeed, her own desire for independence sometimes made it difficult to work with others. After the war her main contribution to feminism was through the Women's International League, where she tried hard to arouse women's interest in international affairs.

There is an autobiography, *I have been young* (London, Gollancz, 1935), and an entry in the *DLB* Vol. IV, pp. 168–71.

TAYLOR Harriet 1807-1858

Harriet Taylor was the daughter of Thomas Hardy, a London surgeon, and his wife Harriet Hurst. She was the middle child of seven, of whom four were boys. Her father appears to have been a mean, domineering man, and there is a tradition that she married at eighteen because she was unhappy at home. Her husband, John Taylor, eleven years her senior, was a partner in a firm of wholesale druggists. A kindly if somewhat dull and conventional man, he was active in the Unitarian church and a Radical in politics. Although happy at first, within a few years of the marriage Harriet Taylor was craving a more intellectual companionship than her husband could give. Moreover, she was already conscious of the social disabilities under which women lived, and seems to have been acquainted with the discussions then current on the emancipation of women.

When Harriet Taylor first met John Stuart Mill in 1830 he was twenty-five years old and she was twenty-three. They met through a mutual acquaintanceship with William Fox, the Taylors' Unitarian minister. He was himself a feminist and enjoyed the company of intellectual women. At this time John Stuart Mill, not long recovered from a serious breakdown, was lonely, and Harriet Taylor, beautiful and intelligent, offered him the companionship he craved. Harriet Taylor was equally drawn to him, not least by his sympathy for her own dissatisfaction with the position of women. In spite of the immediate attraction they had for each other, the friendship developed slowly and as late as August 1832 Harriet Taylor wrote to John Stuart Mill suggesting that they did not meet again. The parting was a brief one however, and by the spring of 1833 Mill was spending most of his free time at her house. Towards the end of the year Harriet Taylor persuaded her husband to agree to a trial separation, and there is no doubt that for a time she considered leaving him altogether. In the end a compromise was reached in which the external appearance of a married life was maintained, but no barrier was placed on her continuing friendship with Mill.

Undoubtedly this arrangement was designed to safeguard the reputation of Harriet Taylor and to conform to the wishes of her husband who was also anxious to avoid scandal. But it failed to do this since it did not save them from the gossip and innuendos of friends, many of whom failed to accept that the relationship was in fact a sexually innocent one. John Taylor, too, gained little from the arrangement, since he lost not only any sexual relationship with his wife but even her companionship since, as time went by, she spent less and less time in his home. Indeed, from the end of the 1830s she lived mainly at a house at Walton-on-Thames, visiting her husband only occasionally. Her two sons, born in 1827 and 1830, were then at boarding school and her daughter Helen, born in 1831, remained with her mother. It is characteristic of John Taylor that he made no attempt to deprive her of the children and, when he died, left her his property. John Stuart Mill, meanwhile, continued to live with his mother and younger brothers and sisters, but spent his weekends at Walton-on-Thames. Moreover, from time to time he and Harriet Taylor travelled abroad together. In 1849 John Taylor died from cancer, and two years later Harriet Taylor and John Stuart Mill were married.

Shortly after they met, in 1831 or 1832, they had exchanged essays on marriage which, although intended for their private use, were eventually published in *John Stuart Mill and Harriet Taylor: their Correspondence and Subsequent Marriage* by F.A. Hayek. The essay from Harriet Taylor's pen, although brief, is important because it is one of the few occasions when we can be entirely sure that the ideas are all her own. Compared with Mill's essay it reveals very clearly that her opinions were much in advance of his, and shows to a much greater extent the influence of the Owenite feminists.

For example, Harriet Taylor was much more conscious than Mill of the degrading effect of women's dependence on men for a living, and wanted even married women to be self-supporting. On marriage, too, she was more radical. She hoped that women's economic equality would make possible the end of all marriage laws, and wanted women to take responsibility for their own children. In contrast, Mill believed that although the possibility of independence should be open to women, in practice most would marry and would then be supported by their husbands. Moreover, in a revealing sentence he suggests that a woman's occupation should be 'to adorn and beautify' and that they performed their particular function 'by *being* rather than *doing*'. Like Harriet Taylor he believed that men and women should have equal rights but he wanted to see these expressed in marriages between equals rather than in women's independence. In this respect, therefore, he reveals himself as more romantic and indeed sentimental than Harriet.

Apart from these unpublished essays, neither Harriet Taylor nor John Stuart Mill concerned themselves with feminist issues for almost twenty years. Nor, apart from a few contributions, mainly reviews and poems, to the Unitarian *Monthly Repository* do we have any opportunity to judge Harriet Taylor as an individual thinker. Her ambition seems to have been confined to sharing in John Stuart Mill's output, and during the whole of their association they worked jointly, she contributing suggestions and revisions to what was essentially his work. Moreover, what was very much a collaboration appeared always under his name. In part this was done to avoid scandal, and indeed in 1848 John Taylor did disapprove so strongly of a dedication to her in the *Principles of Political Economy* that it was removed, although a few copies with this dedication were sent to friends. Undoubtedly this disappointed her, but she acquiesced, and this seems to disprove the suggestion made by some people that she was an essentially selfish woman.

It is generally admitted that she did influence John Stuart Mill's thinking in certain specific directions. This applies particularly to his essay *On Liberty* and to his *Principles of Political Economy*. She was also very closely involved in his *Autobiography*, which she hoped would clear her reputation. Of a less philosophical and more realistic turn of mind, she contributed practical suggestions and illustrations. She also influenced Mill in a socialist direction. It was his thinking on women however that showed her influence most markedly. He himself confessed that before he met her his feminism was of a philosophic rather than a realistic variety, and it is almost certain that without her it would have stayed in that mould. Her own strong feelings on the subject made him much more aware of the actual hardships suffered by women and, after her death, his activities on behalf of women became for him an act of homage to her memory.

A few months after their wedding the *Westminster Review* published *The Enfranchisement of Women* which, although offered as Mill's own work, was in fact largely written by Harriet Taylor. The content of the argument closely follows that of her earlier essay, and differs in several ways from John Stuart Mill's early essay, and also from his *Subjection of Women*, published after her death. There is, for example, an emphasis on women's need for economic independence which was foreign to Mill's thinking.

Later in the same year an article on the need for the protection of wives and children from brutal husbands and fathers appeared in the *Morning Chronicle* (28 August 1851). Although a joint production it still, however, appeared under Mill's name. Yet in 1853 a small pamphlet on the same subject was jointly produced for private distribution. In 1858 Mill was at last in a position to retire from his post at the East India Company, but by this time Harriet was in an advanced condition of tuberculosis. They travelled to

France together for her health, but on reaching Avignon she was taken seriously ill and died. Her husband's grief at her death after only seven years of marriage is well known, and he mourned her ceaselessly for the rest of his life. He was, however, comforted to some extent by the companionship of Harriet's daughter Helen who devoted herself to his needs. As ardent a feminist as her mother, she helped to keep alive his own interest in the women's movement, and it was partly her pressure which resulted in the publication in 1869 of his famous essay *The Subjection of Women*. Clearly this was written by Mill and it reflects his ideas rather than Harriet's. Nevertheless, without her inspiration it is highly doubtful if it would have been written at all.

Just as it is not easy to disentangle the contribution to feminism of Harriet Taylor from that of John Stuart Mill, so it is difficult to separate her personality from the highly romanticised image of her presented by Mill himself and which has been the subject of a great deal of not very fruitful controversy. On the whole she was unpopular with her contemporaries, but this was in large part because they disapproved of her influence on Mill. Hurt at the gossip about them, Harriet Taylor and Mill tended to withdraw from society, and even after their marriage saw only a few friends. Harriet, very unreasonably, often got the blame for this, and his friends, aware only of what he had lost, failed to realise how much he actually gained from the relationship.

Moreover, many of Harriet Taylor's critics are demonstrably wrong about her, especially once she is no longer judged in terms of the stereotype of the 'womanly woman'. She was less selfish and more able than they supposed. This is not to suggest that she had any of the perfection of character attributed to her by Mill. She was highly strung and almost excessively sensitive to the opinions of other, and this certainly contributed to the pain the gossip of others caused both of them. More unconventional than Mill in her ideas she was, in practice, a conventional person and this may explain why she was content to remain the power behind the throne. Her abilities were also more limited than Mill believed, but she complemented him in a way that benefited him both psychologically and intellectually.

Her contribution to feminism came mainly from her influence on Mill, but is complicated by their practice of using Mill's name even when she was very closely associated with the final product. 'The Enfranchisement of Women' article in 1851 may well have been more her contribution than that of John Stuart Mill, and this was in fact recognised by many of their friends at the time. There is no doubt that this essay was an important influence on the growing women's movement that developed during the 1850s. She was never part of this movement, but her sympathies were certainly with it, and if she held aloof it was no doubt an aspect of the Mills' social seclusion as well as her health which was failing very rapidly in the 1850s. Her complex contribution to feminism clearly, therefore, deserves much closer study.

There is no biography of Harriet Taylor, but there is an interesting account of her relationship with John Stuart Mill in *Essays on Sex Equality: John Stuart Mill and Harriet Taylor* ed. Alice S. Rossi (Chicago and London, University of Chicago Press, 1970). The *Life of John Stuart Mill*, Michael St John Packe (London, Secker and Warburg, 1954) also gives her a lengthy and sympathetic treatment. See also *John Stuart Mill and Harriet Taylor. Their Correspondence and Subsequent Marriage*, F.A. Hayek (London, Routledge and Kegan Paul, 1951); *The Dissidence of Dissent. The Monthly Repository 1806–1838*, Francis E. Mineka (New York, Octagon Books, 1972); 'The Writing of Mill's Autobiography', A.W. Levi, *Ethics* (LXI 1951) pp. 284–96; *The Early Draft of John Stuart Mill's Autobiography*, Jack Stillinger (Urbana, University of Illinois, 1961); *Autobiography of John Stuart Mill*, ed. John Jacob Coss (New York, Columbia University Press, 1924).

See also FOX William Johnson, MILL John Stuart.

THOMAS Margaret Haig, Viscountess Rhondda 1883–1958

Margaret Thomas, a suffragette and later editor of *Time and Tide*, was the only child of David Alfred Thomas and his wife Sybil Margaret Haig. Her grandfather, Samuel Thomas, had made a fortune out of coal in the Welsh valleys, and his son had been sent to Cambridge before he went into his father's business. Later he entered politics as a Liberal. Margaret was at first educated at home in Wales by a governess, but at thirteen was sent to Notting Hill High School, and later to a boarding school at St Andrews. A lonely child, she was encouraged by her father in freedom of thought and action but found herself trapped by the conventions of young ladyhood. For some years after leaving school she stayed at home, spending three months every year in London for the 'Season', but was never able to enjoy the parties or balls or the life of the drawing room. Unhappy as she was, however, she did not seriously consider the prospect of any life other than a conventional marriage and a large family. She dreamed constantly of romance, and by the age of twenty had developed a horrible fear of spinsterhood. Eventually she spent a period at Somerville, but this did not work either since she found she did not like the restrictions of life at the college and the narrowness of outlook both of dons and students.

By this time, however, she had at last fallen in love, and in 1908 married a near neighbour, Humphrey Mackworth, later the seventh baronet of Caerleon on Usk. They were, however, an ill-assorted couple since she was an avid reader, whereas he was a man who never opened a book and, an enthusiastic huntsman, was content to spend his time with his horses and his hounds. A tolerant man, he allowed her in fact considerable freedom, but this served only to make of her someone very different from the shy girl he had married. Indeed, the process of her transformation started within a few months of her marriage when she joined the Women's Social and Political Union, the militant wing of the women's suffrage movement.

Both her father and mother had long been supporters of women's suffrage, and she herself had accepted it without thinking about it deeply. Some of her mother's family were already involved in the WSPU, and a cousin of her mother had been in prison, and this inspired both Margaret and her mother to attend a suffrage procession. Her enthusiasm aroused, Margaret proceeded to read not merely the suffrage literature but books on politics, economics, sociology and psychology. She not only joined the WSPU but took part actively in the organisation of meetings in Wales. Her husband, at this stage, accepted her involvement but exacted from her the promise that she would not go to prison. She agreed to this at first, but, as the movement moved further into militancy she broke her promise and took part in the campaign to set fire to letterboxes. Sentenced to a month in prison at Usk, she actually served only five days before family influence secured her release and, although she went on hunger strike, she was not forcibly fed. On the whole, therefore, militancy for Margaret Thomas remained something of an adventure. Although there were rough incidents at some of the meetings, she was never hurt and even prison did not involve her in the physical suffering endured by many other women. Her involvement in the movement was probably most significant as a form of political education which awakened her not only to the demands of the women's movement but to the needs of her own nature.

An equally significant influence on her life at this time, and one which was to have perhaps even more far-reaching effects, was her involvement in her father's business. Not very long after her marriage she was asked by her father to act as his confidential 'right-hand man' with a good salary and, with her husband's approval, she began to work for him as a full-time assistant. Gradually certain sections of the business were turned over entirely to her, and her father began to look on her as the son he would have liked to have had. In 1915 her father was involved in Lloyd George's war effort, his first task that of organising a supply of munitions from the

United States and Canada. Later, as Minister of Food, he was responsible for the introduction of rationing. In 1918, shortly before his death, he was made a viscount with the special provision that his daughter succeeded to the title, and Margaret Thomas became Viscountess Rhondda.

Although her involvement in the militant suffrage movement had created problems in her marriage, it seems to have been the war years which finally brought the marriage to an end. If there had been children, as indeed Margaret had hoped for, things might have been different, but at the end of the war they decided to separate, and in 1923 they were divorced.

The death of her father had left Margaret in charge of his business but, like him, she felt the need for something more than business to fill her life. Still a feminist in outlook, she determined that she wanted to do something for women. With this in mind she fought a battle to get accepted in the House of Lords, but her efforts were defeated largely by the opposition of Lord Birkenhead. In 1923 she founded the Six Point Group, which was chiefly concerned with legislative action to remedy inequalities that still remained in such areas as guardianship of children, equal pay, and equal opportunities. She was also closely involved in the foundation of the Open Door Council, a group which attempted to secure for women freedom from protective legislation which harmed their interests, as well as an end to the marriage bar under which women were not allowed to keep their jobs after marriage, and which applied in both teaching and the civil service. Her chief interest, however, was in *Time and Tide*, founded in 1920 to help change the customs and ideas about women. Always heavily subsidised by her, she was also always effectively in control, although she was not its editor until 1926. During the whole of the 1920s it was a highly important centre of feminist thinking, with feminists like Elizabeth Robins, Vera Brittain, Winifred Holtby and Cecily Hamilton as regular contributors.

By the 1930s, however, she had begun to feel that the fight was over. Gradually *Time and Tide* became less and less feminist. It also became increasingly right-wing as she began to believe that communism and socialism were the new enemies, and by the time of her death in 1958 it had changed its character completely.

Margaret Thomas had a largely conventional upbringing, but her father in particular encouraged an independence in her which made it difficult for her to find happiness in a conventional life-style. Although her involvement in the militant suffrage movement oriented her towards feminism, her father's recognition of her business ability was probably the most significant influence on her life. Her marriage, even if there had been children would, as she herself later recognised, never have satisfied that part of herself which craved achievement. Like many militants she lost interest in feminism at the end, but she remained active in its cause longer than most, and during the whole of the 1920s was one of that small band of women who kept the goals of feminism alive. She was, however, never a part of the 'new feminism' associated with Eleanor Rathbone, and remained to the end firmly within the equal-rights tradition. Her move to the Right in politics also isolated her from the feminists of the Left. Her influence, therefore, was perhaps bound to be limited and she has never achieved the recognition accorded to other feminist activists. But her part was by no means an insignificant one, and her craving for achievement and independence represents an important aspect of the feminist movement.

For Viscountess Rhondda's own account of her life see *This was my World* (London, Macmillan, 1933). There are important references to her activities in the 1920s in *Chrystal Eastman. On Women and Revolution* ed. Blanche Wiesen Cook (Oxford, Oxford University Press, 1978). See also *DNB* 1951–1960 pp. 968–9.

THOMPSON William 1775–1833

William Thompson was the grandson of a Protestant divine, and the son of Alderman John Thompson, one of the richest merchants in Cork. His mother's name is not known. On the death of his father in 1814, William Thompson took over the family business with its fleet of trading vessels, as well as becoming the landlord of the family's estate. He had already developed progressive views, and instituted improved methods of cultivation, gave leases on generous terms to his tenants and founded a school. A widely-read man, he also travelled extensively, spending some time in France where he became acquainted with Saint-Simonian theories.

In 1822 he paid a visit of several months to Bentham, and met the leaders of Unitarian thought. He also came into contact with Anna Wheeler, a noted Saint-Simonian feminist, who was herself a friend of Bentham. Although now well into middle age, William Thompson was still a bachelor, and a close relationship developed between them and although marriage does not seem to have been contemplated it is possible that, for a time at least, they were lovers. In the meantime he stayed on in London to work on his first book, *An Inquiry into the Principles of the Distribution of Wealth*, published in 1824. Although he admired Bentham, the main influence on his writing was Robert Owen, whom he had met in 1822, and the Saint-Simonians. An attack on inequality and the evils of competition, his book was to have a profound influence on the Co-operative movement. Nor did it shrink from attacking sexual inequalities, advocating legal, educational and political equality between men and women, and attacking the double standard of sexual morality. More radically still, he went on to advocate birth control, divorce by mutual consent, and 'free love'.

In 1824 James Mill, the father of John Stuart Mill, in an article on government for the annual supplement to the *Encyclopedia Brittanica*, argued that women did not need the vote because their interests were included in that of either their father or their husband. This aroused considerable opposition from John Stuart Mill and many of his young friends, and William Thompson, in association with Anna Wheeler, felt impelled to write a reply. The result was the *Appeal of one half of the Human Race, Women, against the Pretensions of the other half, Men, to Retain them in Political and Thence in Civil and Domestic Slavery* (1825). This appeal, although it has been greatly neglected, remains one of the most powerful feminist documents of the nineteeth century and was an inspiration for the socialist feminism which flourished during the next two decades. It also undoubtedly influenced the young John Stuart Mill, although his own version of feminism developed in rather different ways.

Although William Thompson was the actual author of the *Appeal*, he acknowledged fully the contribution of Anna Wheeler and, indeed, in many places not only the ideas but also the language seem to be the product of a woman's experience. This is particularly so in the passion with which he writes about women's sexual oppression at the hands of men. As the title indicates, the book appeals for the political and legal emancipation of women but also for an equal system of morality, and he was scathing in his attack on the double standard. However, he goes further than a demand for equal rights, and links the emancipation of women necessarily to the transformation of the economic system.

In the remaining years of his life William Thompson's main attention moves towards the establishment of Co-operative communities, although he did not forget his feminism, since he emphasised that community living was the only way to free women from household drudgery and the constant care of young children. Instead these tasks would be undertaken communally and could be in the hands of either men or women. Domestic life, indeed, he regarded as a form of slavery and pointed out that while the husband 'paints it as the abode of calm bliss' he takes care to find for himself an occupation of a more stimulating kind. In 1833 he died, leaving an annuity to Anna

Wheeler but the bulk of his property to the Co-operative movement. But his relatives contested the will and although they won in the long legal battle that ensued, the greater part of the estate was swallowed up in legal costs.

In the long run William Thompson's version of feminism did not survive. There were feminist socialists in the 1830s and 1840s whose ideas were in many respects similar to his, and who may have been familiar with his writings, but the feminist movement that emerged in the 1850s would have been repelled by any attempt to merge feminism and socialism. Nor would it have approved of his advocacy of free love, or of birth control, which he saw as giving women as well as men the opportunity of sexual pleasure. Consequently it was John Stuart Mill's less controversial *Subjection of Women* which provided the theoretical basis of the women's movement, and not Thompson's *Appeal*. Nor did William Thompson's feminism take root within socialist thinking about women, which turned to Marx and Engels for inspiration. If, however, his neglect is understandable, his *Appeal* deserves to be reinstated in feminist history.

There is a biography, *William Thompson. Britain's Pioneer Socialist Feminist and Co-operator*, R.K. Pankhurst (London, Watts, 1954). See also *Eve and the New Jerusalem*, Barbara Taylor (London, Virago, 1983); *Feminism and Family Planning in Victorian England*, J.A. and Olive Banks (Liverpool, Liverpool University Press, 1964); *DNB* Supplementary Vol. III, pp. 380–2; *Biographical Dictionary of Modern British Radicals*, Vol. I, ed. Joseph O. Baylen and Norbert J. Gossman (Sussex, Harvester Press, 1979).

See also MILL John Stuart, WHEELER Anna.

TUCKWELL Gertrude Mary 1861–1951

Gertrude Tuckwell, one of the leaders in the women's trade union movement, was the second daughter of the Reverend William Tuckwell, Master of New College School in Oxford, and his wife Rose Strong. Her father, known as the 'Radical parson', was a celebrated Oxford personality, a Christian Socialist and an advocate of tax and land reform, so that she grew up in an atmosphere of Radical thought. Another and perhaps even more important influence was her mother's sister Emilia, who had married Mark Pattison in 1861 and who was both a noted art historian and critic and an active feminist, interested in both the suffrage and the women's trade-union movement. It was while staying in her aunt's house in 1878 that Gertrude was persuaded by two of her aunt's feminist friends to become a teacher. She spent a period at a pupil-teacher centre in Liverpool and two years at Bishop Otter's College, Chichester, before starting as an elementary school teacher in London in 1884. By the early 1890s however, ill health obliged her to give up this work.

In 1892 she became secretary to her aunt Emilia, now married to Sir Charles Dilke, and she was soon heavily involved in the work of the Women's Trade Union League. On the death of Emilia Dilke in 1904 she became its honorary secretary, and in 1905, in succession to her aunt, its president. An ardent campaigner for the protection of women workers, she was also involved closely in both the Women's Industrial Council and the Anti-Sweating League. For a time, too, she was editor of the *Women's Trade Union Review*. In 1905 she became president of the National Federation of Women Workers. During these years she travelled up and down the country to address meetings of women's groups and to organise union branches. She also wrote extensively for a wide variety of journals. Moreover, becoming known eventually as an expert on the women's trade-union movement, she was asked to serve on many public bodies.

A cause particularly close to her heart was the protection of women workers against lead-poisoning or 'phossy-jaw' and in 1905 she was appointed to the Departmental Committee on the Dangers attendant on the use of Lead. Her campaign took the form not only of the provision of compensation to victims of industrial injury but also the prohibition of the use of lead in pottery glazes. She also campaigned against *'truck'*, and supported the fight for minimum-wages legislation. A firm believer in state provision to curb exploitation, she also emphasised the need for women to become active trade-union members. She saw the women's trade-union movement as a means not only of improving wages and working conditions, but of educating women on the duties of citizenship.

Her retirement from official involvement in the women's trade-union movement in 1918 did not however greatly diminish her activities. She was made a JP in 1920 and helped to found the Magistrates' Association. She was deeply committed to the idea of probation, which she believed might eventually do away with crime, and was for a time chairman of the National Association of Probation Officers. Her other main interest during these years and through which she demonstrated her continuing commitment to women, was the field of maternal health. During the 1920s she had been a member of the Royal Commission on National Health Insurance, had noticed the prevalence of sickness amongst married women, and came in time to support the principle of non-contributory medical care for children and mothers. In 1927, in association with May Tennant, she launched the Maternal Mortality Committee, an unofficial group to watch over women's health. She and May Tennant continued to press the Ministry of Health to examine the problems of sickness and disability amongst women.

Like most women in the trade-union movement she was a strong supporter of equal pay which she believed was the only system which could guarantee fair wages for both men and women. For a time she had also supported the campaign for family allowances, but finally came to doubt them in case they had an adverse effect on wages. She was, however, strongly behind the efforts to secure widows' pensions. Her active political life continued throughout the 1920s and the 1930s, by which time she was almost eighty years of age. She died in 1951 at the age of ninety.

Gertrude Tuckwell was devoted to her aunt Emilia and to her aunt's second husband Charles Dilke, himself an enthusiastic supporter of legislation to protect women workers. After his death in 1911 she became his literary executive and his biographer, but destroyed most of his papers in case they contained material that might incriminate him. She never married, and shared households with a succession of women colleagues. A sociable woman, her many friends included Mary Macarthur and Margaret Bondfield. Most of her writing was in the form of journalism, but in 1894 she published *The State and its Children*. This was largely a study of children in reformatories, workhouses, asylums and hospitals. She also published, with S. Gwynne, *The Life of the Right Hon. Sir Charles Dilke* in 1917.

Although she firmly supported women's suffrage in principle, she was, like Charles Dilke and Margaret Bondfield, completely committed to adult suffrage, and refused to accept the arguments of those who pressed for claims of a limited extension of the suffrage to women, believing that it injured the cause of socialism. During the years of the suffrage struggle she chose instead to devote herself to the women's trade-union movement and to the various campaigns to raise the wages and working conditions of women in industry. She was driven by her Christian Socialist principles, which she always retained, and by a deep sense of compassion for those women less fortunate than herself. Indeed it is doubtful if she herself felt any strong sense of her own subjection. By concentrating on the needs of working-class women she avoided any conflict between her socialism and her feminism, and indeed throughout her life her loyalties remained very firmly with the Labour Party. Nor does she seem to have questioned, as did some of her contemporaries, existing gender relationships within the family. She remains, therefore, a somewhat peripheral figure to the feminist movement, but in the areas in which she operated her sincerity and devotion are unquestioned.

There is no biography of Gertrude Tuckwell, but there is a brief entry in the *DNB* Vol. 1951–60 p. 997 and a lengthy one in the *DLB* Vol. VI pp. 253–9 which contains a list of all her publications. There is also an unpublished autobiography in Tuckwell Papers in the TUC Archives, London. This is also available on microform in *The Gertrude Tuckwell Collection* (Brighton, Harvester Microform 1984). See also 'The Gertrude Tuckwell Collection', S. Morris, *History Workshop* Issue 5, Spring 1978 pp. 155–62, and *The Politics of Motherhood*, Jane Lewis (London, Croom Helm, 1980).

See also BONDFIELD Margaret Grace, DILKE Sir Charles Wentworth, DILKE Lady Emilia Francis, MACARTHUR Mary Reid.

TWINING Louisa 1820–1911

Louisa Twining, a work-house reformer, was the youngest of the eight children, five boys and three girls, of the well-to-do Twining family. Her father was the eldest son of Richard Twining, head of Twinings of the Strand. Although always destined to take over the business, he was also a man of learning who became a Fellow of the Royal Society. Her mother was the daughter of the Reverend John Smithies, rector of All Saints, Colchester. Louisa was educated entirely at home, mainly by her mother and sisters, although she had masters for languages and later attended lectures at the Royal Institution where her father was a member. Early on she showed considerable talent for drawing, and this seems to have been encouraged by her family. In 1852 she published her first book, *Symbols and Emblems of Early and Medieval Christian Art*, and in 1854 this was followed by *Types and Figures of the Bible*.

Meanwhile, however, she became increasingly aware of the sufferings of the poor, and especially of the appalling conditions inside workhouses. Her own first experience of these conditions was in 1853 on a visit to an old nurse and, finding her visits so welcome, she conceived the idea of a system of workhouse visiting by ladies of the neighbourhood. Limited as her scheme was, she was told that unpaid and voluntary effort was not sanctioned by the Poor Law Board, which controlled workhouses throughout the country.

Dismayed but undeterred, Louisa Twining set out on a campaign designed to persuade the Poor Law Board to change its mind, partly by personal conversation, partly by a series of letters to the Press, and by lectures. In 1855 a lecture by her on 'Workhouse Visiting' was published in *Practical Lectures to Ladies* by the Reverend J.S. Brewer, and she also published a pamphlet *A Few Words about the Inmates of our Union Workhouses*. She also organised a petition which was signed by a large number of influential men and women, including eminent doctors. She continued to be told by the Poor Law Board that such visits would constitute 'interference', but eventually the board gave way and the first visiting committee was formed in 1857.

By 1857 she was becoming known as something of an expert on workhouses and in that year she wrote a paper for the first meeting of the Social Science Association. In 1859 she had a number of interviews with the Poor Law Board, and in 1860 was asked to give evidence on pauper schools. In her evidence she asked for women Poor Law inspectors and for the extension of industrial training for girls. This plea was partially answered in 1872 when James Stansfeld as president of the Poor Law Board appointed Mrs Nassau Senior as the first woman Poor Law inspector.

Workhouses were her main but by no means her only philanthropic interest during these years. From 1850 onwards she was involved in teaching classes for women at the Working Men's College organised by F.D. Maurice. She also attended classes herself at the newly-founded Queen's College. Later she became associated with the Society for Promoting the Employment of Women and, as an artist made an unsuccessful attempt to the Workhouse Infirmary Nursing Association in an attempt to provide trained nurses in infirmaries. She was particularly interested in nursing and at one time thought of training as a nurse, but decided that this was not really her vocation.

By the 1880s Louisa Twining, now over sixty, was able to look on with satisfaction at the progress being made in making opportunities available to women. She was particularly impressed by the movement for opening higher education, which she saw as throwing down the 'wall of Chinese prejudice' by which women had been surrounded. She was also able to rejoice that women, from 1875, had been eligible for election to local boards of guardians. She herself was elected in 1884, serving very actively for the next six years. In 1900 she moved from London to Worthing and later to Tunbridge Wells where she spent her retirement until her death in 1911.

Louisa Twining was drawn into the women's movement in the first instance through her concern for the plight of those in workhouses and her steadily growing belief that their lives could be improved if women were involved in some way in workhouse administration. A determined woman with influential friends, she refused to accept the official view that this was 'interference' and, by means of a mixture of cajoling and coercing, her scheme for workhouse visiting was put into operation and the way opened for women eventually to serve as Poor Law guardians. Gradually accepted as an expert in this field, she was drawn into the circle of women who, during the 1850s, began to concern themselves with the limitations of women's educational background and employment opportunities. It is likely that her friend Anna Jameson, who played a significant part in this circle, did a great deal to encourage her to develop in this direction. She had a very strong desire to see women play a more useful part in society, and it was her commitment to this idea which provided the motive force for her feminism.

Louisa Twining wrote her autobiography, *Recollections of Life and Work, being the Autobiography of Louisa Twining* (London, Edward Arnold, 1893).

See also JAMESON Anna Brownell, STANSFELD James.

V

VENTURI Emilie Ashurst ?1820–1893

Emilie Venturi, one of the leading campaigners against the Contagious Diseases Acts, was the daughter of William Ashurst, a Radical solicitor, himself a feminist, who had been a friend of Robert Owen. Unfortunately we know nothing of the background of his wife or her attitudes but it is clear that all his four daughters were brought up in habits of independence and his house was an important centre of Radical activity. Quick to support anyone he believed to be oppressed, his feminism was based on his sympathy with women's inferior position. Emilie herself studied law informally in her father's office, and it was there that she met a young law student, Sydney Hawkes, whom she married in 1844, the same year that his friend and fellow student James Stansfeld married her sister Caroline. In 1850 the two young men abandoned the law as unprofitable and went into partnership as owners of a brewery.

The marriage between James and Caroline was successful but, for some reason not known to us, Emilie and Sydney Hawkes were increasingly unhappy. Possibly there was some instability in Sydney Hawkes' character, since his business partnership with James Stansfeld did not work either and was soon dissolved. James Stansfeld, alone, went on to prosper but Sydney Hawkes went bankrupt in 1854. The final breakdown of Sydney and Emilie's married life came in 1855 and was a bitter blow to Emilie, especially when Sydney Hawkes, apparently having formed another relationship, sought a divorce. The death of her mother, followed by the death in 1855 of her father, left Emilie without a home and there was a suggestion in 1857 that she should share a house with the secularist George Jacob Holyoake and his family, but this eventually came to nothing. Holyoake, however, helped her find customers for her pictures. Deeply unhappy, Emilie turned for consolation to the cause of Italian unity.

Mazzini had first met the Ashursts in 1844 and soon became a close family friend. Emilie and Caroline both admired him greatly, and were convinced of the rightness of his cause. In 1859, on a visit to Italy, Emilie formed a romantic attachment to Carlo Venturi, a young Italian who had deserted from the Austrian Army in 1848 at the age of eighteen, had fled to South America, and subsequently fought under Garibaldi. At the time of their first meeting her divorce proceedings had been started but not yet finalised, but as soon as she was free, in 1861, the two were married. Emilie was now drawn even more closely into Italian affairs, but in 1866 Carlo Venturi died from a heart attack, and her second marriage was over.

In the years that followed Emilie became, for the first time, deeply involved in the women's movement in Britain. From 1870 onwards she was prominent in the campaign for the repeal of the Contagious Diseases Acts, and was editor of the campaign's journal *The Shield* from 1871 to 1886. These Acts, by requiring the examination and if necessary treatment of women in garrison towns believed to be prostitutes, were seen by their opponents as condoning both vice and the double standard of morality. There was, in fact, a family commitment to the repeal campaign, just as there had been to the unity of Italy, and James Stansfeld, her brother-in-law, eventually took over the leadership of the campaign in Parliament. Emilie was also active in several other campaigns during the 1870s. For example she supported Elizabeth Malleson in her campaign for a co-educational adult college, which was founded in 1874. She was also involved with Ursula Bright in the struggle for a Married Women's Property Bill. Although not prominent in the campaign, she was a strong supporter of women's suffrage. She died in 1893.

Although she eventually became a prominent figure in the women's movement, Emilie Venturi was always something of an outsider. As a freethinker she did not fit in with the more orthodox of her colleagues, and the fact of her divorce was also regarded as shocking at this time. So was her habit of smoking cigars. It seems, too, that she had a somewhat abrasive personality, and was often at odds with those who worked with her, although Mazzini regarded her so highly that he made her his literary executrix. Essentially a romantic, she was happiest when she had some great cause to work for and, for most of her life, this need was satisfied by Italy's struggle for freedom. A follower rather than a leader, she turned to the women's movement only when it took on the semblance of a crusade. A woman who by upbringing was already emancipated by Victorian standards, she is an intriguing figure who would repay further study.

There is no biography of Emilie Venturi, and information on her life is scarce. The best source is *Mazzini's Letters to an English Family 1855-1860* edited with an introduction by E.F. Richards (Three Vols.: London, John Lane, 1920-2). See also *James Stansfeld: A Victorian Champion of Sex Equality*, J.L. and Barbara Hammond (London, Longmans, 1932). For her involvement with the Contagious Diseases Acts campaign see *Prostitution and Victorian Social Reform*, Paul McHugh (New York, St Martin's Press, 1980) and *Prostitution and Victorian Society*, Judith R. Walkowitz (Cambridge, Cambridge University Press, 1980). For her relationship with Holyoake see *Life and Letters of George Jacob Holyoake*, Joseph McCabe (London, Watts and Co., 1908).

See also ASHURST William Henry, STANSFELD James.

VICKERY Alice Drysdale 1844-1929

Alice Vickery, a leading birth control campaigner and a physician, was the daughter of John Vickery of Brierly Hall, Yorkshire. Nothing is known of her mother. She became the first woman to qualify as a chemist of the Royal Pharmaceutical Society and studied both midwifery and medicine in London and Paris. In 1880 she graduated at the Royal College of Physicians in Dublin and later developed an extensive practice in London, mainly amongst poorer women. During the 1870s she met Charles Drysdale and in 1874, while she was studying in Paris, a son, Charles Vickery Drysdale, was born. There is no record of a marriage or the birth of a child at Somerset House and it is possible that the marriage took place in France, although there is no information on when it occurred. In 1877 when, with Charles Drysdale, she gave evidence in support of the defence at the Bradlaugh-Besant trial, she was still known as Miss Vickery, but this is not in itself evidence that they were not already married. The suggestion has been made that there was no legal marriage and it is possible that she, like some other feminists at that time, objected to the legal subjection inherent in the position of a wife. It is equally possible, however, that for some reason the marriage was at first kept secret, perhaps in the interest of her medical studies. Later, although she was known as Dr Drysdale Vickery there seems no question that she was accepted as Charles Drysdale's legal wife.

Alice Vickery shared her husband's Malthusianism and worked devotedly for the Malthusian League both before and after his death. Her Malthusianism, like his, was combined with feminism and she saw birth control as the main key to women's emancipation. In 1904 she initiated the Women's Branch of the International Neo-Malthusian League, and, a year later, at its second congress, she argued that only by taking control of their own bodies could women obtain a fair opportunity in life. In the same address she claimed for women not only political equality but economic independence.

In 1907, on the death of her husband, she followed him as president of the Malthusian League, resigning in favour of their son in 1921.

Both before and after she became president, Alice Vickery was involved in active propaganda for birth control, forming a particularly close association with the Co-operative Women's Guild, both sending them literature and speaking at their branches. She pioneered the way, therefore, for the development of birth-control clinics in the 1920s. Although a keen supporter of women's suffrage, she seems never to have taken an active part in the suffrage movement, and it is likely that her emphasis on birth control as the key to women's emancipation cut her off from the mainstream of feminism at that time. It is perhaps for this reason that she is remembered, when she is remembered at all, for her Malthusianism rather than her feminism. Nevertheless she is important not only for her pioneering work on birth control, but also for her recognition of its significance for the feminist movement.

Information on the life of Alice Vickery is very scanty. The main source is *A History of the Malthusian League 1877–1927*, Rosanna Ledbetter (Columbus, Ohio State University Press, 1976). There is a brief obituary with a portrait in *The New Generation* February 1929 Vol. VIII (2) p. 17. See also *The Birth Controllers*, Peter Fryer (London, Secker and Warburg, 1965).

See also BESANT Annie, DRYSDALE Charles Robert.

WHEELER Anna 1785-1848

Anna Wheeler, an Owenite socialist, came from a family of enlightened Irish Protestant landlords and was the youngest daughter of Archbishop Doyle and his wife Anna Dunbar. She had been brought up in an intellectual atmosphere, but was unhappy at home as she felt under the thumb of her mother and the object of her mother's temper. When only fifteen years of age she met the nineteen-year-old Francis Massey Wheeler, a spoilt only child who was the grandson of one of the big landowners in Country Limerick. He conceived a passion for the beautiful but portionless girl and proposed at their second meeting. Her mother strenuously opposed the match, and persuaded her brother-in-law, General Sir John Doyle, to invite Anna and her sister Bessie to London as a distraction. Anna, tragically as it turned out, refused and the marriage took place in 1800.

Francis Wheeler, if superficially charming enough to attract the young Anna, was in fact a dissolute and boorish young man, interested only in his stables. Anna, increasingly dissatisfied, turned to books as a solace, and conceived a special passion for the feminist writings of Mary Wollstonecraft. Meanwhile her husband was slowly but steadily drinking himself to death. At the end of twelve years of marriage, in 1812, Anna Wheeler had borne six children, but only two, both girls, had survived infancy. Unable to bear the conditions any longer, and with the connivance of her uncle General Sir John Doyle, she escaped to Guernsey where her uncle was governor, taking with her her sister Bessie and her two daughters, Rosina and Henrietta.

Although she corresponded with her husband, he apparently made little effort to secure either her return or that of his children. He refused to pay her any allowance and, when he died in 1820, left her nothing in his will. Meanwhile she lived with her uncle in grand style at the splendid Government House and, still only twenty-seven years old and at the peak of her beauty, she was a popular figure who attracted many admirers. By 1816, however, Sir John Doyle's extravagant life-style forced him to return to London.

Anna Wheeler now had no settled home. She spent a period in London, stayed with friends in Dublin and then, in 1818, settled in Caen, where she became the centre of a Saint-Simonian circle, attracted to it by its strong feminist leanings. Rosina, however, was totally unsympathetic to both her Radical and feminist views, and after quarrelling with her mother she left home. In 1827 Rosina contracted a marriage with Bulwer Lytton which turned out as badly as her mother's marriage, and eventually the two women were reconciled. Henrietta, who had always been the 'good' daughter, remained with her mother until she herself died in 1826, scarcely more than twenty years old.

The period in Caen was interrupted by the death of Francis Wheeler in 1820. For a time Anna Wheeler lived in Ireland with a brother, but soon afterwards was in France again where she met Charles Fourier, the French pioneer socialist, then still unknown. Back in England in 1823 she made contact with the utilitarians and with the Owenites, including the socialist William Thompson. A bachelor in his late forties, the two found themselves closely in accord in their views and became close friends and, possibly, lovers. Under her influence, William Thompson became a convinced feminist and his first book *Inquiry into the Principles of the Distribution of Wealth*, published in 1824, contained a strong plea for legal, sexual and political equality between men and women. A year later, angered by an article by James Mill in the *Encyclopaedia Britannica*, which argued that women did not need the vote because their interests were included in that of husbands and fathers, he published *An Appeal of the half of the Human Race, Women, against the Pretensions of the other half, Men, to Retain them in Political and hence in Civil and Domestic Slavery*. Although published in his name, he readily confessed that Anna Wheeler had played a large part in its composition. Not only had she contributed many ideas, but some passages were actually from her pen. Although primarily an appeal for political emancipation, there are many passages on women's legal and sexual oppression, and it calls for an end both to the double standard of sexual morality and women's domestic slavery within marriage.

Spurred on by her collaboration with William Thompson, Anna Wheeler began to take a more active part in feminist as well as socialist propaganda and became a frequent writer in Co-operative and socialist journals. She also delivered a number of lectures on feminist themes. Her best known lecture was given in a Finsbury Square chapel in 1829 and was a rousing appeal to the women in the audience 'not to leave their daughters to the bitter inheritance of ignorance and slavery'. She attacked women's 'stupid servile submission to men's will' and recognised that their faults were due to their servile position in relation to men. A true daughter of the Enlightenment, she believed that the differences that existed between men and women were due to differences in education and environment, and claimed for women equal sexual, legal and political rights. Her articles in the Owenite press were equally outspoken. For example she attacked the doctrine that wives must be loyal to their husbands whatever the circumstances, claiming that women should be given the right to make moral judgements on their own. Moreover, in writing about love she came very close to those modern feminists who see romantic love as a trap to bind women voluntarily into subjection, calling it a symbol of women's degradation.

During these years she maintained her contact with the Saint-Simonians, including the Saint-Simonian feminist Flora Tristan, and also with Charles Fourier. She also did a great deal to keep Robert Owen in contact with the socialist movement in France. She was active, for example, in translating Saint-Simonian manifestos for his paper *The Crisis*. One such article, on the emancipation of women, appeared in *The Crisis* on 15 June 1833. In that year William Thompson died, leaving her an annuity, but his will was contested by his relatives and the annuity was in fact never paid.

After Thompson's death Anna Wheeler became friendly with the Reverend James Smith and was instrumental in converting him to both socialism and feminism, although they always differed on religion, as Anna Wheeler was, like William Thompson, a secularist. The millenium which he envisaged included the emancipation of women from their dependence on men. Although this entirely platonic friendship was maintained throughout the 1830s, Anna Wheeler's public life was gradually brought to an end by illness. She never lost either her feminism or her socialism however, and in 1848, shortly before her death, was deeply stirred by the revolution in France.

Anna Wheeler's feminism clearly had its source in her tragically mis-matched marriage. Strikingly beautiful and highly intelligent, she craved attention and stimulating society, yet her marriage brought her social and intellectual isolation and the company of a loutish husband. Turning to her books for relief she was easily able to identify with Mary Wollstonecraft's arguments and came to believe that her personal wrongs were the wrongs of her whole sex. Later her experiences were to colour her feminism, lending it a tinge of personal bitterness which continued to colour it long after her husband was dead. She never disliked men as such and, indeed, seems to have preferred men as friends, but she hated the institutional arrangement surrounding marriage which, she believed, led to the degradation of men and women alike.

She saw the emancipation of women as linked necessarily to socialism, and she was one of the most important of the feminist socialists who flourished during the 1820s and especially the 1830s. Yet her influence, considerable at the time, was a temporary one and did not outlast the communitarian phase of socialism. The members of the women's movement which emerged in the 1850s, with a few exceptions, had little sympathy with her socialism and she never became a part of the feminist tradition in the nineteenth century. There is, however, much in her writing which should appeal to those modern feminists who want to go beyond equal rights feminism to a critique of marriage itself. Unfortunately, apart from the *Appeal*, which did not appear under her name, her writings are difficult to obtain, but hopefully it is now possible to reinstate her in feminist history.

There is a brief biography in 'Anna Wheeler: a Pioneer Socialist and Feminist', Richard K.P. Pankhurst, *Political Quarterly* Vol. XXV (1954) pp. 132–43. See also *Life of Rosina*, *Lady Lytton*, Louisa Devey (London, Sonnenschein Loury and Co., 1887); *'Shepherd' Smith and the Universalists*, W. Andrew Smith (London, Sampson Low, Marston and Co., 1892); *Eve and the new Jerusalem*, Barbara Taylor (London, Virago, 1983); *Biographical Dictionary of Modern British Radicals* Vol. I, ed. Joseph O. Baylen and Norman J. Gossman (Sussex, Harvester Press, 1979).

See also THOMPSON William.

WILKINSON Ellen 1891–1947

Ellen Wilkinson, a Labour politician, was born in Manchester, the daughter of Richard Wilkinson, a cotton operative turned insurance clerk, and his wife Ellen Wood. There were four children, two boys and two girls, and Ellen was the third child. Soon after her birth her mother developed cancer and there were a number of operations before her death in 1916. Her father was an affectionate and indulgent man, particularly to Ellen, and she always loved and admired him. Although her schooldays were interrupted by illness, she was a clever child, with a reputation for naughtiness, and at eleven won her first scholarship. At the age of fifteen she became a pupil-teacher, but a future in teaching did not appeal to her and instead she worked for and achieved the Jones scholarship in history. This enabled her to go to university instead of a training college. Meanwhile she had become converted to socialism while still at school and joined the Independent Labour Party at the age of sixteen. She also became an active member of the National Union of Women's Suffrage Societies, for whom she distributed handbills, chalked pavements and put up posters.

In 1910 she entered Manchester University to study history, graduating in 1913 with an upper-second degree. While at university she joined the Fabian Society and became closely involved with the Fabian research department. During her second year she became engaged to John Turner Walton Newbold, the son of a wealthy Liberal Irish Quaker. The engagement lasted only a year but his influence was considerable and lasting, turning her in the direction of both pacifism and Marxism. After graduating she spent a short time as an organiser for the Manchester Society for Women's Suffrage and then, in 1915, was appointed national woman organiser to the Amalgamated Union of Co-operative Employees, a job which enabled her to give expression to both her feminism and her socialism. Very critical of the whole attitude of the Co-operative movement to its women workers, she started a women's department in the union to cater for women's special interests.

After the war Ellen Wilkinson took an active part in the formation of the British communist party in large part because of her sympathy with the Russian revolution. Her membership did not last long however, and she soon resigned because of the party's dictatorial attitude. In 1923 she was elected to the Manchester City Council where she tried to secure equal pay for women public health inspectors. Her ambitions were turning to Parliament and she fought her first campaign, unsuccessfully, in 1923, followed by victory at Middlesbrough East in 1924. In her maiden speech she deplored the failure to grant the vote to women voters under thirty, since their lack of political status was reflected in their pay. She also attacked the limitations of unemployment benefit for women, which denied benefit to several categories of women workers including cleaners and laundresses.

During the next few years she seized every opportunity to promote the cause of women in Parliament, often working in harness with the National Union of Societies for Equal Citizenship. She contributed notably in such areas as pensions for widows, and also conducted an ultimately successful campaign to enable British women who married aliens to retain their British citizenship. She also vigorously attacked the assumption that unemployed women could always enter domestic service. Another of her targets was the position of women in the Civil Service and she fought both for equal pay and an end to the marriage bar. Indeed in 1936 she was successful in introducing a motion for equal pay in the Civil Service but the Prime Minister turned the issue into one of confidence and the decision was reversed. A firm supporter of welfare provisions for women and children, she sought the extension of maternity centres, free milk for school children and grants for children's clothing. Her feminism at this time was still forthright and hard-hitting and in 1932 she condemned the 'silent and invincible freemasonry of men'.

The only feminist issue on which she remained somewhat equivocal was birth control. She herself told Dora Russell that she really supported the birth controllers but had to be careful because she was unmarried. Nevertheless, in 1926, when Ernest Thurtle asked leave in the House of Commons to introduce a Bill authorising local authorities to set up birth-control clinics, she was the only one of the four women MPs to vote for it. She also changed her mind completely on family allowances. An active supporter during the 1920s, by 1938 she was opposed, seeing them now simply as a way to avoid paying wage increases to men.

Meanwhile her parliamentary career was progressing and in 1929 with the advent of a Labour government she became parliamentary secretary to Susan Lawrence at the Ministry of Health. In the same year she was appointed to the Donoughmore Committee on Ministers' Powers. Like so many others in the Labour Party, she lost her seat in 1931 but not long after she was adopted as a candidate for Jarrow and was returned to Parliament in 1935. During the 1930s however her concern moved from feminist issues to unemployment, a particularly pressing problem in Jarrow, and, on the international scene, the growth of fascism. During the war-time coalition government she served as parliamentary secretary to the Minister of Pensions and then as parliamentary secretary to Herbert Morrison, Home Secretary and Minister of Home Security. Her chief responsibility was air-raid shelters and later the fire-watching service, and by this time her feminism was peripheral emerging, for example, in her support of the conscription of women for civil defence.

In the Labour government at the end of the war Ellen Wilkinson was Minister of Education with a seat in the Cabinet. She was already in poor health, and her administration was not regarded as a success, although she successfully fought opposition by some within the Cabinet to raising the school-leaving age. Other achievements included widening the opportunities for university entrance and expanding the provision of school meals and milk. During 1946 she was gravely ill, and in 1947 she died as a result of what was probably an accidental overdose of the medicine prescribed for her bronchitis and asthma.

Apart from a large number of articles in newspapers and magazines, Ellen Wilkinson was also the author of several books, although all on themes other than the position of women. Her first publication, in collaboration with Raymond Postgate and Frank Horrabin, was *A Worker's History of the General Strike*. In 1929 she published a novel, *Clash*, which was partly autobiographical, and in 1934, in association with Dr Edward Conze, *Why Fascism?* Her last and most famous book, on Jarrow, *The Town that was Murdered*, was published in 1939.

Throughout her life Ellen Wilkinson placed politics first, and, although she may not have taken any deliberate decision not to marry, marriage, after her early and abortive engagement, seems to have taken second place to her career. Nevertheless she enjoyed the friendship of men and in many respects may have felt closer to men than to women. From her earliest days in politics she enjoyed the friendship of John Jagger, president of the National Union of Distributive and Allied Workers, who was of enormous help in securing her first entry into politics. Frank Horrabin was also a close friend and colleague, and the ending of their relationship in the early 1930s undoubtedly hurt her deeply. She was perhaps closest of all to Herbert Morrison whom she admired greatly in spite of a number of strong political differences. Herbert Morrison was deeply unhappy in his marriage and it is very likely that during the late 1930s he and Ellen were for a time at least in love with each other. Both, however, were totally committed to their political careers, and Herbert Morrison was a man of exceptional caution so that it is unlikely that they ever became lovers.

Although she was too young to play a very active part in the suffrage movement, Ellen Wilkinson's commitment to feminism is not in doubt. While woman organiser to the Amalgamated Union of Co-operative Employees she worked hard not only to bring women into the union but also to negotiate better rates of pay, and later as an MP she pressed a wide variety of feminist issues with spirit and determination. By the 1930s, however, in common with the great majority of women who had been active feminists in the 1920s, she found herself turning to other issues. She never lost her feminism, but unemployment and fascism came to overshadow almost everything else in her mind. During the war moreover the daily responsibilities of office claimed her entirely. As Minister of Education after the war she was in the wrong post, since she had no previous interest in educational policy and was forced to rely on her civil servants. Consequently she lost any opportunity to introduce a feminist policy in education.

After her death Ellen Wilkinson was remembered less for her feminism than for her crusade against unemployment in the 1930s. She was, however, one of the most important feminist activists during the 1920s. Her particular interest was in such issues as equal pay and equal employment opportunities for women, but she also supported improvements in welfare provisions to help both mothers and children. Unlike many women at that time, she was able to combine her socialism with a strong commitment to equal-rights feminism which allowed her to collaborate with women who were not socialists at all, as her association with NUSEC clearly shows. By the end of her life feminist goals had become superseded by other considerations, but this should not allow her services to feminism to be forgotten.

There is a biography, *Ellen Wilkinson 1891–1947*, Betty D. Vernon (London, Croom Helm, 1982). See also *Chrystal Eastman. On Woman and Revolution* ed. Blanche W. Cook (Oxford, Oxford University Press, 1978); *A New World for Women*, S. Rowbotham (London, Pluto Press, 1977); *The Movement for Family Allowances 1918–1945*, John Macnicol (London, Heinemann, 1980); *DNB* 1941–50 pp. 955–6.

WOLSTENHOLME-ELMY Elizabeth Clark 1834–?1913

Elizabeth Wolstenholme, a leading headmistress and later a suffragist, was the daughter of a Methodist minister from Eccles. Otherwise, nothing is known about either of her parents who died while she was still a child. There was one other child, an older brother, a distinguished student at Cambridge who then followed a successful career as a professor of mathematics. His sister, to her regret, was given a solely domestic education, and even reading for pleasure was forbidden. By the age of fourteen she was deemed to know everything a woman need know. By this time, however, she was doubly an orphan, and she was sent for two years to the Moravian school at Fulneck near Leeds. Convinced by this time that she was intellectually as capable as her brother, she tried to persuade her guardians to allow her to attend the newly-opened Bedford College for Women, but they refused, For the next three years she studied at home, at which point, at her guardians' suggestion, she invested her small amount of inherited capital in a high-class boarding school for girls near Manchester under her own management. Thus, at only nineteen years of age and largely self-educated, she found herself struggling virtually single-handed with the problems of working out for herself the most suitable kind of education for the girls of the middle classes.

By 1865 Elizabeth Wolstenholme was sufficiently well known as a headmistress to set up the Manchester Schoolmistresses' Association, and in the same year she read a paper at the Social Science Association meeting in Sheffield in which she stressed the need for better-qualified teachers. She was also one of the small number of women who, in 1865, gave evidence before the Schools Inquiry Commission. In 1867 the North of England Council for the Higher Education of Women was founded with the intention of providing advanced lectures for women and, later, with the provision of special university examinations to provide a qualification of particular value to schoolmistresses. Elizabeth Wolstenholme was active in it from the first, and it was she who devised the original constitution. She also worked incessantly on its behalf, suggesting and negotiating lectures, drawing up memorials and collecting signatures.

Her ideas at this time were clearly expressed in her contribution to Josephine Butler's *Women's Work and Women's Culture* published in 1869. Deploring the lack of interest shown by parents in the education of their daughters, she asked for a system of high schools for girls in every town. Although she had worked with Anne Jemima Clough for a special examination for girls, her own personal sympathies were rather with Emily Davies, who wanted the same system of examinations and qualifications for both girls and boys and men and women.

She was also involved from the start in the campaign for women's suffrage, collecting personally, in 1866, more than 300 names for the petition presented by John Stuart Mill to Parliament. In 1865 she was the honorary secretary of a small group, the Manchester Committee for the Enfranchisement of Women. This later became the Manchester National Society for Women's Suffrage, with Lydia Becker as its secretary.

In 1868 she was on the executive committee of the newly-founded Married Women's Property Committee which secured a small improvement in the position of married women by an Act of 1870. In 1871 she resigned from the committee, but returned in 1880 and for the next two years was one of the most active and determined members. In 1882, when the Married Women's Property Act gave married women possession of their property and earnings, the committee was disbanded and Elizabeth Wolstenholme and Ursula Bright were given a special address of congratulations and appreciation for their work.

In 1869 Elizabeth Wolstenholme was present at the Bristol conference of the Social Science Association where she attended a special meeting organised in opposition to the extension of the Contagious Diseases Acts. These Acts, designed to protect the Armed Forces against venereal disease, provided for the compulsory medical examination and forced treatment of any woman suspected of prostitution. Fired by what she had heard, Elizabeth Wolstenholme sent a telegram to Josephine Butler, whom she knew well, bidding her to 'haste to the rescue'. Although she does not seem to have taken a prominent place in the leadership of the campaign, probably because of her position as an unmarried headmistress, she was fully in accord with Josephine Butler's views that the Acts perpetuated and reinforced a double standard of sexual morality. Indeed in 1871 she corresponded with Kate Amberley in connection with the idea of a Bill to punish seduction and fornication.

By this time Elizabeth had given up her school near Manchester and was in charge of a school at Congleton. In 1872 she decided to move to London to act as a 'Parliamentary watch dog', but in 1874 she married Benjamin William Elmy, from Congleton, a minor poet who was himself committed to women's rights, and returned to Congleton. Sylvia Pankhurst relates that they were persuaded to marry by Ursula Bright when it was found that Elizabeth was several months pregnant. The wedding was a civil ceremony in which no promise of obedience was made by the bride, and a few months later Frank, the couple's only child, was born. Both husband and wife were free-thinkers, and in 1876 Annie Besant in her *Autobiography* recounts a visit she and Charles Bradlaugh made to Congleton in which they stayed with the Elmys. The meetings were rowdy, and stones were thrown at both Annie Besant and Elizabeth Elmy, although the crowd was eventually routed by the combined efforts of Ben Elmy and Charles Bradlaugh. According to Sylvia Pankhurst, Ben Elmy was an unsatisfactory husband, but his wife always referred to him very affectionately. In 1906, when he was dying, she wrote to Dora Montefiore in praise of her 'beloved husband' and his great dream of seeing women's suffrage a reality.

Her marriage seems to have done little to reduce her participation in the women's movement. The years between 1880 and 1882 were busy years in the campaign for married women's property, and afterwards she was deeply involved in the pressure for the 1886 Custody of Infants Act which improved the custody rights of mothers. Meanwhile her interest in women's suffrage had been maintained and in 1889, along with Richard and Emmeline Pankhurst, she and her husband formed the Women's Franchise League, a ginger group which worked not only for suffrage but for married women's rights in general, including equal rights in divorce. When this did not prove successful, the two Elmys founded the Women's Emancipation Union, with Elizabeth as its secretary. It claimed equal rights for women in all areas of life, including marriage.

In 1905 Elizabeth Wolstenholme-Elmy was drawn into the Women's Social and Political Union and she soon became one of Christabel Pankhurst's keenest admirers. She had long despised what she called the 'fiddle-faddling' of the National Union of Women's Suffrage Societies and was delighted by the new mood she found in the WSPU, and in spite of her age she became a familiar figure in London processions and demonstrations. When the WSPU split in 1907 she remained fiercely loyal to the Pankhursts. By 1910 however, her strength had gone, and she died soon afterwards.

Under the pseudonym Ellis Ethelmar, Elizabeth Wolstenholme-Elmy, either singly or, more likely, in collaboration with her husband, was the author of the *Human Flower Series*, a number of books published in the 1890s which were an attempt to popularise the facts of human physiology. Probably also in collaboration with her husband, who may have been the main author, she published as Ellis Ethelmar several poems, of which *Woman Free* (1893) is a long poem dealing with woman's age-long subordination to man. It is particularly bitter on the theme of man's brutality and selfishness, especially his sexual aggression, but ends with a romantic vision of the marriage of the future. Publications under her own name are largely on the suffrage issue, but also include a collection of pamphlets on the guardianship of infants. Her last work was a pamphlet *Franchise, the need of the hour* issued by the Independent Labour Party in 1907.

Elizabeth Wolstenholme-Elmy's activity as a feminist is remarkable for the span of years it covers and the breadth of her interest and concern. She carried on a voluminous correspondence, not only with other feminists but also with anyone who gained prominence in social reform and, at the start of the militant campaign, she deluged members of Parliament with letters threatening an agitation stronger even than that which forced the repeal of the Contagious Diseases Acts. She was not a particularly able speaker and her talents lay chiefly behind the scenes where she was a powerful asset to the various campaigns in which she became involved. By nature she was romantic and impulsive but she was also able to sustain her enthusiasm through long and exhausting campaigns. Most of all, although very much a radical, she was able to work with men and women whose opinions were very different from her own. She remains one of the most overlooked feminists of her generation.

There is a brief portrait in 'A Woman Emancipator. A Biographical Sketch', Ellis Ethelmar, *The Westminster Review* Vol. CXLV 1896 pp. 424–8. See also *Wives and Property*, Lee Holcombe (Oxford, Martin Robertson, 1983); *The Suffragette Movement*, Sylvia Pankhurst (London, Longmans, 1931; Virago, 1977). There are brief references in *Personal Reminiscences of a Great Crusade*, Josephine Butler (London, Horace Marshall, 1898); *Memoir of Ann Jemima Clough*, Blanche A. Clough (London, Arnold, 1903); *The Life of Sophia Jex-Blake*, Margaret Todd (London, Macmillan, 1918); *The Amberley Papers* ed. Bertrand and Patricia Russell (London, Hogarth Press, 1937); *An Autobiography*, Annie Besant (London, T. Fisher Unwin, 1893); *From a Victorian to a Modern*, Dora Montefiore (London, E. Archer, 1927) and *Prostitution and Victorian Society*, Judith R. Walkowitz (Cambridge, Cambridge University Press, 1980). The Wolstenholme-Elmy Papers are in the British Library Department of Manuscripts.

WRIGHT Frances 1795–1852

Frances Wright, a lecturer and journalist, was born in Dundee, the daughter of James Wright and his wife Camilla Campbell. James Wright, a linen merchant, was a man of strong Radical sympathies who contributed to the expenses of a cheap reprint of Paine's *Rights of Man*. Both parents died within a short time of each other during 1798 and the two little girls, Frances and her younger sister Camilla, both heiresses, were separated from their brother Richard and placed in the care of their maternal grandfather Duncan Campbell and their aunt Frances. Later, when Frances was eighteen, they went to a great uncle James Milne, professor of Moral Philosophy at Glasgow College. Frances was to remember her life with her aunt with bitterness but enjoyed the intellectual company at her uncle's house. Soon she was writing a play on the theme of the struggle of the Swiss against Austria.

While still under twenty-one she entered into an engagement with a cousin but this was later broken off. Instead she turned to poetry, and conceived a passion for Byron's work. She also made friends with Mrs Craig Millar, the widow of a political exile to the United States, who had known her father. This friendship was important not only in intensifying Frances Wright's own Radical thinking but in turning her thoughts to America. In 1818, when Camilla came of age, she persuaded her great-uncle to let the two of them visit the United States. During their visit Frances was involved in a brief romance with William Theobald Wolfe Tone, the son of an Irish rebel condemned to death as a traitor, and with his help a play of hers was successfully staged.

On her return the book of her experiences, *Views of Society and Manners in America*, published in 1821, was widely read and brought her into touch with a number of important reformers, in particular Jeremy Bentham. From France, General Lafayette, a hero of the French and American revolutions and now a widower in his mid-sixties, invited her to visit him and a very warm friendship soon developed in which they spent long hours together. The relationship, on Frances Wright's side at least, was mainly that of father and daughter, although it is clear that she was also deeply stirred by the atmosphere of intrigue and revolution still surrounding him. It does not seem, however, that she ever thought of him as a possible lover and, indeed, she soon fell very deeply in love with a young revolutionary known to us only as Eugene. It is not clear how deeply Eugene's own emotions were involved, but in a poem to him later she calls him an unfaithful lover, and the episode, to her great distress, was soon at an end.

Throughout this incident General Lafayette was her confidant and sympathiser. There was even a possibility that he might adopt her as his daughter, but his own children intervened to prevent it. Nevertheless the friendship continued, if more discreetly, and when he went on a tour of the United States in 1824 Frances and Camilla Wright were for a time part of his entourage. It was while on this tour that Frances was converted to Owenite Co-operation and conceived the idea of introducing Owenite ideas on a slave plantation. From this time, although they remained friends, the paths of Frances Wright and Lafayette were gradually to diverge.

Always impulsive, Frances Wright immediately set about putting her ideas into practice. With her own money she purchased a plot of land at Nashoba in Tennessee and set up a community of slaves. It was planned that the slaves, once they had earned their purchase price, would be set free and settled in some suitable country. Very soon however the community was beset with problems, some arising from its unhealthy situation, some from the difficulties inherent in managing such an enterprise. Moreover, Frances herself was taken seriously ill and had to leave the community in Camilla's rather ineffective care. In her absence James Richardson, the white overseer, not only began living with one of the slaves, but made public in a newspaper his ideas on free love which, speedily becoming known even in England, made both the community and Frances Wright herself notorious. Eventually it became obvious that the community was a failure and, although Frances did her best to put it right, it was apparent that it would have to be disbanded.

Meanwhile, in 1828, Frances Wright began a new career as a lecturer. In association with Robert Dale Owen, the young son of Robert Owen, she became part-owner of the free-thinking *New Harmony Gazette* and started a series of lectures in New York. Her ideas were drawn to a large extent from Owenite socialism and included such issues as the abolition of slavery, the education and emancipation of women, birth control, freedom from revealed religion, and socialism. Her lectures attracted a great deal of attention, and indeed she was a first-class orator, although often enough she attracted hostility rather than admiration. Indeed the very idea of a woman lecturer was, at this time, sufficient to draw a crowd.

She was pleased enough with her success however to start a newspaper, still in association with Robert Dale Owen, entitled *The Free Inquirer*, and to follow this up with the opening of a Hall of Science including a lecture room, offices and Sunday school.

The affairs at Nashoba had still to be finally concluded however, and in 1829 she sailed with the slaves to settle them in Haiti, accompanied by William Phiquepal D'Arusmont, a middle-aged eccentric French physician who had been teaching at the Owenite community, New Harmony. Afterwards he went back to France and Frances returned to Camilla in New York. Camilla had married a young Quaker, Rickerson Whitby, who had followed her to Nashoba. A child had been born, but the couple were now separated and the death of the child had left Camilla desolated. There were also dissensions in New York between Frances Wright and some of her supporters, and she decided to take Camilla to France for a visit. The unhappy Camilla, however, whose health had probably been wrecked by the disastrous episode at Nashoba, was unable to recover and died in 1831. Frances, who had always dominated her sister, nevertheless adored her and her death was a staggering blow. She was helped to recover by Phiquepal D'Arusmont, and it was possibly her dependence on him at this time of weakness on her part which led them to become lovers and, once she was pregnant, to marry. Their first child died, but a second and last child, Sylvia, was born in 1832.

It is possible that by this time Frances Wright was already regretting their marriage. Her husband, almost sixty years of age, was completely caught up in his child but Frances was restless. In 1833 she went to England and took up her lecturing again, taking her place amongst the Owenite lecturers who were becoming popular in London at this time. Enjoying her success, she ignored her husband's letters asking her to come home, and in 1834 he fetched her back in person. He could not keep her with him for long however, and a year later, when they both went to the United States ostensibly for a few months on business, leaving Sylvia in France, he returned but she stayed in the United States for four years, giving lectures at a number of towns, including New York and Boston. Indeed, from this time forward they were rarely together. In consequence their daughter Sylvia turned to her father rather than her mother and Frances drifted apart from both her daughter and her husband.

There was, however, no actual break in the marriage until 1844 when Frances Wright inherited some family property. Her lawyers advised her to place it in trust for Sylvia, depriving her husband of any share in its management. Furious, he tried to take over her American property in his name. Previously, although he had a legal right to it, he had not sought to claim it but now he won the right to take it from her. In the end, on the advice of friends, she divorced him, gaining her property rights back in 1850 but losing custody of Sylvia. In 1851 she broke her hip, and died after a great deal of suffering in 1852.

Frances Wright's feminism was an important part of her programme of reforms, but did not take a central place, and in her practical work for reform the freedom of the slave played much the most important part. Nevertheless her feminism was of a distinctly radical variety and she was amongst the earliest advocates of women's suffrage. Her views on marriage, which caused so much notoriety at the time, were vague rather than precise, but she certainly believed that marriage should be dependent on 'mutual inclination'. Above all, however, she wanted women to be free from 'mental leading strings' and placed great emphasis on their need to recognise their own subordination. In her last book, unfinished when she died, she looked forward to the time when women, at last fully emancipated, would come to the rescue of the world.

Very much a product of the Enlightenment, Frances Wright believed firmly in the importance of knowledge, and it is highly significant that she called her newspaper *The Free Inquirer*. She not only wanted free education for all, but also advocated a system of 'state guardianship' which involved sending children at the age of two years to state boardng schools where their parents would be allowed only infrequent visits. The education of the slaves was also an integral part of her plan for the Nashoba community although, like other parts of the plan, it was never actually achieved.

A romantic by nature, Frances Wright loved adventure and excitement. She also had a great desire for independence. At the same time, however, she had a yearning for love, formed probably during her unhappy childhood. There is no doubt that her dead father had a powerful hold on her imagination and she sought him again in General Lafayette, and perhaps too in D'Arusmont, but the love she sought always eluded her in the end. Her need for dependency however always fought with her desire for independence and she was unable to settle down to a life of domesticity with her husband and child. She probably excelled above all as a lecturer, and here she was almost unique, gaining a very wide audience at a time when women had not yet earned the right to speak in public. In this respect she stands out as one of the most outspoken and courageous of the early propagandists who, before there was even a women's movement in existence, made feminism a matter of public debate.

The most recent biography is *Frances Wright and the 'Great Experiment'*, Margaret Lane (Manchester, Manchester University Press, 1972). However, *Frances Wright. Free Enquirer*, A.J.G. Perkins and Theresa Wolfson (New York and London, Harper, 1939) is more comprehensive. There is an autobiography, *Biography. Notes and Political Letters*, Frances Wright D'Arusmont (Boston, P.J. Menden, 1849). See also *The Feminist Papers* ed. Alice S. Rossi (New York, Bantam Books, 1974) which contains some extracts from her writings, and *DNB* Vol. XIV pp. 70–2 under D'Arusmont.

Index

Index

Amberley, Lady Katherine Louisa, (Kate), 1842—1874	3
Anderson, Elizabeth Garrett, 1836–1917	4
Ashurst, William Henry, 1792–1855	6
Ayrton, Phoebe Sarah, (Hertha), 1854–1923	8
Balfour, Lady Frances, 1858–1930	10
Barmby, Catherine Isabella, ?1817–1853	12
Barnes, Annie, 1887–?	13
Beale, Dorothea, 1831–1906	15
Becker, Lydia Ernestine, 1827–1890	17
Belloc, Bessie Rayner, 1829–1925	19
Besant, Annie, 1847–1933	21
Billington-Greig, Teresa, 1877–1964	23
Blackburn, Helen, 1842–1903	25
Blathwayt, Mary, 1879–1962	26
Bodichon, Barbara Leigh Smith, 1827–1891	27
Bondfield, Margaret Grace, 1873–1953	30
Boucherett, Emilie, (Jessie), 1825–1905	32
Brailsford, Henry Noel, 1873–1958	33
Bright, Jacob, 1821–1899	35
Bright, Ursula, ?1830–1915	37
Browne, Stella, 1882–1955	39
Buss, Frances Mary, 1827–1894	40
Butler, Josephine, 1828–1906	41
Carpenter, Mary, 1807–1877	46
Chappellsmith, Margaret, 1806–1883	48
Chew, Ada Nield, 1870–1945	49
Clough, Anne Jemima, 1820–1892	51
Cobbe, Frances Power, 1822–1904	53
Cooper, Selina, 1864–1946	55
D'Arusmont, Frances *see* Wright, Frances	
Davies, Margaret Llewelyn, 1861–1944	57
Davies, Sarah Emily, (Emily), 1830–1921	59
Davison, Emily Wilding, 1872–1913	62
Despard, Charlotte, 1844–1939	63
Dickensen, Sarah, 1868–1954	65
Dilke, Sir Charles Wentworth, 1843–1911	66
Dilke, Lady Emilia Francis, 1840–1904	68
Drummond, Flora, 1879 (c)–1949	70
Drysdale, Charles Robert, 1829–1907	71
Faithfull, Emily, 1835–1895	74
Fawcett, Henry, 1833–1884	75

INDEX

Fawcett, Millicent Garrett, 1847–1929	77
Fitch, Sir Joshua Girling, 1824–1903	81
Ford, Isabella Ormston, c.1850–1924	82
Fox, William Johnson, 1786–1864	84
Garrett, Elizabeth *see* Anderson, Elizabeth Garrett	
Gawthorpe, Mary, 1881–c.1960	86
Gore-Booth, Eva Selina, 1870–1926	87
Greig, Teresa Billington *see* Billington-Greig, Teresa	
Grey, Maria Georgina, 1816–1906	89
Grimstone, Mary Lemon, c.1790–?	90
Hamilton, Cicely, 1872–1952	92
Hardie, Keir, 1856–1915	93
Hicks, Amelia, (Amie), 1839/40–1917	95
Hubback, Eva Marian, 1886–1949	96
Jameson, Anna Brownell, 1794–1860	100
Jewson, Dorothea, (Dorothy), 1884–1964	102
Jex-Blake, Sophia, 1840–1912	103
Kenney, Annie, 1879–1953	106
Knight, Anne, 1792–1862	108
Lansbury, George, 1859–1940	109
Law, Harriet Teresa, 1831–1897	111
Leigh Smith, Barbara *see* Bodichon, Barbara Leigh Smith	
Lytton, Lady Constance Georgina, 1869–1923	112
Macarthur, Mary Reid, 1880–1921	115
MacDonald, Margaret Ethel, 1870–1911	116
Malleson, Elizabeth, 1828–1916	119
Marsden, Dora, 1882–1960	120
Martin, Emma, 1812–1851	121
Martineau, Harriet, 1802–1876	123
Mill, John Stuart, 1806–1873	126
Miller, Florence Fenwick, 1854–1935	130
Mitchell, Hannah Maria, 1871–1956	131
Montefiore, Dora, 1851–1927	133
Morrison, Frances, 1807–1898	134
Nevinson, Henry Woodd, 1856–1941	136
Nevinson, Margaret Wynne, ?1860–1932	137
Nicholl, Elizabeth Pease, 1807–1897	139
Nightingale, Florence, 1820–1910	140
Norton, Caroline, 1808–1877	143
Pankhurst, Christabel, 1880–1958	146
Pankhurst, Emmeline, 1858–1928	149
Pankhurst, Richard Marsden, 1835–1898	152
Pankhurst, Sylvia, 1882–1960	153

Parkes, Bessie Rayner *see* Belloc, Bessie Rayner
Pethick-Lawrence, Emmeline, 1867–1954   157
Pethick-Lawrence, Frederick William, 1871–1961   160
Phillips, Marion, 1881–1932   162
Proctor, Adelaide Anne, 1825–1864   164

Rathbone, Eleanor, 1872–1946   166
Reddish, Sarah, 1850–1925   169
Rhondda, Viscountess *see* Thomas, Margaret Haig
Rigby, Edith Rayner, 1872–1949   169
Robins, Elizabeth, 1862–1952   172
Roper, Esther, 1868–1938   173
Royden, Maude, 1876–1956   174

Schreiner, Olive, 1855–1920   177
Shaen, William, 1820–1887   179
Sharp, Evelyn, 1869–1955   180
Sharples, Elizabeth, 1804–1861   181
Shirreff, Emily Anne Elizabeth, 1814–1897   182
Sidgwick, Eleanor Mildred, (Nora), 1845–1936   183
Sidgwick, Henry, 1838–1899   185
Smith, Mary, 1822–1889   187
Smyth, Ethel Mary, 1858–1944   189
Snowden, Ethel Annakin, 1880–1951   191
Snowden, Philip, 1864–1937   193
Stacey, Enid, ?–1903   194
Stansfeld, James, 1820–1898   195
Stocks. Mary Danvers, 1891–1975   197
Stopes, Marie Charlotte Carmichael, 1880–1958   199
Strachey, Philippa, (Pippa), 1872–1968   202
Strachey, Rachel, (Ray), 1887–1940   203
Swanwick, Helena Maria Lucy, 1864–1939   205

Taylor, Harriet, 1807–1858   208
Thomas, Margaret Haig, Viscountess Rhondda, 1883–1958   211
Thompson, William, 1775–1833   213
Tuckwell, Gertrude Mary, 1861–1951   214
Twining, Loisa, 1820–1911   216

Venturi, Emilie Ashurst, ?1820–1893   218
Vickery, Alice Drysdale, 1844–1929   219

Wheeler, Anna, 1785–1848   221
Wilkinson, Ellen, 1891–1947   223
Wolstenholme-Elmy, Elizabeth Clark, 1834–?1913   225
Wright, Frances, 1795–1852   228

Index of Topics

ABORTION: Henry Noel Brailsford (33–35); Stella Browne (39–40); Cicely Hamilton (92–93).

ANTI-SLAVERY MOVEMENT: William Henry Ashurst (6–7); Barbara Leigh Smith Bodichon (27–30); Josephine Butler (41–45); Anne Knight (108); Harriet Martineau (123–26); Elizabeth Pease Mitchell (139–40); James Stansfeld (195–97); Frances Wright (228–30).

BIRTH CONTROL: Lady Katherine Louisa (Kate) Amberley (1–2); Annie Barnes (13–15); Annie Besant (21–23); Stella Browne (39–40); Selina Cooper (55–60); Charles Robert Drysdale (71–73); Cicely Hamilton (92–93); Dorothea (Dorothy) Jewson (102–3); George Lansbury (109–11); Lady Constance Georgina Lytton (112–14); John Stuart Mill (126–30); Florence Fenwick Miller (130–31); Emmeline Pethick-Lawrence (157–60); Marion Phillips (162–64); Maude Royden (174–76); Enid Stacey (194–95); Mary Danvers Stocks (197–99); Marie Charlotte Carmichael Stopes (199–202); William Thompson (213–14); Alice Drysdale Vickery (219–20).

CONTAGIOUS DISEASES ACTS: Lady Katherine Louisa (Kate) Amberley (1–2); Elizabeth Garrett Anderson (4–6); Lydia Ernestine Becker (17–19); Jacob Bright (35–37); Ursula Bright (37–39); Mary Carpenter (46–48); Charles Robert Drysdale (71–73); Millicent Garrett Fawcett (77–81); Amelia (Amie) Jane Hicks (95–96); Elizabeth Malleson (119–20); Harriet Martineau (123–26); John Stuart Mill (126–30); Florence Fenwick Miller (130–31); Elizabeth Pease Nicholl (139–40); Florence Nightingale (140–43); William Shaen (179–80); Mary Smith (187–89); James Stansfeld (195–97); Emilie Ashurst Venturi (218–19); Elizabeth Clark Wolstenholme-Elmy (225–28).

FAMILY ENDOWMENT: Henry Noel Brailsford (33–35); Ada Nield Chew (49–51); Selina Cooper (55–56); Millicent Garrett Fawcett (77–81); Eva Marian Hubback (96–99); Dorothea (Dorothy) Jewson (102–103); Eleanor Rathbone (166–69); Mary Danvers Stocks (197–99).

FEMALE SEXUALITY: Stella Browne (39–40); Dora Marsden (120–21); Marie Charlotte Carmichael Stopes (199–202).

GUARDIANSHIP OF CHILDREN: Annie Besant (21–23); Eva Marian Hubback (96–99); Dorothea (Dorothy) Jewson (102–103); Caroline Norton (143–45); Elizabeth Clark Wolstenholme-Elmy (225–28).

HIGHER EDUCATION OF WOMEN: Lady Katherine Louisa (Kate) Amberley (1–2); Elizabeth Garrett Anderson (4–6); Barbara Leigh Smith Bodichon (27–30); Emilie (Jessie) Boucherett (32–33); Frances Mary Buss (40–41); Anne Jemima Clough (51–53); Sarah Emily (Emily) Davies (59–62); Sir Joshua Girling

INDEX OF TOPICS

Fitch (81-82); Sophia Jex-Blake (103-105); William Shaen (179-80); Emily Anne Elizabeth Shirreff (182-83); Eleanor Mildred Sidgwick (183-85); Henry Sidgwick (185-87).

MARRIED WOMEN'S PROPERTY: Lady Katherine Louisa (Kate) Amberley (1-2); Lydia Ernestine Becker (17-19); Bessie Rayner Belloc (19-21); Barbara Leigh Smith Bodichon (27-30); Jacob Bright (35-37); Ursula Bright (37-39); Frances Power Cobbe (53-55); Sir Charles Wentworth Dilke (66-68); Anna Brownell Jameson (100-102); Harriet Martineau (123-26); Margaret Wynne Nevinson (137-39); Caroline Norton (143-45); Richard Marsden Pankhurst (152-53); Mary Smith (187-89); Emilie Ashurst Venturi (218-19).

NATIONAL UNION OF SOCIETIES FOR EQUAL CITIZENSHIP: Eva Marian Hubback (96-99); Eleanor Rathbone (166-69); Mary Danvers Stocks (197-99); Ellen Wilkinson (223-25).

NATIONAL UNION OF WOMEN'S SUFFRAGE SOCIETIES: Lady Frances Balfour (10-12); Lydia Ernestine Becker (17-19); Helen Blackburn (25-26); Sarah Emily (Emily) Davies (59-62); Millicent Garrett Fawcett (77-81); Eleanor Rathbone (166-69); Maude Royden (174-76); Mary Smith (187-89); Ethel Annakin Snowden (191-193); Mary Danvers Stocks (197-99); Philippa (Pippa) Strachey (202-203); Rachel (Ray) Strachey (203-205); Helena Maria Lucy Swanwick (205-207); Ellen Wilkinson (223-25).

OWENITE FEMINISM: William Henry Ashurst (6-7); Catherine Isabella Barmby (12-13); Margaret Chappellsmith (48-49); William Johnson Fox (84-85); Mary Lemon Grimstone (90-91); Harriet Teresa Law (111-12); Emma Martin (121-23); Frances Morrison (134-35); Harriet Taylor (209-10); William Thompson (213-17); Anna Wheeler (221-23); Frances Wright (228-30).

PROTECTIVE LEGISLATION: Lydia Ernestine Becker (17-19); Helen Blackburn (25-26); Sir Charles Wentworth Dilke (66-68); Lady Emilia Frances Dilke (68-70); Henry Fawcett (75-77); Millicent Garrett Fawcett (77-81); Eva Selina Gore-Booth (87-89); Amelia (Amie) Jane Hicks (95-96); Mary Reid Macarthur (115-16); Margaret Ethel MacDonald (116-19); Emma Paterson (156-57); Esther Roper (173-74); Ethel Annakin Snowden (191-93); Margaret Haig Thomas, Viscountess Rhondda (211-12).

SECONDARY EDUCATION FOR GIRLS: Dorothea Beale (15-17); Frances Mary Buss (40-41); Anne Jemima Clough (51-53); Sarah Emily (Emily) Davies (59-62); Sir Joshua Girling Fitch (81-82); Maria Georgina Grey (89-90); Anna Brownell Jameson (100-12); Harriet Martineau (123-26); Emily Anne Elizabeth Shirreff (182-83); Elizabeth Clark Wolstenholme-Elmy (225-28).

SOCIETY FOR THE PROMOTION OF THE EMPLOYMENT OF WOMEN: Bessie Rayner Belloc (19-21); Emilie (Jessie) Boucherett (32-33); Emily Faithfull (74-75); Harriet Martineau (123-26); Adelaide Anne Proctor (164-65); Louisa Twining (216-17).

TRADE UNIONS AND WOMEN: Margaret Grace Bondfield (30-32); Ada Nield Chew (49-51); Charlotte Despard (63-65); Sarah Dickensen (65-66); Sir Charles Wentworth Dilke (66-68);

Lady Emilia Frances Dilke (68–70); Isabella Ormston Ford (82–84); Eva Selina Gore-Booth (87–89); Amelia (Amie) Jane Hicks (95–96); Dorothea (Dorothy) Jewson (102–103); Mary Reid Macarthur (115–16); Emma Paterson (156–57); Esther Roper (173–74); Gertrude Mary Tuckwell (214–16).

VIOLENCE AGAINST WOMEN: Henry Noel Brailsford (33–35); Josephine Butler (41–45); Frances Power Cobbe (53–55); Selina Cooper (55–56); John Stuart Mill (126–30); Christabel Pankhurst (146–49); Harriet Taylor (208–10).

WOMEN AND THE PROFESSIONS: Elizabeth Garrett Anderson (4–6); Phoebe Sarah (Hertha) Ayrton (8–9); Barbara Leigh Smith Bodichon (27–30); Frances Mary Buss (40–41); Mary Carpenter (46–48); Charles Robert Drysdale (71–73); Sophia Jex-Blake (103–105); Florence Nightingale (140–43); William Shaen (178–80); Ethel Mary Smyth (189–91); James Stansfeld (195–97); Philippa (Pippa) Strachey (202–203); Rachel (Ray) Strachey (203–205).

WOMEN'S SOCIAL AND POLITICAL UNION: Millicent Garrett Anderson (4–6); Phoebe Sarah (Hertha) Ayrton (8–9); Teresa Billington-Greig (23–25); Mary Blathwayt (26–27); Emily Wilding Davison (62–63); Charlotte Despard (63–65); Flora Drummond (70–71); Mary Gawthorpe (86–87); Annie Kenney (106–107); Lady Constance Georgina Lytton (112–14); Dora Montefiore (133–34); Henry Woodd Nevinson (136–37); Christabel Pankhurst (146–49); Emmeline Pankhurst (149–52); Sylvia Pankhurst (153–56); Emmeline Pethick-Lawrence (157–60); Frederick William Pethick-Lawrence (160–62); Edith Rayner Rigby (169–71); Elizabeth Robins (172–73); Ethel Mary Smyth (189–90); Margaret Haig Thomas, Viscountess Rhondda (211–12).

WOMEN'S SUFFRAGE AND THE LABOUR PARTY: Henry Noel Brailsford (33–35); Selina Cooper (55–56); Isabella Ormston Ford (82–84); Keir Hardie (93–95); George Lansbury (109–11); Sylvia Pankhurst (153–56); Philip Snowden (193–94); Enid Stacey (194–95).

WOMEN'S SUFFRAGE AND THE LIBERAL PARTY: Jacob Bright (35–37); Sir Charles Wentworth Dilke (66–68); Henry Fawcett (75–77); John Stuart Mill (126–30).

WORKING-CLASS WOMEN AND SUFFRAGE: Annie Barnes (13–15); Margaret Grace Bondfield (30–32); Ada Nield Chew (49–51); Selina Cooper (55–60); Margaret Llewelyn Davies (57–59); Sarah Dickensen (65–66); Eva Selina Gore-Booth (87–89); Hannah Maria Mitchell (131–33); Sarah Reddish (169); Esther Roper (173–74).

DATE DUE

Demco, Inc. 38-293